The
EVIL HOURS

The
EVIL HOURS

A BIOGRAPHY OF POST-TRAUMATIC
STRESS DISORDER

David J. Morris

An Eamon Dolan Book
Houghton Mifflin Harcourt
BOSTON • NEW YORK

2015

For information about permission to reproduce selections from this
book, write to Permissions, Houghton Mifflin Harcourt Publishing
Company, 215 Park Avenue South, New York, New York 10003.

www.hmhco.com

Library of Congress Cataloging-in-Publication Data
Morris, David J., date.
The evil hours : a biography of posttraumatic stress disorder / David J. Morris.
pages cm
"An Eamon Dolan Book."
ISBN 978-0-544-08661-6 (hardback) — ISBN 978-0-544-57032-0
(trade paper) — ISBN 978-0-544-08449-0 (ebook)
1. Post-traumatic stress disorder — United States. 2. Post-
traumatic stress disorder — Patients — United States — Biography.
3. Morris, David J., date. — Mental health. I. Title.
RC552.P67M68 2015
616.85'21 — dc23
2014034487

Book design by Brian Moore

Printed in the United States of America
DOC 10 9 8 7 6 5 4 3 2 1

Heraclitus's Fragment 62 is from *Fragments: The Collected Wisdom
of Heraclitus* by Heraclitus, translated by Brooks Haxton, translation
copyright © 2001 by Brooks Haxton. Used by permission of Viking
Penguin, a division of Penguin Group (USA) LLC.

This book presents the research and ideas of its author. It is not intended
to be a substitute for consultation with a mental health professional. The
publisher and the author disclaim responsibility for any adverse effects
resulting directly or indirectly from information contained in this book.

This book is not affiliated with or endorsed by the Department
of Defense or other instrumentality of the United States.

How many a brief bombardment had its long-delayed after-effect in the minds of these survivors, many of whom had looked at their companions and laughed while inferno did its best to destroy them. Not then was their evil hour; but now; now, in the sweating suffocation of nightmare, in paralysis of limbs, in the stammering of dislocated speech. Worst of all, in the disintegration of those qualities through which they had been so gallant and selfless and uncomplaining—this, in the finer types of men, was the unspeakable tragedy of shell shock ... In the name of civilization these soldiers had been martyred, and it remained for civilization to prove that their martyrdom wasn't a dirty swindle.

— SIEGFRIED SASSOON

A modern disease, as it is comprehended in a laboratory, is explained to the laboratory technician, the student, and the layman as a phenomenon made up of its own pimples, rash, swelling and development. The disease is never presented as a creature—real or metaphorical—a creature that might have an existence separate from its description, even as you and I have an existence from the fact that we weigh so many pounds and stand so many inches tall.

— NORMAN MAILER

Contents

Author's Note

Out of respect for their privacy, I have changed the names
of some of the people who appear in these pages.

Prologue: The Warning

Have you ever been blown up before, sir?
Everything was fine until it wasn't.
Apophenia: finding patterns where there shouldn't be patterns.

These were the words I wrote in my journal on October 9, 2007, the day before I was almost killed by a roadside bomb in Baghdad. The last line I wrote in the days afterward. Later, I went back and underlined it in a different colored ink, as if to emphasize that I had come back to it in a different state of mind. As if I were leaving a clue for some future version of myself.

I was in Iraq for my third reporting trip and had gone out on a patrol with some soldiers from the First Infantry Division into Saydia, a neighborhood that seemed, at least on the surface, to be relatively peaceful. On our way back inside the wire, one of the soldiers asked nonchalantly if I'd ever been blown up before. I considered the question for a moment, and then, as the silence deepened, I sensed that something was amiss. The words came awkwardly as I explained that while I had spent the summer before in Ramadi, at that point the deadliest city in Iraq, I was still a virgin in that particular area.

It was like my fate had been spoken: I had never been blown up before, but everyone in the Humvee knew that was about to change.

According to the laws of grunt superstition, I was the injured party, but somehow I managed to feel bad for the kid who'd asked the question. As it happened, the soldiers in the Humvee were from all over Latin America—Peru, Mexico, Guatemala—and they began pummeling him in a variety of languages and accents for what he'd done.

At the time, I felt embarrassed more than anything else and just wanted the moment to end. I didn't like being the topic of conversation, and it took everything I had to avoid thinking about being blown into tiny red pieces. This, in fact, was one of the first head tricks I'd learned in Iraq, to systematically ignore the obvious: you were always just about to die—get over it. I was wasted, too, and my mind wasn't right. I had been in Iraq for a total of nine months by this point, and even though I had seen people killed by roadside bombs, I'd never been hit myself, and somehow I'd come to feel that I had my luck under control. But in posing the question, it was as if the soldier had stolen that control, thrown me over to the forces of chance that I had worked so hard to insulate myself from.

Later, I interviewed a prominent psychoanalyst, who told me that trauma destroys the fabric of time. In normal time, you move from one moment to the next, sunrise to sunset, birth to death. After trauma, you may move in circles, find yourself being sucked backwards into an eddy, or bouncing about like a rubber ball from now to then and back again. August is June, June is December. What time is it? Guess again. In the traumatic universe, the basic laws of matter are suspended: ceiling fans can be helicopters, car exhaust can be mustard gas.

Another odd feature of traumatic time is that it doesn't just destroy the flow of the present into the future, it corrodes everything that came before, eating at moments and people from your previous life, until you can't remember why any of them mattered.

What I previously found inconceivable is now inescapable: I have been blown up so many times in my mind that it is impossible to imagine a version of myself that has not been blown up. The man on the other side of the soldier's question is not me. In fact, he never existed.

The war is gone now, but the event remains, the happening that nearly erased the life to come and thus erased the life that came before. The soldier's question hangs in the air the way it always has. The way it always will.

Have you ever been blown up before, sir?

The
EVIL HOURS

Introduction

Over the past four decades, post-traumatic stress disorder has permeated every corner of our culture. A condition that went unacknowledged for millennia, and began its public life with a handful of disgruntled Vietnam veterans "rapping" in the offices of an antiwar group in midtown Manhattan in December 1970, has spread to every nation on the globe, becoming in the words of one medical anthropologist a kind of "psychiatric Esperanto." A species of pain that went unnamed for most of human history, PTSD is now the fourth most common psychiatric disorder in the United States. According to the latest estimates, nearly 8 percent of all Americans—twenty-eight million people—will suffer from post-traumatic stress at some point in their lives. According to the Veterans Administration, which spends more annually on PTSD research and treatment than any organization in the world, PTSD is the number one health concern of American military veterans, regardless of when they served. In 2012, the federal government spent three billion dollars on PTSD treatment for veterans, a figure that doesn't include the billions in PTSD disability payments made every year to former servicemembers.

Since the attacks of 9/11, when public awareness of the disorder gained momentum, PTSD (a condition characterized by hyperarousal, emotional numbness, and recurring flashbacks) has, to the dismay of some international aid experts, supplanted hunger as the primary Western public health concern when a war or other humanitarian crisis hits the news. PTSD is one of the newest major psychiatric disorders to be recognized, and yet today it has entered the public lexicon to the degree that it is not uncommon to hear journalists describing entire countries as being stricken with it and writing lengthy articles debating whether or not Batman might be suffering from it. Consumers who are so inclined can now go online and purchase a commemorative patch for $5.99 that reads P.T.S.D.: NOT ALL WOUNDS ARE VISIBLE. As any trauma researcher will tell you, PTSD is everywhere today.

And yet, like many mental health disorders, there is broad disagreement about what exactly PTSD is, who gets it, and how best to treat it. There remains a small but vocal cadre of researchers who argue that PTSD is a social fiction, a relic of the Vietnam War era foisted upon the global community by well-meaning but misguided clinicians, and that by, in essence, encouraging people to be traumatized, we undermine their recovery. A condition born of strife, PTSD is dominated by conflict in its scientific life as well. There is, however, little disagreement that survivors of rape, war, natural disasters, and torture—the events that are generally recognized to lead to PTSD—experience profound, even existential, pain in the aftermath of such events. This brand of suffering has become so widely recognized that it has in fact permanently altered the moral compass of the Western world and changed our understanding of what it means to be human, what it means to feel pain.

Pierre Janet, a French neurologist writing in 1925, observed that emotional reactions to traumatic events can be so intense as to "have a disintegrating effect on the entire psychological system." This book is about that effect and what it looks and feels like from the inside. Over time, PTSD has changed not only the way humans understand loss but also how humans understand themselves generally; I am interested in it both as a mental condition and as a metaphor. How people respond to horrific events has always been determined by a complex web of social, political, and technological forces. For most of human history, interpreting trauma has been the preserve of artists, poets, and shamans. The ways in which a nation deals with trauma are as revealing as its politics and language. The ancient Greeks staged plays that were written and performed by war veterans as a communal method for achieving catharsis. Today, for better or worse, we deal with trauma and horror almost exclusively through a complex, seemingly arbitrary cluster of symptoms known as post-traumatic stress disorder. In the classical world, the ancients in the wake of trauma might look for answers in epic poetry, such as *The Iliad* or *The Odyssey*. Today, we turn to the most current edition of the *Diagnostic and Statistical Manual of Mental Disorders*. This fact alone is worthy of further exploration: most of us no longer turn to poetry, our families, or the clergy for solace post-horror. Instead, we turn to psychiatrists. This is, historically speaking, an unusual state of affairs.

Before 2011, I had never seriously considered the question of post-traumatic stress, either in myself or as a general subject. I returned home in 2007, as I had returned from all of my reporting trips to Iraq, with a powerful feeling of alienation from my countrymen. Freshly deplaned from what I understood to be the defining event of my generation, I discovered to my great surprise that no one back home held this view or seemed to have given much thought to the war. Like Nick Carraway returning from the East in *The Great Gatsby,* I came home expecting to find the world "at a sort of moral attention." When this didn't happen, I was disappointed. The war had changed me, enlarged me in some way, made me feel as if history was a tangible force in my life, and seeing the workaday world, people with their looks of practiced oblivion, put me on edge. The writer in me secretly wished for something similar to what had happened before, perhaps something out of the Vietnam era: people marching in the streets, students debating the war's meaning on college campuses, the war making itself felt at home in some visible way, the loss given some physical form.

The war had hurt me. I wanted the country to feel some of that hurt. Part of me needed to see that, to remind me that the war had been real, not just something I saw when I closed my eyes. I needed to know that the experience had meaning and that the death I had seen really mattered. What I saw instead was people commuting to work and going to the mall, the gym, and the health food store, making their bodies perfect, exactly as they had before. The yellow ribbons I saw seemed almost like a taunt, a challenge to all the horror I'd witnessed.

I learned very quickly that talking about the war wasn't just pointless but actually damaging in its own right. I could barely begin to describe what I had seen before I would be interrupted by a racist comment about Arabs or by someone stopping me to explain how the war had just been about oil all along and that the important thing, really, was to develop alternative energies so that we could divest from the Middle East. After a while, I realized that the problem wasn't just that they didn't understand the war but that they didn't want to understand it. What I had to say was not only inconvenient to their peace of mind but a tangible threat to it. Americans could no more cope with the reality of the war than they could with the reality of particle physics. Not only was it beyond their ken, but the fact that it might be beyond their ken was beyond their ken. Trying to cut through the various layers of incomprehension, I was confronted by further obscenities. If, by some chance, I could get someone to listen to me about what I had seen in Iraq, they would end up looking at me like I had a speech impediment. They'd meet my eyes, and I'd get The Look, a sort of mirror image of the famous Thousand Yard Stare from World War II, a look that told me more about American innocence than I ever wanted to know. More than once I was asked if I'd killed anyone over there. At times, my sense of alienation was so strong I seemed almost radiant with it, as if a stranger could look at me and tell that something was wrong.

Sometimes I would start to shake when I thought about the war—how wrong it was, how many childish mistakes had been made, how no one in power was held accountable, and how tens of thousands had died in the service of some Beltway egos—or the people who had died in the service of nothing at all, owing to the simplest accidents of space and time. One unit I was with north of Fallujah had lost a guy who was killed while using a Port-a-John in the middle of the night. He'd gone out to take a shit and, out of nowhere, a single mortar round came in and ended him. It was the only incoming they'd taken in days. How do you go about telling a guy who is alive only because he didn't use the shitter at the wrong time that he ought to go back home, go to school, get married and mortgaged, have kids, and commit to the world when he knows for a fact that nothing in this world is real except chance? That his continued existence, his dreams, his plans, his hopes for the future are the product of invisible, ever-changing odds, odds that could shift and turn on him at any moment? What place did human reason have in this world really, after you'd seen what war could do to it? The lesson taught by the war was clear: to be human is to be small, powerless, and subject to the forces of randomness.

Every veteran knows this.

Knowing this is what makes it hard to step onto airplanes. Knowing this is what makes it hard to stand in large crowds. Knowing this is what makes it hard to drive a car.

"The war itself was a mystery. Nobody knew what it was about, or why they were there, or who started it, or who was winning, or how it might end. Secrets were everywhere—booby traps in the hedgerows, bouncing betties under the red clay soil. And the people. The silent papa-sans, the hollow-eyed children and jabbering old women. What did these people want? What did they feel?"; so wrote Tim O'Brien in his novel *In the Lake of the Woods,* a book that traces the aftermath of the Vietnam War through the flashbacks of a traumatized veteran.

Still, at other times, I found myself in pain, missing the field, missing the Marines and the excitement, the profane beauty of their words, the mid-patrol trance I'd slip into, the bump and grind of enemy contact, the feelings I'd had in a place where every second could either save you or kill you, where even the smallest gesture took on a certain weight because you knew it might be your last. Instead, people back home just looked at me as if there was something wrong with me, a look that cost me nothing to return.

That these two worlds, war and home, could be kept isolated, one living in almost perfect ignorance of the other, was an obscenity surpassed only by the obscenity of the war itself. The war had been difficult, but there seemed to be meaning in having survived it. Coming home and feeling the dullness of people, the pride they took in their ignorance, seemed to diminish that meaning, as if it had only been a bad backpacking trip overseas that I'd come back from. How could this be allowed to happen? Could a war really be called a war if nobody back home gave a shit about it? In time, I resolved to hate the country I'd once served: the fat, sheltered land with its surplus of riches, its helicopter moms and real estate agents — narrow-minded, smug, and only dimly aware of any lives other than their own.

Virtually every survivor of trauma, whether or not they experience diagnosable post-traumatic stress, returns to the regular world and quickly recognizes that things are not as they were. People behave differently. There is an element of strangeness, a sense, often uncommunicated, of being marked by a kind of scarlet letter, even if one has not violated any moral code. In fact, in these situations, one's degree of innocence or complicity in events can seem almost beside the point, as if one's luck or simple fate is what is at stake. Often this change of perception is expressed in physical, spatial terms, as if the scope of what has transpired is so vast that it serves to alter one's material position in the world. One British World War I veteran described his postwar existence as one lived in "a mental internment camp." Alice Sebold, in her bestselling memoir *Lucky,* which describes the aftermath of her violent rape at age nineteen, looked out at the faces of her college classmates less than an hour after she had been raped and saw that she "was now on the other side of something they could not understand. I didn't understand it myself."

This palpable sense of not belonging, of being "on the other side of something" after trauma, has in fact been widely noted. Anthropologists who study tribal societies describe this state as one of "liminality," which comes from the Latin word for "threshold." Arnold van Gennep coined the term in his 1908 *Rites of Passage,* a book that draws on his studies of the tribes of southwestern Africa. The liminal state, as observed by van Gennep, was thought to be "dangerous" and "precarious" because of its social ambiguity and the conflicting, paradoxical demands it placed on both the individual and society. In tribal society, liminal states, such as adolescence, were punctuated by ceremonies designed to "accompany a passage from one situation to another or from one cosmic or social world to another." Weddings, graduations, bar mitzvahs, and quinceañeras are all examples of van Gennepian rites of passage, which end dramatically and decisively with the person's new status made clear to the community. Yet as Victor Turner, an influential anthropologist, pointed out, the modern world has no such "rites of incorporation" to mark the transition from the underworld of trauma to the everyday world, saying, "The liminal persona, in this case the returning veteran, is not alive, not dead, but somehow both and neither."

It wasn't until the summer of 2009, some two years after Saydia, that I got the first hint that I was "on the other side of something." I was in a theater watching an action movie with my girlfriend when a black curtain fell over my head. The world disappeared for a few minutes. Looking around, I noticed that I was pacing the lobby of the theater, my head on a swivel, looking at people's hands to make sure they weren't carrying. My mind had gone dark, but my body was back in Iraq.

I managed to slip back into the theater and sit back down next to my girlfriend. I looked around to see if it had happened to anyone else, but they were all engrossed in the movie.

"What happened?" I asked Erica, who seemed as confused as I was.

"There was an explosion in the movie. You got up and ran out of the theater."

Soon after, I began to have dreams with explosions in them. Sometimes they were about Saydia. Sometimes innocent items exploded more or less at random—an apple, a garbage can, a box of Chinese takeout. Over time, I began to see that Saydia was beginning to infiltrate the present, albeit in a slightly disguised form, as with the exploding garbage can, which I understood to be related to the loud garbage truck that jolted me awake every Thursday morning. My dreams about Saydia were frightening, but I sometimes saw them as a kind of debriefing, a way of examining different versions of the past, and as meditations on what had happened, or might have happened, in the street that afternoon in Saydia. Sometimes the gunner was decapitated by the blast. Sometimes a machinegun opened up from the neighborhood and wasted us all. Frequently, a member of my old Marine platoon was in the Humvee next to me, watching, shaking his head in disgust, or providing a sort of color commentary on the action.

The dreams usually ended the same way. Something would explode, unleashing a tidal wave of blackness that obliterated everything, and I would wake up with my heart racing. I was dead. This was what the blackness meant. The movie explosion had gone off, just as it had in Saydia, and it had given me a glimpse of my own death. But before things could go any further, my brain would shut everything down, like an overloaded electrical grid; everything would go dark, and then I would wake up. It was just as Freud had noted nearly a century before: one's own death is unimaginable.

For months after the movie, my unconscious debriefed me like this. It didn't happen every night, but it occurred often enough that sleep became an ordeal, something to be worked up to, like an athletic contest. It got so that preparing for bed was like getting ready for a night patrol. I would set my alarm, put up the blackout curtains, close and lock every door and window in the house, recheck them, and ensure that all the paths in the house were clear and all the shades were drawn. After all that, I would take my sleep medicine, usually a mix of prescription and nonprescription pills, depending on my mood, and then put my earplugs in and my blinders on and pray that my mind would behave itself for the next eight hours. Part of me got a black pleasure from it, as it made me feel that it was somehow an honor to be haunted, as if the war had touched me so deeply that it had granted me access to the darkest chambers of the mind. Part of me was ashamed of the dreams, of the realization that I was trapped inside a cliché: the veteran so obsessed with his own past that even his unconscious made love to it every night.

There were other hints that I was on the far side of something. These usually came in times of uncertainty or stress, such as when I received three ludicrously expensive parking tickets in a single week, when I got the cold sweats during a bumpy airplane ride over Cape Cod, or when I saw the fear on Erica's face whenever I got angry, which was often.

For several years after the war, Erica and I lived in a kind of postwar bliss, happily trapped in the time-capsule of our love. We had met before my final trip to Iraq, and I was immediately taken by her beauty, her wide-ranging mind, her joie de vivre, and her exquisite wit, which made her seem at times like a dame from a hard-boiled detective novel. From day one, we shared a bond that seemed immune to the normal laws of life and career. Coming home to her, my life seemed to make a certain kind of sense, as if the world had kept its promise. When she picked me up at LAX in 2007, I saw her standing behind a gate in baggage claim, blushing hotly, angry at me for the ordeal I'd put her through. Finally, she relented, greeting me with her trademark "Hey, bub!" and kissing me wildly.

Women have always played a pivotal role in the drama of homecoming from war. In Homer's *Odyssey,* Odysseus's ten-year journey back from the Trojan War doesn't end when he sets foot in his hometown of Ithaca, but rather when he is finally reunited with his wife, Penelope. Men, left to their own devices, turn into emotional nihilists: wild, cruel, and death-obsessed. Looking back on those heady days after I returned from Iraq, I can see that the drama of my reunion with Erica was an elemental experience on par with the war itself, a struggle to reconcile the two halves of myself—the dark with the light, the hard with the soft, the very masculine stoicism that war demands with a woman's sensitivity. I'd always admired her tough exterior, but Erica's presence somehow had a softening effect on me in the months after I returned, almost as if her sarcastic demeanor allowed me to lower my guard. I couldn't relate to others after what I'd been through, but Erica had been in it with me from the very beginning. She had seen me preparing my gear for my long months in the field before I left. She had read my strained emails from Fallujah, listened to me on the phone from Baghdad as I tried to reconcile what I was seeing every day with what the media was reporting. It was as if I didn't need to tell her what I'd been through. She already understood, somehow. We had survived the war. Whatever followed would be child's play, surely.

Then, in 2010, right before the holidays, Erica disappeared. Her car was gone and there was no answer when I called her cell phone. Two weeks later, on Christmas Eve, she phoned from Las Vegas to tell me it was over. She was tired of my secrecy, she would explain later. "You go off into this other place, and it's like I can't reach you." Oddly, this turn of events, while certainly disappointing, was not overly shocking to me, and even when it finally sank in that Erica would not be returning and that our pantomime of connubial bliss was over, I didn't cry. Tears had become something beyond my ability. In these sorts of situations, I did exactly as I had been trained: I went numb and waited for the time to pass. When I explained Erica's departure to my friends, their jaws hit the floor. *She just disappeared? Like* poof? *For two weeks? Not even a note?*

It was a rotten deal, no doubt. Yet something in me knew that Erica had been capable of this sort of thing all along. That she would surface with a phone call from Vegas seemed somehow in character for her. I had always admired that hint of the femme fatale in her, so what right did I have to be surprised? I knew in some objective way that I had seen a lot of awful things happen to a lot of people, so when chance turned on me in the form of a capricious woman, it wasn't entirely unexpected. This world was designed from the ground up to hurt us, to break us, all of us, into the tiniest little pieces. What made me think I was so special? Who was I to think that I should be spared? That was like going out into the rain and expecting to not get wet.

There had been other reasons, other complications, to be sure. I was a working writer, a career choice that often came with an unspoken vow of poverty, which put a lot of pressure on our relationship. The writing, whatever else it did, took me to the same place that a lot of veterans ended up: the dark cave of my head, where the only sound was the echo of my own voice. It takes a long time, too long, to learn that the brain's job is to hide the truth of trauma from you and that no amount of thinking, however penetrating and well informed, is going to help you locate it. Nobody ever said that nightmares tell the truth, or even a portion of the truth, though their allure is that we think they do.

I can see now that Erica was simply unprepared for what was coming, the sheer weight of all my unprocessed dread. Not that I was prepared. Who could be? I'd been surrounded by death for so long that I'd forgotten how to live. Living, I was learning, was harder than just surviving. It reminded me of something I'd heard a Vietnam vet say: just because your body was safe didn't mean that your mind was. I had been changed and expanded by the war, but it was an expansion that seemed to have put me out of balance with the world, with Erica. I hated her for leaving, but what could I do?

Relationships, when they end, are not unlike car crashes. Hidden energies only hinted at in regular motion are violently released, demolishing the carefully constructed bodies we depend on every day. With Erica gone, everything became more difficult. I felt for the first time that I was alone in dealing with all the pain and uncertainty in my life. My nightmares and general disaffection with the world seemed to double. Occasionally, at sunset, I would hear the Muslim call to prayer, even though I lived dozens of miles from any mosque. As a journalist in Iraq, my greatest fear had always been that I would be kidnapped and tortured. In Erica's absence, this healthy awareness of my surroundings blossomed into a consuming paranoia that I was being followed whenever I left my apartment.

The morbidity of my imagination was astonishing: disaster and loss were my constant companions. The war had taught me some things about physics, and my mind transformed this knowledge into a series of visions: cars exploding on peaceful residential streets, IEDs welded to innocent light poles, helicopters losing power and crashing into suburban canyons. Sometimes it was willful, and, wondering what residues of the war remained, I would create my own daydreams of destruction. Surveying a bustling mall scene, I would call IEDs into existence, watching as a fireball erupted into the air, eviscerating the shoppers. Wherever I went, there seemed to be legions of amputees, reminders of wounded Marines I'd seen, limbs I'd almost lost. For reasons beyond my ken, when I looked at perfectly normal people, my mind would begin to subtract limbs from them. An arm resting on a hip became a mangled memento of an IED in Ramadi, of the machinegunner I'd seen lose a hand near Karma. Everything became a reminder of death's omnipotence. It was as if my mind was insisting that the war be brought home and that true peace was an obscenity, an affront to life's stark reality. And, always, there were the awful mornings when, suddenly awake, I would wonder where Erica was and why there always seemed to be a helicopter hovering over my apartment.

There was a time when I believed that there was only a certain amount of suffering that a person should expect in life. Essential to this belief was the idea that a person returning from war was basically owed a measure of easy happiness from the world, a peace dividend if you will. As a former Marine who had been in and out of a war zone for years, I felt entitled to my own peace dividend. In the courtroom of my mind, I decided I had suffered enough. The end of my relationship with Erica shattered this illusion, and in the winter of 2010, after finding myself out of work and adrift for a number of months, I began searching for a new way to understand what I was going through, an explanation for why I seemed to have lost control of my memories, why I felt stuck in time, why I couldn't sleep, why I was angry all the time.

Looking back on this post-Iraq, post-Erica period of my life, I'm reminded of Hemingway's early short story "Soldier's Home," in which a World War I veteran, identified only as "Krebs," ponders his predicament on the front porch of his father's house. Over the course of the story, Krebs's obsession with the simpler life turns from a vague expectation into something like a mantra. "He did not want any consequences. He did not want any consequences ever again. He wanted to live along without consequences. Besides he did not really need a girl. The army had taught him that." I, too, wanted a simpler, easier life like Krebs, a man whose odd remove from the daily course of life was something I recognized in myself. Watching the world go by from the porch, he thinks, "He liked the girls that were walking along the other side of the street. He liked the look of them much better than the French or the German girls. But the world they were in was not the world that he was in."

Unexpectedly alone, unsure of the world I was in, I began, tentatively, even skeptically, to explore the idea of post-traumatic stress, first as a historical curiosity and then on more personal terms. Had I really been traumatized? I had paid almost nothing as these things went. Sure, I had nightmares and felt haunted by the past, but who didn't? PTSD? Wasn't that something homeless Vietnam vets had? I'd spent some time in Dora and Fallujah, been blown up and shot at a number of times, but I knew plenty of people who had seen far worse things than I had. However, as I would learn, one of the deceptive things about trauma is that it is usually pretty easy to find someone who has been through something even more awful than what you've been through and thus dismiss your own pain, needlessly prolonging the process. It's easy to find people to place at the top of the pyramid of loss—Holocaust survivors, Bosnian refugees, African child soldiers—but what about all that space below them? Who goes there? Who decides? It reminded me of something a veteran of the battle of Khafji once said to me, a guy who'd lost eleven of his buddies to friendly fire. "It was bad, but it wasn't like Stalingrad or anything."

As a Marine lieutenant, I had always been told in times of uncertainty to go to the library. *Read. Get smart. Don't reinvent the wheel. Look at the history. It's likely that someone before you has faced the same challenges you face now.* So I went to the largest library within a day's drive of my house, in this case at the University of California, San Diego, and began methodically working my way through the stacks. What I found was surprising. PTSD may well be the Esperanto of psychiatry, but its research literature is remarkably chaotic. Taken at a distance, the world of trauma studies resembled an arcade at the state fair. Along one side was a series of stalls populated by psychiatrists, psychologists, and neuroscientists, along the other were poets, memoirists, historians, and anthropologists. The barkers within each stall might call out to you, singing the virtues of their worldview, but there seemed to be little overlap between these various groups, let alone coherence. The result was a wash of statistics and anecdotes that offered no logical point of entry for the common observer.

As I would learn, PTSD, as it is understood today, is a very heterogeneous disease, essentially a junk drawer of disconnected symptoms, which include a numbing of the emotions, hypervigilance (always being "amped up"), social isolation, and a variety of intrusive manifestations, such as nightmares and hallucinations. The field of trauma studies embodies this fragmentation, with each subspecies of researcher rarely poking their head out of their own little stall (to continue the state fair metaphor). This sort of "silo-ing" of expertise is common throughout academia, but with the problem of trauma it is unusually counterproductive, because as Jonathan Shay, a pioneering trauma theorist, likes to point out, "trauma impacts the whole critter," by which he means it affects every aspect of a person's life.

In the months that followed, I would enter therapy at the VA, take part in three research studies, visit three historical archives, and interview scores of researchers from across the country, looking for an answer to one question: What is PTSD? The more I looked, the more I found that my initial impression held true. Mental health is an unusually demanding and at times confounding line of work, but I was astonished to learn that few clinicians were familiar with the literature of the Vietnam War from which PTSD emerged, nor did they possess an even rudimentary understanding of the global War on Terror. One leading VA researcher I spoke to didn't seem to know where Fallujah was, nor, as I learned, had she ever read any of the work of Tim O'Brien. Similarly, many of the leading historians on the subject remained willfully ignorant, and in some cases openly dismissive, of the scientific research relating to post-traumatic stress. One British author of an influential history of military psychiatry went so far as to brush off the neuroscience behind modern trauma studies as "completely dubious."

This lack of synthesis also struck me as odd because, apart from my own personal difficulties, I began to see that much as shell shock (a sort of precursor to PTSD) dominated the post–World War I imagination in Europe and Great Britain, so the phenomenon of PTSD dominates our culture today. As a cultural meme, PTSD is everywhere now, an inescapable part of our historical moment. As an expression of deeper anxieties, it defines our era in a way not unlike female hysteria defined late nineteenth-century Europe, a reality that was not lost on Freud's contemporaries. As Otto Fenichel, one of Freud's protégés, put it, "Neuroses do not occur out of biological necessity, like aging . . . Neuroses are social diseases . . . corresponding to a given and historically developed social milieu. They cannot be changed without corresponding change in the milieu."

It would be foolish to diagnose an entire nation with a mental health disorder, but as Susan Faludi points out in her 2007 book *The Terror Dream: Fear and Fantasy in Post-9/11 America,* the country as a whole continues to exhibit certain aspects of post-traumatic stress, including a compulsion to reenact the events of September 11 in movies and television as well as nurturing obsessions with homeland security and surveillance that, according to many military analysts, is out of proportion with the actual threat and smacks of a kind of national hypervigilance. Moreover, the ongoing militarization of American culture — in the form of first-person shooter video games, the rise of the Navy SEAL "brand" in books, films, and other media, and martially themed endurance races like the Tough Mudder series — points to a fixation with the post-9/11 hyper-masculinity and ubiquitous violence reminiscent of the disorder.

In a related vein, some observers have drawn a connection between 9/11 and the recent helicopter parenting phenomenon, the overweening desire to protect our children from every conceivable danger to the point where we isolate them from the world and prevent them from having experiences that previous generations took for granted. Others point to the rising popularity of zombies in books and films as being symptomatic of a kind of paranoid "cultural PTSD." (Zombies are like terrorists in that they look like us but have been tainted by death and can seemingly strike anywhere and at any time, or so the thinking goes.) Indeed, one can quite easily construct an entire theory of recent American culture using PTSD as a nucleus, all without mentioning the tens of thousands of veterans and their families who suffer from post-traumatic stress or the millions of rape victims who live every day amped up, numbed out, and generally haunted.

PTSD has become a bit like Prozac in the nineties: if you hear about it once, you hear about it a thousand times. We live now in an aftermath culture, a culture where being traumatized is presumed to be the appropriate response to just about any overwhelming event. "These are the days after. Everything is now measured by after," a character in Don DeLillo's 9/11 novel *Falling Man* says. This leads to the bigger questions: Why now? Why in the United States, a country that is, by any standard, one of the least traumatized on the planet? Is there something about the War on Terror, a war that directly involves less than 1 percent of us, that has made us all a little nuts? Is there something about the larger war against Islamic extremism that has made us fear the outside world? If war is a kind of symbolic violence, is PTSD a kind of symbolic penance? Do we so easily embrace the diagnosis out of a sort of "white guilt" about not having served overseas ourselves, as some have suggested? Or are PTSD and the threat of it simply another example of how modern therapeutic culture has forced its way into our lives and taught us how to perceive normal human adversity?

In trying to address these questions and balance the various academic disciplines that inform our understanding of post-traumatic stress, these pages may display a bias toward literature. Part of this is simply the result of my being a writer, but there is also the fact that for the bulk of human history, literature has been *the* primary repository of knowledge about war, famine, genocide, and natural disaster. From *The Iliad* to the Great War poets to the literature of the Vietnam War, writers have been wrestling—and wrestling quite well, I might add—with the mysteries of trauma. In a sense, nothing has changed, and today's trauma survivors can take great comfort in knowing that they are confronting the same horrors that Achilles faced four thousand years ago. Moreover, as practically any therapist will tell you, many of the long-term effects of trauma are the product of the emotional interpretations of events by victims—interpretations that are informed by the archetypal narratives that exist within a given culture, a process that is explicitly literary. As Robert Stolorow, an influential psychoanalyst, argues, "The experience of trauma is context-dependent," meaning its essence lies in the subjective experience of the victim; in other words, their story as *they* tell it to themselves.

By reading the stories of Ernest Hemingway, Alice Sebold, Tim O'Brien, and others, survivors are doing more than simply being entertained, they are reifying literature's essential function: to remind us that we are not alone and in the process demonstrating how trauma was processed by previous generations. Medicine itself is founded upon a kind of storytelling; Siddhartha Mukherjee, in his "biography" of cancer, *The Emperor of All Maladies,* explains that "patients tell stories to describe illness, doctors tell stories to understand it. Science tells its own story to explain diseases." A number of the trauma workers I spoke to over the course of writing this book called my attention to this point; namely, that part of trauma's corrosive power lies in its ability to destroy narrative, and that stories, written and spoken, have tremendous healing power both for the teller and the listener. Stories in the form of literature help us to understand the enigma of survival in a way that no other technology can. In short, literature makes meaning out of chaos. One senior VA psychiatrist I spoke to, who has treated PTSD for over thirty years, went so far as to say that "the central image of post-traumatic stress is that of Ishmael at the end of *Moby-Dick,* floating atop Queequeg's coffin, looking out over the vastness of the sea."

For better or worse, the popular image of PTSD is derived primarily from the image of the war-torn American veteran. There are good reasons for this. The idea for what became known as PTSD sprang from a group of American veterans opposed to the war in Vietnam. This group, a clique within the Vietnam Veterans Against the War (VVAW), embarked on a decade-long campaign to have the disorder officially recognized by psychiatry. Without them, PTSD as we know it would not exist. For the first nine years of its existence, in fact, what we know of as "PTSD" was referred to as "Post-Vietnam Syndrome." Since its inclusion in the *Diagnostic and Statistical Manual of Mental Disorders,* the bible of modern psychiatry, the condition has been somewhat demilitarized, but its connection to the most divisive American war of the twentieth century remains strong. This military connection continues into the present day. While most PTSD sufferers are not veterans and have never seen combat, the Veterans Administration, the second-largest department within the U.S. government, remains a global clearinghouse for PTSD research and has an annual mental health budget that hovers around seven billion dollars.

I have included aspects of PTSD from other causes, including rape, genocide, torture, and natural disaster, but have focused less on childhood and domestic abuse and PTSD arising from events like open-heart surgery and traumatic childbirth. By narrowing my view, I hope to sharpen it to probe into the origins of what some future "biographer" might simply call the problem of adult post-traumatic adjustment. Part of my reasoning behind this is strictly practical: a book attempting to address the causes and consequences of every kind of trauma would run thousands of pages and be filled with so many qualifiers and exceptions to every assertion that it would cease being a story with a narrative arc and become an encyclopedia. Further, as the definition of PTSD has continued to expand, including more and more types of stressors (some U.S. military psychiatrists, for example, have begun diagnosing drone operators with PTSD), the research community has struggled to keep pace. As a writer attempting to create some coherence in a subject sorely in need of it, I have chosen to exclude certain newer forms of the disease that await scientific consensus and focus on what some have called the "classic" traumatic stressors: war, rape, and natural disaster. This is not an attempt to privilege one type of trauma over another (though the field of trauma studies remains heavily skewed toward war trauma); instead, it is an attempt to make meaning out of the cacophony of an emerging scientific field by deliberately limiting my data set.

This book is a biography, woven together with elements of my own autobiography, my attempt to tell the story of PTSD, beginning with the first glimpses of it in the historical record and then continuing as a sort of pilgrim to the battered temples our culture has erected to it, specifically the Veterans Administration, the U.S. military medical establishment, and the various civilian academic edifices that study it. But, before I tell the story of PTSD itself, we need to get a sense of the sorts of horrifying experiences that cause it and how it feels to a person in the middle of such an event. This is the subject of the next chapter, titled "Saydia" after the neighborhood in southern Baghdad where I spent a week as a reporter in 2007. The second chapter, "In Terror's Shadow," takes a slight step back to explore the broader medical questions of PTSD: Who suf-

fers from it? Why do some people suffer from it and others don't?
Chapter 3 takes up the early history of trauma, beginning with the
prescientific view of it, and examines the earliest traces of post-traumatic symptoms in Western history, a history that begins, ironically
enough, in ancient Mesopotamia. In "The Haunted Mind," we turn
to the experiences of trauma survivors, including the hallucinations,
the nightmares, and the altered states of consciousness that often
define the post-traumatic condition. Stories of such hauntings have
a substantial place in the literature of trauma, and in this book I
argue that the post-traumatic state is one of liminality, an existence
between realms that causes great confusion for both the survivor and
the society to which he or she belongs. In Chapter 5, we explore the
modern history of trauma, including its role in the American Civil
War, the world wars, and the Vietnam War, the single most important event in the history of psychological trauma.

This book was written for very selfish reasons, as an attempt to
answer some pretty basic questions: Why does the world seem so different since I got back from Iraq? Why do I feel so out of place now?
What does one do with the knowledge gleaned from a near-death
experience? But as a former Marine, I was also driven by a larger
desire to understand how the current war on post-traumatic stress is
being waged, to get a sense of how it is being run by the VA and the
larger medical community, and to make my own independent assessment, my own reconnaissance, of the field. The second half of *The
Evil Hours* is, among other things, the story of this reconnaissance.
In "Therapy," we look at the leading therapeutic modalities and how
they work, which is based on my first-person experience with them
and on my own research into the science and philosophy that inform
them. In "Drugs," we explore the various pharmaceutical interventions that modern medicine has devised to treat PTSD, a set of interventions that, it turns out, is surprisingly feeble, with one possible
exception—a beta-blocker known as propranolol that is so old its
patent expired thirty years ago. (Big Pharma, it turns out, hasn't yet
figured out a way to make much money off PTSD.) Given this fact,
it is perhaps unsurprising that a wealth of therapeutic approaches
outside the medical mainstream has emerged to treat PTSD. In

"Alternatives," we examine the stunningly fertile field of alternative trauma therapy and how many of these therapies challenge our basic Western assumptions about medicine. Some of the most successful approaches to trauma, in fact, aren't really "therapies" in the normal clinical sense, as they are simply applied practices and activities that someone decided might be worth trying out on trauma survivors. Yoga, for instance, which is increasingly viewed as a powerful PTSD treatment, doesn't really have much to say about trauma as a formal subject. Instead, yoga simply aims to bring the body and mind into greater harmony—full stop.

The overarching design of this book is to take the reader from the underworld of trauma, its dark and confounding depths to the various stages of its aftermath, considering the ways that scientists and other thinkers have conceptualized it over the years, and continuing to perhaps the most radical proposition of all: that many people do, in fact, *grow* from trauma and become better human beings as a result of almost dying. The idea of post-traumatic growth was one I came to grudgingly. Like many of the leading clinicians, I found the idea of essentially flipping PTSD on its head, looking for a silver lining in the emotional carnage, to be insulting at first. Nevertheless, after interviewing a number of survivors of near-death experiences, I came kicking and screaming to the conclusion that much of what we call "post-traumatic stress" is, in fact, the failure of our culture to encourage people to seek wisdom in their loss and adversity and to consider trauma in anything other than a narrow medical context.

I have called this book a "biography" of PTSD, a description that is apt given the life the disease has taken on, a life far beyond what its VVAW architects could possibly have imagined. And as much as this book is an attempt to tell the story of PTSD, to recount the basic history and science of this surprisingly complex condition, it is also an attempt to examine the disease's other life in the culture at large and how it has become a sort of global lingua franca, a label, an identity, a way of understanding the self, a cultural meme, a political interest group, a scientific mythology, and even a theory of time.

SAYDIA

Through the small, thick Humvee window, the city was dirty and gray, a charcoal drawing sketched across the horizon. Sand moved over the blacktop. Along the roadside, the sagging arms of dead power lines hung from one blackened light pole to the next. The sun beat down on everything: the palm trees, the cinderblock houses, the dirty boulevards that led from nowhere to nowhere. There was something almost cunning in the layout of the city, in the way it could swallow entire armies, reduce them to chaos, as if to repudiate the idea that fortresses needed walls.

"When were you in the Corps?" a captain named Vollmer asked from the front passenger seat.

"'94 to '98," I said.

"Infantry?"

"Yeah."

"Ever go to Okinawa?"

"Yeah, I did a pump there with Three-Five."

"I was stationed at Schwab, up-island."

"No shit?"

"Third Recon. I was a jarhead before I went into the army."

I had resigned my commission so long before that it felt almost shameful to bring it up. My time in the Marine Corps had been brief and uneventful, boring even—nothing of consequence had happened, a fact that even now brings a sense of regret. I served in no war, took part in no raid launched under the cover of darkness. Most of my time in uniform was spent in garrison, staging mock patrols into the hills of Camp Pendleton and the jungles of Okinawa; occasionally we rappelled out of helicopters, as if to remind ourselves what real danger felt like. We called this training, but really we were just waiting, waiting for the call that never came. After four years, I left the service feeling vaguely disappointed, incomplete, as if some secret in me had been left unrevealed.

I was an unpromising lieutenant, not the worst, but a slacker. Most of my peers wanted to command, to lead Marines in combat. They believed, as others had before them, that their lives would be freed forever from the trivial and the mundane once the bullets started flying. The idea of "leadership," the endless posing and pretending, the trading of steely-eyed glances, bored me. Military leadership is a solemn responsibility, but in peacetime it can seem ridiculous, an exercise in fascism. Twenty-three and fresh out of college, I didn't want responsibility, I wanted adventure—adventure and the stories that came out of it. I think of one story an old sniper in my rifle company told about being in Beirut in the eighties. From a position inside the city, he had held Yasir Arafat in his crosshairs for several minutes as the PLO leader made his way through a refugee camp. Following Arafat through his scope, he began to cycle through his breathing drill, beginning to imagine the shot, the shot that would change history. He never pulled the trigger, of course, but having the man in his sights for a few moments had given him an almost erotic sense of power. It was a feeling I never forgot.

Looking back, I can see that what I really wanted, as much as the adventure or experience or medals, was something far less noble: I wanted to be like that sniper. Not a killer, really, but a man with a history. I wanted to make other people envious. Envious of my experience. Envious of what I had seen. Envious of the stories I could tell. There were other desires, to be sure, some more honorable than that, but what I coveted more than anything was the power of a certain kind of silence, the silence that fell over a room when a veteran launched into a story that began, "Back in the Mekong . . ."

This desire clings to me still and was even stronger during my first years out of the Marine Corps. I was finishing graduate school, still dreaming of faraway places, when the towers fell. Like everyone else, I woke on September 12 and saw a different world. I had begun working tentatively as a writer, and it was the writer in me, not the Marine, that sensed an opportunity. The world was at war, and I saw that the logical thing to do was to become a war correspondent. It would be a way of revising my past, correcting an oversight in my record; without having to don a uniform or suffer any orders, I could collect the experiences I'd hungered for as a young man. I would be in a war, but on my own terms. It felt like I'd discovered a trapdoor in time.

Now it was October 2007, the height of the surge. I was out with some soldiers from the First Infantry Division, patrolling a Baghdad neighborhood west of the river that I'd never been to before, even though I'd been coming to Iraq for three years. Saydia had been Sunni for as long as anyone could remember, but it was being taken over by the Shia, block by block, in a process that the *New York Times* had referred to as "slow-motion ethnic cleansing." This larger narrative of the war, the distinction between Sunni and Shia, the politics of the surge, was of little interest to the soldiers. The real reason behind their presence here seemed beyond them; they were here simply to make sure that their part of the city didn't explode completely and that was all.

It was one of those seasons in Baghdad when you could set your watch by the first firefights of the evening. Usually it was just a bunch of kids in a pickup hosing down the neighborhood with AKs. I didn't mind the shooting so much. Shooting had a logic that I understood. Either you were in its way or you weren't. My problem was with the bombs buried in the street. If you ran over a rigged 155 round, it didn't matter how much you knew about the war, how patriotic or well-trained you were, or if you'd been the honor man at boot camp. The year before, I'd seen a three-ton Humvee blown right off a bridge and into a canal by a pair of 155 rounds that had been flawlessly cemented into the roadway. The Humvee bucked like a startled horse and landed facedown in the filthy water, and two men inside drowned. The rest of us fanned out in a circle, waiting for an ambush that never came. The war happened in collections of seconds, but the memories of it echoed forever.

I shifted in my seat, the Humvee creaking like an old ship. The houses scrolled by. The occasional eucalyptus, the high gray walls, the mysterious chalk markings written in Arabic. The secret life of Iraq that no outsider could penetrate: the life of street soccer games, mullahs, the names of dead uncles. Moving my head left to right, I could make the image of the street bend and warp in the thick armored glass until it dissolved into blue nothingness at the edge of the window frame. It was like everything in Iraq: your perception of events depended on your angle of vision. Nothing was indisputable in Iraq except death and the heat. I tried to imagine the people who lived in the houses but could not, even though I'd spent months going out on patrols in streets just like this and drinking tea in the same sort of houses we drove past. Even the dogs seemed to view us with suspicion, watching us from under the bellies of burned-out cars as we passed.

"Time," the soldier next to me was saying. "What the fuck is time in a place like this?"

His name was Jonah, but everyone called him Reaper, after his radio callsign. He wore a blue bandana that stuck out the back of his helmet, giving him a small ponytail. An American infantry platoon is a haven for characters. Even more than the military in general, it serves as a sort of laboratory for the creation of personalities: court jesters, field preachers, paranoids, grunt magicians, and blessed ne'er-do-wells. Reaper was the platoon philosopher.

"Time," he said, pausing melodramatically, "time is in the eye of the beholder. I go to sleep in May, I wake up in September. Okay, now it's September. I go to sleep at nineteen-hundred. I wake up a month later, and it's nineteen oh-one."

"How long has it been this way?" I asked gamely.

"All day, sir."

Time was an issue with Reaper because he, along with the rest of the platoon, had been in Iraq for thirteen months, a virtual eternity in war. How long was thirteen months when even a second in Iraq could lose you in its vast expanse, its limits stretching outward beyond the grasp of imagination? And, as Reaper had explained to me the night before, the entire war was really just a battle between two different kinds of time. In huge swaths of Iraq, people patterned their lives around the ritual predawn prayers, sunup, sundown, spring, and summer. In America, we lived by the tick of the clock, by the drumbeat of capitalism, the forty-hour work week, the binary code of the internet. As if to reinforce his point, when we'd left the patrol base that morning, I'd spotted a plywood board bolted to a concrete barrier that announced the day's theme, like the subject of a Sunday sermon back home. Painted on the plywood was a simple Godot-like assertion: EVERYDAY IS DAY ONE.

"I think I might be a pacifist, sir."

"Oh, really, how's that working out for you?" I said.

"Okay, not a pacifist, but what's it called? An expatriate."

"You've got a running start being over here."

"I'm serious, sir. I can't stand Americans."

You could feel it, Reaper needed to be talked to. It was like we were long-separated siblings, and now that we were finally together again, there was some catching up to do. Deep down I understood in a way that didn't need expressing: the work of soldiering was numbing and having a reporter along for the ride presented a huge opportunity. I was both entertainment and an audience.

Reaper was twenty-six, a geezer for the infantry. His unit was stationed in Germany, and he had married a local girl, a tall Nordic wonder whose head was practically aflame with fine blonde hair, or so he said. He was from East Texas, so, of course, the first thing out of his mouth when he met her was a joke about her being a member of the Master Race and how he was fated to procreate with her. The way he described her, I imagined her in a convertible Mustang trailing clouds of glory, her hair whipping in the breeze. You got the sense that Germany had shown him something of the world and had dimmed his enthusiasm for the army, the annoyance showing in his face.

Talking back at the patrol base, he told me the one thing he imagined over and over again was taking his wife to Iraq ten years from now, maybe up in the northern part of the country, up where grass grew over rolling hills. "Just to be back here and actually talk to the people. You know, as people."

"Sir, have you read any Sartre?" he asked, fiddling with his bandana.

"Hey, Reaper." It was Vollmer.

"What?"

"Give it a rest, we got work to do."

Vollmer had an odd face, fixed and expressionless. The feeling must have left it long ago—perhaps during his first tour—and now his features were formed, and he would look like that until the day he died. The lack of emotion gave everything he said a certain authority. Like the broken streets we drove down, you wondered what had happened to make him look this way. It was a mystery that tickled at first, and then it burned: Was it one horrible day in particular, or was it the procession of one bleak day added to the next, until the differences between them no longer mattered? In between answering radio calls, he dipped tobacco, spitting into a Coke can in his hand, a habit left over from his days as an enlisted man.

"You must be desperate for a story if you're here," Vollmer said, dully, his eyes never leaving the road.

I didn't like being called desperate, but he wasn't far off. I'd just spent a month in Dora, a place that Al Qaeda, in their charming way, had been advertising on the internet as their "last castle in Baghdad," and my nerves needed a break. My first patrol in Dora, which was supposed to be an intelligence-gathering operation, had been interrupted by a nearby platoon getting ambushed. When we arrived at the ambush site, I saw that a Korean-American soldier had been shot in the genitals. I took cover in the shade of a nearby retaining wall, trying desperately not to think about what had happened. I overheard him talking quietly to his first sergeant, saying that while he'd had his doubts before, he was definitely an atheist now, because what sort of God would let a guy get shot in the dick? Every day in Dora had been a variation on this unreal theme: one day it was a guy getting shot in the dick, the next day it was our Humvee driving right over a metal "pizza box" IED that failed to explode for some reason, and the next day it was a patrol I was accompanying being sent to inspect the ruins of a mansion that had been laced with explosives so that it would collapse on anyone who walked inside.

The close calls. They were like boils in the ocean that held, churning the water for a moment, hinting at something below. You sailed on, but the image of what could have been your last sight stayed with you. War has always been uncanny. For me, however, it was a siren song — the odd occurrences and esoteric knowledge that came from living so close to death for so long, the hope for deeper wisdom, my near-deaths in towns with names like Karma, Fallujah, and Qaim. Places so out there, so far off the map of normal morality, that anything seemed possible. Anything at all.

Have you ever been blown up before, sir?
Finding patterns where there shouldn't be patterns.

The soldiers in Dora were different, too. From a famous airborne unit, they were like an old aristocratic family trying to live up to former glories. They were driven to take chances, as if to prove their worth. It was a self-serving cycle. Each close call they survived confirmed their status as blessed men. Each man who was killed reminded them of the special work they were undertaking. Could there be any more exalting work in this life? To challenge death day after day? I found myself excited and exhausted by my time there, by my brushes with death, a deep tiredness in my bones. Walking away from the battalion command post in Dora the last time, the blood felt different in my veins. It was a lesson the war taught me: the body knows things long before the mind catches up. And the month I spent waiting for "my" IED to go off had taken its toll, the dread accumulating in my body like a toxin.*

I had some time to kill before I was due out west in Anbar, where I had arranged an embed with the Marines, my old tribe. Back in the Green Zone, someone had told me that Saydia was a quiet sector, and so I decided to hang out there until my time came to head into the desert. I was tired and needed some time to myself. A quiet couple

---

* Later, I would learn that I wasn't the only one changed by Dora. In his 2010 book *Lethal Warriors: When the New Band of Brothers Came Home,* journalist David Phillips describes how Dora veterans suffered a PTSD rate more than three times higher than that of a similar army battalion deployed to a different part of Iraq.

days in a quiet sector to fill in some of the gaps in my knowledge of Shia Baghdad, which was weak at best. As we rolled drowsily along in the heat, I decided this would be my final patrol in Baghdad. After that, I'd take a week out west, catch a flight home, stir in some quotes, and collect a paycheck.

The radio crackled on the dashboard of the Humvee. Vollmer picked up the handset and quietly took in the situation. After a minute, he said something that sounded like "Roger that. Out."

"All right, listen up, gents. There are some houses on fire north of us. We're gonna go take a look and see what's what."

Most likely some Shia had set the fires, their way of encouraging their Sunni neighbors to seek accommodations elsewhere. It was one of the maddening things about Iraq. There was almost never any direct combat. Almost never was a day decided by enemies duking it out toe to toe. The fighting, when it happened, was always indirect—a sniper shooting at you all day from an invisible spider hole that you could spend weeks searching for and never find—or by proxy—an Al Qaeda fixer paying an unemployed local to emplace a bomb, its detonation something he would never see.

We drove for a long time, the heat leaking in through the cracks in the Humvee chassis. I had been down so many roads in the city that after a while it became hard to tell if you were awake or asleep. The roads just went on and on, leaving your mind somewhere in the dust trailing behind the Humvee. At some point, I noticed that the streets seemed emptier, paper cups and trash blowing in the flame-thrower heat. After a while, I heard the Bradley armored personnel carrier ahead of us turning. I could feel the tracks grinding the blacktop under the Humvee.

"All right, slow up a bit," Vollmer told the driver as we turned onto a side street.

Ahead of us, the street was on fire. Black smoke poured diagonally out of a row of houses to our left, darkening the entire block. The Bradley punched a hole in the wall of smoke and disappeared. It was like we were entering a cave. The driver pointed us into the lowering dark without a word, seemingly dumb to his course.

"Once we're in, ease off," Vollmer said.

"Roger," the driver said, repeating the word as if to reassure himself.

I concentrated on taking photos, putting the lens of my SLR up against the armored glass to reduce the distortion. We passed under the roof of smoke, and suddenly it was as if a heavy net had been thrown over the sun, everything around us taking on a sepia quality. I could still hear the thunder of the Bradley ahead of us, wavering and distant like a receding train. The smoke parted for a second, and I was able to get a better look at the street. Slate gray and ringed by high cinderblock walls, the houses were basically middle-class dwellings, nearly identical to the homes I had seen in Mexico years before. I half-expected to see kids in Chivas jerseys chasing a soccer ball down the block. The street itself was ominously empty, only the usual trash and palm leaves decorating the blacktop. There was a strange lost feeling to it all, as in an empty house, the rooms without furniture. The world seemed deserted, the last humans having abandoned the earth. The smoke thickened again, mysteriously. Beside me, Reaper was quiet. I looked up at the gunner in the turret. I had been told that it would be up to me to pass him ammunition if he needed it. Without knowing why, I began to tighten up a little and then a little more. I didn't have a thought in my head, but something was happening in there.

"Hey, Vollmer, dude, I know I'm just baggage, but this street sucks, and now we can't see shit."

He ignored me. Alone with his thoughts, he turned his head from side to side. We began to slow down. There was some talk about stopping and dismounting some scouts to investigate the fires. We had come to a halt when someone in the Bradley called back to us. We were in a cul-de-sac, boxed in. "We're turning around," they said.

"Roger," I heard Vollmer say tiredly. "So are we."

The driver put the Humvee in reverse.

"Scan our six o'clock," Vollmer yelled up at the gunner, grasping his calf. "We're gonna pivot and let the Bradley—"

And that was as far as he got.

• • •

Virtually everyone who survives a traumatic experience recalls that certain details surrounding the event have a special vividness, seeming to glow in the imagination with an inexplicable intensity. Extreme events require extreme explanations, and it is as if the mind cannot, even for a moment, tolerate the idea that such absurd things can be allowed to happen, that the universe is random, a cacophony "of sound and fury, signifying nothing." In the wake of trauma, the mind seems to develop a ravishing hunger for meaningful facts, the raw materials from which a story can be fashioned. As the novelist and compulsive storyteller Isak Dinesen once wrote, "All sorrows can be borne if you put them in a story, or tell a story about them."

Sometimes, and particularly with respect to traumatic narratives, these stories take the form of portents and premonitions, as if the trauma in its unalloyed power is able to reach forward through time, disrupting the present; in *The Hour of Our Death,* Philippe Aries observed that in Arthurian mythology, "death does not come as a surprise, even when it is the accidental result of a wound or the effect of too great an emotion, as was sometimes the case. Its essential characteristic is that it gives advance warning of its arrival." Western literature, he points out, is full of such warnings: auguries, omens, doppelgangers, *memento mori,* reminders to the faithful that death is forever on the horizon. In the *Chanson de Roland,* the stories of the Round Table, the knight Gawain is asked, "Ah, good my lord, think you then so soon to die?" Gawain replies, "I tell you that I shall not live two days."

Have you ever been blown up before, sir?

Had I remembered the soldier's question simply because of what happened next? Because of some need to make a meaningful story out of a meaningless event?

To scientists, these sorts of ideas are typically viewed as examples of *apophenia.* An extension of the normal human impulse to find patterns in life, apophenia is an aberrant form of sense-making that can, in its extreme form, merge with the pathological, as in paranoid schizophrenia. The classic example of apophenic thinking that is usually given is that of the NASA scientists who in 1976 discovered a geologic formation on the surface of Mars that seemed to resemble a human face. Some observers saw this as evidence of intelligent life on Mars, a greeting card left on the surface of the red planet by a previous civilization. More recent images from the Mars Explorer show that the apparent face was, in fact, the result of unusual light conditions at the time of the initial photographs, and it is actually shaped more like a lump of cookie dough.

Over my months in Iraq, I became obsessed with the idea that there was something behind apophenia, reasoning that because being close to death necessarily heightened one's perception, then the right sort of person in Iraq might be in a position to achieve a higher form of consciousness, almost like a physicist staring into the glow of a particle accelerator. It was this line of thinking that kept me coming back to the war, year after year, to the bewilderment of my friends and colleagues. In my own peculiar way, I felt like the German painter Otto Dix, a veteran of World War I, who wrote, "I had to have that experience: how someone near me suddenly fell and was finished. . . . I am a man of reality. I must see everything. I need to experience all the abysses of life. That is why I volunteered."

Later, this habit of needing to see everything, of trying to make sense of my experience through intense examination, came to dominate my postwar existence. In time, I came to think of myself as devoted to a sort of Kabbalah, a cult of one whose mission it was to discover what the others had missed, the pattern hidden in the loom, the hand of God, if you will. This habit of rumination, of pattern seeking, of needing to make sense of it all, is present in everyone, but it can kick into overdrive in the wake of trauma.

It was this type of obsessive sense-making, of unintentional apophenia, that vexed Freud when he first observed it in the dreams of World War I veterans, an observation that changed the course of psychology. In *On Metapsychology,* written not long after the guns had fallen silent, Freud saw that sufferers of war neuroses "were endeavoring to master the stimulus retrospectively, by developing the anxiety whose omission was the cause of the traumatic neurosis." (In some translations of Freud's work, this phenomenon was even referred to as "fate neurosis," because it seemed to dominate his patients to such a degree that it became a sort of destiny, a pattern of trauma and retrauma that seemed likely to govern the rest of their lives.) Prior to the war, Freud's theory of the unconscious had been dominated by what he called "the pleasure principle," the idea that all people ultimately desire the gratification of their biological impulses, the need for sex and the need for mastery of their environment. The idea that some people would obsess over such unpleasurable memories flew in the face of everything that Freud believed. And as he observed, the call of such moments becomes something akin to a moral obligation, in the way that some widows are drawn to the graves of lost spouses. One can see this sort of obligation in the words of the poet Wilfred Owen, who in a letter to his mother shortly before his death wrote that "I confess I *bring on* what few war dreams I now have, entirely by *willingly* considering war for an evening. I do so because I have my duty to perform towards War."

This sense that the life-threatening experience is "unmastered" or somehow beyond the survivor's control is one of the central problems of post-traumatic stress. Normal, nontraumatic memories are owned and integrated into the ongoing story of the self. These are, in a sense, like domesticated animals, amenable to control, tractable. In contrast, the traumatic memory stands apart, like a feral dog, snarling, wild, and unpredictable. This is, in part, what the psychoanalyst I interviewed meant when he said that "trauma destroys the fabric of time." These unincorporated memories insist on being noticed, and in their insistence, they come to haunt the minds of survivors, destroying their perception of time.

In *Slaughterhouse-Five*, Kurt Vonnegut's novel about World War II, it is the main character's near-death experience during the bombing of Dresden that causes him to "come unstuck in time." Over the course of the book, which one VA administrator described as "the ultimate PTSD novel," it is as if the space-time continuum has been destroyed along with the city of Dresden. As far as the protagonist Billy Pilgrim is concerned, that is certainly the case. The novel opens: "Billy has gone to sleep a senile widower and awakened on his wedding day. He has walked through a door in 1955 and come out another one in 1941. He has gone back through that door to find himself in 1963. He has seen his birth and death many times, he says, and pays random visits to all the events in between . . . Billy is spastic in time, has no control over where he is going next, and the trips aren't necessarily fun. He is in a constant state of stage fright, he says, because he never knows what part of his life he is going to have to act in next."

One of the perceptual mechanisms that can cause people to become unstuck in time, preventing the incorporation of experiences into the normal web of memory, is what psychologists call dissociation, essentially a splitting of the mind in two. An altered state of consciousness, dissociation allows you to distance yourself when a life-threatening situation occurs, as when a driver suddenly sees his car from a distance, almost like a spectacle in a theater, with a sense of being an observer rather than a participant. This was, in fact, a common refrain I'd heard from soldiers in Dora when they described the combat they'd been through—"It felt like I was watching a movie." One particularly bloody day was insistently referred to as the "*Black Hawk Down* day," as if the only way it could be recalled was through the narrative frame of an action movie. Curiously, this distancing seems to hold even after the event. "Our own death is indeed, unimaginable," Freud wrote in 1915, "and whenever we make the attempt to imagine it we can perceive that we really survive as spectators." Such existential threats must be mutated, converted, or otherwise altered so that the mind can continue to exist.

One of the most commonly reported forms of dissociation is that of time seeming to move differently, as if the brain is processing the world at a different speed than before. For most, this begins at the moment of maximum danger. Virtually everyone who has ever experienced trauma describes the world beginning to move in a kind of "slow motion." Aron Ralston, a hiker exploring the slot canyons of southeastern Utah in 2003, was trapped beneath a huge boulder. He wrote about the rock rolling toward him, saying that "time dilates, as if I'm dreaming, and my reactions decelerate," and in his memoir, *Between a Rock and a Hard Place*, Ralston describes the entire process as seeming to happen in "slow motion." One Marine I interviewed from the Gulf War recalled being under fire and how the tracer rounds seemed to be crawling through the desert air toward him like fireflies. His left leg, which was poking outside of the Humvee he was riding in, suddenly felt like it was on fire, as if he'd been hit already, even though the rounds had yet to reach his vehicle. Instinctively, he pulled his leg inside the vehicle before the bullets zipped by. All of this happened in under a second.

Dissociation can also take on more extreme forms that seem downright supernatural. One study conducted by the U.S. Navy on survival school trainees found that under extreme stress, more than half of them reported experiencing "unreal events that could not be accounted for rationally." Stories of dissociation have a substantial place in the canon of war literature. Michael Herr, in *Dispatches,* his classic work of Vietnam reportage, describes the combat he experienced at Khe Sanh: "It came back the same way every time, dreaded and welcome, balls and bowels turning over together, your senses working like strobes, free-falling all the way down to the essences and then flying out again in a rush to focus, like the first strong twinge of tripping after an infusion of psilocybin . . . And every time, you were so weary afterward, so empty of everything but being alive that you couldn't recall any of it." Dissociation of this sort leads to some of the most intimate, deeply personal experiences that a person can undergo, and descriptions of it are filled with the language of the infinite, as if in moments of trauma the universe pulls back the curtain for a few moments. Herr's *Dispatches* echoes with such glimpses of dark wonder: "the rapture of the deep," "time outside of time," and describing "stories you'd hear out of a remote but accessible space where there were no ideas, no emotions, no facts, no proper language, only clean information." It is little wonder that such states of consciousness continue to haunt the minds of survivors of extreme events.

Dissociation is not a bad thing in itself. People often "space out" in moments of stress, finding themselves obsessively staring at a wall calendar during a tense conversation or being captivated by thoughts of old lovers during a turbulent airplane ride. Psychiatrists think that dissociation may, in fact, have a protective, opiate-like effect on the brain, shielding consciousness from the pain of hideous events.

(Herr seems to allude to this idea in the final pages of *Dispatches*: "Opium space, big round O, and time outside of time, a trip that happened in seconds and over years.") But if the dissociation is profound enough and becomes chronic, it can create problems down the road. As the popular neurologist and writer Oliver Sacks observed in *Hallucinations,* "the dissociations of PTSD are of a more radical kind, for the unbearable sights, sounds, smells, and emotions of the hideous experience get locked away in a separate, subterranean chamber of the mind."

PTSD is often thought of as being a syndrome of remembering things too well, of the memory working itself into a kind of frenzy, overrecording events that are best left forgotten. In fact, in the case of peritraumatic dissociation, or dissociation during a traumatic event, the opposite may be true. It is almost as if the threatening event remains underexperienced or misremembered because it's so toxic. Too hot for the brain to handle, the experiences get stashed in a dark corner of the warehouse, off on layaway, the mind seemingly oblivious to the interest that accrues. This inversion of the expected logic remains one of the paradoxes of survival — that which was unperceived returns to haunt, as if to reiterate Nature's first commandment: Thou Shalt Attend to Danger. As Ben Helfgott, a concentration camp survivor, put it succinctly, "The ones who 'forget,' they suffer later."

Sometimes I can remember the explosion, sometimes I cannot. When I think of it quickly, I can recall the sound, but if asked to recount the story of being blown up, all that comes back is a kind of mental static, as if my ears are still waiting for the noise to arrive. My first stable memory of "my" IED is of Vollmer in the front passenger seat, snapping his head back and yelling stupidly "What was that?" as if it weren't obvious. We were on terror's clock now. Disoriented by the smoke from the burning homes and trapped in a cul-de-sac, we had backed over an IED hidden in the trash on the side of the road.

The force of the blast rocketed past Reaper's right ear, buckling the metal behind his head. I looked at him, his head wreathed in smoke, and felt alien and empty inside. When I turned my head back, it was like I wasn't there anymore. I suddenly saw myself as if from behind, floating above the whole scene. There I was, sitting motionless in my seat, my black digital camera resting on my leg. The ghost-me hovered there, unable to move or to speak, unable to connect with that other person, as if an invisible wall had been thrown up between us. In the air behind my head there was no sound, just an underwater rush, like I was swimming inside the explosion, holding my breath and waiting to come out the other side. In later years, I would come to see that there were two of me created in this moment: the one who heard the explosion and knows it fully, and the other, more slippery one, harder to make out, who did not hear. Which one was the real me, which one the imposter?

The moment passed, and when it was over, I was back in my seat again, just as before. Time hadn't slowed down so much as it had become denser, richer in detail. I sat up and looked around. I could see that we were on fire and that thick smoke was pouring into the cabin from a gash in the metal behind Reaper's head. He appeared to be okay, and looking past him, I could see the smoke moving in a thick current, like a wide mountain stream, the edges curling, the center continually flowing. Segments seemed to break off and reach out toward the front of the cabin in long articulated arms. Elaborate curls were born like small galaxies in the darkening air, thickening and stealing light as they turned.

My eyes adjusting, I looked through the window and saw that the homes to our left were still burning, the smoke migrating over the blacktop. It occurred to me that someone ought to be shooting at us from behind the wall of smoke. This thought began to irritate me. We were off the script, somehow. This was supposed to be an ambush, so why wasn't the enemy playing its part and finishing us off? With all of our attention focused inward, on the bomb that had just gone off, we were in perfect position, practically begging to be annihilated. As if by magic, just then a line of muzzle flashes began winking at us through the smoke almost whimsically, like carnival sparklers. I sat there for a moment, bracing for the bullets' impact. My ass welded to the seat, I was trying to believe in what was happening: any moment now and it would be over. The agony of the end, it seemed to go on forever. There was a moment of regret, clouds of dust billowing from the houses.

Blinking, suddenly I felt different, as if a long moment had passed in my head. I looked over at the houses, and I realized that no one was shooting at us. We were safe and yet all was profane, all was going and coming at the same instant.

And just like that, I got pissed. Here I was, trapped in a Humvee full of buffoons who were practically begging to be murdered by a bunch of half-assed insurgents. Was there ever a bigger ship of fools?

"Why the fuck isn't someone busting down doors, looking for the trigger man? Where the fuck is the Bradley? Why hasn't someone launched the QRF?" I yelled at no one in particular, using the military term for the rescue squad that every unit kept on standby in case of attack.

Vollmer turned his head around. "Everyone okay?" he yelled. He didn't seem to have heard a word I'd said.

I patted down my legs, first doing a quick once-over, then squeezing near my groin, my armpits, and my neck for the arteries. Remembering the dick-shot soldier in Dora, I double-checked my crotch, just to be sure. All clear. I got my gear in order and found the door handle with my hand, just as a reference point. I looked over at Reaper, somehow making out his eyes burning red through the haze. He was cursing violently. "Two months left in this bitch and then this!" And so on.

"Everybody stays in the vehicle! Nobody gets out!" Vollmer yelled at no one in particular. Then he was yelling up at the gunner, craning his neck up into the turret, asking him if he could see where the smoke was coming from. The gunner didn't say anything.

As John le Carré observed, somewhere in every bomb explosion there is a miracle. For some, it is the tiniest of details that saves a life: the shrapnel that penetrates a guy's helmet only to exit the other side, leaving him unscathed. With every IED that went off, there were a dozen stories, some dark and some redeeming and transcendent, but all of them flew in the face of human reason. The year before, I'd interviewed a navy corpsman who told me about a Marine who'd been killed in Fallujah the same hour that his son was born back in the States. Our miracles were more common. The first was the twelve inches that saved Reaper, sending the force of the blast through the trunk of the Humvee instead of through his ass. The second miracle was that somehow everyone in the Humvee was deafened by the explosion except me, even though it had gone off less than three feet from where I sat.

At some point, I can't remember when, someone from the Bradley ran up to our Humvee and doused the flames with a fire extinguisher. A second later, he wrenched open the door and yelled, "You morons, there was a shitload of machinegun ammo in the back that was on fire." Before the soldier could get another word out, Vollmer hollered at him to get back in the Bradley before someone took a potshot at him.

This seemed to wake Vollmer up, and he yelled at the driver to put it in drive and take us back to the patrol base. The driver did as he was ordered, though Vollmer had to yell at him twice to be heard. It was then that we discovered our next problem: the IED had destroyed our right rear wheel, and when the driver floored it, nothing happened except the grinding of the wheel rim inside the remnants of the tire. It took forever, but somehow the driver, alternating between forward and reverse, was able to extract our Humvee from the blast crater and aim us toward home, toward our patrol base, which shone in my mind now like a holy city.

Somehow we got back safely, somehow the Humvee held together, somehow no one else decided to light us up, somehow we managed to not hit another IED on the way. My memories of the drive back are erratic, like snapshots in a lost photo album. There were checkpoints manned by Iraqi soldiers that we ignored, local traffic moving blindly through the streets oblivious to our presence, the ruined rim of the Humvee grinding on the pavement.

One memory remains clear, however. I could feel Reaper's eyes on me, and when I glanced over at him, he let me have it.

"What the fuck are you doing here anyway?" he yelled. "I don't fucking get it. They must be paying you some serious bread to be here." He turned his head away but not before I got a look at his eyes, which blazed with a sort of fury. It was like the IED had soured things between us, and whatever connection that had existed had been destroyed in the blast. There was an unmistakable tone of disgust in his words. He began again. "You're a reporter, man! You could be anywhere, and of all the places in the world, you chose this one. I have to be here. I don't know if you've noticed, but none of us wants to be here in this bullshit. You think I'm here because I love America? Dude, I joined the army 'cause I'm poor. I joined the army 'cause I had nowhere else to go."

I started to answer him but gave up. What could I say? The blast had shaken me enough that I could barely think straight, let alone argue coherently, and what really was the point in trying to argue with a Humvee full of deaf soldiers? And besides, he had a point, and even though it wouldn't sink in for years, I didn't have any words for him. Turning away, I looked out the window and watched the hot city stutter past. Reaper had been wounded three times before and had handled it with equanimity, or so I had been told by his buddies, but there was something about my presence in Saydia, on this particular patrol, that seemed to have pushed him over the edge, as if the IED had shaken loose some secret doubts within him, as if he couldn't fathom what sort of person had so little use for his life that he would voluntarily go to a place like Baghdad in the middle of a war.

Later, I would realize that Reaper had been on to something, that this was exactly what it was all about, this and several other things. I was here to cover the war, it was understood, but why was it understood? The war had granted Reaper a certain measure of early wisdom, this much I had seen prior to the explosion. Now, shaken by this fourth near-death, he had aimed some of this wisdom back at me, and it hurt, though it took a long time to understand why. Maybe he wouldn't have said anything under normal circumstances, maybe he shouldn't have. The IED had stolen so many things, including his restraint. Or perhaps this was a gift, really, the gift of candor, the bomb's final miracle.

When, after what seemed like hours, we made it back inside the wire, I looked up and saw the sign again. EVERYDAY IS DAY ONE. I looked away as quickly as I could. One part of the war was over, another just beginning.

Thirty minutes later, I was back at FOB Falcon, in an air-conditioned surgical clinic, having my head examined. A week after that, I was back in California.

IN TERROR'S SHADOW

W E ARE BORN in debt, owing the world a death. This is the shadow that darkens every cradle. Trauma is what happens when you catch a surprise glimpse of that darkness, the coming annihilation not only of the body and the mind but also, seemingly, of the world. Trauma is the savagery of the universe made manifest within us, and it destroys not only the integrity of consciousness, the myth of self-mastery, and the experience of time but also our ability to live peacefully with others, almost as if it were a virus, a pathogen content to do nothing besides replicate itself in the world, over and over, until only it remains. Trauma is the glimpse of truth that tells us a lie: the lie that love is impossible, that peace is an illusion. Therapy and medication can ease the pain but neither can suck the venom from the blood, make the survivor unsee the darkness and unknow the secret that lies beneath the surface of life. Despite the quixotic claims of modern neuroscience, there is no cure for trauma. Once it enters the body, it stays there forever, initiating a complex chemical chain of events that changes not only the physiology of the victims but also the physiology of their offspring. One cannot, as war correspondent Michael Herr testifies in *Dispatches,* simply "run the film backwards out of consciousness." Trauma is our special legacy as sentient beings, creatures burdened with the knowledge of our own impermanence; our symbolic experience with it is one of the things that separates us from the animal kingdom. As long as we exist, the universe will be scheming to wipe us out. The best we can do is work to contain the pain, draw a line around it, name it, domesticate it, and try to transform what lies on the other side of the line into a kind of knowledge, a knowledge of the mechanics of loss that might be put to use for future generations.

Trauma is not exotic, nor is it something belonging only to poorer regions of the world. It is not unique to the modern era, and while history tells us our responses to it evolve, trauma itself, what one pioneering researcher called "the death imprint," is immortal and ubiquitous. "Trauma is democratic," Yale historian Jay Winter observed in a volume on the cultural history of World War I, as "it chooses all kinds of people in its crippling passage." It is little wonder that the ancient Greeks included a god of war in the pantheon of the universe: the historian Will Durant calculated that there have been only twenty-nine years in all of human history when there wasn't a war going on somewhere in the world.

The numbers are staggering: a 2010 study undertaken by the Department of Justice found that 18 percent of women in the United States have been raped and that around half of them will suffer from PTSD, some fourteen million women in all. The most cited research study on the incidence of trauma, a sort of Census of Misery known as the *National Comorbidity Survey* (completed before 9/11), found that approximately 55 percent of the U.S. population will be exposed to at least one traumatic event in their lifetime in the form of military combat, rape, physical assault, natural disaster, or automobile accident, roughly the same number of Americans who own smartphones. Alice Sebold, when asked why she chose to write about the rape and dismemberment of a fourteen-year-old girl in her bestselling novel *The Lovely Bones,* replied, "Because it's part of life. It's very much a part of the experience of what it is to live in this culture. It happens all the time." Pulitzer Prize–winning novelist Cormac McCarthy makes a similar point when he begins *Blood Meridian,* his dark masterpiece of violence in the American West, with a reference to a June 13, 1982, article in the *Yuma Daily Sun* that describes the discovery of a 300,000-year-old fossil skull that had been scalped.

Trauma defies description, but as an analogy it can be useful to think of it as a transfer of energies: like a bullet, it enters the body, angry, and with a surplus of power, eager to transmit it to whatever flesh it finds, doing its work and then exiting, leaving the troubled body behind, dragging a comet's tail of memory, hope, and innocence through the air, looking for another body to complicate. Logic tells us that the larger the bullet, the greater the damage. In fact, one of the cardinal principles of modern trauma studies is built on this big-bullet little-bullet idea, which is what researchers refer to as the "dose-response curve." In plain English, the dose-response curve says that the more terrifying the event, the greater the potential for harm. To use a real-world example, the dose-response curve tells us that a thirty-one-year-old woman named Linda who is pinned beneath a heavy bookcase after an earthquake for an hour is more likely to survive without post-traumatic symptoms than if she had been pinned under a bookcase for twenty-four hours next to the body of her dead husband.

The dose-response curve explains a lot. It explains, for instance, the somewhat obvious fact that not all traumas are created equal and that trauma has a certain cumulative quality, in the sense that one terrible event can serve to "soften up" a person and make him or her more vulnerable to a later trauma. But as with all elegant theories, something gets lost in the translation to real life; some overlooked truth remains hidden. For anyone who has ever been to war or watched a brushfire consume the dreams and family histories of an entire suburb, the problem with this theory is obvious: How exactly does one go about quantifying trauma? What exactly qualifies as a "dose" in this theory? Put another way, exactly how many cc's of pain, loss, and moral vertigo can one fit into a laboratory beaker?

There is also the challenge of how to factor in the identity of the person undergoing such a "dosage." As one Vietnam vet turned advocate practically yelled at me one day, "Combat doesn't happen to inert bodies, it happens to *people*." In our falling-bookcase example, the question thus becomes: *Who is Linda exactly?* What sort of family does she come from? What sort of childhood did she have? A safe, protected one or one marked by sadism and abuse? Was she extroverted? Open to new experiences and sensations? Was she someone who was easily hypnotized? What happened to her immediately prior to the earthquake? To what degree was she exposed to the elements during her ordeal? Did she lose consciousness at any point? How did her friends and family, her social support system, respond after the temblor? And perhaps most importantly, what story did she tell herself in the wake of this seismic event? How did she incorporate the terror into the ongoing tale of her life? How did she go about creating a narrative from the disparate images of her actual experience, arranging them into a shape that she could recognize as uniquely her own?

This quagmire of questions would seem to overwhelm the scientific mind and to a certain extent it does. Fundamentally, we do not know why some people are damaged by terror and some are not. Part of trauma's power lies in its mystery, in the fact that it remains outside the range of normal human perception, like a distant galaxy beyond the reach of even the most powerful telescope. It remains an enigma because human beings are an enigma. Nevertheless, scientists have in recent years developed what amounts to a recipe for post-traumatic stress, for lack of a better word. If you surprise someone, trap them, physically violate them in some way (as with rape), and expose them to the elements for some period of time, you will soon see the hallmarks of what we call PTSD. According to the *Comprehensive Textbook of Psychiatry,* the common thread in psychological trauma is a feeling of "intense fear, helplessness, loss of control, and threat of annihilation."

Chief among the crimes that trauma commits against the mind is the distortions of memory it introduces. In the face of terror, the mind skips straight over some things and perversely overrecords others; one pattern that researchers see is that during terror the mind's normal capacity to record novel visual stimuli tends to go into overdrive, creating what early psychologists called the *idée fixe.* One of the most unsettling features of trauma is the odd sense — which one gets when visiting war zones and automobile accidents — that the mind functions as a sort of mad curator of the grotesque and the bizarre, documenting in painstaking detail the most repulsive scenes of violence and human violation. The mind, which recoils at the thought of its own extinction, adheres to visions of the extinction of others, as if to collect clues to its own demise. Here one is reminded of the tragic cry of the overexperienced—"If I could just get that sight out of my head!" I cannot, for instance, get out of my head the sight of the soldier in Dora who'd been wounded in the groin. Nor can I unsee the red Igloo Beverage Container floating in a filthy canal next to an overturned Humvee north of Fallujah that contained the bodies of two dead Pennsylvania National Guardsmen. The sight of the bodies being loaded onto a medevac chopper is paradoxically less vivid, less real, than that of the red Igloo, an American symbol of portable leisure, floating in an eddy next to the Humvee, occasionally brushing against some bracken on the shore.

It is almost as if certain types of events—the bloody, the melodramatic, the spectacular, the incongruous—are somehow biologically protected from the normal degradations of time, permanently seared into the gray matter. This, in fact, is one of the more disconcerting things one learns in the first month of war: the same obscene impulse that compels civilians to rubberneck at a highway accident exists in a war zone in even greater force. You don't want to look, and yet you have to. And so you do, and you're stuck with what one Marine buddy of mine calls "a mind tattoo." In the end, such things turn out to be one of the strange tricks of human perception, another object lesson in the idea that "PTSD is a disease of time"—the worst things in the world enter your brain in an instant, though it may take you the rest of your life to understand what you saw.

From a certain vantage point, it is tempting to say that trauma is trauma is trauma, when in fact something like the opposite is true. Trauma is much like cancer in that each individual subspecies has a different impact on the individual. Some of the most intriguing insights into the human experience of trauma come from looking at how people react to natural disasters. For reasons that defy explanation, so-called acts of God like tsunamis and hurricanes are somehow less aggravating to the psyche than acts of man, such as rape and combat, and result in substantially lower PTSD rates for survivors. It is as if, somewhere deep within, there remains an animal part of us that accepts the omnipotent caprice of the physical universe without question. Though they retain the ability to drive people mad, natural disasters are interpreted by the mind as less of a betrayal than man-made disasters or interpersonal violence, a relationship that speaks to the idea that it is not merely the blunt force of trauma that matters so much as how it impacts one's social environment and one's *interpretation* of the social environment. On some lower substrate, the body understands that nature is always a killer. With people, one can never tell.

One study published in the *New England Journal of Medicine* found, for example, that the PTSD rate for female victims of natural disasters was 5.4 percent, whereas 45.9 percent of female rape victims suffered from persistent PTSD. Sonali Deraniyagala, writing about the 2004 tsunami in her memoir *Wave,* never curses God or the sea, reserving her anger for the Dutch family who moved into her old house, cruelly sold by an uncle while she grieved for her lost family. The idea never seems to occur to Deraniyagala to blame the universe or look for evidence of God's hand in the holocaust of her life. In the face of nature, there is a curious moral suspension: she simply pines for her lost sons, crying when she sees their empty juice boxes in the back of her sedan. Similarly, if we think back to Linda, our notional thirty-one-year-old woman pinned beneath her bookcase, and compare her with another thirty-one-year-old woman who was "pinned down" for hours by continuous mortar fire in Iraq, the woman who was pinned down by mortar fire is roughly three to four times more likely to develop post-traumatic stress symptoms.

There is, it seems, almost a comfort to be found in the majesty of savage nature. One never discusses the "crime" of a tornado or the "violation" of a storm at sea, and in fact the impulse to savor the sublime power of nature, even at its most dangerous, seems almost restorative, as if the sight of it reminds us of our place in the universe. Every year, parents pay millions of dollars for tickets to zoos in order to point out tigers, bears, and sharks to their children. Returning home from Iraq in October 2007, my brother and I visited our old neighborhood in San Diego, which had just been decimated by a wildfire. Touring the devastation, hours after President Bush had declared it a national disaster area, I was overcome by an awful sense of nostalgia for my lost childhood, a feeling that persisted for several days. The surreal image of our house, the lone surviving structure on our street, still resonates. Nevertheless, I understood somehow that such a disaster was to be expected. My brother and I had grown up watching giant plumes of smoke rising from the hills surrounding our suburb, and the fact that this particular fire had simply gotten out of hand seemed perfectly reasonable to me.

Not so with manmade trauma, especially if the perpetrators are well known to you, in which case the likelihood of lasting harm is even greater. In fact, the governing principle with social traumas seems to be that the greater the intimacy, the greater the "dose." If, in our example, Linda is being mortared by friendly troops by mistake, an incident of so-called friendly fire, then the traumatic dose is generally regarded as being even greater than if the barrage were being inflicted by the enemy. Together, all of these various factors reveal a rarely acknowledged tension within the field of trauma studies: the tension between the logic of nature and the logic of culture. These crimes, which are in essence interpersonal crimes, reflect the degree to which post-traumatic stress, a disorder that is so often viewed as a problem of neuroscience, is perhaps better thought of as a social wound, a damaging of the intricate web of relations that keeps a person sane and tethered to the world.

Perhaps the easiest way to understand how all these epidemiological factors play out in the lives of real people is to look at one of the most famous and thoroughly documented episodes in the field of trauma studies: the "Hanoi Hilton" prisoner-of-war camp in North Vietnam, which held a group of 591 American servicemen, including the future senator and presidential candidate John McCain. This group of men, most of whom were pilots, was the longest-detained group of POWs in American history, with some men being interned for the better part of a decade. (McCain was held for five and a half years.) To say that the prisoners held at the Hanoi Hilton endured horrific conditions would be a vast understatement. Prisoners were routinely tortured and survived extended periods of solitary confinement, an unusually potent form of abuse. One of the methods favored by the North Vietnamese was a local variant of the *strappado*, a technique dating back to the Spanish Inquisition, which involved being hung from the ceiling by one's arms for hours. Repeated application of the *strappado* is the reason why Senator McCain to this day cannot raise his arms above his shoulders.

Unbelievably, the survivors of the Hanoi Hilton have one of the lowest lifetime PTSD rates ever recorded, a mere 4 percent. (By comparison, one study on the Americans held by the Japanese during World War II found that more than 85 percent developed PTSD.) More surprising is that a substantial number of these men consistently report that they actually benefited from the experience. Describing what he called his "transforming" time in the Hanoi Hilton, McCain wrote, "Surviving my imprisonment strengthened my self-confidence, and my refusal of early release taught me to trust my own judgment. I am *grateful* to Vietnam for those discoveries, as they have made a great difference in my life. I gained a seriousness of purpose that observers of my early life had found difficult to detect."

How do we explain such a response to barbarity? Were McCain and his comrades superheroes, blessed with a supernatural ability to transcend brutality? How, when confronted with circumstances that would have destroyed most men, did they not only endure, but also, in many cases, actually seem to grow as human beings?

The story of John McCain's survival has been told and retold so many times that it has become something of a secular American sermon, and it is tempting, on a certain level, to simply chalk up the entire Hanoi Hilton episode to the mysteries of heroism. The truth of the matter, however, is more complicated and fascinating. In fact, McCain and his comrades enjoyed a number of measurable psychosocial advantages that enabled them to survive and stay sane in the face of unspeakable horror. If scientists had set out to engineer a group of men designed to withstand the pain and furies of trauma, they might have created the men of the Hanoi Hilton. As a group, they were older, higher-ranking, and more mature than the average draftee. (The typical prisoner was fifteen years older than the average American servicemember.) Virtually all of them had been to college, and as pilots and flight crew, they were the products of one of the most rigorous military training systems in existence at the time, a training regimen that typically included over a year of flight school and a comprehensive medical screening. A substantial number of them had even attended a mock prisoner-of-war school designed to help captured personnel survive enemy captivity. The U.S. government had literally spent millions training each of these men.

Second, the Hanoi Hilton is unique in the annals of military prisoner-of-war camps for its relative geographic stability and for the emotionally supportive prisoner culture that developed there. Admiral James Stockdale, one of the highest-ranking prisoners, who was later awarded the Medal of Honor, described his role in the prison as one "presiding over a unique society." This society was built upon mutual care, unity, and optimism in the face of adversity. Newly captured prisoners would later speak of being "mentored" by the more experienced prisoners.

Importantly, when the men of the Hanoi Hilton were finally released at the end of the war, they were given a lavish hero's welcome. In a time when many Vietnam veterans were met with suspicion and hostility when they came home, these men were treated like returning astronauts. President Nixon, who had campaigned extensively on the issue of their repatriation, hosted a special dinner at the White House in their honor, which included performances by Bob Hope, John Wayne, and Sammy Davis Jr. Most of them returned to find their marriages, families, and finances intact. Each man was given a complete medical exam, free access to medical care, and even lifetime passes to Major League Baseball. Many of the former POWs, like George Coker, a navy pilot captured in 1966, were given their own welcome-home parades and the "keys to the city" of their hometowns. Most of the Hanoi Hilton "alumni" chose to remain on active duty and were generally regarded as something like celebrities by their comrades. They were frequently called upon to deliver motivational speeches, imparting the life lessons they had learned while in captivity. In short, while their traumatic "dosage" was exceedingly high, this group of survivors was not simply told they were heroes upon return and sent packing; their suffering was acknowledged, processed, meditated upon, and even celebrated by their culture. Trauma workers often talk about the post-trauma reintegration process being dictated by the "opportunities to be understood." From this standpoint, the POWs from the Vietnam War were uniquely blessed.

As John McCain later wrote,

> In the many years since I came home, I have managed to prevent the bad memories from intruding on my present happiness. I was thirty-six years old when I regained my freedom. When I was shot down, I had been prepared by training, as much as anyone can be prepared, for the experiences that lay ahead. I wasn't a nineteen- or twenty-year-old kid who had been drafted into a strange and terrible experience and then returned unceremoniously to an unappreciative country.

The Hanoi Hilton experience is a unicorn in the literature of trauma, a case in which a perfect storm of circumstances converged to produce a group of people who defied the odds and, as such, would be exceedingly hard to duplicate. The episode does, however, highlight the myriad factors, both personal and cultural, that dictate who suffers post-traumatic stress and who does not, as well as the special role that reacculturation plays in the process. In most post-traumatic situations, survivors are viewed by "normals" with confusion, suspicion, and in some cases outright hostility. For a psychologically wounded person returning to the regular world, it is only natural to return this suspicion and hostility, virtually guaranteeing their own social isolation. One group of VA investigators, summarizing twenty-five years of research, wrote that "the major posttraumatic factor is whether the traumatized person received social support. Indeed, receipt of social support, which appears to be the most important factor of all, can protect trauma-exposed individuals from developing PTSD."

Therapists like to talk about "small-t" traumas and "Big-T" traumas. Small-t traumas are not really traumatic in the formal sense of the word, but they are enough of a stressor to alter your perception of time and shake you up for a few days, like being woken by a bear rummaging through your campsite in the middle of the night. After your bear encounter, you may have trouble sleeping in your campsite, and the smallest sound, like a branch snapping, will send your heart racing. Small-t traumas, or danger for that matter, trip the guard-dog part of your brain known as the amygdala, a tiny almond-shaped piece of gray matter that deals with immediate threats (the Greek word for almond is *amygdale*).* Whenever you encounter a similar set of circumstances—a similar-looking or similar-smelling campsite—your amygdala will remember that first bear. These little details, many of which go unnoticed at the time, become what clinicians call a trigger, and you will probably not sleep well that night. Small-t traumas set up shop in the brain, altering your response to anything that reminds you of the bear, creating an emotional bookmark. Create enough bookmarks and you can begin to have a problem. During a small-t trigger, the amygdala initiates an incredibly complex series of chemical events that causes your heart rate to spike, your blood vessels to constrict, and your adrenal glands to secrete epinephrine and cortisol, two very powerful stress hormones. Outwardly, this process is often described by psychologists as one of "fight, flight or freeze." During a small-t trauma, and the triggers that follow, your IQ is reduced to that of an ape and your body chooses one of those three outcomes before your conscious brain even has a chance to notice what's going on. Time dilates, things happen on autopilot, and you notice things that were invisible before. You react, you don't think.

Erich Maria Remarque, author of *All Quiet on the Western Front,* has written about this effect with amazing clarity, especially since, at the time of its publication, knowledge of the amygdala was limited to only a handful of scientists:

> At the sound of the first droning of the shells we rush back in one part of our being, a thousand years. By the animal instinct that is awakened in us we are led and protected. It is not conscious; it is far quicker, much more sure, less fallible, than consciousness. One cannot explain it. A man is walking along without thought or heed—suddenly he throws himself down on the ground and a

---

* I'm simplifying here. The human fear response implicates many other parts of the brain, but this is the gist of what researchers have found.

storm of fragments flies harmlessly over him—yet he cannot remember either to have heard the shell coming or to have thought of flinging himself down. But had he not abandoned himself to the impulse he would now be a heap of mangled flesh. It is this other, this second sight in us, that has thrown us to the ground and saved us, without our knowing how.

Of course, Remarque wasn't exactly describing a "small-t" trauma in this instance. What he was describing was a mortar attack taken in isolation from all the other stressors one finds in war, one where everything went right and no one was killed or wounded or tripped and kicked in the face by his buddy hitting the deck right in front of him. But tallied over the course of months and years, such small-t events can add up and become something entirely different.

Big-T traumas can destroy the soul. Big-T traumas are the stuff of madness, permanent insomnia, and hallucination. Big-T traumas don't merely trip the amygdala into a short-term survival response, they actually overload it, damaging its ability to respond in a predictable fashion, almost like a broken thermostat. If we imagine small-t traumas as setting up shop in the body, then Big-T traumas are like massively expanding multinational franchise chains, a series of big-box stores, each supported by a large invisible workforce that never sleeps. In time, this franchise can begin to crowd out other parts of the community. People with chronic, long-term PTSD are often described as having multiple personalities, as if the trauma hasn't just fragmented their psyches but created separate identities within them. This is, in a manner of speaking, the franchise effect. Rape, physical assault, airplane crashes, extended military combat, natural disasters—hurricanes, earthquakes, tsunamis, and tornados—all qualify as Big-T traumatic events. The salient factor with these traumas is their ability to make you feel helpless and overwhelmed. When resistance and escape from terror are no longer possible, consciousness tends to become fragmented and disorganized, almost as if the mind, in order to effectively handle the spectacle of one's own annihilation, has to slice or break up consciousness into smaller, more manageable pieces. This fragmentation, or in some cases dissociation, which happens in the moment of maximum terror, has big implications down the road.

Terror, like beauty, is in the eye of the beholder. If, when confronting a three-hundred-pound assailant, a potential rape victim recalls a jiujitsu class she took, she will likely feel less helpless than one of her peers who went to Pilates instead. In essence, one's perceived sense of control dictates the likelihood that one will develop a harmful traumatic reaction. This highly subjective sense of one's predicament creates some odd juxtapositions. On average, combat units suffer one psychiatric casualty for every physical one. During the 1973 Yom Kippur War, most frontline Israeli units conformed to this ratio. Yet, strangely, Israeli logistics units, who were exposed to far less danger, suffered three psychiatric casualties for every physical one.

Major traumas are both a death and a rebirth, the end of one kind of consciousness and the beginning of another. As practically any survivor will tell you, the day of their rape or "their" IED serves not merely as the end of a chapter in their lives, such as the end of puberty or bachelorhood, but the actual disappearance of their previous identity and the emergence of something altogether new and unknown. After trauma, your mind works differently, and your body has been altered to the extent that an entire new understanding of it must be negotiated. In time, as people enter therapy or simply reflect back upon the course of their lives, on the turning points in the stories of their time on earth, such days grow in power and take on a totemic quality, seeming to contain not only some portion of the mystery of their new being but also some key to the structure of the universe. Cormac McCarthy, describing one such haunted survivor in his classic novel *The Crossing*, wrote that

> men spared their lives in great disasters often feel in their deliverance the workings of fate. The hand of Providence. This man saw in himself again what he'd perhaps forgot. That long ago he'd been elected out of the common lot of men. For what he was asked now to reckon with was that he'd been called forth twice out of ashes, out of dust and rubble. For what? You must not suppose such elections to be happy ones for they are not. In his sparing he

found himself severed from both antecedents and posterity alike. He was but some brevity of a being. His claims to the common life of men became tenuous, insubstantial. He was a trunk without root or branch.

Trauma exists in time even as it destroys it; the numerals of such dates can become like curses, and because they recur, both in the mind and on the calendar, they take on a timeless quality, as in 9/11 or 7/7, the date of the terrorist attacks in London in 2005. The language that Western survivors use in these instances is so consistent as to constitute a law of some kind, and it reveals, to a surprising degree, how religious images of rebirth and resurrection still govern the imagination. World War I veteran Max Plowman, describing his feelings when taken off the front lines, said, "It is marvelous to be out of the trenches: it is like being born again." Reunited with his family at Clark Air Base in the Philippines, Hanoi Hilton survivor Dick Tangeman was moved by the "warmth and sincerity of all the wonderful people who welcomed us home and witnessed our rebirth." Alice Sebold, writing of her return to her parents' home after being raped, seems to echo a verse from First Corinthians: "My life was over; my life had just begun." (Interestingly, this theme of rebirth takes on a slightly different tone when observed in non-Westerners. One Hindu survivor of the 2004 tsunami in Sri Lanka spoke of her joy in the aftermath of the disaster, for it surely meant that she would be rewarded in her next life.)

In the increasingly interconnected PTSD community, it is common to hear such days referred to as "Alive Days" or "second-birthdays." On March 25, 2010, professional mountaineer Steve House was climbing Mount Temple, an 11,600-foot peak in Western Canada, when he fell eighty feet and broke his pelvis and six ribs, an event he would later describe to me as a "rebirth." To this day, House and his wife Eva observe this day as a special event in their lives. House, who still climbs widely and is by temperament keenly attuned to the physical world, finds himself uniquely sensitive to the environment every March 25, as if he were being observed by the universe in some special way. On what he described as the "third anniversary of his second birthday," he wrote on his blog, "On my way to Canada to celebrate my third year of life since my accident in the best way I know how: to climb and share experiences with the Alpine Mentors crew. [House founded a climbing training organization shortly after his fall.] The weather forecast seems to be a good omen that we're doing the right thing."

The death and rebirth that traumas constitute do not happen simultaneously, though the sequence is something familiar to us. One might catch a glimpse of death in an instant, but the process of emerging from that instant can take years, even decades. One friend of mine, who was raped as a young woman, speaks of having completely lost the five years after the rape; it was only after many years of wandering, taking odd jobs overseas, that she was able to return to the United States and regain a kind of consciousness. Nor is this rebirth a linear process. Robert Stolorow describes how for a survivor time often takes on an almost circular quality: life moves forward, but one reencounters memories of one's loss over and over again, finding its fingerprints in situations seemingly unconnected to the past. In some instances, it is possible to imagine life not as a single rebirth but as a series of them, as a new aspect of the original event is unearthed.

The science bears out this idea of rebirth. After a traumatic experience, the body gets locked into a state of permanent alert, hypersensitive to any stimuli that might constitute a threat. In this state of chronic arousal, which is one of the principal symptoms of post-traumatic stress, the victim startles easily, is constantly irritable, and sleeps poorly. In fact, during World War I, some of the first psychiatrists who looked into the origins of war trauma believed the entire basis for postwar mental health disorders lay in this chronic mobilization of the autonomic nervous system, a system triggered by our watchdog, the amygdala (which you could almost imagine here as an aggressive pit bull barking wildly at every passerby). A number of recent studies examining the sleep patterns of combat veterans confirm this early impression. Simply put, people who have been exposed to traumatic events sleep differently than those who have not. As psychiatrist Judith Herman explains in *Trauma and Recovery*, "People with post-traumatic stress disorder take longer to fall asleep, are more sensitive to noise, and awaken more frequently during the night than ordinary people. *Thus traumatic events appear to recondition the human nervous system.*"

Traumatized people often feel fragmented, with their nervous systems living in the past, while other parts of their body continue to live in the present. This sense of temporal disorientation is strong enough that it is difficult to describe such feelings as merely memories. (When your heart starts to race and your eyes start scanning rooftops for snipers in downtown Phoenix, is this really the same as remembering your high school graduation?) Put another way, if on a chemical level your body is essentially still in Iraq, is that still memory? Isn't it something more than a memory? Poet Robert Graves recounts how in civilian life he continued to behave as if he were in the trenches of World War I: "I was still mentally and nervously organized for War. Shells used to come bursting on my bed at midnight, even though Nancy shared it with me; strangers in the daytime would assume the faces of friends who had been killed." In order to be happy, people have to be able to enjoy life as it happens, in the present. In its worst forms, trauma can almost completely destroy not only a person's sense of time but also the very Western idea of time as a linear concept, of moving from one minute to the next and so on.

For some people, a traumatic event is so compelling that it takes on a hypnotic power. While the definition of what exactly qualifies as trauma is a discussion for another time, this hypnotic effect seems to apply to all kinds of powerful events. To some degree, what we call post-traumatic stress is merely an extension of a psychological principle that is obvious to anyone who reflects upon it: our bruises define us. Researchers at the University of California at Irvine, who interviewed survivors of the 1993 Laguna Beach wildfires, found that people who had been evacuated from their homes reported disturbances in their orientation in time: the past felt like the present. The future seemed disconnected from the present. People who reported a strong feeling of such temporal disorientation immediately after the firestorms were especially likely to continue ruminating on the past after six months. Here, we see one of the many paradoxes of trauma: damage occurs when you remember too much, and damage occurs when you remember too little.

Major trauma is a death and a rebirth; in some cases it kills the present, but it also gives rise to a second self, a doppelganger, a shadowperson with its own distinct body chemistry and sense of what is past and what is present. *He was never the same after the war.* This is the common refrain of the loved ones of the traumatized, followed closely by *He came back a different person.* Both of these sentiments are, it turns out, empirically accurate. Post-trauma, a person is essentially forced to begin all over again and retrain their body to deal with the stimuli the world throws at them. This overremembering makes sense from a survival standpoint. The parts of the brain dedicated to survival, such as the amygdala, store away as much information as possible for future reference. You might want that information to go away, but these deeply seated survival mechanisms, wired into the oldest regions of the brain, are simply not open to human reason. They are, as one researcher called them, "zombie subroutines of the brain."

In my new post-Iraq life, I saw myself doing a kind of survivor shuffle, alternating between hating the past and missing it with an intensity that warped the present into a kind of extended flashforward. The past was always present, just like with Reaper, EVERYDAY IS DAY ONE, forever, or even worse, Tomorrow Is Day One. 2014 is 2004. Bodily, what I thought were two separate conditions I now know are one: withdrawing from the world and feeling like part of you is always on patrol in a sort of adrenalized present. Though I didn't notice it until years later, I became irritable whenever someone walked behind me on the street, feeling their presence like heat on my back. On the street, I watched rooftops without even meaning to and searched the roadway for IEDs, taking note of potholes and irregularities in the asphalt. At times like this, I never felt like I was literally back in Iraq, but for a very long time I felt on edge, and I was not pleasant to be around. Average Americans, undisciplined and shambling through life without a care in the world, never failed to get on my nerves. My survival brain, trained and retrained by my years in the Marine Corps and Iraq, had wired a protective carapace of memories, many of which had outlived their usefulness.

The war is over, but it will live forever in the cipher of my brain. It is a part of me. To wage war against a memory is to fight against an old dream and, for me, an old way of looking at the world, the idea that "what does not kill me only makes me stronger." Some ideas die the hard way: I can see now how foolish that notion is. Like many of my friends, I used to cherish my near-death experiences, collecting them like Boy Scout badges. A close call wasn't simply a brush with mortality, it was an experience, a story, an episode from a novel in which I was featured as the hero. Now, when I think about getting shot or being vaporized by an IED or burned to death in the fiery crash of a helicopter, all the various ways of shuffling off this mortal coil, a certain melancholy settles in. The first time you see someone shot, it's the most amazing day of your life; by the third time it begins to seem sad, sad and oddly boring, because you realize that there is nothing inherently meaningful or of metaphysical import in random enemy contact. As modern, technologically enhanced humans, we may live like gods, but we die like animals.

It is easy when you are young to believe that you have a date with destiny and to assume that the universe is waiting to reveal its deepest secrets to you if you choose to put yourself in harm's way. When I decided to go to Iraq, like many Americans, I was young and had mistaken my lust for danger as real insight into the nature of existence. I never supported the war, but I did believe that it would grant me a clarity and fix what was wrong with my life. In the end, Iraq did give me a certain clarity, it did force me to come to grips with my own human frailty and the frailty of others, but this insight, which has guided the writing of this book, didn't happen simply because I went to Iraq. It happened because of what transpired afterward, in the years after I came home. Whatever knowledge or wisdom I might have achieved came in the aftermath as I began to read, to introspect, and to consider the choices I made in my life and how I fit into the larger world.

There are so many ways to think about PTSD. As a construct, it touches on so many things, but the most important of these might reside in the simple meaning of the first letter of its formal name, the *P*. The loss, the insight, the fragmentation, the moral vertigo, all of these things only happen *post-*, after The Event has come and gone and we discover to our shock and surprise that we are not who we used to be. It is perhaps a facile thing to say, but it seems to me that the first duty of every survivor is to simply acknowledge the existence of trauma, to accept that there are things in this world that can break us. Only then can we begin to make meaning out of everything that comes after.

TOWARD A GENEALOGY
OF TRAUMA

M OST PEOPLE, when they first learn about PTSD, assume that the hypervigilance, social isolation, flashbacks, and nightmares of the condition are universal complaints, as old as the hills. In fact, the opposite is closer to the truth, in that the collection of symptoms and concepts that we call PTSD is a relatively new historical entity that emerged from a very particular point in time and space—1970s America, a period lived in the long shadow of the Vietnam War, a period notable for its social upheavals, its crises of faith, its questioning of gender roles and modes of thought, what Joan Didion called its "febrile rhythms." The seventies were, after all, the years that brought us Watergate, Patricia Hearst, Kent State, Jim Jones, the Weather Underground, and, perhaps most importantly, the end of the Vietnam War, a conflict that radically altered not only the way Americans looked at trauma and the role of the veteran in society but also the way America looked at the world.

Even with these data points to anchor us, trying to understand how PTSD fits into the larger sweep of history is a surprisingly difficult task because the human response to war and disaster changes in the way that Texas weather changes: constantly, capriciously, rapidly. To give just one example of the way that culture has influenced how we think about trauma, consider the flashback. Commonly thought of as a signature symptom of PTSD, the flashback is, in fact, a term borrowed from the world of film. Originally coined by early twentieth-century filmmakers to describe a jump between different points of time within a narrative, the flashback is so deeply embedded in the public imagination that it is difficult to imagine a world without it, and yet in 2002, researchers at King's College in London, digging through war records dating back to the Victorian era, found that flashbacks were virtually nonexistent among veterans who fought before the age of film. (Civil War veterans who suffered from involuntary intrusive images didn't refer to them as flashbacks, and they were more likely to describe being visited by a host of spirits, phantoms, demons, and the ghosts of fallen comrades.) Adding to the confusion, a variant of the term was also in wide use in the LSD culture of the sixties and seventies. In all likelihood, the reason that the flashback is an essential part of today's understanding of trauma is that an influential San Francisco psychiatrist with an interest in stress syndromes and psychedelia, Mardi Horowitz, served on the working groups that oversaw PTSD's eventual introduction into the *Diagnostic and Statistical Manual of Mental Disorders* (DSM) in 1980.

Some scholars, such as Roger Luckhurst of the University of London, have even gone so far as to say that cinema's claim on the imagination is so strong that it serves to "shape the psychological and general cultural discourse of trauma into the present." Looking back on my experiences in Iraq, it isn't hard to see where Luckhurst might derive such ideas. There were, wherever you went in Anbar province, continual references by Marines to *300,* a film about ancient Sparta, and then there were the soldiers in Dora who insistently referred back to their *"Black Hawk Down* day" when describing a series of ambushes they'd survived, as if the casualty count wasn't enough to lend it gravity. Thinking back on the soldiers' stories from that day, it is tempting to wonder if film, television, and, increasingly, video games don't provide the lion's share of our modern traumatic vocabulary, teaching us how to see our memories in the way that photography taught us how to see (and not see) sunsets, in the way that the minds of British soldiers from World War I were dominated by the poetic images of Kipling and Hardy, and in the way that Protestant Christianity guided the attitudes toward death and dying in the Civil War.

In fact, the more you dig, the less secure PTSD's place in history becomes and the more it seems to be a product of culture as much as a hardwired biological fact. Indeed, it is this historical slipperiness that led Allan Young, a medical anthropologist at McGill University, to declare that PTSD is an "invention," arguing that "the disorder is not timeless, nor does it possess an intrinsic unity. Rather, it is glued together by the practices, technologies, and narratives with which it is diagnosed, studied, treated, and represented and by the various interests, institutions, and moral arguments that mobilized these efforts and resources."

The earliest appearance of the word "traumatic," according to the *Oxford English Dictionary*, dates to 1656, and was used to indicate something "belonging to wounds or the cure of wounds." (The modern, multimillion-dollar trauma centers we hear about at large hospitals today refer to this early definition.) Indeed, for the greater portion of its life in the English language, "trauma" adhered to this earlier meaning, and it took more than two centuries before the word was first used in any way resembling its current usage as something "emotionally disturbing or distressing." Tellingly, the catalyst for this shift in meaning was technology, in this case the railroad. In 1866, a London surgeon named John Erichsen published a book titled *On Railway Spine and Other Injuries of the Nervous System,* in which he described, in a way characteristic of the Victorian period, how the shock of railway accidents "depleted the nervous energies of victims," comparing the damaged spine to a magnetized horseshoe that has had its attractive force "jarred, shaken, or concussed" out of it.

In other words, our current, deeply felt ideas about post-traumatic stress, what it means to be a survivor, and the basic vocabulary we use to communicate the aftermath of violence — ideas that are staples of the modern American media and seem so fundamental to the human condition as to be beyond question — are in fact not even as old as the United States of America, not even as old as the railroad.

Nevertheless, some of the concepts that make up PTSD do have historical antecedents, and these traumatic responses have in some cases persisted in a manner not unlike traumatic memory itself — through long periods of ignorance and willful amnesia — and this reality makes the job of tracking down PTSD's past that much more challenging. In the great class photo of mental health disorders, post-traumatic stress is like the odd kid at the edge of the frame who always moves just as the shutter trips, leaving him permanently out of focus, forever fuzzing into his neighbors: depression, grief, and generalized anxiety. And a late bloomer, too! His pre-1980 existence is seemingly dominated by a confusing series of name changes, misbegotten identity crises, denial, and flat-out ignorance before passing through the crucible of Nixon's America, finally coming of age in 1980 with his induction into the DSM.

Compared to depression, for instance, which enjoys a clear and almost aristocratic lineage within psychiatry, traceable directly to Hippocrates and the dawn of Western medicine, post-traumatic stress is a dim figure shuffling before the lens of history, often existing as little more than an intriguing irregularity in the negative or a fascinating anecdote that refuses to be linked to any larger phenomenon, such as the Athenian soldier, reported by Herodotus, who went permanently blind from fear during the battle of Marathon in 490 BC, a case that for millennia was consistently described as being so unique, so extraordinary, so far outside the vein of practical experience as to be unfit for deeper examination.

And yet, amazingly, in spite of the shape-shifting ideas of post-traumatic stress, the changing attitudes and cultural schemes and the general fickleness of the language used to describe it, a few unifying themes do hold across the centuries, as we shall see.

Most of what we know about trauma's past comes from military history. The never-ending ebb and flow of war has produced a corresponding cycle of traumatic history, a cycle of societal ignorance followed by denial, a brief period of understanding, and then another interval of ignorance. The bullets fly, the bombs explode, the body of knowledge about the effects of terror on the mind expands generously for a period of time. Previously uninterested doctors and other learned folk are drawn into the war effort. New treatments and technologies emerge. Then the guns fall silent, and the body of knowledge relating to trauma contracts with surprising violence as society moves on, leaving the survivors to more or less fend for themselves.

The change that broke this cycle, or at the very least seriously altered its periodicity, was PTSD's introduction into the DSM in 1980. With a mere three pages, some fifteen hundred words in a telephone book–sized manual published by the American Psychiatric Association, the West embarked on a new relationship with trauma, medicalizing what in previous eras had been a spiritual, moral, or artistic concern, inviting survivors to enter into the modern transactional relationship that exists between patients and doctors, expecting them to do what all good patients do: go to their health care provider, undertake a course of treatment, take their medications, and get well.

Frustratingly, there is no equivalent cycle for survivors of sexual trauma, whose existence, if it can be historically detected at all, is largely defined by society's insistence that they remain invisible, an insistence that no doubt worsens the harm immeasurably. As sociologist Georges Vigarello argued as recently as 2001, "The history of rape has never been written." Moreover, as Susan Brownmiller indicates in her study of sexual assault *Against Our Will,* the systematic erasure of rape can be seen throughout human history. "Thou shalt not rape" is not one of the Ten Commandments, whereas adultery and coveting thy neighbor's wife are both forbidden. As she points out, this blind spot continued through the modern era: Freud, Jung, Adler, Marx, and even Karen Horney discuss rape only glancingly in their work.

The other reason for this dearth of knowledge is the simple fact that women are far more likely to be the victims of rape than men (91 percent of all rape victims are female), and the struggles of women have long been considered less worthy of the historian's attention than the struggles of (generally male) soldiers. Unsurprisingly, one of the primary goals of seventies feminism was to force society to recognize the fact that rape is more common than our history textbooks would lead us to believe. By and large, this gendering of trauma continues today. Despite the fact that rape is the most common and most injurious form of trauma, the bulk of PTSD research is directed toward war trauma and veterans. Most of what we know about PTSD comes from studying men: the eight-hundred-pound gorilla in PTSD research is the U.S. Department of Veterans Affairs, a governmental body designed to serve an overwhelmingly male population. Even the beginning student of trauma will find this bias evident in this book: to explain various aspects of post-traumatic stress, I have been forced to rely on a deeply biased body of literature. I have attempted, whenever possible, to ungender these forms of trauma, to include stories from female veterans and rape victims, but for the sake of clarity I have been forced into many of the same regrettable habits that have gendered the history of trauma for so long. For this, I beg the reader's forgiveness.

"PTSD is a disease of time," anthropologist Allan Young tells us in his history of modern trauma, *Harmony of Illusions.* While Young was speaking of the personal experience of trauma, his idea of trauma as something that disrupts the normal flow of time touches on one of the central problems of attempting to write a history of trauma; namely, where should it begin? One possible beginning is at the dawn of time itself, in this case the prehistorical hunter-gatherers of Siberia and the Huichol people of central Mexico, as both belong to a grouping of cultures thought by anthropologists to be shamanic in character. These and other prehistorical groups have at the center of their cultures a figure known as the shaman, what one researcher described as a sort of "sacred politician." These types of societies, some of which still exist today, are apt to look at crisis journeys and traumatic passages — near-fatal accidents, severe illnesses, extreme exposure to the elements — as being part of a larger cycle of human life, essentially flipping the contemporary disease model of trauma on its head.

The shaman, a figure who emerged during the Upper Paleolithic period, had a broad, loosely defined role within tribal society. Anthropologist Joan Halifax, describing shamans in her book *Shamanic Voices,* saw them as "healers, seers, and visionaries who have mastered death." Initiation into this sacred caste required that applicants survive a direct experience of death or passage through an extreme terrain of the psyche. Such boundary crossings or experiences of being "catapulted into the territory of death" were thought to grant the potential shaman special knowledge of "the inner workings of human crisis," a knowledge which could be applied to the treatment of other sufferers. This view of trauma not only formed the bedrock of tribal medicine but also gave shape to the traditions of wisdom that guided such societies. In the late 1800s, during the golden age of polar exploration, a Caribou shaman known as Igjugarjuk told the Arctic explorer Knud Rasmussen that "all true wisdom is only to be learned far from the dwellings of men, out in the great solitudes; and is only to be attained through suffering. Privation and suffering are the only things that can open the mind of man to those things which are hidden from others." In other words, trauma, which obviously leads to great pain, can also lead to deeper knowledge about human existence.

Such ideas do not directly inform our modern understanding of trauma, but this vision of it as a transformative life experience, a source of supernatural knowledge, exists as a sort of rarely verbalized undercurrent to the prevailing view of terrible events. Our current understanding of trauma, along with the secret suspicion that survivors are somehow tainted or poisoned by sexual violation and violence, traces its origins to another ancient river of knowledge, which is best exemplified by early Jewish law and its paranoia of free-flowing blood, which included menstrual blood and any blood spilled on the battlefield, as seen in the Old Testament in Numbers 31:19, which commanded, "All of you who have killed anyone or touched anyone who was killed must stay outside the camp seven days."

Because such shamanic societies existed (and in some cases still exist) in their own cycle of time, apart from the normal course of Western history, and pass their traditions orally in the form of mythic tales, it is difficult to place them within a normal historical context or to determine the extent of their influence on us today. Nevertheless, it's fascinating to consider how these societies, whose cultures were free of the influence of technology and Judeo-Christian beliefs, essentially invert our contemporary view of trauma: it is the survivors of trauma, not the "normals," who are considered to be the possessors of special knowledge. It is the traumatized who are the doctors and the untraumatized who are the patients. This conversion of traumatic knowledge into a kind of religious commodity is less surprising the more you think about it: What could be more mystical than visions of old wounds that you cannot escape much less put into words? It is the boundless blackness, the Void, the forever unknown that lies at the edges of human consciousness, and early man, lacking any other insights into the mind or nature or the universe, might have understandably accounted for the nightmares and frights of post-traumatic experience by converting them into a sort of religious medical tradition.

Now, at this point, I should be clear, I am not arguing that such an arrangement is preferable to the current way of dealing with trauma. I am not, for instance, suggesting that psychologically scarred veterans would be better served by being told that they possess mystical powers and can heal the sick. And now is probably a good time to point out that these same ancient cultures also tended to look upon neurological disorders, such as epilepsy, as being somehow blessed or sacred as well. (Epilepsy was, in fact, often referred to as the "sacred disease" during the time of Hippocrates, a characterization he ridiculed.) However, it's worth considering the distinctive way that some ancient societies chose to frame the narrative of the survivor and their ability to see that, as an experience at the boundary between life and death, trauma holds within it the potential for wisdom, a formulation one almost never hears today. War equals trauma equals loss equals pity and nothing else. As one well-spoken Iraq veteran told me recently, "Sometimes, it feels as if the American civilian population has pathologized the entire veteran experience. Somebody said to me the other day, 'I can't see how anyone could go to Iraq and *not* come back with PTSD.'"

Interesting, also, is the degree to which these mythic shamanic journeys seem to parallel the cycle of death and rebirth that so many traumatic survivors describe today. (Recall Alice Sebold's feeling her life had ended after her rape, only to feel "reborn" later.) Thinking about the question of trauma mythically for a moment, it is tempting to wonder if, on a certain level, what we call PTSD doesn't represent an incomplete passage from the underworld of death and darkness back to a more fully realized consciousness of one's role in the universe, a knowledge of the hugeness of existence and of the value of safety and comfort and social connectedness. Modern medicine, like any other culture, has its mythologies, and who's to say that this mythology doesn't have its blind spots, its failures of imagination, its false gods, just as the Huichol mythology does?

The soldier turned writer is something of a cliché in American culture (Norman Mailer, for instance, complained that everyone in his World War II rifle company was working on a novel), but most of the veterans I know, in addition to finding major parts of their war surpassingly awful, also found a lot of it to be sublime, and more than a few of them woke up after being home for a few months and were suddenly *consumed* by a need for answers to life's great questions. It was as if the war had deeply unsettled them, forcing them to confront aspects of themselves that had been ignored for too long. This contemporary yet ancient way of looking at trauma is almost completely absent in the clinical literature on the subject.

War is always ironic, the literary historian Paul Fussell observed, and something similar is probably true of trauma, because the first glimpse we get of post-traumatic stress in the historical record comes from the land of Sumer, an ancient civilization that existed for around a thousand years in a place that we today refer to as Iraq. Four thousand years before the United States invaded Iraq, ostensibly because of weapons of mass destruction, two converging armies, those of the Ilamites and the Subarians, invaded the Sumerian city of Ur looking for booty. (Some scholars think that the land of Ur, or Uruk, is where we get the place-name "Iraq.") The aftermath of this event is recorded on stone tablets in an anonymous account known as the *Lamentation of Ur.*

> *The city they make into ruins; the people groan.*
> *Its lady cries: "Alas for my city," cries: "Alas for my house."*
> *In its lofty gates, where they were wont to promenade, dead bodies*
>   *were lying about;*
> *In its boulevards, where the feasts were celebrated, scattered they lay.*
> *. . . At night a bitter lament having been raised unto me,*
> *I, although, for that night I tremble, fled not before that night's*
>   *violence.*

The storm's cyclone like destruction — verily its terror has
filled me full.
Because of its affliction in my nightly sleeping place,
In my nightly sleeping place verily there is no peace for me.

Obviously, the author of this account isn't available to be interviewed about the nature of this "affliction" and why exactly there
was no peace in their "nightly sleeping place," but it's fascinating
to note that the author of the *Lamentation of Ur* did, apparently, see
a relatively direct cause and effect relationship between "terror" and
subsequent "affliction," linking such an event with a lack of sleep.
Today, encountering such an ancient fragment, it is tempting to look
at it as a case study in the history of science — one gets the sense that
one is observing the birth of the clinical mindset, the ability to observe a phenomenon in the abstract, connecting a physical event to
a resultant pattern of symptoms. At the very least, from this archaic
example we gain proof of the existence of perhaps the most vexing
of post-traumatic symptoms, insomnia, which is a problem that remains largely unchanged today. As one VA psychologist, who has
treated hundreds of Iraq and Afghanistan veterans, told me recently,
"Sleep is one of the last areas to resolve in PTSD."

The Greeks, by contrast, took a notably unclinical approach to
war's effect on the psyche. Some contemporary researchers have even
gone so far as to look at the ancient Greeks, with their encompassing
mythology, as representing something of a dark age in the study of
trauma. And yet, as with so many things relating to the mysteries of
life, the ancient Greeks have a lot to teach us about terror and loss.
In his pioneering studies on *The Iliad* and *The Odyssey,* books which
helped launch a renaissance in classical trauma studies, retired VA
psychiatrist Jonathan Shay argues that "Homer saw things that we
in psychiatry and psychology had more or less missed." Homer's epic
poems are virtual warehouses of knowledge about war-born psychological injury, yet as the poet himself proclaims in the opening lines
of *The Odyssey,* his intent is to celebrate, to sing of the deeds of Odysseus, not to educate or to provide a clinical taxonomy of any kind.
For the Greeks, the heroic ideal was literally a religion, and Homer's

works focused on combat and the clashing of spears in a way that might seem juvenile to some today were it not for his very Greek insistence upon depicting the losers of such contests in great detail. (As the legendary Oxford classicist C. M. Bowra put it, "The Greeks thought victory glorious and a defeat heroically endured only a shade less glorious.") Strife, and one could say terror, were at the heart of the Greek worldview, a belief system that is so pervasive in their writing that it is likely they viewed war in a way that is similar, in a moral sense, to the way natural disasters are viewed today—as events outside the realm of human agency, as acts of God or, in this case, acts of the gods. The poet Heraclitus described how conflict defined the age:

> *Justice in our minds is strife.*
> *We cannot help but see*
> *War makes us as we are.*

To die nobly in battle was the surest route to fame and honor in Greek society, and while *The Odyssey* delves unflinchingly into the costs of heroism and the aftermath of war, the idea of linking such tribulations even tangentially to madness would likely have been at odds with the basic Greek view of life.

Curiously, the Greeks had a rather sophisticated view of other forms of mental illness, such as depression. Medicine at that time was based upon humoral theory, which viewed character as a balancing act between four basic elements: phlegm, blood, yellow bile, and black bile. The ancient physician Empedocles, for instance, thought that depression was caused by too much black bile (the Greek words for black bile are *melaina chole,* which is where we get the word "melancholy"). Hippocrates, the father of medicine, held a surprisingly biological view of mental illness. "It is the brain which makes us mad or delirious, inspires us with dread and fear, whether by night or by day, brings sleeplessness, inopportune mistakes, aimless anxieties, absentmindedness, and acts that are contrary to habit." This divide between the philosophical/religious view of madness and the psychological costs of war and disaster was clear and inviolate, which helps explain why trauma remained outside the circle of medicine for millennia. It was, for lack of a better word, a matter of politics. To treat venerated warriors like the insane would have been unthinkable to the Greeks.

Similarly, the rather brutish politics of the ancient world help to explain why there are comparatively few accounts of rape in the historical record. Women in antiquity were treated as something like property, and while incidents of rape do appear in ancient literature, they were often recorded in the manner that one might record the theft of livestock or the damage caused by a passing storm. (Or, as in the case of the rape of Lucretia, described by Livy in the *History of Rome,* the victim announces that she has been dishonored and commits suicide in front of her husband and father.) To make an obvious point, rape victims were not treated as heroic survivors worthy of veneration in antiquity. In fact, in one notable instance of rape in ancient literature, the writer seems to dwell on the lamentable weakness of women as something needing correction. We see this in the Roman poet Ovid's *Metamorphoses,* in which the victim, a mortal named Caenis, is raped by the god Neptune. Afterward, Neptune asks what he might do to please her, to which she responds: "What I want is not to be ravished again, ever . . . I have a serious prayer that matches the serious wrong you have just now done me. I want you to make me a man so that nothing like this can happen again." Neptune grants her prayer. And as she spoke, "her voice began to resonate deeper and fuller . . . Her body was turning to that of a male and, to make it an even better gift, Neptune allowed it the further favor—that never should swords or weapons wound it. Caenis, renewed as Caeneus . . ." Thus was rape transformed into a boon in the ancient world.

Western literature begins in strife and trauma, in the sweat and spear clashing, the agony and exertion of *The Iliad.* In his epic poem, written eight and a half centuries before the birth of Christ, Homer depicts Achilles, the hero of *The Iliad,* as the ideal warrior, a surpassingly talented soldier and stalker of men, a man capable of intense feeling who, not coincidentally, also appeared to suffer from at least two symptoms of what today might be called post-traumatic stress. (One of the biggest differences between the Greek world and our

own is that public displays of emotion by men were not only toler-
ated but also considered highly dignified, an appropriate response to
an overwhelming event.) His best friend, aide-de-camp, and comrade
(and, some say, lover) Patroclus is killed in battle. Having tended to
his body, honoring Patroclus in accordance with the strict martial
rites of the time, Achilles found himself unable to simply put the
loss behind him:

> Achilles went on grieving for his friend, whom he could not ban-
> ish from his mind, and all-conquering sleep refused to visit him.
> He tossed to one side and the other, thinking always of his loss, of
> Patroclus's manliness and spirit . . . of fights with the enemy and
> adventures on unfriendly seas. As memories crowded in on him,
> the warm tears poured down his cheeks.

Whenever I read lines like this from Homer, I think of friends
who lost buddies in Iraq and Afghanistan, men who despite having
strived mightily to protect their comrades saw them die anyhow. I
have watched, over the years, as these good and honorable people
then proceeded to eviscerate themselves with guilt, convinced that
they had somehow violated the holiest and most sacred of warrior
bonds. One of the most psychologically wounded trauma survivors
I've ever met was a Marine who lost seven of his closest friends in
a single IED blast near Fallujah in 2004. The fact that he'd had an
argument with one of them right before he was killed only deepened
the blow. "Kevin wasn't the same guy who'd shipped out to Iraq
seven months before," his sister told me.

When I first met him at a restaurant, his eyes locked on me the
second I stepped through the door. We sized each other up like boxers
as I made my way to his table. Sitting down, I could see clearly the
anxiety, the guilt that possessed his frame almost like rictus. He sat as
stiffly as a man about to get a root canal. The only things that moved
were his eyes, which missed nothing, and his right leg, which worked
up and down like a sewing machine needle the entire meal. We got
to talking, and more of his story emerged. He was in a kind of reverse
basic training for the most afflicted sorts of post-traumatic sufferers.
"Boot camp with smoking privileges," he called it. He told me he'd

been addicted to crystal meth, a drug he knew to be the worst of them all. "The only time my symptoms go away is when I'm high."

Post-traumatic stress is a slippery thing, a ghost that haunts history, but it isn't hard to imagine what happened to Kevin. The instant that the IED had gone off, killing his buddies, the moral universe he'd inhabited for the first nineteen years of his life essentially ceased to exist. Virtually everything he assumed to be true and right and just came to an end in that moment. (Recently, a number of researchers, many of them close readers of Homer, have begun calling this sort of thing "moral injury.") What happened next is harder to understand, but somewhere deep in Kevin's psyche, in a dim place beyond the light of reason, an insistent voice began whispering a secret message to him until it was the only thing he heard. The message was simple and unmistakable: *Bad things don't happen to good people.*

Out of the Corps a year later, it wasn't long before Kevin lost his way. Looking back on it, one could say he tried to make true that secret lie he heard within. *Bad things don't happen to good people.* Alcohol, drugs, rampant paranoia, and the life of a shut-in soon followed. In such moments, when one's social horizon shrinks down to a pinhole, the idea of palliative human warmth can seem untrue, wrong, like a heat on the skin. Self-damage becomes inevitable. This unnerving human impulse to reflect one's inner pain with outer damage runs across cultures. As Homer shows us in *The Iliad,* there's an immortal species of self-torture that demands physical expression. Learning of Patroclus's death,

> *A black storm cloud of pain shrouded Achilles.*
> *On his bowed head he scattered dust and ash*
> *In handfuls and befouled his beautiful face,*
> *Letting black ash sift on his fragrant khiton.*
> *Then in the dust he stretched his giant length*
> *And tore his hair with both hands.*

Perhaps unsurprisingly, Homer anticipates other ideas in contemporary psychological research that we are only now coming to terms with. In *The Odyssey,* for example, we find a depiction of survivor's guilt, written 2,760 years before the term "survivor's syndrome" was coined by Holocaust researcher W. G. Niederland. As Odysseus faces a deadly storm, which threatens to sink his ship on the way home from the Trojan War, he finds himself wishing that he had been killed with his buddies in Troy instead of dying ignominiously at sea:

> There is nothing for me now but sudden death. Three and four times blessed are those countrymen of mine who fell long ago on the broad plains of Troy in loyal service to the sons of Atreus. If only I too could have met my fate and died the day the Trojan hordes let fly at me with their bronze spears over Achilles' corpse! I should at least have had my burial rites and the Achaeans would have spread my fame abroad. But now it seems I was predestined to an ignoble death.

Reading these old poems, *The Odyssey* in particular, one cannot help but be struck by what appears to be the more than metaphorical inability of these survivors to go home. It is less the enigma of survival at stake in *The Odyssey* than the enigma of homecoming, the frustrated transit between worlds: the world of savage, warring nature and the world of civilization. Indeed, the entire narrative structure of *The Odyssey* is built around this basic fact: the Trojan War ends, and in the face of all reason Odysseus hits the road for ten years in what amounts to history's greatest road trip, in the process bedding the beautiful sea goddess Calypso and narrowly escaping a mind-killing drug habit in the Land of the Lotus-Eaters. It is impossible to know what dark, self-destructive impulses were at work in Odysseus's postwar heart, but it isn't hard to imagine that after the brutality and capriciousness of war, Odysseus might not have felt fully prepared to return to a buttoned-down domestic life back in Ithaca. This deep-seated, even existential, feeling of having been cut loose in the world, transformed by the cruelty of fate into a rootless wanderer without a relational home, a theme familiar to readers of Jon Krakauer or Jack Kerouac, has little place in the modern psychiatric canon and is not generally included in discussions of PTSD. Still, one sees this theme echoing throughout the literature of trauma, predating even Homer. (In *The Epic of Gilgamesh*, Gilgamesh, who is generally regarded as the mythic predecessor of Odysseus, looks on his dead comrade Enkidu and cries, "I cannot bear what happened to my friend. Then I was frightened, I was terrified by death, and I set out to roam the wilderness . . .")

This impulse to wander, to leave the awful past behind and kill time in a strange place, is written across the lives of so many survivors that it could easily stand as a literary genre all its own. It is, in essence, a form of resurrection. Alice Sebold, describing her postrape roamings, said, "Syracuse was over. Good riddance, I thought. I was going to the University of Houston in the fall. I was going to get an MA in poetry. I would spend the summer trying to reinvent myself. I had not seen Houston, never been south of Tennessee, but it was going to be different there. Rape would not follow me."

Trying to outrun shame, even perceived shame, is perhaps a universal human impulse, and it should come as no surprise that *The Odyssey* is but an early example of what can be found in every era of human history. After the Civil War, the number of veterans, both Blue and Gray, who hit the road after Appomattox is beyond counting. In fact, once you start looking into the number of Confederate veterans in Jesse James's gang, that roving band of gunslingers who terrorized the American West throughout the 1870s, an entirely new theory of how the American West was settled opens up. The Wild West was filled with scarred young men whose only skills in life included killing, sleeping on hard ground, stalking, and looting. Closer to home, a dear friend of mine, who was drugged and raped on Long Island as a nineteen-year-old, left America as soon as she could, cut off all of her hair, and wandered around Europe for months, eventually moving to a small island off the coast of Italy. One Iraq veteran I interviewed for this book has moved almost every year since his unit returned from Baghdad in 2003, an odyssey that has taken him to three different continents.

The urge to reinvent one's moral and physical universe through travel is so common that some students of trauma think it might be biological. Laurence Gonzales, a *National Geographic* writer who has written extensively on the science of survival, wrote that "travel is a time-honored strategy for healing. It forces the unconscious re-

organization of a number of areas of the brain, especially those involving the hippocampus, which has the special function of creating
spatial maps. Every time you travel to an unfamiliar environment,
your brain undergoes an important transformation." The neuroscience behind this claim hasn't been firmly established, but the point
remains: Homer was on to something.

Homer died some four hundred years before Hippocrates, the father of medicine, was born, and the bodies of knowledge they pro-
mulgated were as separate then as they are today. Hippocrates, as
with Plato and his idea that the quality of one's childhood influences
the quality of one's adulthood, formulated notions of the self that
have, over the centuries, exerted a powerful influence over the field of
psychiatry, not to mention our general view of human development.
Some students of depression have even gone so far as to argue that
Hippocrates is, in effect, the grandfather of Prozac, viewing the body
as the originating point of mental ills.

Nothing remotely similar can be said of Homer, whose works
have largely remained under a sort of house arrest in ever-shrinking
classics departments across the United States (most of the classical
scholars I know are forced to scrape by, struggling to find teaching
work). Even today, when so many Greek assumptions about life and
society are woven into the fabric of our lives (such as their faith in
human reason, individuality, and democracy), the Greek views of
postwar life and heroic loss remain oddly removed from our modern
view of trauma. In Denis Johnson's epic Vietnam novel *Tree of Smoke,*
the dominant character, a towering army colonel turned CIA pup-
petmaster named Sands, observes that "war is ninety-percent myth,"
a truism that was never more resonant than with our Greek heritage
and trauma. War, it seems to me, *is* mostly myth, ancient ideas and
dreams handed down to us by our fathers, stories we live out un-
knowingly, often having no idea of the invisible stories and arche-
types that guide us from day to day.

Unfortunately, whatever psychological insights Homer has be-
queathed to us remain hidden behind the wall of a more recent, very
unclassical sort of mythology, obscured by our society's need for heroes who are somehow immune to normal human weakness, which

conversely views survivors as damaged goods, aliens, and walking time bombs rather than as people burnished by adversity. In my own life, my experience has always been that the joys of survival, the exuberant embrace of life that seemed to emanate from my deepest cells, was always greatest on my way home, neither here nor there, in the remote airfields and transient barracks that are every war correspondent's postwar odyssey. Home: that was always another matter entirely, and it was almost as if some deeper sense of life's preciousness leaked out in transit, hour by hour, in between the world of the war and the world of the protected.

If, as Siddhartha Mukherjee argues, "every era casts illness in its own image," there can be few clearer examples of the way that a particular age has cast the image of psychological trauma than the Middle Ages, an era dominated by the Catholic Church. During this period, the post-traumatic condition, such as it was, was treated as a question of theology and, secondarily, as a matter of tending to the moral needs of warriors returning to their communities after war. In a world viewed as God's Kingdom on Earth, where little distinction was made between the natural and the supernatural, the first challenge was how to conceptualize violence in a religion whose messiah's teachings strongly emphasized pacifism over bearing arms. Keeping this in mind, leaders in the early Christian church assumed that warriors returning from battle would be racked by feelings of guilt and shame over their role in breaking the "Truce of God," and they paid an unusual amount of attention to their plight, providing them with what could generously be described as a sort of religious medicine. Veterans today are often encouraged to undergo therapy and deal with their conflicted feelings about their wartime experiences, but returning warriors during the Medieval period were encouraged, and in some instances commanded, to undergo various rituals of repentance and reconciliation, cleansing themselves before the Lord. In the eyes of the church, warriors were, in essence, sinners until they got right with God. As Pope Gregory VII put it, "It is impossible to engage in military service without sin." In particular, church leaders were concerned with those warriors who had broken or believed they had broken the Sixth Commandment, which declared without qualification that "Thou Shalt Not Kill."

Dying and suffering exemplified Christian devotion, as Jesus showed on the cross, but actual killing presented a number of theological problems that vexed the church for hundreds of years. Oddly, while church leaders at the time acknowledged war's horrors and worried that it rendered men "more savage than wild beasts," the officially stated concerns were almost always of the cosmic variety, ensuring that the potential sins associated with warfare were properly understood and accounted for and that a sort of balance could be maintained between the politics of the time and the need to please God.

Apart from the theological concerns with killing, there was also a deeper sense that the act of killing somehow soiled the killer, even when the killing was justified by the powers that be, a sentiment found in *The Odyssey* as well. (After slaughtering Penelope's suitors, Odysseus calls fire and brimstone down upon the hall in order to cleanse it.) Whether or not the clergy were aware of this primitive belief regarding "blood pollution," they often insisted that warriors who had killed stay away from church for a period of time. The Archbishop of Canterbury in the seventh century, for instance, ordered that "one who slays a man by command of his lord shall keep from the church for forty days."

Throughout the Middle Ages, religious authorities imposed penances on returning warriors, requiring, among other things, periods of prayer, fasting, and abstinence from communion. These edicts, which came down in a manner not unlike Supreme Court rulings today, were designed to work within a larger body of Christian theology, which, among other things, created the first "just war" philosophy in the West. The severity of the penances that were imposed depended upon the kind of war the soldier in question had participated in and on the number of people they had personally killed or wounded. One church document from the tenth century, the "Arundel Penitential," ordered a penance of one year if the killing was committed in a battle ordered by a king, whereas in the case of a war ordered by a lesser prince, where some doubt existed as to its "justness," the penance required was two years, which was the same penance required of someone involved in a homicide.

Church records from the Middle Ages are rife with such "penitentiaries," or holy requirements, imposed on soldiers who had killed during a war. These edicts were often surprisingly detailed, outlining the specific alms and acts of contrition required of those who had fought. In 1068, in one of the most dramatic decrees of the time, an official gathering of Norman bishops instituted a set of penances upon all ranks of the army who had fought with William the Conqueror at the battle of Hastings:

> Anyone who knows that he killed a man in the great battle must do penance for one year for each man that he killed.
>
> Anyone who wounded a man, and does not know whether he killed him or not, must do penance for forty days for each man he thus struck (if he can remember the number), either continuously or at intervals.
>
> Anyone who does not know the number of those he wounded or killed must, at the discretion of his bishop, do penance for one day in each week for the remainder of his life; or, if he can, let him redeem his sin by perpetual alms, either by building or endowing a church.

Of particular relevance today, this set of commands, which are sometimes referred to as the "Hastings Articles," goes on to say,

> The archers who killed some and wounded others, but are necessarily ignorant as to how many, must do penance as for three Lents.

The psychological experience of war during the Medieval period was, needless to say, quite different than the experience of war today. Combat at that time was, generally speaking, far more personal and intimate than it is today, being almost exclusively a hand-to-hand affair. It's possible that, for many warriors at the time, the primary psychological concern was to understand the slaughter they had been a part of and to come to terms with it through the dominant moral authority of the time, the Catholic Church. Physical distance between enemies in war is significant, and it is likely that the act of killing another person in the Medieval period, because it was generally done by the sword, would have been more distressing than the act of killing today. Studies of soldiers throughout history confirm the judgment of Dave Grossman, a retired U.S. Army lieutenant colonel and former West Point psychology professor, that "man is not by nature a killer." Modern wars, while more destructive, are far less intimate, a fact that increases the death toll, greatly reduces the burden on the individual soldier, and helps to explain why grappling with guilt over killing was a preeminent concern during the Middle Ages.

Today, the idea that a religious ritual of some kind could somehow resolve the myriad conflicts that arise after combat might seem ridiculous to many. Psychology has by and large replaced the church as the arbiter of inner conflict. The therapist, in some ways, plays the role of the priest today. And yet the questions of one's guilt and culpability in war and in other traumatic events remain. In times of extreme stress, one's moral horizon contracts to the size of a pinhole. One is captive to the needs of the moment and nothing else. In time, survivors are forced to pay for what the moment made them do. A soldier, if he kills, kills for his buddies. Later, the soldier comes home, and in the absence of his buddies must face what he has done. As Ernest Hemingway wrote in *For Whom the Bell Tolls,* "Never think that war no matter how necessary nor how justified is not a crime. Ask the infantry and ask the dead."

In the wake of overwhelming events, after the fateful moment has passed, the mind is often consumed by questions of cosmic responsibility and the dimensions of one's role in the world. For the veteran, in particular, these sorts of questions carry a special weight because, as a device of the state, the fateful responsibilities of soldiering were never intended to be borne alone. As one army sniper, who had killed dozens of Iraqis in Baghdad, said several years after coming home, "I should never have been given that much responsibility." A community belief system that works to take some of the weight of these questions off the shoulders of the individual can do wonders, as recent research has shown. As Jonathan Shay argues at length in *Achilles in Vietnam,* communalizing the guilt and shame over one's conduct in war can have a powerful effect on the psyche, especially if the war or traumatic event in question is controversial. Soldiers are ultimately vessels and vassals of the state, and they do not go to war of their own accord, so why shouldn't the state or the community help relieve them of their guilt when they return home? While this method of addressing post-traumatic responsibility has no direct descendant in the modern world, it did have an impact. Arthur Egendorf, a Vietnam veteran and one of the architects of the PTSD diagnosis, invoked the Hastings Articles of 1068, noting that "modern communities no longer provide ritual cleansing for their surviving warriors . . . The healing we sought in the rap groups, although new in form, was not original in spirit."

Give it away, give it to God, this theory of loss seems to say. For the Medieval church, these matters were confronted in an unusually direct manner, one that stands in marked contrast to how guilt and shame are handled today. And in a world lit only by fire and the mind of God, perhaps such a moral feat was more easily achieved. In other times and other places, it seems fair to say, the prospects for reconciliation aren't so simple.

In historical terms, technology is the great transformer of trauma.* The Civil War, the first modern industrialized war, produced carnage on a previously unprecedented scale, presaging the colossal slaughters of the twentieth century and transforming the American imagination in the process. Pre–Civil War Americans had long understood the terrors of the wilderness that encircled them and had fought an endless series of campaigns against the American Indian, but the Civil War changed the way Americans understood violence, death, and their place in the world, a world where unspeakable destruction could be visited upon common citizens. As one South Carolinian declared in 1863, "The world never saw such a war." Prior to the Civil War, Americans held a view of violence that fit with their previous experience with conflict generally—as an event limited by

---

* As the classical scholar and Jesuit priest Walter J. Ong put it, "Technologies are not mere exterior aids but also interior transformations of consciousness."

time and space that impacted a relatively small circle of dedicated combatants. While visiting Union hospital ships moored along the Virginia Peninsula, Frederick Law Olmsted declared that the war had, in fact, created a veritable "republic of suffering." The Civil War remains the central catastrophe of the American experience, and in stark contrast to virtually every conflict that followed, it forced Americans of every station and class to grapple with the widespread effects of trauma.

The major technologies that made such a cataclysm possible were the railroad, the telegraph, and the rifled musket. The rifled musket allowed troops to deliver accurate volleys of fire at greater range, and it heralded a revolution nearly on par with the machinegun in World War I. As Arnold Toynbee observed, every invention of a new weapon is a disaster for society, and the Civil War is a case in point: the number of soldiers who died during the conflict—around 620,000—is roughly equal to the number of American soldiers killed in the Revolutionary War, the War of 1812, the Mexican War, the Spanish-American War, World War I, World War II, and the Korean War combined. The sheer kinetic intensity of Civil War combat is impressive even by modern lights. A British observer who visited the battlefield at Antietam ten days after the fighting wrote that "in about seven or eight acres of wood there is not a tree which is not full of bullets and bits of shell. It is impossible to understand how anyone could live in such a fire as there must have been here."

Such violence had a powerful psychological impact on soldiers, both Blue and Gray. For many men, the shock of "seeing the elephant" (the term used for one's combat initiation) was simply overwhelming. The opening engagement of the battle of Shiloh, an early morning Confederate charge that caught a number of Northern units eating breakfast, sent thousands scampering to the rear. A number of them, estimated by General Grant to be eight thousand, cowered under the bluffs of the Tennessee River, "panic-stricken." One observer at Shiloh noted, "Such looks of terror, such confusion, I never saw before, and do not wish to see again." Luckily for the Union side, thousands of Southern troops also ran from the battle with horror in their eyes.

William Tecumseh Sherman, also at Shiloh, was similarly impressed. One historian, describing Sherman's tortured recollections of the battle, wrote that "for all its absorption, his mind—perhaps his subconscious mind—was photographing hideous pictures, sharp negatives, and storing them away. Later on they would become vivid positives: 'our wounded mingled with rebels, charred and blackened by the burning tents and grass, crawling about begging for some one to end their misery . . . the bones of living men crushed beneath the cannon wheels coming left about . . . 10,000 men lying in a field not more than a mile by half a mile.'"

Unfortunately, the American medical establishment of the time lacked even the most rudimentary knowledge of psychology, and its ability to understand, let alone treat, the terror created by industrialized violence was extremely limited. It is a commonplace among historians that the American Civil War was an instance where technology had outrun tactics, and the same can be said for the medicine of the period. Such terrors had never been seen before. Civil War doctors were innocent of virtually every psychological principle we take for granted today. It would be another thirty-nine years before Freud published *The Interpretation of Dreams.* Noting this, one researcher writing in 2012 described Union Army physicians as simply "psychologically naïve." Basic distinctions made today between psychiatric and neurological disorders were nonexistent. Characterizing the state of medicine as a whole, the Union surgeon general, William Hammond, later observed that the war was fought at the "end of the medical Middle Ages." Both sides in the Civil War were desperate for personnel, and soldiers who today might be treated as psychiatric casualties were often ignored or punished as malingerers or evacuated far from the battlefield.

The medical field as a whole struggled to keep pace with the violence the war unleashed, and psychiatric casualties, who existed as a problem without a name, were relegated to the margins of the field hospital. A proper ambulance service was only established at the very end of the conflict, and given the perennial shortages of infantrymen, only around twelve hundred Union troops were ever admitted to the one federal institution dedicated to the treatment of mental illness, the Government Hospital for the Insane in Washington. An asylum in the classic nineteenth-century tradition, the hospital, which later became known as St. Elizabeths, was in many respects simply a warehouse for the sick and demented.

In the mid-nineteenth century, before any formal system of psychiatric classification existed, many Civil War doctors fell back on the four-thousand-year-old Greek diagnostic categories of mania, melancholia, and dementia. In addition to the Greek terms, a minor dictionary of colloquial descriptions for traumatic stress emerged. War has always driven linguistic innovation, and the Civil War was no different. Soldiers suffering from what today might be called "acute stress reactions" were described using a rainbow of epithets, including having "the blues" or being "nervous," "played out," "used up," "worn down," "worn out," "depressed," "dispirited," "rattled," or "badly blown." In a time when spiritual matters were foremost in the minds of Americans, discouraged troops and deserters were frequently characterized as being "demoralized" or "dis-spirited." Another subgenre of these descriptors had a cardiac component, as with traumatized soldiers who were referred to as being "downhearted," "disheartened," or suffering from a "trotting heart."

In 1871, six years after Appomattox, Jacob DaCosta, a physician who had served with the Union Army, wrote a famous article describing three hundred cases of what he called "irritable heart." In it, he described a number of postbattle symptoms that today would be recognized as a simple reaction to overwhelming stress, or what psychiatrists today would call "hypervigilance," one of the cardinal symptoms of post-traumatic stress. DaCosta, also present at the battle of Shiloh, observed men suffering from palpitations, chest pain, a rapid pulse, and a host of respiratory and digestive disorders brought on by "quick and long marches, heavy work . . . or even slight exertion in those whose constitution has been impaired." Oddly, DaCosta never attributed these symptoms to the peculiar terrors of combat; believing them to be caused by an overstimulation of the nerves at the base of the heart, he treated them with a host of drugs, including opium, digitalis, belladonna, and cannabis indica. (Interestingly, in 1998, researchers at Boston University found the heart's reactivity to certain traumatic stimuli to be a useful indicator of combat PTSD in patients, so while DaCosta's explanation may not have been correct, his observations were.)

In the case of the Union troops at Shiloh who broke and ran, several thousand of them were later evacuated to the rear, with an uncounted number claiming to suffer from a condition known as "nostalgia." A word that has taken on different meanings over the centuries, *nostalgia* during the Civil War was used to indicate a number of mental conditions that today might be called clinical depression or simple panic. ("Nostalgia" has its roots in Homeric Greek and means "home-ache.") Based on the French diagnostic category *nostalgie*, which had been in the medical lexicon since the 1700s, the term was often applied to soldiers serving far from home who suffered from a kind of mental deterioration while campaigning. Incidents of nostalgia were recorded as far back as 1633 in the Spanish Army, and they reached their apogee among Swiss soldiers fighting on the plains of France who were forbidden by their commanders from singing or even whistling the traditional "kuhreihen" alpine folk songs. (The phenomenon was even referred to as the "Swiss illness" for a time.)

By the 1860s, the term as a medical category was on the decline in Europe, but accounts of the Civil War are filled with references to it. In a time when few Americans traveled beyond their home states, the stresses of fighting far from one's home and family were real indeed. The Union Army recognized nostalgia as a mental disorder and included it in the handbook issued to medical officers. *A Manual of Instructions for Enlisting and Discharging Soldiers* describes it as "a form of mental disease which comes more frequently under the observation of the military surgeon . . . The extreme mental depression and the unconquerable longing for home soon produce a state of cachexy, loss of appetite, derangement of the assimilative functions, and, finally, disease of the abdominal viscera . . . As Nostalgia is not unfrequently fatal, it is a ground for discharge if sufficiently decided and pronounced."

By war's end, the Union's surgical rolls listed some 175,000 men, or around 8 percent of the army, as victims of nostalgia, "insanity," and other "nervous" disorders, though in an era when military record keeping was flawed and inconsistent, such a figure only hints at the true psychological toll. Interestingly, because Civil War soldiers tended to look at themselves as civilians in uniform, the shame attached to those who did succumb to the stresses of war was less intense than what one sees in professional armies today. Desertions, especially after battlefield reversals, were common. Hundreds of thousands of soldiers from both sides deserted at various points during the war, often returning home to protect and sustain their families. Commanders, especially in the South, were desperate for bodies to fill the ranks and often declared amnesties, permitting such "AWOLs" to return without charging them under military law.

This openly acknowledged fear of battle was on display during the early years of the war when Union commanders, plagued by paranoia about the enemy's intentions, quarreled with their superiors at every level of command, often hesitating rather than committing their troops to action. William Tecumseh Sherman, who later earned a place in history by declaring that "War is all hell," first rose to prominence in October 1862, when his immediate superior resigned because of the "mental torture of his command." A month later, Sherman asked to be relieved for the same reason. Given a second chance by the army, his cool handling of the Confederate charge at Shiloh restored his reputation, reestablishing his career, even though he had initially dismissed a number of reports indicating that an attack was imminent.

When the war finally ended in 1865, the U.S. government, which had grown to an unprecedented size in response to the hostilities, oversaw a number of projects designed to manage the aftermath of the conflict. Included among these were the establishment of national cemeteries and a pension system to provide for the physically wounded and for the survivors of the fallen. Counseling psychology and biological psychiatry did not exist as the disciplines we know today, and the idea that veterans of the Civil War might require formal adjustment counseling simply didn't occur to Americans. The Veterans Administration, a fixture of modern American life, wouldn't emerge for another sixty-five years. Veterans of the Civil War who weren't physically wounded were expected to return home to their farms and neighborhoods and more or less pick up where they had left off. A number of states operated asylums, such as Indiana, which saw a peak in admissions from 1876 to 1890, a period from eleven to twenty-five years after the cessation of hostilities. The idea of the "veteran experience" as a popularly accepted social category was a largely unexplored notion to Americans who had never before lived through a mass conflict like the Civil War.

Stephen Crane, as an up-and-coming newspaper reporter in the 1890s interested in the experience of the common soldier during the war, was frustrated by the lack of such accounts. Like many young men of the time, Crane had grown up hearing veterans' stories and had read many articles about the war. After consulting the widely quoted *Battles and Leaders of the Civil War,* he found himself disturbed not by what he'd read but by what he hadn't read. "I wonder that *some* of these fellows don't tell how it *felt* in those scrapes," he complained. What came out of this wonderment was the first proper American war novel, *The Red Badge of Courage.* Seemingly fated to be a classic, the novel, which recounts a soldier's baptism by fire (including his brief desertion), essentially established the coming-of-age war novel genre in the United States. Following a year later was a lesser-known tale, "The Veteran." The story ends with Henry Fleming, a survivor of Chancellorsville, charging into a burning barn to save some trapped horses and disappearing in a "great funnel of smoke." When Fleming first learns of the fire, his humanity seems to end. "His face ceased instantly to be a face; it became a mask, a gray thing, with horror written about the mouth and the eyes." Created by one conflagration, the "veteran," it seemed, was fated to meet his end in another, transformed into a "rose-hue'd" spirit swelling from the flames.

In fact, the violence loosed by the Civil War did not end after the South's surrender at Appomattox. As other historians have pointed out, the war "let the genie out of the bottle," leading to a wave of criminal violence that spread to every corner of an already blood-soaked nation. It was almost as if the war had untamed men to a certain extent. Thousands of men deranged by the fighting found themselves unable to return to their old lives and civil society. The widespread habit of violence cultivated by the war, combined with a lack of economic opportunity, particularly in the South, created a culture of lawlessness that defined the post–Civil War era. Jesse James, the West's most famous outlaw, learned his trade as a guerrilla fighter in Missouri during the war, and he operated in a similar fashion until he was killed in 1882.

Throughout the postwar South, newspapers reported a "frightening increase in crime," driven by what were thought to be roving bands of former Confederate soldiers. In the North, two-thirds of all men sentenced to prison were war veterans, and in some states the number of men serving time shot up 400 percent. The postwar period also saw the rise of organized racial violence in the form of the Ku Klux Klan, an organization founded by another Confederate guerrilla fighter, Nathan Bedford Forrest.

While not technically criminal in nature, the Plains Indians wars, fought over the course of the 1870s, were dominated by the genocidal "total war" strategy devised by General Sherman. The Civil War's impact on the American Indian can be easily understood by a simple comparison of the strategies pursued by the U.S. Army. Before the war, the army followed an informal policy of containment, making and breaking treaties as was convenient. After the war, a scorched earth strategy prevailed, exemplified by General James Sheridan, a veteran of Shiloh, who declared that the only good Indian was a dead Indian.

The idea that war might promote crime and violence throughout society has occurred to many thinkers throughout history. Although the exact origins of this notion are difficult to trace, Erasmus, Sir Thomas More, and Machiavelli all speculated that wars lead to increased crime and violence. As researchers at the University of California, Santa Cruz, noted the year after the fall of Saigon, "During the Vietnam War, the murder and nonnegligent manslaughter rate in the United States more than doubled." The U.S. Navy's Health Research Center, looking into a similar set of issues among return-

ing Iraq War veterans in 2010, found a "significant association between combat exposure and subsequent arrests and convictions that
persisted when preservice background factors were controlled." The
implications of these sorts of studies aren't hard to understand. Violence changes people in mysterious ways, and when the normal human prohibitions against murder and cruelty are lifted on a wide
scale, it unleashes violent impulses that are not easily controlled. It
should come as little surprise that the bloodiest era of lawlessness,
racially motivated violence, and genocide in American history came
immediately after its bloodiest war.

In many ways, the catastrophe of the American Civil War was merely
a preview of the horrors to come in World War I. The same technological elements that made the Civil War an era-demolishing blood-
bath—improved firearms, motor transport, and the telegraph (now
wireless)—were all present in World War I but in greater force. This
bigger, bloodier, more thoroughly industrialized conflict, which was
widely referred to as "The Great War" until relatively recently, destroyed over eight million lives outright and demolished four European empires, while putting a fifth—the British—on the road to
bankruptcy. To a degree that is difficult to appreciate in America,
which entered the war only in its last few months, World War I
changed the course of history. More than that, the war was so disil-
lusioning, so corrosive to the public spirit, that it actually destroyed
people's belief in the *idea* of history as it had been understood up to
that point. As Paul Fussell, one of the war's preeminent chroniclers,
would say, "It reversed the Idea of Progress."

The central metaphor of the period is, tellingly, a psychological
one: shell shock. A post-traumatic phenomenon that one can, with a
bit of poetic license, plausibly describe as the grandfather of PTSD,
shell shock essentially began as a response to the horrors of twentieth-century technology—"the shock of the shell." Partly because of
its catchiness as a phrase, it went on to become something of a catchall for any English-speaking soldier suffering from a war-related psychiatric disorder, even after its early champions distanced themselves

from it. (The Germans and the French both had their own versions of shell shock—*Kriegshysterie* and *choc traumatique*—but the terms never quite caught on.) Many of the symptoms associated with shell shock would be familiar to today's PTSD sufferers—a coarse shaking of the hands, nightmares, jumpiness, and in the worst cases hysterical deafness, blindness, and mutism.

In addition to its gross historical impact, the war changed our basic view of human endurance. Before the war, a man was, in large measure, the captain of his fate. After the war, this view was colored by the fact that against the iron tide of industrialization, the lone man didn't stand a chance. The war killed eight million people, and in the process it killed off a number of popularly held beliefs about martial glory, manly honor, and the benefits of military service. From a psychological standpoint, the war destroyed the idea that a determined person can survive any adversity with their mind intact, that a "good" person can and will always overcome their circumstances. The war severely damaged the notion that post-traumatic sanity was a choice and that simply by not dwelling on the past, by "moving on," one could remain healthy and whole.

While World War I did not bring PTSD into existence, it is inconceivable without it. The war disillusioned tens of millions of people, and in retrospect it can be seen as the opening engagement of a "war of nerves" that culminated sixty-six years later in PTSD's introduction to the DSM. The first conflict where war neuroses were officially identified and treated, World War I is one of the premier examples of what terror can do to the mind and how human memory, even when damaged in battle, can work to influence history.

One of the primary means for wounded minds to convey their experiences is through literature. Perhaps unsurprisingly, the icons of shell shock are the poets Wilfred Owen and Siegfried Sassoon, figures who have come to represent not just the tragedy of the Great War but of modern war as a whole. This effect is most pronounced in Great Britain, where people still wear poppies every November in remembrance of the fallen. As Pat Barker, the author of a Booker-winning trilogy of novels dealing with shell shock, said in a 2004

interview in the *Guardian,* "I think the whole British psyche is suffering from the contradiction you see in Sassoon and Wilfred Owen,
where the war is both terrible and never to be repeated and at the
same time experiences derived from it are given enormous value . . .
No one watches war films in quite the way the British do."

Owen and, to a lesser extent, Sassoon continue to occupy a unique
place in the imagination of the English-speaking world. Through
the power of their poetry and the pity they arouse in readers, they
helped to cement ideas about war trauma in the public sphere and
legitimize later generations' attempts to document their own traumas. The most conspicuous beneficiaries of their eloquence were the
veterans of the Vietnam War, many of whom drew inspiration not
from their fathers' war—World War II—but from the war that pre-
ceded it. Robert Jay Lifton, one of the leading theorists behind the
campaign to have PTSD recognized, invoked Owen's poem "Mental
Cases" in 1973, saying, "No wonder that Vietnam veterans sometimes express strong identification with certain veterans of World
War I—more so than, say, with those of World War II. Wilfred
Owen . . . put his death guilt to powerful use in the moving 'survivor formulation' contained in his poems."

The first hints that the war was impacting soldiers' minds in a new
way came in the winter of 1914. The German offensive, intended
to take Paris in six weeks, had ground to a halt less than a hundred miles from the city. This opening stage of the conflict, which
would later be called the last "nineteenth-century war," was one of
high drama and unprecedented casualties on both sides. The war
of maneuver ended in November with both sides deadlocked, each
unable to turn the other's flank. Having suffered unspeakable casualties, both sides began digging in. The result was a line of trenches
running diagonally across the European continent from the Belgian
coast to the Swiss border. The trench system created forms of human
misery that the world had never seen before. Wet, filthy, and exposed
to harassing artillery fire for months on end, soldiers broke down in
bizarre ways. The most damaging aspect of it seemed to be the pas-
sivity required of soldiers. Standing in muddy trenches and waiting

for an artillery strike or stray mortar round to end your life took an indescribable toll, even on those who were visibly spared. Describing the miseries of trench life, Wilfred Owen wrote,

> *Watching, we hear the mad gusts tugging on the wire,*
> *Like twitching agonies of men among its brambles.*
> *Northward, incessantly, the flickering gunnery rumbles,*
> *Far off, like a dull rumour of some other war.*
> *What are we doing here?*

Soon, strange cases began appearing in field hospitals and aid stations across France. These soldiers didn't appear to be physically wounded but were exhibiting a host of sensory disorders. Some couldn't see. Some couldn't smell or taste normally. Many had odd gaps in their memory or were vomiting uncontrollably. More than a few were suffering from "the shakes." It was as if some invisible force, unleashed by the new form of war, had taken possession of these men, disturbing their basic biological functions.

One twenty-year-old private had been caught in a German artillery barrage while moving between trenches and gotten tangled up in barbed wire. Charles Myers, a Cambridge psychologist working at the base hospital at Le Touquet, later wrote about the case: "Immediately after one of the shells burst in front of him, his sight, he said, became blurred. Another shell, which then burst behind him, gave him a greater shock, 'like a punch on the head without any pain after it.' The shell in front cut his haversack clean away and bruised his side."

This unnamed soldier was the first documented case of shell shock. In February 1915, Myers published a paper in the *Lancet* describing three such cases, titled "A Contribution to the Study of Shell Shock." The term seemed to be an apt description of the phenomenon — most of Myers's cases had "followed from the shock of an exploding shell," leading to the soldier's collapse. With Myers and other doctors, it almost seemed to be a case of the Victorian tendency toward scientific analogy expressing itself, a way of making concrete a decidedly abstract idea, that of post-traumatic stress. However, the fact that the term rolled off the tongue with such ease, and as a result stuck in the public imagination, was to become problematic later.

That Myers had taken notice of these odd cases was itself unusual, so strong was the desire to dismiss the soldiers as malingerers. Qualified as a physician, Myers was an example of that very British species of intellectual, the gifted dabbler. Along with W. H. R. Rivers, another notable member of Cambridge's fledgling psychology department, Myers had taken part in a groundbreaking anthropological expedition to New Guinea, applying modern scientific techniques to the study of the tribal societies there. As an academic and a Jew, he was a double outsider within the Royal Army Medical Corps, a body noted for its attention to the needs of discipline over the needs of medicine. Nevertheless, Myers possessed a surplus of networking ability and was eager to find a role for himself in the war. While visiting Salpêtrière, the famous French neurology institute, he noticed several soldiers who had lost the power of speech or been partially paralyzed after German artillery barrages. It wasn't long before British soldiers with similar symptoms began arriving at Le Touquet, a hospital sponsored by the Duchess of Westminster. With the publication of his *Lancet* piece, Myers ignited a fierce debate within British society about masculinity, honor, and the rights of the individual.

On one side of the debate were the army's hardliners, who according to one historian possessed "a rough and ready model of human psychology, with its own clear-cut labels. Men were either sick, well, wounded or mad; anyone neither sick, wounded, nor mad but nonetheless unwilling to or incapable of fighting was necessarily a coward." And if the force of tradition weren't enough to persuade, the British Army, in the early years of the war, adhered to a draconian policy toward such "moral invalids." During World War I, more than 2,200 British soldiers were condemned to death for cowardice and desertion. Though only around two hundred soldiers were actually executed, the threat of the firing squad had a powerful impact.

Regardless of the policy, shell-shocked soldiers kept appearing at casualty clearing stations. Soon their stories filled the medical press. One Oxford professor of medicine serving in the army wrote to a colleague that "I wish you could be here in this orgie of neuroses and psychoses and gaits and paralyses. I cannot imagine what has got into the central nervous system of the men . . . Hysterical dumbness, deafness, blindness, anaethesia galore. I suppose it was the shock and the strain but I wonder if it was ever thus in previous wars?" The trenches were only nine months old, but it was becoming clear that doctors were facing an epidemic. According to one estimate, at least two hundred thousand British soldiers were eventually discharged because of shell shock. By the middle of 1916, Myers had personally seen over two thousand shell-shocked soldiers.

As a phenomenon, shell shock confounded the prevailing theories of the day. Within the annals of military medicine there was simply no precedent for it. In the first reports on the subject, one detects a sense of bewilderment at the grotesque symptoms being encountered. One British military doctor wondered if the explosions of the shells weren't damaging the entire central nervous system. A distinguished neurologist, F. W. Mott, speculated that carbon monoxide poisoning or tiny particles from the shells might be the source of the trouble. Industrialized warfare was new, and the understanding of the effect that it might have on the mind was still dominated by the stark images of exploding shells and the mysterious forces they presumably released. As a result, most of the explanations for shell shock centered on physical causes. The psychiatrists were, in a sense, trapped in the same predicament as the generals: just as the military tactics of the time had yet to catch up to the weaponry, so too had medicine yet to catch up with twentieth-century high explosives.

Myers, who was familiar with French thinking on hysteria, treated the first case with hypnosis and sent the man back to England after ten days of treatment. In his *Lancet* article, he argued that "the close relation of these cases to hysteria appears fairly certain." Hysteria, derived from the Greek word for uterus, was until the late nineteenth century thought of as basically a female disorder. The idea that men could be reduced to weeping, spasming shadows of their former selves was practically unheard of. Freud's ideas on hysteria, which could have been of great service, were not widely accepted at the time, being largely confined to a group of disciples clustered around Vienna. Twenty years before the war, Freud had argued that hysteria was caused by unpleasant memories and experiences. These repressed memories were "flung" into the unconscious in an attempt to avoid mental conflict. In extreme cases, repressed memories were "converted" into physical symptoms, which bore some resemblance to shell shock. Later, Freud would theorize that war neuroses were caused by an internal conflict between self-preservation and the need to maintain one's sense of honor and duty to comrades.

Some contemporary trauma workers, such as Bill Nash, a retired U.S. Navy psychiatrist, have suggested that these sorts of "conversion disorders" were related to the stigma associated with not doing one's duty and not being "manly," a powerful motif in British society at the time. (This was, after all, an era that saw women handing out symbolic white feathers of cowardice to men not in uniform.) The fact that hysterical blindness and mutism, common during World War I, are almost nonexistent today seems to confirm Nash's thesis, as "stigma reduction" with respect to PTSD has become a part of the medical culture within the military. This issue of stigma is, in fact, one of the great points of divergence between the Great War era and our own.

By late 1915, the British Army, realizing that something had to be done, broke with its old policy and officially admitted to the existence of a gray area between cowardice and madness. This new policy, enacted by the Army Council in London, established what amounted to a two-tier system: shell shock caused by enemy action and shell shock resulting from a simple breakdown. In official reports, this distinction was to be recorded as either "Shell-shock W" or "Shell-shock S." In the minds of many, including Myers, this system was ripe for abuse. One medical officer complained to him, "We have seen too many dirty sneaks go down the line under the term shell-shock to feel any great sympathy with the condition." Six months later, Myers proposed that the term shell shock be abandoned and replaced with two new categories, "concussion" and "nervous shock," but popular opinion both inside and outside the army was fixed. In part because of its power as a metaphor, shell shock was here to stay.

Confusion about how to treat war neuroses was reflected in this confusion about what to call it. The nineteenth century had seen the development of a number of psychological theories, and when the war came, these theories were put to the test. More than a few doctors saw the war as an opportunity to experiment. Military doctors on both sides unleashed an arsenal of therapies on the shell-shocked soldiers, including hypnosis, drugs, talk therapy, milk diets, bed rest, physical exercise, "military discipline" (which frequently meant shouting insults at shell-shocked soldiers), and a crude form of electroshock therapy.

Unsurprisingly, the use of electricity on soldiers was controversial. One French soldier, Baptiste Deschamps, punched a physician when he tried to apply electrodes to his body. Because he had struck an officer, Deschamps was court-martialed. Eventually, the French press, which had been growing increasingly skeptical of the war, seized on the story, and Deschamps's case became a *cause célèbre*. He was given a light sentence in the form of a suspended six-month prison sentence. The doctor who had attempted to electrocute him, Clovis Vincent, whose center at Tours was infamous for its electrocution technique, known as *torpillage* (literally, "torpedoing"), voluntarily stepped down and asked to be reassigned to the Western Front. While a few other doctors continued to experiment with it, by 1918 *torpillage* had been discontinued and its leading proponents excoriated in the press.

One doctor who championed a more liberal approach was Myers's old mentor at Cambridge, W. H. R. Rivers. A doctor who seemed ill at ease in uniform, Rivers was a member of the same New Guinea expedition as Myers, a trip that epitomized both his wide-ranging intellectual interests and his deep human sympathies. His medical knowledge, while not as technically polished as many of his peers', ran deep. If later generations would come to idolize him, converting him into a sort of iconic doctor-hero, as novelist Pat Barker did in her award-winning *Regeneration* trilogy, it was not without reason. With his myopic, reserved demeanor and humanistic sensibility, he seemed the embodiment of the modern physician as Renaissance man.

The son of a Kent clergyman, Rivers possessed a sort of puremind-edness and omnivorous curiosity about the human psyche that has fallen out of fashion today. This curiosity took him through a variety of investigatory incarnations, including that of international anthropologist, general practitioner, ship's surgeon, and house physician to two famous neurologists in Queen Square, London, all prior to heading to Cambridge as a lecturer in psychology in 1893. One colleague was later to say of him, "Perhaps no man ever approached the investigation of the human mind by so many routes."

After the war, Rivers would conduct a study of war neurosis published in the War Office's inquiry into shell shock. His conclusions were fifty years ahead of their time. Examining the incidence of neurosis in the air corps, he found that neurotic symptoms were best correlated not to the intensity of the action seen nor the amount of time spent in combat but to the relative physical immobility of the victim. In the air corps, as in the infantry, neurosis was a function of having control over one's surroundings. Examining medical records, Rivers found that, among other things, the pilots, who enjoyed a degree of control over their fate, suffered far fewer cases of neurosis than artillery observers in the balloon service, where men were tethered to the ground, essentially sitting ducks. Incredibly, he found that in the balloon service, the psychiatric casualties actually outnumbered those who were physically wounded. In short, the more helpless the patient felt, the more likely he was to be traumatized, a finding that remains essentially unchanged to this day.

Rivers was fifty-one and serving as an army physician at Craiglock-hart Hospital in Scotland when he treated his most famous patient. In July 1917, a few weeks before arriving at Craiglockhart, Siegfried Sassoon, a decorated infantry officer and celebrated poet, had published a statement in a newspaper denouncing the war, and it had been read aloud in the House of Commons. The declaration ended by saying that "on behalf of those who are suffering now I make this protest against the deception which is being practised on them; also I believe that I may help to destroy the callous complacence with which the majority of those at home regard the continuance of agonies which they do not share, and which they have not sufficient imagination to realize." That Sassoon was speaking (and continued to speak) for many soldiers went without saying; from the point of view of the army, he was dangerous, and after some deliberation, they declared him shell shocked and had him sent to Craiglockhart, where he was soon under Rivers's care.

It was a meeting of the minds that became the stuff of legend: two noted intellects clashing over *the* question of their time. Whether or not Sassoon was technically suffering from shell shock is open to doubt (he suffered from nightmares, and at one point left the front claiming to suffer from "trench fever"), but in the long run such a technical question is almost irrelevant. What the Sassoon–Rivers dyad came to address was nothing less than the central questions of trauma, questions that continue to echo today: How does one reconcile the self with the often inhumane demands of society? How does one communicate to society the conditions that constitute the underworld of trauma? How does one face death with dignity and authenticity?

At first, it seemed far from an ideal match. Sassoon, aware of how the army was attempting to marginalize him with the shell-shock label, was indignant, even truculent, toward Rivers. Sassoon had a tendency toward snobbishness, and he scorned the other patients at Craiglockhart, referring to the place in his letters to friends as "Dottyville." Rivers met Sassoon's rebellion with an avuncular tone that he had probably perfected in dealing with Cambridge undergraduates. Rivers's method, such as it was, seemed to be a sort of medically guided social conversation. They spoke as peers. As Sassoon would later write in his heavily autobiographical novel, *Sherston's Progress:*

> One evening I asked whether he thought I was suffering from shell shock.
>
> "Certainly not," he replied.
>
> "What *have* I got, then?"
>
> "Well, you appear to be suffering from an anti-war complex."
>
> We both of us laughed at that. Rivers never seemed elderly; though there were more than twenty years between us, he talked as if I were his mental equal, which was very far from being the case.

Rivers had been influenced by Freud, but he was no Freudian. He saw little use for Freud's theories on infantile sexuality in treating war neuroses. Nevertheless, he looked at dream analysis as an important part of understanding the workings of the mind. Whatever his theoretical leanings, he took an individualized approach with Sassoon. They saw each other every day at first, and then Rivers cut it down to three times a week. It wasn't long before Rivers was trying to convince his patient to return to the front as a means of strengthening his argument about the war's injustice.

The director of Craiglockhart believed in the therapeutic value of sport, and daytime saw the officer-patients playing tennis, croquet, and cricket, a curriculum that lent the place a buoyant atmosphere. The ever-aloof Sassoon took to the links, brooding his way over the Scottish countryside. The nights were a different story. As Sassoon saw it, the place was divided into two spheres, the enforced bonhomie of the day followed by the dismal night, a division no doubt familiar to many veterans today. "By day the doctors dealt successfully with these disadvantages and [Craiglockhart] so to speak, 'made cheerful conversation.' But by night they lost control and the hospital became sepulchral and oppressive with saturations of war experience. One lay awake and listened to feet padding along passages which smelt of stale cigarette smoke . . . One became conscious that the place was full of men whose slumbers were morbid and terrifying — men muttering uneasily or suddenly crying out in their sleep. Around me was that underworld of dreams haunted by submerged memories of warfare and its intolerable shocks and self-lacerating failures to achieve the impossible." In time, Rivers began to win Sassoon over.

Also at Craiglockhart was another troubled infantry officer and poet, Wilfred Owen. He had fought with the Manchester regiment and been blown up by an artillery shell near Fayet. Dazed and unresponsive, he was eventually sent back to England. Seven years younger, Owen was as yet unpublished, and after hearing that Sassoon was at Craiglockhart, he went to his room and sought his writing advice. Stammering out his admiration for the older officer, Owen asked him to autograph a book of his poetry. Over the course of their residence at Craiglockhart, Sassoon mentored Owen, helping to polish the work that would become the defining poetry of the war. Many of Owen's greatest poems were written during this period, including "Anthem for Doomed Youth" and "Dulce et Decorum Est." The two agreed about a number of things, including the "apparent indifference of the public and press" toward the war.

If Sassoon was expecting a kind of martyrdom at Craiglockhart, he was to be disappointed. Over the course of their time together, Sassoon went from sparring ineffectively against Rivers to seeing him as a kindred spirit, despite Rivers's lack of combat exposure. Years later, he would describe him as a "dream friend." Ashamed by the comforts of the hospital, by the end of the summer Sassoon seemed to accept his fate, saying, "Reality is on the other side of the Channel, surely." In an extraordinary act of sublimation, Sassoon came to believe that offering up his life to the pacifist cause in the trenches was the proper course. In November, Sassoon appeared before an army medical board and was declared fit for general service.

It was never entirely clear how Rivers was able to alter the trajectory of Sassoon's life, apart from simply talking thoughtfully with him about his predicament. On a certain level, there seemed to be something curative about the respect Rivers accorded him, an act of creative compassion that seems almost magical, considering the pressure both men were under. Sassoon later wrote, "Shutting the door of his room for the last time, I left behind me someone who had helped and understood me more than anyone I had ever known. Much as he disliked speeding me back to the trenches, he realized that it was my only way out. And the longer I live the more right I know him to have been."

By May, Sassoon was back in France. Returning to friendly lines after an incredibly risky two-man reconnaissance of a machinegun position, he was shot in the head by a British soldier who mistook him for a German. Despite his protests, he was evacuated back to England. After the war, he lived as a lettered country gentleman and continued to write poetry, though his style was much changed. The war was never far from his mind, and decades later he would continue to dream of returning to the front, echoing the experience of other veterans, such as Ivor Gurney, a Great War poet and composer who died in a mental hospital in 1937 convinced that the war was still going on.

Owen's luck was of a different sort. He was killed in action a week before peace was declared. Word of his death reached his parents as church bells announced the Armistice on November 11, 1918.

For all its pathos and drama, World War I represents something of a lost opportunity for the cause of trauma. The war took an unspeakable toll on soldiers' minds, and for a time, the world sat up and noticed. In Britain alone, there were twenty shell-shock hospitals and numerous "Homes for Recovery" by the end of the war. Shell shock was the first instance of a trauma-caused mental disorder being acknowledged, and while the term itself became confusing, it offered a chance of recognition, of adding to the store of knowledge about post-traumatic stress.

Oddly, no veterans movement ever coalesced in Great Britain. Prominent veterans of the war, such as Harold Macmillan and Clement Attlee, were known to reminisce about the war "at the drop of a hat," but they did so as individuals, never as members of any kind of movement. Some have argued that the issue broke down as a matter of class. The most high-profile sufferers of shell shock were anything but inclined to make a political cause out of it. Sassoon is again useful as an exemplar: always somewhat aloof, he wrote extensively about the war, but the idea of agitating for what amounted to a psychiatric issue was simply not in the cards. After the war, Rivers returned to his academic work at Cambridge; his research on physical immobility and trauma was scarcely read.

Across the Atlantic, the American Legion, established in 1919 by veterans who had fought in France, became a powerful voice for the treatment of returned soldiers, though like the Grand Army of the Republic, the dominant post–Civil War veterans organization, the Legion focused on pensions and the funding of local veterans hospitals rather than on a mental health agenda. The political meaning of the veteran experience was a dominant motif in the interwar politics of Germany, France, and Italy (Mussolini used veteran support when he took power in 1922), but the trauma narrative itself was politicized in a way that rarely served the psychological needs of the individual veteran.

The one exception to this vast amnesia was an American who never saw the war firsthand, Abraham Kardiner. A sometimes obsessive man, Kardiner's long medical education culminated with a personal analysis by Freud himself in Vienna. In 1922, he began work at No. 81 Veterans' Bureau Hospital in the Bronx. Over a four-year period, he saw over a thousand war-related neuroses. He later described the experience as "the most instructive and the most dramatic" of his entire career, but also very disturbing. There was nothing in the medical literature to explain the "tortures and discomforts" he was attempting to treat.

In 1939, as war was again breaking out across Europe, he began work on a comprehensive theoretical study, *The Traumatic Neuroses of War,* in which he noted the episodic amnesia that dominated the field, saying, "The subject of neurotic disturbances consequent upon war has, in the past 25 years, been submitted to a good deal of capriciousness in public interest and psychiatric whims. The public does not sustain its interest, which was very great after World War I, and neither does psychiatry. . . . In part, this is due to the declining status of the veteran after a war."

The book would be almost completely ignored for over thirty years. Kardiner's message was one that no one wanted to hear: for war-damaged men, unless active, systematic treatment was undertaken, the prospects for recovery were slim. In the 1970s, as American medicine confronted an epidemic of mental disorders among Vietnam veterans, Kardiner's work was the only resource psychiatrists could turn to. His predictions about the capricious public interest in war neurosis proved all too accurate.

4

THE HAUNTED MIND

IN TREATING SHELL-SHOCKED soldiers, doctors during World War I were at first inclined to address the ailment strictly as a physiological phenomenon, as if the concussive force of the shell had damaged something in the body of the sufferer. While people suffering post-traumatic symptoms may experience their distress as forms of somatic dysfunction, they are just as often experienced as paranormal, uncanny phenomena or compulsive returns to the past. Survivors look back and see messages written into the world. Warnings, omens, sermons in the form of premonitions. Clues. Survivors look back and remember the unanswered email, the curious out-of-the-blue remark from a stranger, the way the traffic aligned the moment before impact, putting five red cars together in the same lane. The unused plane ticket, the trees whose leaves were out of season, the freakish weather, the odd journal entry. What is it to be a person who notices such things, to become a detective of one's own life? What is it about terror that makes us into creatures so lacking in normal faith that we begin looking for a deeper order in the world, drifting into a kind of gnostic wonder? What happens at the moment of horror that makes us so lonely that we begin to see the world as haunted, to keep such details as company? Does terror in its total mystery awaken some need for pattern making, some more ancient way of understanding the world?

What is it that makes us want to believe that a traumatic event has a life of its own? That it is searching for a place in time to express itself, to make itself known to the world?

The day before I hit an IED in Baghdad, I went out on a patrol with some soldiers who couldn't believe that I had never been blown up before. A month before that, while waiting for a helicopter to Dora in a cooling hut next to the flight line at Camp Fallujah, I had what I believed at the time to be an intimation of death. It came in the form of a man whom I recognized even though we'd never met.

He was waiting, like me, for a helicopter out of Anbar, beginning the endless journey home or, like so many other citizens of the war—contractors, retired shooters, wanderers, and mercenaries—making their way from one assignment to another, hitting the line of bases strung along the Euphrates like old frontier towns. I was on my way to the latest in a series of embeds and filled with a fatigue that seemed to stretch back into childhood, making me feel that I might spend the rest of my life trying to get on the other side of it. It was the sort of fatigue that went beyond simply making you feel exhausted and took on an aggressive character, actually causing you to question certain fundamental principles in your life.

I'd been living hand to mouth with the infantry for months, and opening my eyes after a nap inside the cooling hut, my heart froze. There I was, stretched out a few feet away on the filthy plywood floor, eerily still, head resting on a backpack, immersed in a book whose title I couldn't make out. The floor seemed to turn to liquid beneath me. It was impossible: my double in brown-canvas utility trousers.

He had the same build as me. We both possessed an unmistakable college boy look, a wholesome angularity that almost seemed designed to anger first sergeants. Like me, he was a dandy with a taste for the old world adventurer. He wore tastefully scuffed Italian mountaineering boots, displaying his (our) weakness for needlessly technical gear in a war that required no such extravagances. It was as if I were seeing myself for the first time. Nevertheless, it is a man's books that tell the inner story, and if it wasn't for the book he held, I might have been temporarily fascinated and then fallen back to sleep. Once my eyes adjusted to the light of the hut and I made out the book's title, I went from being intrigued to a sort of fearful wonderment: he was reading the very book that rested inside my identical Canadian-made rucksack: an out-of-print Black Dog & Leventhal copy of T. E. Lawrence's *Revolt in the Desert* (the précis of his magnificent *Seven Pillars of Wisdom*), available only through certain rare-book dealers in Great Britain. It was the only copy I'd ever seen apart from the one I owned. Seeing the book, I felt ill. The idea came to me that he, whoever he was, wasn't an accident, that he had been *inserted* here for some purpose.

The fear grew, clenching and unclenching itself like a fist inside my ribs. I knew that in certain mythologies the appearance of a double was viewed as a warning, a premonition of coming death. If this were true, then it was possible that a version of him had been following me throughout Iraq, lurking in my peripheral vision, waiting for the right moment to present himself. I saw him watching from inside a hovel in Karma, through the parting of a window curtain, through a half-cracked doorway, through the dark of a peephole, almost as if he were not just a warning but an actor in the drama of my demise. Was it possible that I'd seen him before but hadn't recognized him? Was this how it worked? Did a man take on a heightened perceptive power the closer he moved toward death? Was this why so many men were overtaken by a feeling of calm when they passed, as if the end were something like a learning process, an acknowledgment of a lost memory? Why was I being allowed to see him now?

Then, as if he'd felt my gaze, he stood up, collected his gear, and stepped out of the hut. Without thinking, I rose from the plywood floor and hurried after him, out into the assembled crowd of Marines, contractors, and weary straphangers, hundreds of them on their way in and out of theater, piling off trucks and Humvees, carrying with them the body heat of the vast war and their own small reveries and agonies, the unspeakable melancholy of all their gear stacked into long moraines that stretched along the edge of the landing zone. Almost at once, I experienced a strange elation, the kind of thrill that seizes every chase. I ran toward him, taking brisk, overstated strides, but he was already weaving himself into the knots of men crowding the gravel field between the hut and a wall of seven-ton trucks. For a moment, I felt free, tethered to him, enmeshed in mysterious adventure.

I could feel the fatigue draining, the lava in my limbs burning away in the pursuit. I saw him slip behind a tall SAW gunner, catching a final glimpse of the exquisitely weathered backpack dancing on his frame, his impeccable gait, the bulk of Lawrence still in his hand, middle finger marking his place. Then he was gone.

Looking back, I found myself thinking that he was a vision of myself already returned, a doppelganger in the Norse tradition who arrives before his twin departs. But I saw him before Dora, before The Question, before I met Reaper, before the IED in Saydia. Did I know something without knowing how I knew it? If he was here for me, what message was he carrying? Was he just the embodiment of how I really saw myself: a vagabond beholden to no one, a grown boy who'd read his Lawrence with a little too much enthusiasm, a guy who'd taken it all a little too seriously and found himself rootless, wandering through a war that seemed to grow more meaningless by the month?

Sometimes I think that he came from the same fund of superstition I had been drawing on ever since I started going to Iraq, a fund that had been augmented by all the books I'd read and movies I'd seen where soldiers carried lucky charms, stuffed animals, and rabbit feet. All those previously mundane objects made holy by the war. I'll wonder if those talismans and alternative beliefs about life are what drew me to the Marine Corps in the first place. A knowledge of them gives you a great sense of power that stays with you long after you get out and makes you think you've mastered something about life itself.

And in that way, maybe the other me was just a messenger sent to show me who I was or dreamed myself to be, a dispatch rider bearing the same questions that Reaper would pose *in extremis* a month later. What was I doing in Iraq? Who was I now? Who was the war making me into? What exactly was I trying to prove to myself, to the world, by being over here when I didn't have to be? Why did I keep coming back, putting myself in more kinds of danger than I could understand, trying to write about a war that people back home had only the dimmest interest in, people that increasingly seemed to me to live their entire lives like fish in an aquarium, insulated, glassed off from the real world? Was there some other force at work, some invisible magnet that kept drawing me back? Some sense that there was an honor, a distinction, to be found in mortal danger?

Modern science tends to look on such episodes as, among other things, examples of apophenia, events meaningful only in retrospect, or as the product of an altered state of consciousness, like the doppelgangers that mountaineers often report seeing at high altitude. An omen, properly understood, is like the foreshock of a major earthquake. A foreshock only becomes a foreshock in the wake of the temblor that follows it, as seismologists begin creating a model of what happened. In the absence of an earthquake, what might be described as a foreshock is instead simply called a tremor, one of the dozen-odd minor seismic events that happen across Southern California on any given day. Or so the thinking goes.

And yet there is something to these uncanny events, these mental foreshocks and aftershocks. If, as Freud argued, dreams are the royal road to the unconscious, then perhaps there is practical meaning to be found in these visitations, even if they are only mirrors made by the self. Stories, self-fulfilling prophecies, hallucinations. Flashbacks. It is tempting to look at such phenomena as negative symptoms, as deficits of perception, but keeping in mind how common hallucinations are in all cultures, perhaps—once we acknowledge their surreality—we can use them as tools, as lenses into the mind of the survivor, rather than seeing them only as evidence of pathology. Perhaps, as Laurence Gonzales wrote in his book on disaster and resilience, *Surviving Survival,* there is a useful neurological correlate at work, a negotiation that happens during such hauntings between the lower, older parts of the brain and the neocortex. Perhaps there is something of value to be found in this conversation, this call and response between instinct and imagination.

The year after she was raped in a tunnel in Syracuse, Alice Sebold felt "sharp, stabbing pains" in her abdomen at 8:56 p.m. while at a poetry reading the week before Thanksgiving, which was the same time, as the Syracuse Police Department later reported, that one of her friends was being raped in Sebold's apartment.

"We've got an exact time," the female detective said. "She looked up at her digital clock. It was eight fifty-six p.m."

"When I felt sick," I said.

"What?" The female detective looked mystified.

This event, we learn later, was part of a larger feeling about her postrape life. "My whole world was turning over; whatever else I'd had or known became eclipsed. There was no chance to escape, I realized; from now on this would be it. My life and the lives of those around me. Rape." Not merely obsessed with it or defined by it, Sebold had been overtaken, *eclipsed* by her rape, as with a celestial body whose reflected light has been blocked by another body. Within the space of a year, Sebold had been raped and one of her best friends had been raped. It was as if her entire world had been raped.

The literature of trauma contains a wealth of similar unsettling phenomena, and because trauma can tattoo the imagination and disrupt our normal powers of narrative, it can create episodes that seem supernatural in origin. Ambrose Bierce, the most important American writer to actually fight in the Civil War, wrote that he was haunted by "phantoms of that blood-stained period" and continued to see "visions of the dead and dying" for the rest of his life. Freud, a passionately secular man, discussed the tendency of World War I veterans to repetitively relive their traumas in their dreams, which he described as having a "daemonic character," having first broached the subject of such repetitions in an essay titled "The Uncanny." Seventy years later, Cathy Caruth, a writer with seemingly no reservations about the supernatural's relationship to trauma, declared in *Trauma: Explorations in Memory* that "to be traumatized is precisely to be possessed by an image or event."

Beliefs about trauma's connection to the spiritual realms remain strong even today. Bear Creek Ranch, a Pentecostal Christian organization located in Portal, Georgia, and profiled in a 2013 book by journalist Jen Percy, offers exorcisms for 199 dollars, asserting that PTSD can be cured only through "deliverance." The proprietors of this retreat claim to have conducted five thousand such exorcisms, including casting out the demons of army veteran Caleb Daniels, who lost eight of his buddies in a 2005 helicopter crash in Afghanistan. Daniels, who is no longer associated with the group, described being visited by a "destroyer demon," intent upon punishing him for both "killing and living." Consumed by survivor's guilt, he began to hallucinate that his dead buddies had crowded into his bedroom. "Everywhere he went, he saw them, their burned bodies, watching him," wrote Percy. Eventually, he was haunted by a demon he called "Destroyer," a six-foot-five buffalo with horns. "It was a shadow. It was death. It was the gathered souls of all his dead friends." According to Percy, the owners of the ranch believe that "people are in bondage to a pattern of sin. Trauma is the doorway through which demons can pass."

That such possessions occur is, on a certain level, unsurprising. Everyone carries with them arresting memories of particular events that come to define them, both positive and negative, events that can seem to enshadow everything that follows. Graduations, road trips, breakups, broken bones. Such are the raw materials of life, the stories we tell ourselves about ourselves. We are our scars, it seems. Neuroscientists have long known that not all memories are created equal. James McGaugh, a pioneering memory researcher at the University of California, Irvine, recalls his grandson Tristan saying, as his mother pulled a T-shirt over his head, "Remember when I fell at Kirby's house and cut my chin? I had this shirt on." Tristan had fallen a year earlier. According to McGaugh, "Significant experiences create strong memories."

But the extraordinary flashback memories associated with PTSD are more than just strong memories, and psychologists think that flashbacks may be stored in the brain in a different "format" than normal autobiographical memories. According to Chris Brewin, a researcher at University College London who studied the memories of sixty-two civilian PTSD patients, there is a radical difference between autobiographical memories, which can be verbalized, and flashback memories, which remain beyond the reach of language and can flare up if there is any reference to the traumatic event or any sensory stimuli associated with the event. This "dual representation theory" posits that the most toxic memories remain sequestered even from other memories of the same traumatic event. That such un-controllable memories of the dead and dying might, in the case of Bierce, have been construed as "phantoms" isn't hard to imagine.

Perhaps such flashback experiences are the root of the human belief in ghosts and the supernatural, our faith in revenants that return to torment us, to demand answers to questions that remain unresolved in the mind of the survivor. Such ghosts have a way of forcing their way in. They break in. They insist. They *intrude*, in the language of the DSM. "Memories gone wild," one Marine veteran told me, describing his memories of the Iraqi girl he killed. In the worst cases, such memories can intrude so often and with such power that the entire life story of the survivor becomes warped over time, the autobiographical memories overshadowed. This can even affect memories that precede the event.

Traumatic time doesn't just destroy the flow of the present into the future, it corrodes everything that came before.

In 2010, Sonali Deraniyagala, writing about the aftermath of the 2004 tsunami that killed her family, felt compelled to rethink her entire past in light of the subsequent horror. "In the past six years I've recoiled from remembering my childhood. I felt foolish about my youthful contentment, was niggled by a notion that even as an unsuspecting child I must have been marked, doomed." Notice the language. *Marked. Doomed.* As if a scheme had been worked out in advance, a plan made, targets selected. Not the work of an anonymous force, but an alien intelligence.

A suggestible person, a writer, in the wake of terror can begin to see their imagination hijacked by The Event until, in time, everything flows from it and to it; the world itself, the past, the future are all an expression, an extension of what happened, what continues to happen, what has always happened. Like a virus, trauma writes itself into the world, hijacking the cells of memory in order to replicate.

Have you ever been blown up before, sir?

The day I was asked that question, I worried about what it might mean. Further, I knew that I needed to be worried. I knew that a question like that was not a question without consequences. To ask it was, in some sense, to defy the will of the war, to defy its absolute control of your existence, its total ownership of your every moment. To ask it was to assert a kind of independence from the workings of fate, an independence that said one could exist apart from the mysteries of the war, that one had control, and that one needn't worry about one's luck. A luck that was seemingly determined by what you said about IEDs and when and where they actually went off.

I knew this, in part, because I had written in my journal a nearly identical line about apophenia in 2004. That year, those early groping months of the war after the statues had fallen and before Abu Ghraib, when the war still held a certain novelty even back home, I had been at a remote Marine outpost on the Syrian border. On patrol one day, I'd heard a master sergeant mutter that something felt off, that it felt like the convoy we were riding in was going to get hit.

"Today just doesn't feel right," he said after talking with some other Marines on the radio. This, it seemed to me later, was not mysticism. This was a guy, an unusually talented soldier as it happened, who had, over his months in-country (he was on his second deployment at this point), gotten so close to the war that he knew things without knowing how he knew them.

When an IED went off ahead of us later that day, he was unsurprised.

Patterns where there shouldn't be patterns.

This was, of course, an atypical episode, what might be described as a case of *positive* apophenia. A case where one Marine's unconscious pattern making turned out to be correct. Had he been wrong, had there been no IED, I almost certainly wouldn't have remembered it. But this event, coming when it did in the early months of what turned out to be a very long war, months which in retrospect came to seem like a primer in Iraq for me, drove me to take the master sergeant's behavior that afternoon as an object lesson in survival: sometimes you have to attend to the invisible in a way that might seem crazy at first. Stay long enough in the war and you begin to grow antennae for the invisible, the unspoken, for the sometimes weak, staticky signal of intuition, the signal that says *I don't feel safe here. Why is that?*

By 2007, at the height of the surge, the existence of such antennae would, in fact, be recognized by the Pentagon and enshrined in *FM 3-24 Counterinsurgency* (a manual coauthored by General Petraeus), which encouraged commanders to pay attention to the "atmospherics" of a given area of operations. But what happens to these antennae when you come home, when you don't need them anymore? How does one adapt to the "atmospherics" of San Diego? For many veterans and civilian first responders, these antennae can become a problem; an armature that was lifesaving in one context can become destructive in another.

Back in California, I didn't immediately see the problems that could arise from having developed such antennae. Mostly what I felt was anger. Anger at the apathy and smallness of mind that had allowed the war to happen, anger at the same apathy and smallness of mind that allowed most Americans to act as if the war had never happened. But there were other, less intelligible concerns. For reasons that became clear once I thought about them, driving in alleys and on dirt roads became problematic. In theory, driving on virtually any paved road was permeated with bad associations for someone who'd been blown up in Iraq, but for reasons that remain unclear to me, driving on most surface streets, even driving in Tijuana, only rarely activated my antennae.

Driving down the alley behind my apartment one morning, late for an appointment at the VA, I looked ahead and saw a flatbed work truck blocking my path. Without thinking, I stopped my truck, got out, and rushed toward the flatbed truck, yelling for the owner of the truck, whoever they were, to move it.

"This is not a fucking parking lot, you piece of shit!" I remember yelling.

Not for a second did I think that I was back in Iraq. Not for a second did I think that I was about to be ambushed, that there was an IED buried in the dirt of the alley. This was my neighborhood, North Park, San Diego, a neighborhood I had lived in for years after I had left the Corps the decade before. Three blocks away was a house that a friend of mine, a former drill instructor, had owned for years. Three blocks beyond that was Claire de Lune's, the coffee shop where my friend Mitch had worked to pay his way through San Diego State. I knew by instinct how far away I was from the 805 freeway, could judge the traffic on it by sound, could tell the time of day simply based on the behavior of drivers on the nearby surface streets. In 2011, for my birthday, Erica had in fact blindfolded me and, according to a prearranged plan with a group of friends, driven me to my best friend's house in nearby University Heights for the beginning of what would prove to be a two-day party. When I began calling out the street names as we drove by them, she got angry.

"Damn it, Dave! You're ruining the fucking surprise!"

This was *terra cognita,* in other words, a place that as much as anywhere else on the planet I would consider home, and yet when I saw that truck, part of me was somewhere else.

Mercifully, the owner of the truck, a handyman who resembled Jeff Bridges in *The Big Lebowski,* appeared and quickly moved it onto the street, clearing the alley. I was free. My face was hot, the blood suddenly loud in my ears.

After the same truck blocked the alley a week later, I was able to piece it together. Explaining it to a graduate student who was briefly my therapist at the VA hospital in La Jolla, it struck me. It was an ambush. The truck blocking my way, the dirt piling up at the verges, the heat coming off the concrete, the smell of old garbage, the diesel smell of the truck; these various stimuli had put a part of my brain back in Iraq. There had been no particular moment of transport, no feeling that I was leaving my body, no bad flash, no patter of radio traffic in my ears, no explosion, no sound of Reaper's voice. Just a blocked alley, the truck seeming momentarily to be in color while everything else was in black and white.

Scan our six o'clock.
We're gonna pivot and let the Bradley —

My brain was making patterns, in other words, where there shouldn't be patterns. Or more accurately, one part of my brain, the amygdala, that was governed by one principle, the danger principle, was making what at one time were the right patterns, but my body was now in another time. This was not an ambush. This was not an attempt to channelize an American patrol by blocking the escape route. This was not a key element of the enemy's scheme of maneuver. This was an inconveniently parked work truck in San Diego.

This was, I would see later, yet more evidence for the idea that "PTSD is a disease of time."

This situation was not, needless to say, governed by a rational process on my part. I was not thinking it through, lucidly deciding that I was in an ambush and responding accordingly. This was, I would learn, what amounted to a contest between two different parts of my brain, the old part and the new part—the amygdala and the neocortex—a contest between what I was feeling and what I was seeing. Laurence Gonzales, describing this sort of contest in *Surviving Survival,* wrote that "the brain can seem at times like a confounding bureaucracy with different departments arguing with one another. The amygdala is not in the Rational Department."

Episodes like mine in the alley behind my house are essentially an altered form of perception, and because they are typically fleeting in nature, they elude scientific observation. Reminiscent experiences like this, especially when they are chronic and delusional, can be difficult to distinguish from full-blown psychosis. For this reason, cases of chronic PTSD are frequently misdiagnosed as paranoid schizophrenia. So powerful, so transporting, are these intrusive memories and flashbacks that Dewleen Baker, a researcher at the University of California, San Diego, who has studied PTSD for decades, refers to them as "affective seizures," though she is quick to point out that they are not actually seizures in the neurological sense. PET scans done on patients in controlled settings have shown that the most active part of the brain during an induced flashback is the amygdala, the bundle of cells that serves as our guard dog, warning us of approaching danger, a finding that would indicate that while flashbacks can represent a number of past experiences, the overwhelming theme seems to be one of fear for one's safety. Interestingly, these neuroimaging studies also show that one area that is conspicuously inactive is a region of the brain known as Broca's area, one of the brain's speech centers, which may help explain why flashbacks remain so mysterious, so beyond the powers of language.

Such hauntings or "reexperiencing" of symptoms, as such events are sometimes called by psychiatrists, play a major role in PTSD and exist along a continuum from recurrent images, thoughts, and dreams about a traumatic event to persistent misperceptions, hallucinations, full-blown dissociative flashbacks, and in the rarest of cases permanent psychosis. (One famous case of such a psychosis is that of Ivor Gurney, the World War I poet, who was wounded and gassed in 1917 and died in a mental hospital twenty years later convinced that the war was still going on.) These sorts of alterations in consciousness can also be caused by overwhelming guilt for a crime or perceived sin that the conscience cannot tolerate, as in the ghost of Hamlet's father. Like death itself, death's "ghosts" have a million ways of making themselves known. Some recurrent images and thoughts are responses to specific environmental stimuli, such as the sudden appearance of women dressed in traditional Islamic clothing in the United States for veterans who served in Iraq or the fear felt by rape victims who find themselves alone in a dark alley. In each case, environmental stimuli associated with the traumatic event, even the most trivial and spurious stimuli, like the smell of diesel fuel, can become triggers.

Flashbacks, as they are experienced by survivors of trauma, tend to be dominated by the visual sense, but they are often triggered by smells. One woman, who had been molested as a child and then assaulted as a teenager, wrote that "for both events smell will bring back strong flashbacks." She continued, saying,

> I had my first flashback of being assaulted as a child when a man sat next to me on a bus. Once I smelled [his] sweat and body odor, I was not on that bus anymore. I was in my neighbor's garage and I remembered everything. The bus driver had to ask me to get off the bus when we arrived at our destination. I lost all sense of time and place.

Nearly all survivors report that certain traumatic memories communicate an uncanny feeling of timelessness, as if, as Tim O'Brien described in his novel *In the Lake of the Woods,* "the unities of time and space had unraveled." Joe Simpson, a British mountaineer who survived a catastrophic fall while climbing in the Peruvian Andes in 1985, returned to the site of the original accident to film a reenactment of it, only to find himself hallucinating that he had never left the mountain and was still crawling his way back to base camp. Writing about it in an epilogue to his bestselling book *Touching the Void,* Simpson said,

> I felt as if I was about to be attacked from behind at any moment. The feelings became most powerful when I was on the moraines or the glacier and the familiar cirque of mountain ridges dominated my every view. It was a memory that had been seared into my consciousness. Seeing it again all these years later was the trigger that brought back my worst memories and associations. This was the place where I had known I was going to die. Those ridge lines should have been the last thing I would ever see. It was not cathartic. It was terrifying . . .
>
> For me memories came rushing back with such a clarity and startling vividness that I became convinced at times that the last seventeen years had not passed by and I was back in the terrible reality of 1985 trying to crawl my way down the mountain.

As Simpson later explained to me, this hallucinatory episode triggered by his return to the Andes caused him to suffer from PTSD, whereas the original trauma did not, an unusual instance of being re-traumatized by environmental stimuli. (Though psychologists think that one traumatic event can "soften up" a person for a subsequent trauma.) Interestingly, before this episode, Simpson had "always been a little sceptical about the very idea of post-traumatic stress disorder. It seems that everyone gets it nowadays and I was suspicious that it had become a catchall to provide exculpation from the past and a convenient way of suing for compensation." Needless to say, Simpson, who considers himself something of an "enlightened stoic," is no longer skeptical about PTSD.

While intrusive symptoms are most often visual, people with PTSD may experience auditory hallucinations as well. One study of

115 combat veterans with PTSD published in *Traumatology* found that fully 65 percent of those studied reported hearing voices, often the voices of dead comrades. Some veterans in this study reported hearing "command voices," which the veterans felt compelled to obey. Douglas Bremner, a researcher at Emory University, makes the point that post-traumatic hallucinations, while easily confused with traditional psychotic hallucinations, are quite different, saying, "Auditory hallucinations in PTSD are related to the traumatic event, and often consist of a buddy talking to a patient, voices crying out in pain, or actual traumatic memories. Psychotic auditory hallucinations, on the other hand, commonly consist of an unrecognized foreign voice with specific types of content, such as making disparaging comments about the individual."

Once, after interviewing an Iraq veteran on the phone for several hours, I heard the *maghrib,* the Muslim evening call to prayer, from my front porch in San Diego, even though there were no mosques in my neighborhood. My strongest associations with the *maghrib* pertain to Fallujah, a town known to some Iraqis as the "city of mosques," and from Marine patrol bases within the city, you would hear the calls to prayer broadcast over loudspeakers throughout the day. ("God is great/I bear witness that there is no God except the one God.") That many Marines were convinced that the mosques were insurgent sanctuaries that used their PA systems to coordinate attacks seemed almost irrelevant: hearing the *maghrib* never failed to send a chill up my spine. Spooky is just a word in your mouth until you have heard the sunset call to prayer in a half-rubbled city surrounded by Al Qaeda fighters.

The veteran and I had been talking about Diyala province, a mixed sect region east of Baghdad. The consensus among Marine officers was that the Sunni insurgents who had been driven out of Anbar in 2006 had largely relocated to Diyala, and I had been half-heartedly planning a reporting trip there before finally ending up in Dora. Somehow Diyala had come to represent a missed opportunity in my mind, a challenge unmet, and as we spoke I felt a certain disappointment in myself, along with a number of other complicated feelings about the war. Shortly after hanging up, I stepped out of my apartment to take a walk. When I returned, I heard a distant PA system turn on, followed by the strains of the *maghrib*. This went on for nearly a minute, continuing even after I went inside my apartment and shut the door.

Hearing the *maghrib,* sung in the distinctive Iraqi style, while in San Diego reminded me that, like many veterans, I have a number of disturbing, unresolved memories lurking in the depths that can be reactivated under certain conditions. Interestingly, the *maghrib* is not associated with any particular traumatic event for me but rather with the string of weeks I spent in Fallujah, beginning in May 2004. It is common within the clinical literature on trauma to focus on superlatives—on the singular moments of greatest terror and helplessness, such as the instant the IED went off or the moment the building collapsed during the earthquake—as if the process of traumatization must be reduced to a single point in time in order to be understood. In this vein, clinical descriptions of traumatic hallucinations are nearly always told as corresponding to a moment of maximum horror, a point of near-death. During my worst times post-Iraq, times when I felt the most alienated and angry at the world, it felt like my body was back in Dora and Ramadi, places where I lived on the knife-edge of fear for weeks at a time. It was, in short, a *cumulative* feeling of stress and fear that came back to me, not unresolved memories relating to a specific close call. Arabic music has always been evocative for me, and I wonder if hearing the *maghrib* in San Diego when I did wasn't a misperception that related to a broader stretch of time in Iraq, when I felt lost inside the war, like a fugitive from a regular, grounded life back in the States.

Post-traumatic hauntings require no such invitation from the senses, however. John Bumgardner, a Union soldier in the Civil War who survived a near miss from an exploding shell, is one such case. After the war, he took up farming with his new wife, Charlotte. Several weeks after they were married, however, she noticed that something was amiss. John would be sitting quietly and then suddenly blurt out, "Don't speak to me; don't you hear them bombarding?" On one occasion, he came running in from the fields, yelling, "They are coming, they are coming. See the bombshell." Soon after, he ran to an upstairs room, where his wife found him shivering in fear and saying, "Be still. Don't you hear them?"

Michael Ferrara, a veteran wilderness first responder in Aspen, Colorado, describes being overtaken out of the blue by what he called the "slide show," a procession of mental images he couldn't control: eviscerated bodies, a father riding in the back of an ambulance with his dying skateboarder son, burned figures on a runway. In a 2011 article in *Outside* magazine that recounted Ferrara's struggle, Hampton Sides wrote that "it was a horror show, crowded in his head like a Hieronymous Bosch scene, and the images wouldn't stop. He reacted to them with a surge of adrenaline, a stab of fear, a complex of real and present emotions. His eyes would drop, he'd lose visual contact with his surroundings. His blood pressure would spike and he'd find himself hyperventilating. He wasn't just remembering these traumas; he was reliving them."

"The pictures were burned into my mind," Ferrara said. "They were happening right here, right now. My subconscious didn't know it wasn't actually real."

If the daytime is the occasional stalking ground of Freud's *daemons,* then the nighttime is their lair, an underworld of mystery and metamorphosis where they have free rein. Unsurprisingly, many trauma survivors report that it is at night that they feel the most vulnerable, both to their memories and the outside world. The daemonic night and its chief product, the nightmare, have always been a special hell for survivors. As we saw in the previous chapter, Siegfried Sassoon noted this soon after beginning treatment for shell shock in 1917, observing that there were in essence two hospitals at Craiglockhart, the "elaborately cheerful" hospital by day and the "sepulchral and oppressive" hospital at night, where he found himself submerged in the "underworld of dreams" and "memories of warfare." One Civil War veteran, after visiting the battlefield at Cold Harbor after the war, remarked that "skeletons and ghosts haunt us in our dreams." An Indiana physician who treated Newell Gleason, a Civil War veteran who had recently been released from an asylum, observed that Gleason's sleep was "laborious" and "filled with dreams that seemed to make sleep exhaustive rather than refreshing."

The dead seem most likely to visit us at night, as happened to Michael Herr, a reporter for *Esquire* in Vietnam. "During my first month back I woke up one night and knew that my living room was full of dead Marines. It actually happened three or four times, after a dream I was having those nights (the kind of dream one never had in Vietnam), and that first time it wasn't just some holding dread left by the dream, I knew they were there, so that after I'd turned on the light by my bed and smoked a cigarette I lay there for a moment thinking that I'd have to go out soon and cover them."

In fact, it was the modern war nightmare that forced Freud to revise his theory of the unconscious in 1920. Unable to explain their painful and repetitive "daemonic" character, Freud struggled to fit these nightmares into his theory of dreams as unconscious wish fulfillments. In time, this observation caused him to posit an entirely new facet of psychoanalysis, a counterweight to Eros that he called the death drive or *Todestriebe*. Noting that traumatic nightmares seemed to repeat themselves for years, Abraham Kardiner in 1939 described the repetitive traumatic dream as "one of the most characteristic and at the same time one of the most enigmatic phenomena we encounter in the disease" of combat neurosis. More recent research has confirmed Kardiner's thesis. Peretz Lavie, in an article in the *New England Journal of Medicine* a few months after 9/11, wrote that

> trauma-related anxiety dreams appear to be the most consistent problem reported by patients with PTSD. Studies involving veterans of combat, survivors of Japanese imprisonment during World War II, and Holocaust survivors indicate such dreams persist, sometimes for more than 40 years after traumatic events.

One Vietnam veteran, "Mr. D.," who was quoted in an early conceptual study of PTSD, continued to have dreams that repeated his wartime experiences. In the dream, he was on a hill being overrun by the Vietcong. The dream was dominated by images of death. Looking around and seeing his friends die, Mr. D. then kills a Vietcong fighter by smashing the man's forehead with his rifle. Another Vietnam veteran, who served on a U.S. Navy "swift boat," still dreamed about his experiences in the Mekong Delta some twenty years later. The lone survivor of a boat that was destroyed by enemy fire, at night he revisited various scenes from the Mekong, picking up the wounded bodies of his buddies and the Vietnamese that they tortured. "In my nightmares I can't stand the screaming," he said.

In many cases, the fear of these nightmares prevents the sufferer from falling asleep, or even trying to fall asleep, which leads to chronic insomnia. Over time, this lack of sleep can develop into a kind of ghoulish survivor lifestyle. One Vietnam veteran I met, who worked as a security guard at an office building in downtown Los Angeles, told me he hadn't slept more than two hours at a stretch since the 1970s. Numerous studies, dating back to the advent of the PTSD diagnosis, have confirmed what the spouses of veterans have known for millennia: survivors of trauma sleep differently than other people. They have trouble getting to sleep, they wake up constantly, and they are more easily disturbed by noises. (My experience certainly bears out this thesis. Any sharp or unexplained noise when I am in bed will send my heart racing.) Interestingly, Richard Ross of the University of Pennsylvania has even suggested that PTSD nightmares might represent a new phenomenon called "REM sleep without atonia" or REM sleep without the usual low muscle tone experienced by most people.

The prevailing theory among researchers today is that traumatic nightmares are mostly "instant replays" of the original trauma, an idea that is surprisingly congruent with Freud's original "repetition-compulsion" theory, which says that survivors tend to reenact old traumas. "The bad stuff never stops happening: it lives in its own dimension, replaying itself over and over," Tim O'Brien wrote in *The Things They Carried.* Proponents of this belief look at these nightmares as being essentially sleeping flashbacks and even less significant than normal dreams because of their repetitiveness. For this reason, and the fact that nightmares are difficult to produce in sleep labs, little research is currently being done on nightmares. The 2007 *Handbook of PTSD,* edited by a group of leading VA researchers, contains but a single reference to nightmares in its 592 pages. (This holds true for similar heavily cited scientific anthologies on PTSD published in 1996, 2000, and 2009 as well.)

Why this seeming lack of interest in nightmares? The answer lies in the recent history of psychiatry. "Psychiatry," says William Normand, a practicing psychoanalyst in New York, "has gone from being brainless to being mindless." Clinicians who once neglected physiology in favor of emotionality now neglect the emotions in favor of brain chemistry. The study of dreams and nightmares, once the centerpieces of mainstream psychiatry when it was dominated by Freud and his many disciples, is now in decline. Today, researchers increasingly look to neuroscience to explain and manage PTSD symptoms. The most cited studies on traumatic nightmares today relate to the medications used to reduce them, principally Prazosin, a drug that blocks some of the effects of adrenaline, which the body releases during PTSD nightmares.

Nevertheless, interviews with survivors and historical accounts of post-traumatic nightmares give us a richer picture of this nocturnal world and can reveal aspects of trauma that may not necessarily have a neurological correlate. Further, because nightmares tend to be less transient than flashbacks and often have a narrative quality to them, studying them within the larger context of a PTSD sufferer's life can offer insights into the nature of the condition and how survivors really feel about what has happened to them.

One common theme in traumatic nightmares is that the horrific event has never ended, that it lives on and evolves, melding with the present, or, conversely, that it has come to encompass one's entire history: past, present, and future. Veterans of combat often describe dreams involving fallen comrades who have returned to judge them or to join seemingly non-war-related aspects of their past. In a study conducted by therapists at the West Los Angeles VA hospital, one Vietnam veteran, who claimed "his dreams were only about the war," reported a dream in which he shot an attacking Vietcong soldier on a rooftop. When the Vietcong fell dead, the patient recognized the man as his brother.

Richard Fox, a therapist who worked with over one hundred Vietnam veterans in the 1970s, observed that the loss of a friend frequently led to the most powerful traumatic nightmares and other stress syndromes. He felt that these sorts of visitations were especially likely to occur if the deceased had been a close companion with whom the survivor had a "mirror relationship," and that there was something intolerable about this because it represents such a close encounter with one's own extinction. This theory helps explain how Caleb Daniels, the Afghanistan veteran who lost his best friend in a 2005 helicopter crash, was so profoundly disturbed that he came to feel that he was being pursued by a buffalo-shaped "Destroyer" demon.

One Iraq veteran I interviewed, who now runs a successful printing company in Virginia, described his war-related dreams as happening on a "circuit." Mentioning how his nightmares seemed to correspond to his general stress level, he said, "Most of the time they involve being attacked, and my weapon misfires." When I asked him if they were simply "instant replays" of traumas from Iraq, he responded, "[The] dynamics of the dream stay constant, the situation/environment changes. My takeaway is 'You're not ready,' or 'You're not prepared.'" Audie Murphy, the most decorated American soldier to emerge from World War II, had similar dreams. A line of Germans advancing toward him, "men running and shooting and hollering and then my gun would fall apart when I tried to pull the trigger."

Some researchers look at nightmares as playing a potentially beneficial, integrative role, helping the survivor to make sense of what happened or to construct meaning out of the chaos of war and other traumatic events. Zahava Solomon, a pioneering Israeli researcher, describes one such case in her 1993 book, *Combat Stress Reaction:*

Something of the working-through process can be seen in a repeated nightmare of Eli, who developed PTSD after participating in intense fighting in the Lebanon war. Among the many harrowing experiences that he underwent, one that cut very deeply was of being shot at by 10-year-old "RPG kids," named after the [*sic*] automatic weapons they carried. What made this experience so terrible for Eli (and other Israeli soldiers who described it) was not only the inherent threat of injury and death but also the moral conflict it evoked in these soldiers, who were trained not to harm children. With the onset of his PTSD, Eli began to have repeated nightmares of RPG kids shooting at him; these were so frightening that he would jump out of bed with the image before his eyes. The nightmare appeared with all sorts of variations, quite frequently at first, then less and less so. Parallel to the decrease in frequency, a process of working through took place in which Eli found "practical solutions" to the problem. In the early versions of the nightmare, he generally stood by helplessly as he was shot at. In later versions, he took cover or cocked his weapon.

Sometimes, in the darkness of dreams, traumatic events can fuse with the present, creating a kind of permanent midnight; past and present become one, and it is the life itself that is enshadowed. One comments on, ridicules, ironizes the other. "Forty-three years old, and the war occurred half a lifetime ago, and yet the remembering makes it now. And sometimes remembering will lead to a story, which makes it forever," wrote Tim O'Brien in *The Things They Carried,* perhaps the best novel to emerge from the war that produced PTSD, a novel that, as many critics have pointed out, repeatedly embodies and enacts the disorder in its 224 pages.

In the winter of 2007, while writing a series of stories on the surge in Iraq, I began to have dreams involving my old rifle platoon. In the dreams, my Marines are on patrol with me, asking me why I was doing this or that while we walked the streets of Ramadi. Sometimes they are with me in a Sea Stallion getting lit up over Fallujah, the air outside the crew chief's window bright with tracers. Sometimes my radioman, a thin reed of a man named Dougherty, is behind me in the Humvee in Saydia. I'm driving. He doesn't say anything. He just looks at me. His eyes are more than enough.

Perhaps no one has inhabited this shadowland of dream and reality more completely, or imbued it with greater meaning, than Siegfried Sassoon. For decades after World War I, Sassoon continued to dream that the war was still going on and that he would be called back to active service. After leaving the army, he moved back to the English countryside, published several books, joined the Labour Party, became the literary editor of the *Daily Herald,* began a close friendship with E. M. Forster, fell in love with a man, finally marrying a woman named Hester. But it was the war that stayed with him, it was the war that populated his dreams. Indeed, Sassoon spent the rest of his life writing about the war and the youth that led up to it, a period from 1895 to 1920. In a trilogy of autobiographical novels, culminating in *Sherston's Progress,* whose pages provide the title of this book, he revisited the earlier stages of his life, with the war and Craiglockhart serving as the turning point. As a writer, Sassoon turned this backward-looking impulse to good use, though the perversity of what he called "my queer craving to revisit the past and give the modern world the slip" was not lost on him.

These types of obsessions and revisitations all highlight the degree to which many survivors remain in a liminal state, alternating between *now* and *then,* between *here* and *there.* The veteran, the rape victim, the repatriated political prisoner all carry aspects of the trauma with them forward into the present. This is another way in which the literary habits of describing a traumatized person as being "haunted," or "unstuck in time" (to use Vonnegut's phrase from *Slaughterhouse-Five*), are consistent with how post-traumatic stress is physically experienced by the survivor. When I speak of liminality, I mean it not as the fancy of a poetic imagination but as a state of being with a clear biological correlate: in the instance of the rape victim, whose nervous system reverts back to the traumatic state — mobilized to confront an attacker, the adrenaline flowing, the heart rate elevated, the pupils dilated — there is an observable physiological manifestation of this liminality. Herein lies the problem: the liminal person who returns to society (physically at least), with what one anthropologist described as "more alert faculties" and an "enhanced knowledge of how things work," possesses a knowledge that is of little use in the everyday world.

These facts alone may explain some of the pain that survivors feel upon return. They aren't merely seeing things that others don't, they are, at varying times and to varying degrees, living in different times and in different places. Like Billy Pilgrim, the main character in *Slaughterhouse-Five,* who survived the bombing of Dresden only to lose his footing in the universe, they have become "spastic in time." Dizzied by these spasms in time (and space), they lose the normal narrative compass that most people rely on to guide them through their lives, the compass that tells them where they are and what they need to attend to.

Eric Leed, a historian at Florida International University writing about World War I, spoke of veterans as being trapped in a kind of "No Man's Land," applying the military term for the terrain between friendly and enemy lines. Having been unmade and remade by the war, paradoxically disgusted and defined by the slaughter of 1914–1919, the veteran was, in Leed's view, "a man fixed in passage who had acquired a peculiar 'homelessness,'" belonging neither to the war nor to the society he fought for. As Leed points out, many veterans remained transfixed by the image of this shadowland for the rest of their lives. In 1965, one such veteran wrote that "in fifty years I have never been able to rid myself of this obsession with no-man's land and the unknown world beyond it. On this side of our wire everything is familiar and every man is a friend, over there, beyond the wire, is the unknown, the uncanny."

To Leed, this betweenness wasn't simply an obsession, it was a complete reshaping of the survivor's identity. "The figure of the veteran is a subcategory of what might be called 'the liminal type.' He derives all of his features from the fact that he has crossed the boundaries of disjunctive social worlds, from peace to war, and back. He has been reshaped by his voyage along the margins of civilization, a voyage in which he has been presented with wonders, curiosities, and monsters—things that can only be guessed at by those who remained at home." While Leed's focus in *No Man's Land* is on the World War I veteran, it is not hard to imagine how this state of liminality, this feeling of apartness, pertains to survivors today. As one female Iraq veteran explained to me, "I feel like a Martian."

This change of identity also creates a dilemma for the society to which the survivor returns. As every military spouse can attest, the soldier who returns from war is different than the one who left, and it is perhaps this sense of a combatant's differentness that led the Israelites to impose a strict weeklong period of exile on warriors returning from battle, as described in the book of Numbers. ("Anyone who has killed someone or touched someone who was killed must stay outside the camp seven days.") Interestingly, in the cases of returning warriors and survivors of near-death experiences found in history, it is the survivor who is most often expected to do the work of the ritual cleansing. Having been "stained" by death or rape, the survivor is looked on as being out of place.

This deep sense of separation from the normal world, this sense of, in the words of World War I veteran Charles Edward Carrington, "possessing a great secret which can never be communicated," leads to the awkward conversations and misunderstandings that survivors often report when they return home. It is, as so many veterans have noted, as if they no longer speak the language of their countrymen. This language barrier, this inability on the part of the untraumatized to understand the existence of a place like No Man's Land, further alienates the survivor. It is this language barrier that makes it possible for an otherwise thoughtful person to openly question whether a rape victim might have secretly wanted to be violated, might have in some way "been asking for it." It is this language barrier that makes an unbloodied suburbanite ask a veteran whether or not he'd killed anyone in Iraq.

To Leed, this liminal person, having journeyed to the boundaries of society and back, having seen it at its most extreme, has been granted a unique moral perspective. Examples of veterans, and of survivors of genocide and rape, who have become great critics of society abound. Indeed, as we shall see, the core group that fought to have war trauma officially recognized by psychiatry was a group of Vietnam veterans who, having taken part in war atrocities, felt compelled to make them known to the world. In Leed's view, "As a man who had lived for years in No-Man's-Land, he knew the nation and its pathologies from an exterior perspective."

Though he wrote *No Man's Land* in the late seventies, Leed mentions Vietnam but once, quoting Chaim Shatan on how basic training is really about psychological restructuring, an argument that certainly rings true for me. Often my dreams about Iraq get mixed up with Texas A&M, where I enrolled in ROTC, first donned a uniform, first learned the Marine Corps hymn, and first chanted *Kill, Kill, Blood Makes the Grass Grow!* In that way, my dreams don't really belong to me, they belong to that No Man's Land that remains forever beyond my control, untamed, on the furthest margins of what might be called the self. They refuse my will, they touch and turn my past, they bend it into new and unforeseen shapes.

One of the strangest things about war is that you never dream about it when you're in it. Instead, you dream about holidays in the tropics, vast dinners with friends, the way your dad's Impala looked in the sunshine, old lovers. It's almost as if your mind knows the score, knows that you aren't ready yet, and so it serves up these terrific entertainments, even as the war seeps into the bloodstream, the veins and capillaries, the synapses. Later, sometimes much later, is when the dreams come, good and bad. Sometimes they feel like intel briefs, updates from the unconscious telling you what's up outside the wire, what really happened. It's like the old story told by Michael Herr about the bullet that almost killed him. The bullet came so close that he never even heard it, so close that it took ten years before the sound finally reached him. That's how it goes sometimes. *Everything is fine until it isn't.* Shit happens, but you're cool. Years later, in a Greyhound station in Green River, Utah, the fear finds you and changes everything.

Sometimes I think that's what happened to me in the movie theater that day. Before the movie, I'd had a good idea how close I'd come to dying in Iraq, all the close calls, the pizza box IEDs I'd run over that didn't go off, the booby traps I'd stepped around. But, really, I didn't know, or I should say that part of me knew, but I didn't know that it knew. The movie explosion was a reminder, an all too realistic one, almost like a dispatch from that part deep inside of me that had recorded it all: here is what it would've looked like. Enjoy.

One war-reporter friend of mine, who spent a year in Mosul with the National Guard before getting out and moving to Egypt to study

Arabic, has one dream where he's helping insurgents bury IEDs under the streets of Baghdad. When I asked him about it, he seemed to think that it had something to do with divided loyalties, about not always feeling like a "true" American, whatever the fuck that is, as if a conversation was happening between two very different chapters of his life, which is how I think life and war and loss work: your youth happens and you spend the rest of your life trying to figure out what it means.

It's a truism among psychologists that trauma messes with your sense of time, that it breaks your internal clock in some way. But to describe it as simply destroying your sense of time doesn't quite do it justice. Post trauma, there are probably as many experiences of time as there are survivors. I'm frustrated by the fact that I have essentially lost years to my obsession with the war. To say that I am "haunted" by it doesn't sound right to my ears, though in a certain sense it's probably true. Something I say to friends a lot is that it still feels like 2004, the year I first went to Iraq, the year that the biggest lies about the war began to unravel, the year of Fallujah One and Fallujah Two, the year of Abu Ghraib, the year that Bush was reelected, the year my relationship with America changed forever, the year that was so full it seemed to drain the entire decade. The year, as well, that I watched Marines from my old regiment being sent to die in the streets of Fallujah because of an incompetence and duplicity that make me so angry I can scarcely begin to describe them. There comes a point in every man's life when he sees that the magician's hat is empty, that the government and the church are run by fools, and that virtue is far rarer than he'd been led to believe. It was my misfortune to see this at a comparatively young age and in an unusually dramatic fashion, one that was not easily forgotten. To forget what had happened and who was to blame seemed like an affront to memory itself. Time stopped that year, and looking back, I can see that I wasn't really growing older so much as I was taking on a new version of time, a new way of being in the world.

Since 2004, I have learned to trust people less. I have learned to trust America less. I worry that life is completely random, without center or cause, and that the world could blow up at any time.

I drive slower, eat out less, drink more. I walk carefully over broken asphalt. I avoid crowds. I don't go to action movies. Sometimes, when someone is following me on the sidewalk, I stop and let them pass. Sometimes, maybe when I hear an old song, I find myself missing the old America, the one that existed before 9/11. Sometimes I find myself missing the nineties, me in my twenties, fresh out of the Corps and loose in the world for the first time.

Elise, my friend who was raped, said something similar. Thinking back on her wandering years, years when she'd forgotten how to trust people, when she'd chopped off all her hair so she could pretend to be someone else, she said something you hear a lot of trauma survivors say. She said, "I want those years back." Now, I can't say I feel exactly that way, in part because rape and war are two very different things to go through, and war is more than just terror. War is also thrilling and revelatory. War is an adventure. War is history in fast forward. But I want something equally impossible. I want a different world. A better, less venal world, one where stupid wars aren't started and then forgotten about when they lose their entertainment value, and sometimes I play a game with myself that historians like to play; it's called creating a counterfactual, a what-if realm where the Germans won World War II, Lee Harvey Oswald's shots missed JFK, or the Supreme Court ruled in favor of Gore instead of Bush. You change just one thing and imagine the different world that would result.

And so I build a world where three Blackwater contractors don't get lazy and decide to take a shortcut through downtown Fallujah in March 2004 and get ambushed and killed and burned and strung up from the pedestrian bridge over the Euphrates west of the city. A world where their charred bodies aren't filmed, don't make the evening news back home, and don't cause the president to order the Marines into Fallujah to punish its citizens, against the advice of commanders on the scene. A world where we don't invade Iraq, a world without a 9/11, without a Gulf War, without an Islamic Revolution in Iran, without Allen Dulles in charge of the CIA in 1953, and so on.

It's fun to see how far you can take it, to see how they look, these alternate worlds. And it teaches you some things, too. It teaches you that the world depends, has always depended, on the smallest details, every single last one of them needing to happen the way they do so that the world ends up the way it does, to make us the way we are. Accidents. Statistics moving through space.

But in the end, it's still just a game, a dressed-up kind of nostalgia, and really it's a dodge, a way to not think about what's really bothering me, and sometimes I have to rely on my involuntary memories, memories I forgot I had, my dreams, my nightmares, to remind me.

Which they always do. Almost every night I'll have a dream about a thing that happened over there, a thing I'd forgotten about, something hilarious or cruel or wonderful a grunt said; the cigarette I shared with a wounded soldier from the 10th Mountain as we watched my first *shamal* come in, turning the sky blood red; the *Aladdin* songs I sang with a bunch of Marines in a seven-ton on the way to reinforce a platoon that had been wiped out near Saqliwiyah. Usually when it happens, I wake up smiling and excited because I know that I have the rest of the day, the rest of my life, to think about it, to figure out what it means. And then I thank God that I survived.

5

MODERN TRAUMA

I. The Good War?

WITHIN THE HISTORY of psychological trauma, the era that remains most shrouded in myth and misapprehension is World War II and its aftermath. In the popular imagination, the war, which lasted from 1939 to 1945 and ended the lives of an estimated sixty million people, is still somehow remembered as "The Good War," and the veterans who fought in it are generally regarded as having returned home, put their uniforms in the closet, and simply gotten on with their lives. For the United States, the war came on the heels of the Great Depression, and the soldiers who fought the Nazis and the Japanese came from a culture that had little patience for people who dwelled on their personal problems. Karl Shapiro, the poet laureate who served in the Pacific theater, described the group of young writers who'd fought, saying, "We all came out of the same army and joined the same generation of silence." Included in this generation of silence was J. D. Salinger, who in one of his early stories wrote that "I believe, as I've never believed in anything else before, that it's the moral duty of all men who have fought and will fight in this war to keep our mouths shut, once it's over, never again to mention it in any way."

In America, stories of veterans who came home and kept their mouths shut are commonplace. In *Flags of Our Fathers,* James Bradley describes how his father, who famously helped raise the Stars and Stripes on Iwo Jima, avoided discussing his role in the battle, instructing his children to wave off reporters and curiosity seekers with a cover story that featured him on a fishing trip to Canada. It was only after the senior Bradley died that his son, while arranging his father's effects, discovered a trove of old letters that revealed how much the war had tormented his father.

In October 1945, my maternal grandfather returned from the Pacific, where he'd served as a Seabee, and never uttered a word about the war. For most of her life, my mother knew almost nothing about her father's military service, never for instance knowing why he had a large puffy scar on his left hand, nor understanding why he never spoke of the war. This near-perfect state of ignorance reigned until 2011, when we requested his records from the military's storage facility in St. Louis. While no shocking revelations emerged from his personnel file (he spent most of the war on a tiny atoll in the middle of the Pacific; the scar on his left hand was caused by an accident with a power saw), it nevertheless highlighted the degree to which my grandfather had lived as a stranger to his family, silent and unknown. A cipher. "He came from the Midwest," my mother explained. "People just didn't talk about their problems then. It was considered impolite."

The refusal of the average veteran to talk about the war was one thing, but the larger, enduring problem with the trauma of World War II, historically speaking, stems from how this silence was viewed by the culture. As psychiatrist Judith Herman explains in *Trauma and Recovery,* "As long as they could function on a minimum level, they were thought to have recovered. With the end of the war, the familiar process of amnesia set in once again. There was little medical or public interest in the psychological condition of returning soldiers." Nearly sixty years after the Japanese surrendered, this idea that keeping your mouth shut helped you recover was still being promoted. In the November 8, 2004, issue of *The New Yorker,* Malcolm Gladwell, in an article titled "Getting Over It," examined the evolving attitudes toward trauma, utilizing Sloan Harris's iconic novel about a veteran turned business executive, *The Man in the Gray Flannel Suit.* At the beginning of the article, Gladwell posed the following question: "The Man in the Gray Flannel Suit put the war behind him. Why can't we?"

In fact, the evidence indicates that many World War II veterans were unable to put the war behind them. Millions of veterans were haunted by the war for the rest of their lives, returning to a culture that celebrated them in ceremony but preferred not to trouble itself with the messy details of their service. (The U.S. government encouraged this ignorance. In 1945, when the U.S. Army learned of John Huston's plan to screen his war trauma documentary *Let There Be Light* for some friends at the Museum of Modern Art, it had the film seized and banned, claiming that it violated the privacy of the soldiers shown.) During the war itself, the incidence of psychological breakdown in the U.S. Army was three times that of World War I. Over half a million men were permanently evacuated from the fighting for psychiatric reasons, enough to man fifty combat divisions.

At the end of the war, General Eisenhower ordered a commission to look into these "lost divisions." The authors of the official report, titled *Combat Exhaustion,* concluded that

> there is no such thing as "getting used to combat" . . . Each moment of combat imposes a strain so great that men will break down in direct relation to the intensity and duration of their exposure . . . psychiatric casualties are as inevitable as gunshot and shrapnel wounds in warfare . . . Most men were ineffective after 180 or even 140 days. The general consensus was that a man reached his peak of effectiveness in the first 90 days of combat, that after that his efficiency began to fall off, and that he became steadily less valuable thereafter until he was completely useless . . . The number of men on duty after 200 to 240 days of combat was small and their value to their units negligible.

Most of these casualties didn't improve once they got back home, either. While the mental health of the Greatest Generation was almost completely ignored for thirty years, the few inquiries that were made showed a clear pattern of what today would be labeled "chronic post-traumatic stress." One such study, published in the *American Journal of Psychiatry* in 1951, examined two hundred World

War II veterans and found that 10 percent of them still suffered from "combat neurosis." Subsequent studies into the traumatic experiences of World War II veterans in the eighties found some of the highest PTSD rates ever recorded. One study, which zeroed in on Pacific theater POWs, discovered that nearly forty years after the war, more than 85 percent of them suffered from PTSD. In a 1987 study, eight out of ten former Pacific POWs had a form of "psychiatric impairment," more than one in four had PTSD, and nearly one in five were clinically depressed. As Matthew Friedman, the first executive director of the VA's National Center for PTSD, explained, "World War II occurred in a different generation and society didn't acknowledge the psychological consequences of war in the forties any more than it did in the sixties . . . People [at the time] didn't talk about what they called 'traumatic neuroses,' or combat stress . . . Yes, there were all kinds of dollars given to the VA, 'hire a vet,' the G.I. Bill, the ticker tape parades and all that. But when you get down to the nitty-gritty, in terms of the nation's willingness to acknowledge the devastating consequences of World War II, that's only happening retrospectively." The postwar years were dominated by this paradox: Americans were, on the one hand, surpassingly proud and supportive of their veterans, but on the other, they took almost no interest in their inner problems. Part of this was just human nature. People simply wanted to move on, and if some vets were struggling, then that was their own problem, as it had been before the war and during the Depression.

If anyone embodied this paradox, it was Audie Murphy, the most decorated American soldier to emerge from the war. Born into a large sharecropper family in Hunt County, Texas, Murphy was abandoned, along with his siblings, by his father during the Depression, forcing Murphy to hunt game to put food on the table. After he was rejected by the Marine Corps because of his age, his sister helped him falsify the enlistment papers for the army. A supremely talented soldier, he was awarded the Medal of Honor after killing fifty Germans during the Allied invasion of southern France and was later profiled in *Life* magazine. His battlefield prowess bordered on the mythic. One time, he'd heard that a group of officers was leaving on a reconnaissance patrol beyond friendly lines. Unbeknownst to them, Murphy trailed after the group. He said, years later, "I figured those gentlemen were going to run into trouble; so I tagged along, about twenty-five yards to their rear, to watch the stampede." When the patrol found itself pinned down, Murphy charged the enemy position, killing five Germans and wounding another three.

Back in the States after the war, Murphy found himself without any marketable skills and bored by civilian life. "War robs you mentally and physically," he said in 1962. "It drains you. Things don't thrill you anymore. It's a struggle every day to find something interesting to do." He flirted with the idea of going back to school—he wanted to study veterinary science at Texas A&M—but his restless energy seemed to prevent him from settling into an academic routine. Like so many, he was tired and glad to be home, but he missed the war terribly and didn't know how to fill his days. Complaining that he couldn't find a job that left him any self-respect, he eventually decided that the only thing he had of value in a market economy was his fame. Exploiting the connections he'd made as America's most celebrated war hero, he managed, after a long struggle, to find work as an actor in Hollywood, eventually starring in dozens of films. In 1955, he even played himself in a movie based on his war exploits, *To Hell and Back.*

Despite his fame and outward success, Murphy struggled with his memories of the war and, according to his first wife, was frequently suicidal. For the rest of his life, he suffered from insomnia and nightmares. At one point, he became addicted to the sleeping pills the VA doctors prescribed him. Ten years after he returned from the war, he began sleeping alone in his garage in order to be farther away from the noises of the house. He traced this habit back to the war: "In combat, you see, your hearing gets so acute you can interpret any noise. But now, there were all kinds of noises that I couldn't interpret."

As Murphy later admitted in interviews, the war had never really ended for him, and for years after it, he would criticize the army for the way it treated an entire generation of veterans, taking them from the killing fields of the war and dropping them into civilian life, equipped with little more than a bus ticket home. "They took Army dogs and rehabilitated them for civilian life. But they turned soldiers into civilians immediately and let 'em sink or swim."

This sink-or-swim mentality would dominate the veteran's experience and the societal notion of trauma for decades.

Until Vietnam.

II. Vietnam

As many observers have pointed out, the intervention in Indochina instigated a second American civil war, altering the political and social landscape in ways so vast they are difficult to perceive today. Among the many things that Vietnam changed is the way that people talk about trauma. Before Vietnam, the terms used to describe the psychological disorders of war came and went, each one beholden to the conflict from which it emerged. Five years after the fall of Saigon, there was an entirely new psychiatric category designed to address the needs of *all* trauma survivors, not just war veterans. This category — post-traumatic stress disorder — is a product of the American experience in Vietnam and the feverish political environment it helped create. Its emergence represents a revolution in trauma, one that continues to inform how millions of people all over the world — who have faced a wide variety of extreme events — are diagnosed and treated. This revolution in thinking has even extended into the past, as Jay Winter, a professor of history at Yale, explained in an article on shell shock: "One of the most powerful stimuli to a new generation of historical thinking on World War I has been the Vietnam War."

But even beyond the "invention" of PTSD, the Vietnam War changed the public's perception of extreme events, ushering in a new way of thinking and talking about violence and death, creating what some critics have called a "culture of trauma." Before Vietnam, *trauma* was a term generally used to describe a life-threatening event experienced by an individual. After Vietnam, *trauma* was applied widely and was increasingly used to describe a broader range of experiences, many of which might have, in other eras, simply been called "rough going" or "tough sledding," as in "I'm still recovering from the trauma of getting laid off."

Within the American imagination, the words "Vietnam" and "trauma" are practically synonymous. Among veterans who served in Vietnam, it is not uncommon to hear the other word used as a means of encapsulating the entire experience, as if the conflict was so complicated, filled with so many confounding events, that a word that could summarize the psychological fallout without explicitly taking a side was needed. Hence, *trauma.* The war is technically over, but its meaning remains unknown. It has lost none of its power to anger and confuse. As Tim O'Brien would later write in his novel *In the Lake of the Woods,* "The war itself was a mystery. Nobody knew what it was about, or why they were there, or who started it, or who was winning, or how it might end." It is this sense of uncertainty that has helped keep the memory of Vietnam alive and malleable within the American mind. Every manner of lesson can be derived from it. For a young Marine lieutenant in training at Quantico in the mid-1990s, for instance, it was not uncommon to hear officers who had fought at Hue City or Dong Ha talk about the "trauma of Vietnam" as a way of introducing a short lecture on the importance of small unit leadership or the "offensive spirit"—or any other practical topic for that matter.

Vietnam has come to represent many things to Americans. For people on the left, it is the ultimate symbol of American hubris and the catalyst for a new kind of political consciousness. On the right, it is often viewed as a just war lost because of a lack of American resolve or a disloyal press. It is this sort of ongoing disagreement over basic themes and facts regarding the war, the sense one gets from historians that the jury is still out on Vietnam, that might have led Bill Nash, a psychiatrist who would go on to lead the navy's PTSD task force in Washington, to declare in 2006, at a presentation to a group of military social workers, that "we are still fighting the Vietnam War." Despite the war's uncertain place in history, one thing is clear: Vietnam and the political climate it created made a public conversation about trauma possible.

One of the great students of this climate was a Yale professor of psychiatry named Robert Jay Lifton. Lifton had served as an air force psychiatrist in Korea, an assignment that began a lifelong fascination with psychological responses to war. By 1970, Lifton was one of the most famous psychiatrists in America and had won the National Book Award for his study on Hiroshima survivors, *Death in Life.* A practitioner of an unorthodox academic field known as psychohistory, which sought to explain historical events using a mixture of principles drawn from psychology and the social sciences, he was the consummate dove. (At one point, Lifton said, "I was opposed to the Vietnam War before it even began.") Indeed, his entire life was an embodiment of psychohistory: as a public intellectual, he was always on the move, shifting between leading problems of the day, forever probing into the fault lines between public issues with a constant stream of lectures and articles. He seemed to take world issues like nuclear disarmament personally, as if the integrity of his intellect was on the line. He was less focused on a tangible political outcome than on the process of insight itself. Somber, well mannered, and somewhat patrician in his bearing, Lifton was in his manner, if not his worldview, an unlikely advocate for a group of disgruntled veterans.

The change for Lifton came in November 1969, when on a flight to Toronto, where he was to deliver a lecture on the arms race, he read an article in the *New York Times* about My Lai, where American G.I.s had massacred hundreds of unarmed Vietnamese. Later, he would write of his "shame and rage" at My Lai. The rage, he said, "was directed partly toward the warmakers in power, and partly toward myself for not having personally done more to confront or resist American slaughter of Vietnamese." Soon, Lifton was speaking out against the war in public lectures and before Congress, arguing that the war with its "permanent free-fire zones," industrialized slaughter and focus on enemy body counts was fundamentally evil, an "atrocity-producing situation."

In November 1970, Lifton received a letter from Jan Barry, the leader of a group called Vietnam Veterans Against the War. Formed in the late 1960s, VVAW's membership was small, but because it was composed entirely of veterans, the group enjoyed a prestige denied other, larger protest groups. Of them, Hunter S. Thompson would later write that "There is no anti-war or even anti-establishment group in America today with the psychic leverage of the VVAW." In the letter, Barry asked for Lifton's help, describing "the severe psychological problems of many Vietnam veterans because of their experiences," caused by "the military policy of the war which results in war crimes and veterans' nightmares."

Barry saw the politics of the war and the psychological problems suffered by veterans as inseparable. He and other VVAW members felt exploited and abused by a war that had, according to one like-minded veteran, "turned them into animals." As animals, they no longer knew how to fit into civil society, a society that, while loosely familiar with the horrors of Vietnam, was far more concerned, in Barry's words, about "making a buck." This collision of realities jolted many veterans into a kind of identity crisis. Unlike their fathers, who had fought in World War II, they felt little sense of accomplishment. Some VVAWers, like Joe Urgo, an air force veteran who had seen action during the Tet Offensive, felt that the very basis of their upbringing, their belief in American civilization as a unique force for good, had been destroyed by Vietnam. All wars are damaging, went the reasoning, but Vietnam was especially damaging because it was built on lies, and far from being simply unjust, it represented a crime against humanity. Along with John Kerry, the VVAW's most famous member, they felt compelled to take action on a number of fronts.

Part of what troubled veterans like Urgo was the rank inability of stateside Americans (the "normals") to grasp what they had been through, a feeling echoed by many Iraq and Afghanistan veterans today. They were, in a sense, trapped in Van Gennep's liminal state, caught between worlds: they were in some ways welded to the war, defined by it, but they didn't belong to it anymore, nor could they make their own countrymen understand where they'd come from, which showed them that they didn't belong to their country anymore either. Some of them described the experience as feeling like they were tumbleweeds. They didn't belong anywhere. (Lifton would later say that this restlessness was "a constant subject of discussion.")

"You couldn't explain to people how you just got through murdering people, that you were nothing more than a murderer, a rapist, a baby killer," Urgo spat. "You couldn't come back to the society—with its bread and circuses, with *The Beverly Hillbillies*—and tell people, 'This is what we were doing over there.'" One Marine veteran said to a therapist, "I want to scream at friends and relatives that people are still dying while the NFL is playing—but how can I?"

Over the course of their activism against the war, Barry and other vets found themselves rocked by emotions that they couldn't understand. They were committed to ending the war but found that their personal issues were often taking center stage, sabotaging their ability to live coherently, let alone work. All this was right up Lifton's alley, classic psychohistory. According to Lifton, Barry said two things in his letter: "Guys are hurting. They're opposed to the war, and they want to deal with their hurt, and they don't want to go to the VA. They also want to make known to the world what the war was like. Can you help us in some way?"

Along with Chaim Shatan, a New York University psychoanalyst and friend, Lifton met with Barry and a handful of VVAW members after delivering a lecture at NYU titled "My Lai and Kent State." Hearing how intensely the veterans "rapped" about their feelings toward the war and American society, along with their desire for psychological insight into their struggles, Lifton suggested they schedule a regular series of meetings on "their own turf." In Shatan, Lifton had, by sheer accident, stumbled onto the perfect partner. A working therapist who'd treated a number of returning veterans through NYU's free psychoanalytic clinic, Shatan was practical where Lifton was cerebral. Both were appalled by Vietnam. Before he became involved with the VVAW, Shatan, who was a French-Canadian Jew, had been thinking about moving back to Canada so that his children wouldn't be drafted and sent to Vietnam, going so far as to visit Vancouver to look into the possibility of relocating there. His meetings with the VVAW convinced him that there might be a reason to stay in the United States.

The first "rap group" met on Saturday, December 12, 1970, at the cramped VVAW headquarters at 156 Fifth Avenue in midtown

Manhattan. Arthur Egendorf, a Vietnam veteran who would become a pillar of the group, walked into one of the early meetings and saw "about twelve guys, most of them in fatigue shirts, with beards, unkempt hair and heavy looks." What happened next shocked everyone. "The explosion of feeling that occurred, associated as it was with a war whose pain pervaded all of our lives, rendered those first meetings unforgettable in their emotional power," Lifton would recall. The rap groups, originally scheduled for two hours, stretched into the evening, sometimes going on for seven or eight hours.

Shatan recalled one early meeting: looking around, he saw men sitting on packing cases and filing cabinets in the run-down VVAW office. The group that day included Bob, a former Marine gripped by "unpredictable episodes of disorientation and panic." Another was a former helicopter door gunner who tried to forget his "pleasure in killing [his] first 16-year-old Commie for Christ" by racing down the freeway at night on his motorcycle.

Needless to say, the first meetings were intense, with veterans unleashing feelings that had been bottled up for years, the charged atmosphere heightened by the fact that the war itself was still going on and seemed, in fact, to be metastasizing—the invasion of Cambodia had taken place just a few months earlier. For many of the veterans, these rap sessions were a life-altering experience. One former army sergeant remembered that "here was the first opportunity that I really had to talk with guys who had gone through the same thing. They were having the same doubts about themselves, you know, and digging inside themselves—and you didn't want to do that with just anybody . . . I said, Wow! You got something here." Egendorf, who was an outlier in the group, having served as a counterintelligence sergeant after graduating from Harvard, said, "When I found myself sitting in a rap group with fellow veterans—and my veteranness, and my understanding of this, and my going through the same business . . . I didn't know to pray or say something like that, but it was like an inner relief: *Ah! This is like heaven-sent.*"

For Egendorf, the rap groups represented a pivotal step in a personal odyssey that had begun for him in the crucible of Vietnam. From a privileged Philadelphia family, he had planned on going to law school before the war happened. In Vietnam, he had worked as a "spy-handler," running a network of local informers, a job that kept him out of the line of fire but showed him how the entire war was built on a series of lies. Even more disturbing to him was the fact that his work in intelligence had forced him to live behind a façade of deceptions. It became hard for him to let anyone get close. About the only thing that got past the façade and elicited something resembling a human emotion was the sight of the prostitutes on Saigon's Tu Do Street. One night, atop his hotel in Saigon, he was looking down at the women in their *ao dais* working the street below when another soldier on the roof yelled out, "Goddamn, now that's a gorgeous sight!" Looking over at him, Egendorf realized that the other man was, in fact, watching a flight of helicopter gunships shooting up a neighborhood in the distance. In *Healing from the War,* his memoir about the experience, he wrote that "in a flash I saw beyond the flames, to the people being incinerated like trash. I knew then that something had touched me, and that I'd never be the same."

The structure of the rap groups was unusual in that they had no structure. Lifton's suggestion that they take place on the veterans' home turf turned out to be a small act of genius. (The VVAW crew, like many of their Vietnam veteran peers, were deeply suspicious of the Veterans Administration, which refused to acknowledge their psychological problems. Part of this was due to the fact that in 1966 the Pentagon had declared that psychiatric casualties in Vietnam were lower than in any previous war.) At ease in their own territory, the veterans cut loose, channeling the dark feelings of the era into the group. In line with this accommodating atmosphere, Lifton and Shatan abandoned the traditional labels, referring to themselves as simply "professionals" rather than "therapists," though the vets dispensed with both, referring to them as "shrinks." From the beginning, Lifton and Shatan had the feeling that they had stumbled into a new group form, one that transcended the hierarchical medical model of doctor and patient and pushed into some new higher plane of social consciousness. It felt like the beginning of a revolution of some kind.

In fact, what the VVAWers were doing had some precedent in

the "consciousness-raising" small groups of the women's movement as well as being part of the exploratory spirit of the late 1960s. As Egendorf explained in an interview years later, "The idea for rap groups came from the rap groups in therapeutic communities for drug treatment, Synanon and . . . encounter groups. But most prominently, where guys encountered it most frequently, was with their girlfriends going to women's groups." These groups, like San Francisco's "Sudsofloppen" collective, held "Free Space" sessions that offered women a forum to "think about our lives, our society, and our potential for being creative individuals and for building a women's movement." Like the rap groups that followed them, these women's groups held to a philosophy that said "the personal is political," a belief that would play a crucial role connecting the pain that vets were feeling with the need for larger social change. Both traditions emphasized openness and an agendaless discussion. Egendorf, who later spoke of the need for male veterans to embrace the healing power of women and to see VVAW as a way for male vets to, in a sense, "catch up" with feminism, wrote in *Healing from the War* that "we had the women's movement as a constant example, with their use of consciousness raising groups as a major organizing tool."

The women's movement of the 1970s not only helped give form to a growing veterans movement, it also began to tackle the great invisible problem that had plagued society since the dawn of history: rape. In 1971, the first rape crisis center opened its doors in Oakland. After her fifteen-year-old foster daughter was raped, Oleta Kirk Adams took her to the hospital. "She was treated like a piece of meat," another daughter remembered. "There was no compassion, nothing that helped her deal with the emotion" of the experience. Livid over her treatment, Adams, along with two other women, founded the nonprofit organization Bay Area Women Against Rape. It was all part of a vast national phenomenon. The Civil Rights Movement of the fifties and sixties had opened the door to a grassroots movement, but it wasn't until the seventies that the women's liberation movement took to the national stage. Confronting reported cases of rape, which had seen a 121 percent increase over the course of the sixties, was one of the movement's first priorities. "Rape is only a slightly forbidden fruit," feminists charged in 1971.

Around the same time, Ann Burgess and Lynda Holmstrom, researchers at Boston College, began studying the psychological effects of rape. There were hundreds of studies about rape as a crime, but they noticed that no one had ever spoken to the victims. The two made an arrangement with a local hospital to be on call day or night in order to interview any rape victim admitted to the emergency room. They noticed almost immediately that, with few exceptions, the victims they spoke with looked at being raped as a life-threatening event. After a year, they had interviewed 92 women and 37 children. Looking over their interviews, they noticed a pattern of postrape symptoms: sleeplessness, paranoia, an exaggerated startle response, nightmares, and a host of phobias related to the circumstances of their attack. Deciding to call this phenomenon "rape trauma syndrome," they noted that the same symptoms they had observed had been described thirty years before in survivors of war.

The rap groups, which had begun as an explosion of feeling, evolved into a more exploratory forum for vets to synthesize their feelings in an open, nonjudgmental environment, something that was not available at the VA. As Egendorf described it, "One vet would usually begin the conversation by talking about a problem he was having. Before long, another guy would respond, then a few more would take turns, almost like a jam session. There was nothing you were supposed to say, except that everybody shared a few common ideas: The war was a horror, and it's good to talk it out . . . the inquiry would frequently unfold as men recalled an event, then realized that although they were detached when it first happened, they were much closer to it looking back. Suddenly emotions would come, often pain, anger, or sorrow, as the men ceased feeling removed and let what happened touch them, as if reflecting on the moment at some later time allowed for a more intimate reinterpretation."

One problem that emerged early on was Lifton's compulsive note taking. When one veteran complained that Lifton couldn't be an equal member of the group and write about it at the same time, he put his notepad away. Still, despite their wide-ranging backgrounds and experiences, the group began to bond. A large measure of this was simply due to the novelty of the group: from a veterans' standpoint, nothing like it had ever happened before. Veterans in American history have often held to an unspoken code of silence. This phenomenon is most easily seen in the World War II generation, where veterans, in part because they grew up in the Great Depression, believed that dwelling on one's personal struggles was unseemly. Not so with this generation and with the VVAW, which viewed the war as a moral catastrophe that had brought their lives into crisis and changed everything. It had to be stopped. Suddenly, everything was on the table. Their inner lives, the morality of the war, questions about what it meant to be a man, feelings that they didn't even know the names of. Topics that had never been addressed before were right in front of them now. The normal divisions, where the questions stopped, were gone. No one knew where it would all go. Egendorf, reflecting on the feelings of the time, remarked that there was an almost utopian impulse at work, to "make it new right here and now."

One person who was very concerned about where such newness might lead was Richard Nixon. Like Hunter S. Thompson, Nixon was keenly aware of the political leverage that an organization like the VVAW had, and as the group continued to garner public attention, he launched a broad campaign to blunt its impact. In particular, Nixon was concerned about the group's public statements about the war's atrocities and the havoc it wreaked on the minds of veterans, which fit into a larger trend of media reports suggesting that the Vietnam War was creating a "different breed" of veteran, as the *Capital Times* of Madison, Wisconsin, reported in February 1971. One statement from a VA psychologist in the *Capital Times* article, which was forwarded to Chuck Colson, Nixon's point man on the VVAW, was particularly damning. "Vietnam combat veterans tend to see their experience as an exercise in survival rather than a defense of national values. The majority, given the opportunity in [the] company of their peers, express both intense anger and much guilt." The article, which reads almost like an advertisement for the rap groups, went on to describe a host of other symptoms that VA doctors were beginning to see in Vietnam veterans, including a general paranoia and "uptightness," "shaky masculine identity," and of greatest concern, a "hostility toward authoritarian figures and institutions."

The man who forwarded the article to Colson was Donald E. Johnson, director of the VA under President Nixon. Along with the article, Johnson included a note that read, in part, "Attached is a news story from Madison, Wisconsin, which explains in some detail the problems we in the Veterans Administration are encountering . . . As a country, and particularly the Government, we have failed to adequately inform these young men that their service has indeed been a defense of national values. We in the VA have noted a profound difference between the dischargee of 1967 and the dischargee of 1970." Tellingly, the dates Johnson listed roughly correlate to the ruinous Tet Offensive of 1968, after which American attitudes toward the war, both stateside and in-theater, began to shift dramatically.

Two months later, soon after the VVAW's highly publicized "Dewey Canyon III" protest in Washington, which saw hundreds of veterans throwing their medals onto the steps of the Capitol, Nixon ordered Colson to look into having the IRS revoke the group's tax-exempt status. Colson, who later went to prison for his role in the Watergate scandal, also took a number of steps to try to publicly discredit the VVAW, encouraging leaders of the "Big Four" veterans organizations (the American Legion, the Disabled American Veterans, the Military Order of the Purple Heart, and the Veterans of Foreign Wars) to speak out against them. At Colson's request, Herbert Rainwater, head of the VFW, held a press conference in Washington, where he charged that groups like the VVAW were communist inspired.

The effort to undermine the group went well beyond these overt steps and in time would come to include the FBI's infamous "Counter-Intelligence Program," or COINTELPRO, which infiltrated and surveilled a number of left-wing organizations. At one point, certain parts of the organization were filled with so many informers and agents provocateurs that they actually outnumbered the bona fide members. Soon after Chaim Shatan began working with the VVAW, he noticed that his mail was being tampered with. In an article in the *American Journal of Orthopsychiatry*, describing what he called the "grief of soldiers," he appended a "note of caution" to other clinicians interested in working with veterans, explaining how his mail from veterans' organizations and Lifton was being opened and then resealed with sticky paper and stamped DAMAGED IN HANDLING AT U.S. POST OFFICE. (Lifton reported this irregularity as well.) Shatan later described an incident where a VVAW member had dropped by their New York office on a Sunday afternoon and found a man he didn't recognize riffling through their files. The man had flashed an FBI badge and made a hasty exit.

Despite Nixon's attempts to disrupt the VVAW, veterans kept showing up to the New York rap group. Eventually, the group got so big they ran out of room, forcing it to split in two, with Lifton staying with the original Fifth Avenue cohort. By Lifton's count, around 115 veterans eventually cycled through the group during his tenure, including a number of the VVAW's leaders, who were frequently crisscrossing the country, spreading the word about the group in the course of their organizing against the war.

The veterans movement was building, slowly, incrementally, working openly to end the war while at the same time trying to make sense of the violence in-theater that they'd been a part of, but what really lit a fire under it was the violence at home. On April 30, 1971, Dwight Johnson, a recently discharged army Medal of Honor winner, was shot and killed while trying to rob a Detroit liquor store. Unemployed and angry at the army, Johnson had been diagnosed by VA doctors as suffering from "depression caused by post-Vietnam adjustment problems." Ordinarily, a death like this wouldn't have attracted much notice, but because Johnson had been awarded the Medal of Honor by the president in a White House ceremony, the story of his postwar struggle was soon on the front page of the *New York Times*. Shatan, reading of Johnson's death, was deeply moved, and he quickly wrote an op-ed for the *Times* and prepared a longer scholarly article for publication. The *Times,* for a variety of reasons, waffled on Shatan's op-ed, with the opinion editor saying he had reservations about it.

Nevertheless, a year later, on May 6, 1972, the *Times* published the piece, titled "Post-Vietnam Syndrome." In it, Shatan described the work of the rap groups, opening with the story of "Steve," a Marine veteran of Vietnam, who after being discharged from the Corps for psychiatric reasons still suffered from "unpredictable episodes of terror and disorientation." Shatan also described the emotional numbing many vets experienced, how they felt alienated "from their feelings and from other human beings: after systematically numbing their humane responses, veterans find it difficult and painful to experience compassion for others." The trauma of Vietnam finally had a human face.

According to Shatan, once the op-ed hit newsstands, "the telephone started jumping off the wall."

In April 1973, just as the Watergate scandal was picking up steam, Shatan, Lifton, and a grab bag of veterans' advocates held a summit in St. Louis hosted by the Lutheran Synod of Missouri. The brainchild of Mark Hanson, a Presbyterian minister and friend of Arthur Egendorf, the conference included ninety vets, sixty shrinks, thirty chaplains, and a handful of VA staffers who, according to Shatan, jumped on at the last minute. Impressed by Egendorf and the work of the New York group, Hanson, who worked at the National Council of Churches building in upper Manhattan (known at the time as the "God Box"), had launched a one-man offensive, setting up rap groups across the country. Also in St. Louis were Shad Meshad and Ron Kovic from Los Angeles, a former military chaplain from San Diego named Bill Mahedy, and Jack McCloskey and Chester Adams from San Francisco, who had started a group called Twice Born Men that ministered to a group of veterans recently released from prison.

Participants spent much of the three-day conference describing the various methods they used in dealing with veterans' issues. Shatan and the New York cohort held workshops on the rap groups, emphasizing the need to let veterans "take charge of their own lives as part of the treatment." They also established a coordinating committee composed of vets and shrinks whose mission it was to mobilize the various rap groups for political action and to designate experts to testify before Congress or in the media. By all accounts, the St. Louis summit was a huge success. In Shatan's words, there emerged an ethos of "no leader and no followers—we were all peers on an equal footing." Meshad, who would go on to found a number of influential veterans organizations, called it "the pivotal turn in American history for mental health on PTSD."

The lone exception to this was the contingent of VA people, led by Charlie Stenger, a World War II veteran and former POW, and Dr. Jerome Jaffe, then chief of medicine for the VA, the man who Nixon had claimed the year before would "solve" the heroin problem in America. According to Shatan, "The VA guys wanted to pooh-pooh the whole thing; and even if it was so [that the war caused some stress disorders] hardly anybody was suffering." While they were in St. Louis, Lifton and Shatan gave an interview to a reporter from the *Chicago Tribune,* where they argued that 20 percent of Vietnam veterans were afflicted with some form of delayed stress caused by the war. The same reporter spoke to Jaffe, who claimed that at most 5 percent of veterans were mentally ill, and that clearly Lifton and Shatan were obsessed with the war. Moreover, he added, it was what the two were saying to the veterans that was the real problem, not the war itself, stating that their work was "an insult to brave men."

Despite these official objections, which were unsurprising to the rap group crowd, St. Louis was a big step forward. A consensus of a sort had been reached, a network had been formed, and tellingly, a line in the sand had been drawn. On one side were the rap group insurgents with their bad war and their new ideas, while on the other side were largely members of what would later be called the "Greatest Generation" with their "good" war and wholly different ideas about how trauma should be borne. Speaking of the event years later, Jack Smith, a Marine veteran from the New York rap groups, said,

There were many friendships that were formed that exist to this day which came out of that conference . . . [But] it was a knockdown, dragout battle at that. I remember very vividly . . . Charlie Stegner getting up and saying, you know, "I'm a World War II POW and I really understand what's going on and I'm one of your brothers." And I got up and launched into a tirade about how . . . everything he had written indicated he didn't have the foggiest notion of what was going on with us and how the hell could he call himself a brother? It was the beginning of a long and hostile relationship.

As the conference drew to a close, the attendees created an organization to carry on the work. Called the National Veterans Resource Project (NVRP), they elected twelve of the St. Louis participants to a board, which a few weeks later chose Jack Smith as their president.

Around the same time, a number of rap group–inspired bodies began sprouting up around the country. In Detroit, a Holocaust survivor and psychiatrist, Emmanuel Tanay, began working with vets at nearby Macomb College. Soon, another Holocaust survivor, Henry Krystal, was collaborating with Tanay. Back in New York, Al Singerman, a VVAW member and the son of Holocaust survivors, started organizing rap groups for Holocaust survivors and their families. All of this opened up Shatan's eyes to the "commonality" among all traumatic survivors, a connection that would become a tenet of modern trauma research.

While the movement had achieved a measure of success — they had some therapeutic ideas and a bare bones organization — what they seemed to lack now was money and a clear direction for their clinical agenda. With passage of the Case-Church Amendment in Congress two months after the St. Louis conference, which ended all U.S. aid to and involvement with Vietnam, the war was clearly and finally over, at least from an American standpoint. While certainly a boon for the VVAW, the war's end diminished the overall sense of urgency. The war was over, so what was the point of the organization anymore?

It would be years before the members of the VVAW would learn of the effect they had had on the White House, and in the meantime, there remained the burning question of what in the press had become known as "Post-Vietnam Syndrome," after Shatan's *New York Times* op-ed. Because of its still-speculative nature, Post-Vietnam Syndrome became something of a media catchall, a junk drawer for fears about returning veterans. Ever since the early 1970s, there had been stories in the press about homeless, drug-addicted, violent, and in some cases suicidal vets, but as fears over this new breed of veteran continued to mount and fuse with the public's more general paranoia about hippies and the drug culture, it began to resemble something like an epidemic in the public mind. "Vietnam Veterans Called Time Bombs" read one *Baltimore Sun* headline of the time. Lifton, Shatan, and the VVAW had done historic work bringing attention to the readjustment problems of veterans, but the illness, whatever it was, remained largely undefined.

In a way, what had happened thus far was just a repeat of shell shock and the high drama of Craiglockhart. You had a few conscientious veterans who had found their way into the public consciousness (a harder task than it might seem at first, because the public tends to see the military as a faceless mob) and there was a new name for war-made madness that the press liked, in this case a neat little acronym that fit easily in a newspaper column: PVS. With the war winding down and Nixon on his way out, it all could have stopped right there, with PVS frozen in the amber of history along with the rap groups, an intriguing footnote to a deeply unpopular war. The NVRP's efforts in the beginning were scattered and ineffective, the interest in the cause waning.

In moments like these, on both the micro and macro levels, the tendency is toward a kind of amnesia, driven by powerful forces within the culture whose greatest desire is to achieve a sort of status quo antebellum. This deep-seated need of nations to forget, to simply "move on," is universal and understandable and, coincidentally, one of the major drivers of combat-related post-traumatic stress. It is, perhaps, the fatal flaw of humankind, this failure to learn from conflict, and even after history's greatest catastrophes, as in the Soviet Union after World War II, there is evidence of this drive toward willful ignorance. Randy Floyd, a former Marine attack pilot who flew fifty-five missions over North Vietnam, was interviewed in 1973 and said, "I think Americans have tried, we've all tried very hard to escape what we've learned in Vietnam, to not come to the logical conclusions of what's happened there." Needless to say, the historical deck was stacked against the NVRP.

What the movement and Shatan, in particular, hadn't counted on was a revolution in psychiatry on par with Freud's "discovery" of the unconscious. In response to a series of scandals that had rocked psychiatry in the sixties and early seventies, the American Psychiatric Association decided in 1973 to let Robert Spitzer, a Columbia psychiatrist, oversee the next revision of the *Diagnostic and Statistical Manual of Mental Disorders,* which was due for its third edition. Spitzer, who had volunteered for the job, had never really liked Freudian psychoanalysis, even though he'd been trained in it, and felt the time was right to introduce a new guiding philosophy for the DSM, one that emphasized close observation of symptoms and clinical data collection over the Freudian theory that had dominated the DSM-II. An empiricist to the core, Spitzer had, during his childhood summer camp, graphed his attraction to various female campers. He also had a proven track record with tricky assignments. Prior to taking on the revision job, he had refereed the process that had deleted nearly all references to homosexuality from the DSM, which had for decades listed it as a mental disorder. "I love controversy! I love it!" Spitzer would say years later.

Spitzer had had a number of opportunities to indulge this love of controversy during the homosexuality debate, and while psychiatry has always been a fraught discipline, the questions that the homosexuality debate raised continued to resonate in a way that gave fuel to psychiatry's many critics at the time. Chief among the questions was how politics and lobbying by outside groups had driven the revision process. The removal of homosexuality was, taken in the larger context, the sort of clash that was deeply characteristic of the times: a minority group had for the first time found itself in a position to organize and mount an almost military-style campaign for redress. The difference in the case of homosexuality was that instead of the government being the target of the lobbying effort, it was a struggling medical discipline that was searching for a new identity and was only just finding its way out of Freud's long shadow. In

1973, it was the National Gay and Lesbian Task Force leading the charge, and while the APA's membership had voted decisively to delete almost all reference to homosexuality from the DSM, far from everyone was happy about it. "If groups of people march and raise hell, they can change anything in time. Will schizophrenia be next?" one psychiatrist complained.

In June 1974, Shatan got a phone call from a public defender in Asbury Park, New Jersey, who was trying to use a "traumatic war neurosis" defense to clear his client, a Vietnam veteran who'd been charged with breaking and entering. The judge had thrown out his defense, saying there was no such disorder listed in the DSM-II. Shatan told the public defender to call Robert Spitzer, certain that the DSM czar had something in mind for the upcoming edition. Eventually, it came out that Spitzer had no plans for a "post-combat reaction" in DSM-III. Shatan was horrified. He, along with Lifton, had dealt with so many veterans at this point that they simply assumed that their case had already been made. The idea that they would have to grapple with this new diagnostic cognoscenti had never occurred to them. Part of this disconnect could be chalked up to the growing cultural rift within psychiatry. Lifton and Shatan had both been trained in the psychoanalytic tradition, where the well-written case study, which owed as much to anthropology as to psychiatry, was the lingua franca. To Lifton, this new sort of empirical approach was a form of psychiatric "technicism," akin to the body counts the military had kept in Vietnam. Spitzer's vision for the new DSM was more in line with the work of Emil Kraepelin, the father of psychobiology. Given that Kraepelin had once said, "Trying to understand another human being's emotional life is fraught with potential error . . . It can lead to gross self-deception in research," Lifton and Shatan had their work cut out for them.

This clash of philosophies came to a head at the annual APA meeting at the Disneyland Hotel in Anaheim. "You don't have any evidence. You don't have any figures. You don't have any research," Shatan recalled being told by Spitzer. It was a grim time, and Shatan recalled that most of the researchers there seemed more interested in getting their pictures taken with Mickey Mouse than in talking about Vietnam. Also at Anaheim was a group of researchers from Washington University in St. Louis led by Lee Robbins, a psychiatrist who had conducted a study on Vietnam veterans and drug abuse. According to one psychiatrist sympathetic to Shatan's view who was there, Robbins essentially argued that "these guys are all character disorders. They came from rotten backgrounds. They were going to be malcontents and dysfunctional anyway. Vietnam probably just made them worse, but Vietnam is not the cause of their problems. They're alcoholics and drug addicts." This Washington University group, which from Shatan's point of view clearly had Spitzer's ear, was, in essence, making the same argument that the Nixon administration had been making all along: the people who are having problems with the war were troublemakers. In other words, there is no need for a delayed stress entry in the new DSM.

Virtually everyone from the VVAW camp who attended the Anaheim conference remembers it as one of the most demoralizing experiences of their lives. In the minds of Shatan, Lifton, Smith, and others, they had the moral high ground. They had spent years grappling with the inconvenient truths of Vietnam and had unearthed some deep insights about trauma only to find themselves on the losing end of an institutional power play within the APA. There was a new game in town, and the game, in Shatan's view, was about the rise of a biological model of human behavior. According to Shatan, "They were reluctant to accept the idea that social, psychological, political, and economic factors could have an influence on psychiatric symptoms in people." To this way of thinking, there could be no traumatic stress category in the DSM because the idea that an external event could cause mental illness didn't fit within their model.

Shatan was bruised by the Anaheim experience, but once back in New York, he set to work gathering data to support the VVAW position. He and Lifton had spoken with Spitzer and grasped that the battle would now turn on the numbers, on hard data that would support their position. With the help of Jack Smith and Sarah Haley at the VA hospital in Boston, the new Vietnam Veterans' Working Group began amassing data. What they found was astonishing. Sifting through stacks of VA records after hours, they discovered that, in the case of Boston, 90 percent of the Vietnam veterans admitted to the psych ward had been diagnosed as suffering from either a "depressive reaction" or "anxiety reaction." Because many of the veterans were hearing voices and occasionally hallucinating, a number of them were diagnosed as schizophrenics. After the official APA-approved diagnosis, Haley almost always found a working diagnosis provided in parentheses by the VA psychiatrist—"TWN," an acronym for the old World War II term "traumatic war neurosis." Sending out questionnaires, the group was eventually able to collect records on 724 veterans.

Invited to the APA's annual convention in Toronto the next year, Shatan, Lifton, Haley, and Jack Smith came armed. After presenting their paper and a series of detailed tables, Spitzer called a meeting of the Reactive Disorders Subcommittee, including the VVAW cohort, a researcher from the University of Iowa, and a respected family therapist from Syracuse. After hearing their arguments, Spitzer finally relented, though he made it clear that the new DSM entry would not be called "post-catastrophic stress disorder," as Shatan and Lifton wanted. When the committee finally released its findings to the APA a few months later, it recommended a new diagnosis, which deemphasized the distinction between manmade and natural disasters and made no reference to Vietnam, but otherwise was almost exactly as Shatan had dictated it to Spitzer. It was called "post-traumatic stress disorder."

It would take another two years before the APA published the official version of DSM-III (which had more than tripled in length over the previous edition), but as word got out and preliminary drafts began circulating, a smattering of VA hospitals across the country began diagnosing veterans with PTSD. Shatan would later complain that the diagnosis had been depoliticized, but the publication of the early drafts was a victory that could scarcely have been imagined almost a decade prior when the first rap groups had met. Ironically, much of what ended up in the DSM's entry for PTSD was simply a clinical elaboration of the work that Abraham Kardiner had outlined forty years before.

III. The Culture of Trauma

The post-1980 history of trauma has, to a certain extent, been a continuation of the methodology championed by Robert Spitzer in the early 1970s. As Matthew Friedman, executive director of the VA's National Center for PTSD, explained in a 1988 interview, most of the early pioneers of the PTSD diagnosis perceived it as a "psychological disorder, rather than a biological disorder." According to Friedman, the first director of the National Center for PTSD, a seven-campus system created in 1989, his job was to bring PTSD into the psychiatric mainstream, which by the 1980s had become increasingly focused on the biological characteristics of mental illness. Accordingly, the global research agenda for PTSD, heavily influenced by the budget priorities and interests of the U.S. Veterans Administration and the Department of Defense, has tended to favor exploring the neurological and biological foundations of PTSD rather than the psychoanalytic, cultural, and cross-cultural aspects of the condition. The narrative of trauma has become less about politics and inner psychic conflict and more about stress hormones and the chemical dance of synapses. These stark budget realities have also resulted in a tendency to study the struggles of the individual American military veteran and to apply the results to the global population.

In 1983, as the nation continued to struggle with a number of painful issues related to Vietnam (including the legacy of Agent Orange, a toxic defoliant used extensively by the U.S. military in Southeast Asia), Congress ordered the VA to conduct a comprehensive study to assess the war's impact on veterans. Covering more than one thousand male subjects, the seminal National Vietnam Veterans Readjustment Study found that 15.4 percent of Vietnam veterans had diagnosable PTSD at the time of the study and that 31 percent had suffered from it over the course of their lives. The first study of its kind, the NVVRS helped to create a statistical foundation for the modern study of trauma and is still widely used as an epidemiological benchmark.

However, as with all things Vietnam, the NVVRS remains con-

troversial, its numbers and meaning open to more or less continuous reevaluation in the same way that the Warren Report on the
assassination of President Kennedy remains open. In 2006, a Columbia University epidemiologist reworked the data in the study
and concluded that the lifetime PTSD rate for Vietnam veterans was
closer to 18 percent. A subsequent reexamination by a Harvard psychologist, who had served as a field interviewer for the original study,
found that the NVVRS overstated the PTSD rates by nearly 300
percent, arguing that many of the veterans included in the study
were "generally functioning pretty well." To hear the debates about
the study (which was covered extensively in *Scientific American*) is to
get a visceral sense of how elusive our knowledge of trauma is and
how subjective the art of psychiatric diagnosis remains despite all
the advances of modern neuroscience. And there is, in these statistical debates, something that goes beyond the numbers, something
that goes beyond the particulars of what was, until very recently,
America's longest war.

At issue in the NVVRS is nothing less than the creation myth of
PTSD itself, the widely accepted narrative of a war that was so obscene and so damaging to the psyche that it forced society to finally
sit up and acknowledge trauma as a part of the human condition.
Much like the Civil War in the nineteenth century, the Vietnam
War opened up rifts in American society that remain unhealed. We
visit and revisit these old wounds in somewhat the same way that
individual sufferers of PTSD revisit their old wounds. Going to Iraq
and seeing an American war fought in the first person taught me
many things, one of which is that Vietnam and the divisions it created will probably always be with us. Vietnam and its aftermath
opened up a number of new avenues of intellectual, political, and
cultural experience, avenues we are still mapping today. In 2000,
Robert McNamara, the divisive secretary of defense under President
Johnson, published his second reconsideration of the war, titled *Argument Without End,* an appellation that seems to describe the debate
about the psychological aftereffects of the Vietnam War as well.

Beyond the recent emphasis within psychiatry on biology, there
is a larger social interest in saying that PTSD is primarily a brain

event dominated by internal chemical processes. If an underlying biological basis for PTSD were discovered, if it could be described, as depression is so often described today, as "a chemical imbalance in the brain," then the stigma associated with it could be virtually eliminated. Further, if a "cure" for post-traumatic stress can be found, then society as a whole won't have to bother with trying to deal with the events that cause trauma, which have deep roots in social justice issues. More often than not, it is the powerless and the disenfranchised who are traumatized, and as Arthur Egendorf liked to point out, any honest attempt to deal with the problem of PTSD must begin with a commitment to reduce the sources of trauma that are under human control: war, genocide, torture, and rape. Robert Lifton, echoing this sentiment, said, "There are always moral questions, which are inseparable from political questions that are at issue. I think some psychologists may make the mistake of imagining that it's all a technical matter." A number of the original leaders of the VVAW, in fact, worried about this very thing, that post-traumatic stress would in essence become viewed as a manageable medical condition, like lupus or arthritis, an outcome that would encourage governments to wage wars and commit torture and genocide.

An influential 1995 article in the *American Journal of Psychiatry*, by Rachel Yehuda and Alexander McFarlane, seemed to address this tension, arguing that a conflict has arisen between "those who wish to normalize the status of victims and those who wish to define and characterize PTSD as a psychiatric illness. The future of the traumatic stress field depends upon an acknowledgment of the competing agendas and paradigms that have emerged in the last 15 years since the inception of the diagnosis, a clarification of theoretical inconsistencies that have arisen, and a reformulation of the next generation of conceptual issues." Perhaps unsurprisingly, the authors, after acknowledging the work of Lifton, Shatan, and company, come down on the side of privileging hardnosed science over other forms of inquiry into post-traumatic stress, concluding that "now that PTSD's place in psychiatric nosology is safely established, it is the scientific process that must provide the organizing philosophy for the field."

This renewed focus on the hard stuff of brain science is not without its drawbacks. Chief among them is the lack of emphasis placed on the highly subjective experiences of survivors, experiences that are difficult to listen to and do not easily lend themselves to scientific measurement. And because it is instigated by an external agent, PTSD is, almost by definition, less of a "brain event" than schizophrenia or manic depression or virtually any other mental illness. Yet to look at the field of trauma research today, one gets a clear sense that brain-imaging technologies are not seen as useful instruments in a larger toolkit but as actual windows into the mind of the survivor. It is not uncommon to hear researchers today voicing the hope that such technologies will be able to "prove," once and for all, the existence of PTSD. We live in an era where the hard sciences are valued far and above other academic disciplines and where the humanities are frequently treated as luxury pursuits. This has resulted in a clinical culture, especially within psychiatry, that tends to treat neuroscience as the only rubric for understanding human experience, a clinical culture that applies the language of chemistry to describe patients' suffering, as in "titrating" a patient's emotional response to "prolonged exposure" therapy, as if a person suffering from a mental health disorder can be balanced like a chemical equation.

This surge in biological thinking has, in the minds of some, reached the point of absurdity. As one senior VA clinician with the National Center for PTSD joked with me recently, "So tell me about the war, so I can better work on your hippocampal transplant." As William Normand, a practicing psychoanalyst in New York, said succinctly, "Psychiatry has gone from being brainless to being mindless." Oliver Sacks, the popular author and neurologist, put it this way: "All of us have our own, distinctive mental worlds, our own inner journeyings and landscapes, and these, for most of us, require no clear neurological 'correlate.'" In 1979, at the dawn of contemporary neuroscience, Nobel laureate Eric Kandel argued a similar point, saying that all academic disciplines require "antidisciplines" in order to advance human knowledge: "The hard-nosed propositions of neurobiology, although scientifically more satisfying, have considerably less existential meaning than do the soft-nosed propositions of psychiatry." The human mind is perhaps nature's most complex creation, and no single academic discipline, however promising, should be relied upon to explain it in its totality.

Around the time that Yehuda and McFarlane's article was published, there was an increasing recognition of what some observers have called the coming of the "Age of Prozac," an age dominated by both a biological materialism and a growing faith in modern pharmaceuticals and their ability to solve a growing number of personal problems, many of which hadn't previously been considered mental illnesses. In his bestselling book *Listening to Prozac,* psychiatrist Peter Kramer described a number of his patients who under the influence of the drug "were not so much cured of illness as transformed." Based on his experience with such transformations, Kramer began referring to Prozac as a "cosmetic pharmaceutical," a term that neatly described the driving force behind a new mental health culture in the United States, a trend that increasingly sees patients as consumers and seeks ways to serve their needs. This new orientation has had an impressive effect on psychiatry. Between 1987, the year Prozac was introduced, and 2007, the number of Americans diagnosed with a mental disorder increased by almost 250 percent.

Modern trauma psychiatry has been influenced by this sea change in American attitudes toward mental illness, and not long after Prozac's debut, doctors who had heard about the extraordinary results their colleagues were getting with depressives began prescribing SSRIs (Selective Serotonin Reuptake Inhibitors, the class of drugs that Prozac belongs to) to PTSD patients. This type of prescription is sometimes referred to as happening on an "off-label" basis, and this happened in the case of SSRIs because the drugs have few known side effects and it seemed likely that they might work, reducing the emotional numbing symptoms associated with PTSD. Zoloft, an SSRI fielded in 1991, is now the most prescribed drug for PTSD and was the first medication to receive FDA approval for such treatment.

This accidental discovery, of a drug associated with a particular mental illness being effective with another disorder, is, it turns out, typical of modern pharmaceutical research, where the major drugmakers today will admit that they have no biological "targets" to shoot for in developing new drugs. This lack of a scientific basis for using SSRIs to treat PTSD confused more than a few practitioners, and in 2007, after the VA asked it to, the prestigious Institute of Medicine investigated the situation and found that "for all drug classes reviewed, the evidence is inadequate to determine efficacy in the treatment of PTSD." In other words, regarding the use of drugs to treat PTSD, the jury is still out.

Despite these huge gaps in scientific knowledge, public faith in the idea that biology is destiny continues to grow. Along with the dramatic growth and popularity of "cosmetic pharmaceuticals" like Prozac has come a dramatic lowering of the threshold for what people define as mental illness and an increasing popularity of the PTSD concept in the culture at large. As one Oxford University psychiatrist put it recently, "Society has rejected the stiff upper lip." In 1992, the World Health Organization included a slightly modified version of PTSD in its International Classification of Diseases compendium, one of the most widely used diagnostic tools in the world, a step that virtually guaranteed that post-traumatic stress would see global acceptance. As an institutionalized form of compassion and a concept by which victims of violence can connect, PTSD has proved to be a formidable concept indeed. One Manchester, New Hampshire, physician and lawyer argued mid-decade that "post-traumatic stress disorder is *the* mental illness of the nineties." Adding, "With the number of cases of PTSD being diagnosed today, it can almost be called a growth industry."

Since 1980, one of the greatest challenges for the field of trauma studies has been one of growth management. Like Prozac in the 1990s, PTSD began its life as a psychiatric trend and has become a cultural phenomenon, not only a way of understanding the self, but also a way of interpreting culture and history itself. Indeed, much of the recent criticisms of the PTSD "project," as it is sometimes known, has focused on whether the diagnosis on an individual level has become too popular, too powerful, too readily exploited by the legal profession and whether it has, in essence, served to medicalize normal human adversity. In 1995, Cathy Caruth, a trauma scholar at Emory University, hinted at PTSD's seemingly boundless expansion, saying, "This classification and its attendant official acknowledgment of a pathology has provided a category of diagnosis so powerful that it has seemed to engulf everything around it: suddenly responses not only to combat and to natural catastrophes but also to rape, child abuse, and a number of other violent occurrences have been understood in terms of PTSD, and diagnoses of some dissociative disorders have also been switched to that of trauma."

That the power of the diagnosis would expand even as the war that spawned it was receding into history is noteworthy. In retrospect, it seems that PTSD spoke to something in us at the end of the twentieth century, as if the diagnostic concept held up a fractured mirror to ourselves, revealed how fragmented human consciousness had become. In time, PTSD would break out of the VA clinics and begin to insinuate itself into the dream life of the culture in a distinctly civilian fashion. Every age finds its disease. Borderline personality disorder, a diagnosis common during the 1960s, seemed to capture the growing unease many parents felt about their children, their daughters in particular. During the 1980s, the specter of AIDS haunted Americans in part because the country was struggling with the legacy of sexual liberation that began the decade before. By the 1990s, PTSD as a concept had outgrown its close association with Vietnam and become a cultural meme, its various symptoms represented in a variety of media, including the memoir boom of the 1990s, African-American fiction, the "poetry of witness," fine art photography, and cinema.

"After the formulation and extension of PTSD in the 1980s," according to writer and trauma scholar Roger Luckhurst, there was a "marked disruption of linear temporality in 1990s cinema—with plots presented backwards, in loops, or disarticulated into mosaics that only retrospectively cohere—[a technique] partly driven by attempts to convey the experience of traumatized subjectivity." Films like Quentin Tarantino's *Pulp Fiction* and Harold Ramis's *Groundhog Day* shuffled narrative sequences in new and disjunctive ways, splicing the story into a series of repetitive loops, mixing time signatures, making the flashback not only a cinematic technique but the conceit of the entire narrative.

In Christopher Nolan's innovative *Memento*, released a few months before 9/11, the main character, Leonard Shelby, suffers from anterograde amnesia after being assaulted in his home, rendering him incapable of creating new memories. Forced to live his life in a series of fifteen-minute segments, he exists, according to Luckhurst, in "the timeless time of the post-traumatic condition, whereby time seems arbitrary but is in fact undergirded by a repetition-compulsion that he cannot know or master." (Repetition-compulsion is an idea, introduced by Freud, that says that survivors tend to reenact their traumas, both in real life and in their dreams.) The only sustaining memories he retains are haunting, disjointed flashbacks of his dead wife, whose death he is driven to avenge. In one poignant scene, Leonard asks, "How am I supposed to heal if I can't feel time?" The film ends on a repetitive note, signaling that the loop of the story will continue, perhaps into infinity. Leonard kills one of his wife's "murderers" and then selects another for elimination. Before the next loop begins, he asks, "Now, where was I?"

By September 11, 2001, PTSD as a cultural phenomenon was so widely accepted, had so infiltrated the helping professions, that almost immediately after the towers fell, an estimated nine thousand trauma counselors flooded lower Manhattan in order to address what was expected to be a tidal wave of post-traumatic stress. The Federal Emergency Management Agency spent 155 million dollars to make psychological counseling available for the quarter of a million people who would need help dealing with their trauma and grief. To the shock of many, a mere three hundred people turned up, a development some observers chalked up to the national need to clean up lower Manhattan and gear up for the war to come.

While this particular epidemic failed to materialize, it is now broadly assumed that survivors of traumatic events, and even those watching them remotely, will suffer some form of post-traumatic stress. To the dismay of infantrymen who fought in Iraq and Afghanistan, drone operators, piloting unmanned planes over Pakistan from air-conditioned trailers in the continental United States, are now being diagnosed with PTSD by air force doctors. In 2004, in the wake of the deadly tsunami that struck Sri Lanka, one Duke University professor of psychiatry told a reporter, "Based on prior experience from other mass disasters, we can expect that between 50 and 90 percent of the affected population will experience conditions like post-traumatic stress disorder and depression which, if left untreated, may last for years." Robert Gates, the secretary of defense under Presidents Bush and Obama, in his memoir *Duty* wrote that he came to believe "that no one who had actually been in combat could walk away without scars, without some measure of post-traumatic stress."

Once the dream of a handful of Vietnam veterans, PTSD is now, as one observer examining the Sri Lanka tsunami described it, "the lingua franca of suffering."

6

THERAPY

To REACH THE San Diego VA hospital from downtown, you drive fourteen miles north on Interstate 5 past a gleaming Mormon temple, exit at Nobel Drive, and pass the Whole Foods Market. Then turn right onto Villa La Jolla Drive and head up a steep hill, passing the Rock Bottom Brewery and UCSD's Skaggs School of Pharmaceutical Sciences on the left, make another right, and there it is. The hospital itself is a white five-story building that has been retrofitted and expanded so many times that it has begun to resemble a giant Lego sculpture. Not all the parts match up. The parking lot is filled with Harley-Davidsons, RVs, pickup trucks, and SUVs, many of them with out-of-state plates. Located less than a mile from the beach, it is seemingly always sunny and seventy-two degrees, and you can smell the ocean while standing in the parking lot. Situated on the central coast of San Diego County, home to the largest constellation of military bases in the United States, including Camp Pendleton twenty miles to the north, the hospital is the centerpiece of the VA San Diego Healthcare System. The original building, completed in 1972, boasts an authorized capacity of 304 beds. It serves a regional veteran population of over a quarter million, including the largest concentration of Iraq and Afghanistan veterans in America.

Inside the building, the beach feels a million miles away. Visiting a major American VA hospital is, ironically, a lot like arriving at a foreign airport; one immigrates through a maze of confusing signage and punishing bureaucratic rituals. Eye contact is avoided. Documents are inspected. Time slows. One is immediately surrounded by long-suffering faces, faces of a sort not seen in the typical American suburb. Entire families can be seen, three generations deep, clinging to one another like shipwrecked passengers. And there is, of course, a discernible sadness and resignation in the air.

This is the VA story we all expect to hear if we bother to venture past the headlines, variations on the same three themes: the veterans are tragic, the facilities are outdated, and the staff are callous. To say that the VA hospital is where the final bill for every American war is paid is to state the obvious. The VA is like a morbid version of Disneyland: even if you've never been there, you feel like you have. And yet, as I would learn, the truth about the VA, an institution that serves as Ground Zero for PTSD, is far more complex and confounding and, for lack of a better word, *fascinating* than I had imagined. Joined at the hip to the academic medical establishment, the VA, the second-largest department in the federal government, is where the public and the private, the military and the civilian, and the real and the symbolic all meet. Yes, the VA is often a sad place, but then so are many foreign countries when you first arrive, a fact that makes them no less startling and enriching once you actually open your eyes, start looking around, and start talking to people.

The first time I visited the San Diego VA hospital, I was going to see the coordinator of a study looking for the best combination of Zoloft and individual psychotherapy for the treatment of PTSD. The week before, having waited for months, I had finally been screened by a psych intern at the nearby Mission Valley clinic. This screening appointment, I would learn later, was the key to the realm. Once you made it through a basic introductory interview, you were in the system. You existed. Dealing with the VA, I would learn, is basically a patience marathon. If you give up, nobody stops and the race just moves on around you. At the conclusion of the hour-long interview, the intern told me that the fastest way, and really the only way, to see a therapist one on one was to volunteer to be a subject for one of the twenty-plus PTSD studies being conducted at the La Jolla hospital.

"La Jolla. You mean the Death Star?"

"Yes, the Death Star," she replied, laughing.

I entered the building in a state of rising awe, watching the generations of veterans walking and in some cases rolling by. It was history in motion. Old Filipino men in guayaberas and embroidered VFW hats. An amputee, who from the waist up resembled a college sophomore; from the waist down, he was pure science fiction, a half-android making his way down the bright corridor on a composite limb that resembled a stealth fighter wing. The generational strata were more or less recognizable by their clothing. The Iraq and Afghanistan vets were easy to spot. They were the ones with the skate shoes and the digital camouflage backpacks, looking like they subsisted on a diet of powerbars and Red Bull. Then there were the T-shirts, many of them displaying a variety of avenging bald eagles, terrorist hunting licenses and proclaiming their indifference toward their own mortality. The fashion grew progressively more formal as you went deeper into the strata until eventually you reached someone who looked like very much like your grandfather and was dressed in a tie and coat with elbow patches, procured in the dark ages before irony became a primary mode of communication.

In a restroom off the main corridor, my breath caught. There was a piece of graffiti written in black laundry marker.

> *"MAKE PEACE OR DIE"*
> *1/5 A. CO. 3D PLT*
> *FALLUJAH RAMADI KARMA*
> *THE LORD IS MY SHEPHERD*
> *EAS 15 AUG 05*
> *PEACE. I'M DYING.*

It seemed to say it all in just a few lines. The poetry of places and dates. Unit names, the lies you told yourself over there in order to make it through. Everything that was supposed to happen but didn't when you got home. "Fuck this place, man. This war is over once I get home." You heard this kind of thing every day in Iraq. There was the fever and afterward the long sleepless evenings, the emptiness of the return, or the refusal to return at all. First Battalion, Fifth

Marines, or "1/5," was the sister battalion to my old unit and was the second battalion I had visited in 2004. Karma, a small town just north of Fallujah, was where I had seen my first IED ambush, which resulted in two dead Pennsylvania National Guardsmen.

After waiting at Two North, the same-day psychiatry clinic, for a merciful twenty minutes, I was met by Mark, the study coordinator. A spectacled man with the genial confidence of an executive, he explained the study to me. Designed to find the best combination of Zoloft and individual psychotherapy for PTSD, it was one of the largest of its kind ever done and would take well over a year to complete, involving hundreds of patients at four separate VA sites: San Diego, Ann Arbor, Charleston, and Boston. A therapist with an MBA, Mark loved doing research and spoke of the investigators running the study like they were rock stars. "The primary investigator for this study has a résumé that is thirty-six pages long."

As he explained to me later, "This study includes some of the very best researchers in the world. It's interesting because I like working on studies where you're not trying out new things. I mean, you have to try new things out but I like working on stuff where I can say to people 'Look, this is research but our treatments aren't experimental.' That's the cool thing about Prolonged Exposure [the form of psychotherapy being investigated in the study]. This is a treatment that we know absolutely works for PTSD. I know it sounds arrogant but if you get into this kind of treatment and do the work that your therapist tells you to do, you'll have a huge improvement in your symptoms. If you don't, you won't. The research behind Prolonged Exposure, for example, says it works in about 85 percent of people. Those are some pretty darn high odds if you ask me."

After guiding me through a thick stack of surveys and consent forms, Mark passed me off to Sarah, a VA employee who, after giving me a water break, opened up a thick binder and gave me what is known as the Clinician-Administered PTSD Scale or CAPS. The most widely used diagnostic tool for PTSD, the CAPS is a structured interview format created by the National Center for PTSD that is often referred to, in the dialect of the VA, as the "gold standard in

PTSD assessment." Derived from the DSM-IV diagnostic criteria for PTSD, it consists of a thirty-item survey that takes around two hours to complete. For a trauma survivor, it can be a stressful experience.

To complete the CAPS, the patient is asked to identify one or two traumatic events. The patient is then given a series of questions relating to these events, such as "Have you ever had unwanted memories of the event? What were they like? What do you remember?" After working through this first part, the patient is then asked to rate their answers in terms of frequency and intensity on a four-point scale. As with most things related to the treatment of PTSD, the patient is expected to condense their traumatic experience down to one or two distinct events that can be verbalized and subsequently recorded and scored by the interviewer.

Here is where I struggle. There are certain moments from my months in Iraq that stand out from the others. These moments journey away, return, speak to me, on some level consume me, flood me with joy. Others continue to break my heart. There is the moment in Saydia, for example. There is the moment on the bridge near Karma, the long minutes waiting for the medevac helicopter. But there are other, less easily described moments. Moments with no clear narrative line. Moments of moral chaos. Moments when anything became possible. Moments where nothing was real. Moments that occurred over the course of months. Moments I am still waiting to end. Moments that have yet to be tamed by language.

For my first CAPS, I chose one of the easy ones. An incident where I was riding in a Marine helicopter over Fallujah that was taken under fire, an event that has made it difficult for me to fly on some occasions. Shortly after I began describing this event, about which I have had nightmares, my blood began to heat up. My breathing became shallow, more rapid. It was as if someone, invisible to me, was turning up a heating element inside my chest.

I told my story, lifting off in a Super Stallion stuffed with gear and Marines, seeing the window across from me suddenly turn bright green with tracer fire, the contractor next to me seizing my arm in panic, the helo swinging wildly in the air, the two crew chiefs returning fire, the spent brass rolling around the floor of the cabin, the sound of the incoming mixing with the outgoing, taking my helmet off and sitting on it.

Across from me, Sarah sat with her binder perched at ninety degrees in her lap like a high school student trying to prevent her answers from being stolen. My body was ramping up, going back, even as the rational part of me tried in vain to race ahead. My body was in the helicopter. The higher parts of my brain were trying to tell the story. Sarah was cooler than me, protected behind the battlement of her binder, her pencil calmly hovering over the pages.

The rest of the interview went smoothly, as smoothly as a string of real-life horror stories can go. Something in me had decided to like Sarah despite her naiveté, despite all the reasons I was supposed to hold her in contempt: her innocence, her inexperience, all the privileges her remove gave her, a remove that made her a kind of royalty, free to care as little or as much as she wanted. She was like a number of VA trauma workers I would meet, all of them seemingly young women: bright, almost terrifyingly sweet, their faces unmarred by cynicism.

A part of me still wanted, almost needed, to live by a line Jack Nicholson delivers in *The Two Jakes*, the sequel to *Chinatown:* "You can't trust a guy who's never lost anything." But another part of me knew that a time was coming when I would need to start making exceptions to this rule.

And I thought maybe that time was now. And so I did.

I could see that it wasn't her job to make me feel better or to collect my life story or political philosophy. Her mission was to complete a form, filling in the bubbles as she had been trained, as efficiently and with as little drama as possible. She was a census taker. I could see as well that this wasn't cakewalk for her. She was a trained professional doing her job, but it didn't take much for me to see that hearing these stories for hours, day after day, had to take a toll.

Later, I would see that the CAPS, whatever else it did, took a huge load off the interviewer. As a morally neutral instrument, it possessed what amounted to an antibiotic quality. It kept the blood, the filth, the squalor, and the trauma off the interviewer and kept the contagion of PTSD from spreading. It was as if Sarah were a laboratory technician administering a throat culture—putting on a latex glove and, without contaminating the sample or infecting herself, carefully placing the contents into a plastic tube and sealing them inside.

After a while, I found my mind drifting, and I began to describe other things that had happened in Iraq that had nothing to do with the Sea Stallion. There were other, more important things that needed airing, and being forced to limit my answers to just one isolated event felt wrong, like reading pages from a novel at random. She had told me we would talk about a couple of events, but so far we'd just spent an hour working our way through the story of the helicopter over Fallujah.

And so I told her a story that had happened in Saqliwiyah in 2007. One evening, shortly after embedding with 1/1, I had been talking with a young Marine sergeant when he stood up and told me that he had to get ready for his first patrol in-country. An hour later, I sat listening to the radio traffic in the company operations center as his patrol ran into one IED after another, killing one Marine and wounding six others. A "TIC" was declared. A "TIC," which stood for "Troops In Contact," meant that every available aircraft in-theater would divert to the incident to provide support, an eventuality that would lead to a dozen sections of birds being stacked in the air, one upon the other, awaiting instructions from the ground. In time, a second patrol from 1/1 was launched, a patrol that also hit an IED, wounding another six Marines. Six Marines, all first-termers, who had been in-country for all of a week. Teenagers, in other words.

After another hour, the Marine I had been talking to was evacuated back to the company area. As I walked over to his litter to see if I could get him anything, a cigarette, a Red Bull, some water, he began cursing at me, a long stream of obscenities that echoed in the lobby of the large commandeered hotel that served as the company command post. For years, I had puzzled over this and the long conversation we'd had before he'd left on patrol. Toward the end of this conversation, he'd confided that one of his biggest goals this deployment was to find a way to tell his wife everything that happened in Iraq.

"If I keep stuff from her, it just makes things harder in the long run. I need her to know who I am," he'd said. Among my various CAPS-worthy moments in the war, this story had come to symbolize so many things: the mystery of wartime love, the paradox of intimacy, the impossibility of explaining the war to someone who'd never been there, the secret feeling that every soldier carries with him, learned through hard, searing experience, that every time you let your guard down and acted like a human, you got fucked.

He had revealed a small part of himself to me. An hour later, his legs were full of shrapnel. There seemed to be a pattern, a sequence, one thing leading to another thing, a linking of ideas, a connection both in form and content: the sergeant talking to me about talking to his wife. Then: boom, him seeing me and yelling "Fuck you, motherfucker!"

I wondered if there was a relationship between the sergeant and Erica. Had I made a connection in my head without realizing it? Was there something that had happened at Saqliwiyah, some other clue that I had missed? Was I remembering it right? Why didn't I tell Erica about it when I got back? Why didn't I tell her anything at all? Why did I keep so many secrets from her? Did I need to keep her as a kind of haven, untouched by the war?

It took me a few minutes to get through the Saqliwiyah story and what I thought it meant. It felt good getting it out. I'd never told anyone that story before. Something inside felt that Sarah, or someone like her, needed to hear it. In fact, I needed her to hear it. When I looked back at her, her face was blank, as if she had been waiting for me to finish. Her pencil, I noticed, was not moving. Later, I would learn that because my story about the wounded sergeant from 1/1 wasn't the moment I'd selected at the start of the CAPS, Sarah would not be including it in her bubblings.

"So, how many times in the last thirty days have you been reminded of the . . . helicopter event?"

This went on for another hour, as we made our way through the seventeen symptoms listed in the DSM-IV, one by one. Every question began "In the last thirty days, have you . . . had recurrent distressing dreams about the event . . . had difficulty falling or staying asleep?" and so on. Followed immediately by an identical set of questions, which began "How many times in the last thirty days . . ."

Then suddenly we were done. Leafing through her binder, Sarah seemed to be checking my answers. "You must be tired," she said.

I was exhausted. I thought about trying to give her something else for her binder, but I felt like I'd spilled enough blood for one day. I left the interview room in a kind of delirium. Later, I would think back on all the things that hadn't made it into my CAPS. The week at a remote Marine outpost between Ramadi and Fallujah where we'd been mortared every day, the bridge at Karma, walking into the battalion command post at Dora and seeing eighteen pictures on the wall, one for each soldier who had been killed, all those no-contact patrols in bad country where the Marines looked at me like I was crazy for not carrying a weapon. The peace I'd felt when I knew I was going to die among Marines from my old regiment. The disappointment I'd felt when I didn't.

I didn't hear anything from the VA for several weeks until Mark phoned to apologize and explain that because of a clerical error, they'd allowed a month to go by, a fact that invalidated my CAPS. I would need to come in and do it again. So I went back in and spent another afternoon with Sarah, this time selecting the Saydia attack as my moment.

A week later, Mark called back and explained in his usual brisk manner that because I'd reported in one of their surveys that I occasionally had more than three drinks in one day that I had been disqualified from the study.

"People with PTSD drink," he said, laughing. "Anybody who does research, or I should say, anyone who does *good* research understands why people with PTSD drink, or why people drink more than they did before they had PTSD. We know that people with PTSD drink and use other kinds of drugs because the period of time they're under the influence of those drugs is literally the only break they get from their symptoms unless they're fast asleep and not having nightmares. So, the bad news is, you're out for our study but there is another very good study starting up that is looking for people who fit your profile. Just make sure for this study that you don't underreport your drinking. The other bad news is that you'll have to do the CAPS again."

The next week, I went back and completed another CAPS with a different interviewer, along with an hour-long battery of cognitive assessments for which I was paid twenty dollars. This study, like the one before it, was being conducted by the National Center for PTSD with support from the Department of Defense. This particular study, which would take eight weeks of my time, was looking into combining a therapy known as Prolonged Exposure with counseling designed to curb drinking.

Finding out that you are suffering from post-traumatic stress is often surprisingly anticlimactic. The fact that Mark kept calling me back and describing for me the next step of the process confirmed what I suspected. Most of the trauma survivors I've spoken to met their diagnosis with a mixture of relief and excitement: their suffering has a name. One Iraq veteran I met later told me, "When I started to read the symptoms online on the VA website, I started to cry because I was like oh my God, all this stuff is happening to me, it's not in my head. It's real. Other people have that numbness. I remember telling friends 'I know I love my daughter but I can't feel it. I can't feel anything.' And sensing that my thoughts were disorganized and that I couldn't keep them straight, I was going right down the checklist saying 'Yep, yep, yep.' I felt relieved that there was an explanation for it, that it wasn't just me losing my mind."

Several years after being raped, Alice Sebold sat in the main reading room of the New York Public Library, working her way through the literature on PTSD. She had struggled with her symptoms for years but didn't really pay much attention to labels like PTSD, dismissing them "as so much psychobabble." Nevertheless, reading about sleep disturbances in Judith Herman's *Trauma and Recovery,* she wrote, "Paragraphs like this began the most gripping read I had ever had: I was reading about myself," she said. "There was a collection of first-person accounts of Vietnam that I read over and over again and kept on reserve. Somehow, reading these men's stories allowed me to begin to feel."

Back at Two North a week later, six months after I had first contacted the VA, I met with Scott, my new therapist.

Scott was a graduate student, finishing his PhD in clinical psychology. Serious, but with a quick smile and a single stud earring, he was the son of a retired air force officer. One of his grandfathers had served as a medic in Korea. Working with veterans, he explained, was his "way of giving back."

He had worked with vets before, but one of his first acts was to admit his inexperience. "Now, I'm gonna make mistakes and say some stupid things. Are you gonna be okay with that?" Like a young salesman, he turned every other statement into a question, as if to underline that these sessions were to be about me, my experiences, my responses, my choices. Underlying his questions was an awareness that he needed to convince me. Given my bad experience with the CAPS, I was guarded at first, determined to say as little as possible. Having spoken to a number of trauma workers at the VA by this point, I'd come to believe that they were almost completely illiterate about the War on Terror. So, for our first session, I brought with me a copy of *Fiasco,* a history of the Iraq War, as a gift for Scott. To me, this seemed only fair. I was being asked to take part in their study and learn some things about their world, was it too much to ask that he learn a little bit about mine?

After the usual introductions, we chatted briefly about rock climbing and Chicago, where he had done his graduate work. Then we dove in.

Prolonged Exposure, one of the VA's "gold standard" PTSD therapies, has two major components, both of which are designed to extinguish fears arising from trauma and allow the patient to regain control of their environment by ridding themselves of "avoidant" behaviors. A form of flooding therapy, "PE," as it is known, is based on classical learning theory, which has its origins in the work of Ivan

Pavlov, the famed Russian physiologist, who noticed, by accident, that dogs became conditioned to salivate when they heard the sound of a bell they associated with food. The first part of the treatment, to be done at the hospital, was known as "imaginals" and would involve me closing my eyes and retelling the story of a traumatic event of my choice a number of times. This would continue until I was no longer afraid of it, and it no longer activated a fear response in my body, until in the sometimes-confusing language of conditioning it became "habituated."

For the second component, known as "in vivos," I would be asked to do things in the real world that in some way resembled the traumatic event in question. The theory behind this was that by reactivating the fearful memories in the safety of a therapist's office and in the relative safety of the real non-Iraq world, I would unlearn bad trauma-related behaviors and learn to incorporate new information about the world. I would unlearn the trauma in a way not unlike the way that Pavlov trained his dogs to associate food with other, unrelated stimuli.

With both of these activities, the governing principle was uncoupling the fear response that had been created by the event from another stimulus, whether it be driving down an alley that subliminally reminded me of driving in Iraq or riding on an airliner that subliminally reminded me of the Sea Stallion over Fallujah. Finally, I would be asked to listen to a recording of our sessions at home at least once a week.

At this point, Scott, ever the salesman, started in fast and heavy with the similes. PE was like knee surgery, he explained. It was like physical therapy, it was like unlearning a dog phobia, it was like learning to surf, because at first you got swamped by the white water, but eventually you learned how to stand up on top of it. Trauma, he continued, was like having a folder full of papers thrown up into the air. "What we're going to do is collect all those papers up and get them sorted and into neater piles." The keys, he said, were working up in intensity and repetition. We would start slow, with me telling my story, and keep at it.

"Think about it like the gym," he said before letting me go.

For our second session, Scott began by describing how the autonomic nervous system worked with respect to PTSD. "Something triggers you, whether it's driving or walking into a crowd, something that reminds you of Iraq and you get that fight-or-flight response going, right? And your autonomic nervous system can only maintain that for about forty minutes. And then that's when you crash, right?" I agreed. To help me control this involuntary response, he took me through what he called a "rebreathing drill," a progressive relaxation technique that reminded me of yoga.

Instructing me to close my eyes, he walked me through several repetitions, slowing my breath down incrementally. "This is your homework for this week. When you're feeling activated, I want you to give this a try. Okay?"

Our sessions, ninety minutes twice a week in a shabby office filled with furniture from Ronald Reagan's first term, were focused on the involuntary aspects of post-traumatic stress. Basically, anything beneath the realm of conscious thought was on the table. Although I didn't know it at the time, what we were doing was zeroing in on the animal aspects of trauma, trying to fix what had happened at the mammalian level of stimulus and response, all the survival instincts that can go awry in the aftermath—sensing stimuli learned in a survival situation and attending to them in a nonsurvival context, the brain making patterns where there are none.

"The body knows things long before the mind catches up to them," novelist Sue Monk Kidd wrote in *The Secret Life of Bees.* The problem is that once the brain learns something in a survival situation, it becomes very difficult to unlearn it, as if it cannot disobey its first commandment: *Thou shalt attend to danger.* Prolonged Exposure is essentially designed to force the brain to do just that, to unlearn the first commandment. This is not an easy task, to be sure, because when an intense life-threatening event happens even once, it is etched into the brain in a way that nonthreatening events aren't.

Joe Simpson, the British mountaineer and author, describes undergoing a crude, real-life version of Prolonged Exposure in his book *Touching the Void.* After being diagnosed with PTSD, he was told he'd have to wait six months before seeing a therapist. "In the meantime

I experienced eight weeks of mild panic attacks, a tendency to cry unexpectedly and a persistent feeling of vulnerability. Then I gave a corporate motivational presentation recounting the 'Void' story and within days the symptoms had disappeared . . . Telling and retelling the 'Void' story had inadvertently proved to be a good treatment for the condition. Apparently it is a common practice for psychotherapists to make a victim recount as vividly as they can the full horrors of their experience. With each telling of their real story it gradually becomes a fiction, becomes someone else's experience, and they can separate themselves from the trauma."

After discussing some of the basics of the treatment and what to expect, Scott and I started in on the imaginals. He asked me to close my eyes and put myself back in the Humvee in Saydia, narrating it all in the present tense, as if I were actually there again. I described driving down the boulevard, turning onto the smoke-covered street, seeing the burning houses, realizing we were in a dead end, hearing the Bradley ahead beginning to turn around, the Humvee starting to back up, and the boom. After this first "repetition," he asked me how I was feeling, if my heart rate and my breathing were up. They were.

"Okay. Let's go through it again," he said.

I closed my eyes and went back into the Humvee and retold the whole story again, picking up a few more details here and there, like forgotten keepsakes in an old house. There was the heavy grinding noise of the Bradley on the street, the low cinderblock wall in front of the burning houses, Vollmer yelling up at the gunner, and the gunner not hearing him. Not hearing him because his eardrums had been blown out. Opening my eyes, I looked down at my feet and realized I was sweating. After a moment's time, I came back more fully, then looked over at Scott, waiting to see what was next.

Telling the story was irritating. It was hardly a gripping adventure story to begin with. It was, in truth, a story without heroes or a moral point of any kind, just some tired soldiers driving on a dirty street and rolling over an old mortar round that had probably been made by the Soviets before most of the guys in the Humvee had even been born. Part of me was glad to finally talk about the war, to have it out, but chopping it down to this one tiny episode felt like an act of vandalism, as if we were turning the war into a snuff film. I decided some context might help set the scene a little better, help explain my emotional state at the time, so I began telling him about Saqliwiyah, what a crazy scene it had been, how I had left the company operations center and walked into the lobby of the old hotel and seen that it was filled with wounded Marines, most of them just six months out of boot camp. Then hearing the sergeant cursing, his *fuck*s and *goddam*s echoing off the high ceiling of the lobby as I walked away. Before I could really get into the meat of the story, however, Scott put a hand up and stopped me.

"Dave, now I know you saw a lot of crazy stuff over there but we need to get back to the imaginals. We need to get you back in the Humvee and get you really engaging those feelings. So, let's do it again but this time I want you to really put yourself back in it, really engage those feelings, okay? Do you think you can do that?"

And so it went. We did another two repetitions before we broke for the day. Before I left, however, we briefly discussed my "in vivo" homework, which involved me walking through a dodgy neighborhood near downtown and seeing if it activated any of my Iraq memories.

When I stood up, I could feel my face starting to do strange things, my fists balling up. Leaving the hospital those early days was confusing, maddening. There were feelings happening that have no names. My blood felt different. Hot. The venom in my veins I'd felt in Dora was back. The whole process was strange, detached from what I considered to be any natural rhythm. In the therapy room, going through the imaginals with Scott, I felt annoyed with the monotony of it, bored even. The story of my getting blown up had never been particularly interesting to begin with, but now it felt staler than month-old dogshit. We would roll through it, and I would be back in Saydia for a few minutes, remembering the fear, then it would be over. But once I stepped out into the fluorescent corridor of the hospital and got a look at the people, a knot of anger and resentment would form in my stomach. My jaw would set itself, and I would begin patrolling my way back to my truck. And there was a bitterness, a sourness to it all, what I would later describe as a kind of "body nausea," as if all the fear from Iraq had been trapped inside all that time, fermenting.

I began to think of the treatment not as therapy so much as punishment. Penance.

It went on like this for weeks. I would show up with some things I wanted to talk about, thoughts I'd had, questions that had arisen when I looked over the journals I'd kept during the war, and after hearing me out, Scott would invariably direct me back to the imaginals. At one point, I went in and out of the cul-de-sac in Saydia eleven times in one afternoon. I say "I" went in and out of the cul-de-sac because I always felt like I was alone in this activity. It soon became clear to me that this was not "therapy" in the sense that one traditionally thinks of it, as a conversation between therapist and patient where issues are raised and worked through, insights achieved. This, I saw, was a far more controlled form of treatment. Scripted even. Stage-managed. I had a role to play. The role was that of the patient diligently repeating his story, *ad infinitum.* The therapist's role was to be "present" and reassuring, armed as he was with a set of calming and validating phrases and rhetorical gestures. It was, I would later learn, a "manualized" therapy. A therapy, in other words, whose results were designed by researchers for researchers, a therapy designed to be touted by medical administrators as being "efficacious" and scientifically tested.

For a few minutes every session, we would talk about my drinking, how I was managing my "cravings," and then we would return again to the imaginals. It reminded me of a Spanish language tutor I'd had in college. I would talk about my difficulties with certain verb tenses: the preterite, the future conditional, and so on. My tutor would listen attentively, and inevitably we would dive straight into the verb charts, working our way through them. The point wasn't how you felt about the verbs, why you were struggling with them. The point was to keep going through the charts. Prolonged Exposure was, I reminded myself, a therapy predicated on repetition.

It was also excruciating. And confusing. It seemed to be altering my body chemistry in ways that I didn't understand. Everything was beginning to feel like an out-of-body experience, as if I were always hovering a few feet away from my body as it went on with its day.

I had sought out this particular therapy because I had been told by Mark, the research coordinator, and others that it was the most effective, that it would be one on one, and that it was "perfect" for someone with my experiences.

It was, I had been told, the "gold standard" of PTSD therapies.

After a month, I complained to Scott.

"I haven't felt this bad in years," I began. "Honestly, I don't remember even feeling this bad in Iraq. Is there something else we can try?"

Scott listened patiently, nodding along as I went through my litany of complaints, how this wasn't helping, how I was having trouble sleeping, how I was unable to work, how I was unable to read, how new symptoms that I'd never even had before were emerging.

"I appreciate your honesty," he said. "I appreciate that you're thinking about all this stuff. Because this is important, what you're saying. What's happening now is we're stirring the pot, activating those memories. It does get better. Trust me, this therapy has helped a *lot* of people."

This argument didn't seem to have the desired effect and brought about one of his trademark metaphor change-ups. "What we're doing right now is cleaning out the wound. So, let's say you have a cut on your arm and it's infected, it's festering, what are you going to do?"

"You're gonna clean it out," I said, playing along.

"Now, when you first take off that bandage to put that antibiotic in there, how's that gonna feel?"

"It's gonna fucking hurt."

"*Right.* So it's gonna hurt for a bit when we first get in there. It's going to burn. But then it's going to get better. We just need to stick with it and clean out that wound."

Then, five weeks into therapy, it happened. One evening, a few hours after our afternoon session, I picked up my cell phone and tried to dial a number and it died. I flew into a rage and began pounding the phone into the corner of a nearby bookcase, knocking it over and making a mess out of my bedroom. Rushing into the kitchen, I grabbed a large stainless steel knife and, like a murderer in a Hitchcock film, began stabbing the phone over and over again, screaming obscenities.

And I continued to stab my phone until I had bent the knife blade fully ninety degrees. Outside the window of my apartment, I could hear my neighbors debating the pros and cons of calling the police.

Prolonged Exposure, one of the VA's top-tier or "Schedule A" PTSD therapies, is one of the most thoroughly researched and empirically validated psychiatric treatments in existence. The body of science supporting its use is over a century old and reaches back to the very dawn of psychology, when the fledgling discipline was still trying to carve a niche from the fields of philosophy and literature. It is no exaggeration to say that PE has the best scientific pedigree of any trauma therapy protocol. Derived from the classical conditioning or "learning" theories first described by Pavlov in the late 1800s, the principle behind PE is very simple: almost all human behaviors are learned, and they can be unlearned by manipulating the stimuli that a person is exposed to.

Applying behavior learning theory to PTSD, researchers have created an extensive model of how the disorder develops and persists. These theorists posit that once exposed to a traumatic stimulus, a person suffering from post-traumatic stress will continue to avoid situations reminiscent of the original trauma, a process that can prevent the victim from ever healing or moving on. In time, the original traumatic stimulus can begin to evolve, metastasize, to include a number of random stimuli associated with the trauma, until vast swaths of the world become fear inducing. This effect is depicted in Jonathan Safran Foer's novel *Extremely Loud and Incredibly Close,* where the narrator, talking about the aftermath of 9/11, says,

> Even after a year, I still had an extremely difficult time doing certain things, like taking showers, for some reason, and getting into elevators, obviously. There was a lot of stuff that made me panicky, like suspension bridges, germs, airplanes, fireworks, Arab people on the subway (even though I'm not racist), Arab people in restau-

rants and coffee shops and other public places, scaffolding, sewers and subway grates, bags without owners, shoes, people with mustaches, smoke, knots, tall buildings, turbans. A lot of the time I'd get that feeling like I was in the middle of a huge black ocean, or in deep space, but not in the fascinating way. It's just that everything was incredibly far away from me.

Within VA circles, it is not uncommon to hear something similar to this "huge black ocean" effect, and one often hears clinicians describing their patients as living inside a "PTSD bubble," a severely limited range of activities that doesn't trigger their symptoms. For one Iraq veteran I interviewed, who lost several of his buddies in Fallujah, this "bubble" consisted of a single bedroom in his apartment and nothing else. Just being out on his balcony triggered bad memories.

One of the more recent therapies derived from classical learning theory is what is known as "flooding." Created by psychologist Thomas Stampfl in 1967, flooding involves exposing a patient to a concentrated dose of a frightening stimulus, such as putting a person with arachnophobia in a room full of harmless spiders. One of the classic examples of successful flooding involved an adolescent girl with a phobia of traveling in a car: she was driven around for four hours until her fear disappeared. During World War II, a group of American soldiers who showed an aversion to loud noises and even music were hospitalized and forced to view documentary war footage that featured an increasingly loud soundtrack of combat noises. Most of the soldiers, while terrified at first, eventually grew bored and all but one showed a decrease in symptoms. Flooding has since been shown to be an effective treatment for a number of phobias and for obsessive-compulsive disorder.

The idea of using flooding on PTSD patients occurred almost immediately after the condition was recognized by psychiatry in 1980. Because putting combat veterans back into wartime situations was not logistically feasible (or ethical for that matter), researchers began hunting for other ways to selectively reexpose PTSD-positive veterans to their traumatic memories. In 1982, Terry Keane, a psychologist at Boston University, began exploring the idea of using a directed reminiscence technique called "flooding in imagination" or "imaginals" to reactivate and, in some way, modify the traumatic memories of Vietnam veterans. A number of investigators continued to study the problem, and by the end of the 1980s, it was clear that flooding, or some derivation of it, held the potential to be a benchmark treatment for PTSD.

However, as any medical researcher can attest, the road from laboratory discovery to the widespread use of a therapy is often very long. Funding constraints, politics, institutional inertia, careerism, along with simple intellectual trendiness, intrude upon the scientific process in ways that can frustrate even the veteran investigator. With the increasing specialization of modern science, it is not uncommon for the most innovative researchers to be overlooked by influential funding bodies and the scientific press because they struggle to lobby for their own work. As one senior VA official lamented to me, "Often what passes for science is just simple popularity."

Proponents of flooding and the various exposure therapies were also confronted with a unique set of challenges. Practicing therapists have always been deeply uneasy about subjecting traumatized patients to such an unusually arduous form of therapy. One of the recurring concerns raised by therapists was the possibility that the therapy might, in fact, be "retraumatizing" to a patient, a prospect that flew in the face of the clinician's credo of reducing human suffering. Opponents of such therapies even theorized that flooding could cause psychosis in some patients, effectively destroying any hope for recovery.

One of those most excited by the possibilities of flooding therapy was Edna Foa, a psychologist at the University of Pennsylvania. Charismatic, media savvy, and possessing a seemingly limitless store of energy, Foa regularly crisscrosses the country delivering lectures and workshops on PTSD treatment. (One participant, describing one of her legendary workshops, said, "I didn't see her sit down for four days.") Born in Haifa, Israel, and trained in clinical psychology at the University of Missouri, Foa began investigating postrape interventions in the early 1980s, cobbling a variety of therapeutic techniques together. But she was frustrated by the lack of progress. It wasn't until 2000, during a sabbatical in Israel with her husband, that the light bulb went on.

Just five days after they arrived, the Second Intifada began. A conflict that killed over four thousand people, it spurred Foa to shift her research toward the treatment of combat PTSD. Building on Keane's work, she went on to refine the techniques of flooding and imaginal therapy, combining them with an "in vivo" component that allowed patients to apply techniques learned in a therapist's office in the crucible of the real world. A number of studies, many of them overseen by Foa, have shown that PE can dramatically reduce PTSD symptoms. Sometimes jokingly referred to as the "doyen" of Prolonged Exposure, in 2010 Foa was named one of *Time* magazine's one hundred most influential people for her work in treating post-traumatic stress.

However, not everyone was convinced about this new therapy, including Stanley Rachman, a psychologist at the University of British Columbia, who in 1985 warned against drawing a direct analogy between "fear acquisition" behaviors in animals and humans. As Jerome Kagan, a professor at Harvard, wrote, "It is not obvious that a rat's display of an enhanced startle reaction . . . [is a] fruitful model for all human anxiety states." The idea that humans enjoy a much richer and more complex inner life than other mammals, and that this fact might influence the onset of PTSD, was noted by a handful of other theorists.

In 1991, Roger Pitman, a professor of psychiatry at Harvard Medical School and an experienced PTSD researcher, released a case study of six Vietnam veterans treated with flooding that raised grave concerns about the approach. During a twelve-week course of treatment, two of the veterans became suicidal. Another, with a history of alcoholism, broke 19 months of sobriety shortly after beginning flooding therapy. Others became severely depressed. One patient began suffering panic attacks between treatment sessions. "Mr. B.," a forty-five-year-old veteran, said, "Your research has worked on one level but has exacerbated problems on another dozen . . . it has opened up horrible holes in my personality that I had been successful in glossing over." In the conclusion of the study, Pitman and his team raised a red flag, saying, "We feel we have accumulated sufficient experience to call into question the reassurance that flooding does not risk retraumatizing the PTSD patient." A lengthier study by Pitman published in 1996 found that applying what amounted to a therapy for simple phobias to a far more complex condition like PTSD had serious drawbacks, asserting that in addition to the unknown side effects of PE, "PTSD may not be amenable to modification by exposure."

Similar research, conducted by Zahava Solomon, a leading Israeli investigator, and published in the *Journal of Traumatic Stress* in 1992, found that after flooding treatment, Israeli army veterans reported an increase in the "extent and severity of their psychiatric symptomology." One of the most cited volumes on traumatic stress, edited by another Harvard researcher, Bessel van der Kolk, concluded its review of PE by saying that "it is important to emphasize that exposure may lead to serious complications." In a recent phone interview, Pitman told me that after releasing his results, a number of his colleagues approached him confidentially, saying, "You're right. We're seeing the same things you are."

In 2008, undeterred by these and other disturbing studies, the VA began a broad rollout of PE therapy that one Yale psychologist called "unparalleled in the mental health field." To support this effort, the VA began holding workshops across the country, enlisting Foa as one of their lead trainers. ("To Foa, spreading the word is what matters most now," wrote Jeffrey Kluger, her profiler at *Time.*)

Since the rollout, a number of trauma workers, both inside and outside of the VA, have expressed concerns about the safety of PE, arguing that it is at best unproven for combat PTSD and at worst unethical. One clinician quoted in *Fields of Combat,* a book-length study of the politics of PTSD treatment authored by a VA medical anthropologist in San Antonio, described its use on recent Iraq and Afghanistan veterans as "unconscionable." Another said that it seemed "too atomized" to be effective on veterans because of its focus on onetime traumatic events. One research assistant at VA San Diego that I spoke to said she had heard other veterans complain about PE, describing the dropout rate as "very high." An independent survey conducted by the health website 23andme.com in 2012 found that among 531 PTSD sufferers, Prolonged Exposure was rated as the least popular and least effective among 31 different treatments. One rape victim I interviewed, who completed a two-month course of flooding treatment, said, "Flooding. That's about right. I am once again flooded with fear and paranoia."

Part of this new, risky campaign against PTSD can be understood by examining the larger political situation that the VA finds itself in. As more veterans from the War on Terror come home and wrestle with PTSD, the VA has come under increasing pressure to respond to the crisis in a dramatic fashion. For leaders within the VA, many of whom came of age in the aftermath of Vietnam, the signs were all too familiar: a huge wave of veterans returning home from unpopular wars, greeted by a health care system whose resources were stretched to the limit. The 2007 Walter Reed hospital scandal, whose political fallout included the VA, helped bring about a sea change in the way PTSD therapies are delivered to veterans. The days when veterans were screened and then assigned to an individual therapist who would work continuously with them for years are probably numbered. (The revelations in 2014 of exceedingly long wait times for veterans at the VA hospital in Phoenix, which resulted in the deaths of several veterans and eventually led to the ouster of VA Secretary Eric Shinseki, has only increased the pressure on the VA to deliver quick and efficient care.)

The focus within the VA now is upon large, scalable, "Evidence-Supported Treatments" like PE and Cognitive Processing Therapy (CPT), which together are frequently referred to as the VA's "gold standard" PTSD treatments. This state of affairs also has a generational component. One senior VA official, who was trained as a psychoanalyst and has been treating PTSD for over thirty years, complained to me, "These new treatments have me worried that clinicians will never learn how to do actual therapy." Jonathan Shay, one of the most highly respected trauma theorists in America, cited the recent focus on efficiency and what amounts to mass-produced therapy as one of the major reasons for his retirement from the VA.

Nevertheless, there are good reasons for the VA's transition to PE and CPT. The science behind them is held in very high regard by a number of experts, and because of their relative simplicity, they hold the potential to treat greater numbers of veterans than other long-term therapies. In 2008, the prestigious Institute of Medicine determined that PE was one of only a few therapies shown to be effective in reducing PTSD symptoms. Dozens of studies confirming the effectiveness of PE have been published in many of the world's top peer-reviewed scientific publications. In an August 2002 study in the *Journal of Consulting and Clinical Psychology,* titled "Does Imaginal Exposure Exacerbate PTSD Symptoms?" Foa acknowledged the widespread safety concerns related to PE but concluded that "prolonged exposure has gained more empirical support for its efficacy than any other treatment for PTSD, and some studies even suggest that it is the most efficient treatment for this disorder."

However, the problem of PE raises a number of questions about how modern research into psychotherapy is conducted. For evidence-supported therapy researchers, who tend to view therapy through the narrow lens of simple empiricism, patient outcomes that can be easily measured in clinical trials are presumed to be indicative of the best therapies. Such results are to be taken at face value, according to a simple tallying of symptoms before and after treatment, a method that makes little allowance for nuance, ambiguity, or the nonspecific effects arising from the rapport between therapist and patient.

In his book *Manufacturing Depression,* therapist Gary Greenberg singled out one of Foa's experiments, which pitted PE against another kind of PTSD therapy, called "supportive counseling," as an example of the flawed psychotherapeutic research that is often published today, arguing that comparative studies of evidence-supported therapies of the sort that the VA favors often fail to objectively compare one therapy against another and end up merely showing that "something intended to be effective works better than something intended to be ineffective." Greenberg also rails against another statistical procedure common to clinical trials: "excluding from the bottom line the subjects who don't complete the study . . . Rather than counting them as failures, most studies simply treat dropouts as if they never enrolled in the first place, which, mathematically speaking, makes the treatment look stronger than it would otherwise." This sort of statistical cherry picking is especially problematic with a therapy like PE, which has the highest dropout rate of any PTSD treatment.

The controversy surrounding PE also resembles in broad outline the problems with another post-trauma talk-it-out therapy that enjoyed a surge of popularity at the beginning of the millennium. The therapy, known as critical incident stress debriefing or CISD, was developed in 1983 by a volunteer firefighter named Jeffrey Mitchell and encourages recent survivors of trauma to talk about it, in some cases as soon as twenty-four hours after the event. The typical CISD session lasts around three hours and has a similar set of clearly spelled-out protocols to PE. As with Prolonged Exposure, the central idea is that openly talking about the worst parts of a traumatic event eases the pain. The problem is that, like PE, research indicates that it often makes matters worse. One U.S. Army study of 952 Kosovo peacekeepers found that CISD did not aid recovery and, in fact, led to more alcohol abuse. Another study, looking at how CISD impacted a group of burn survivors, found that the group that underwent CISD was three times as likely to suffer from PTSD as a control group.

For his part, Roger Pitman remains skeptical of PE, saying that while it is has been shown to be an effective treatment for some forms of trauma, it seems to be less effective for combat PTSD, which is often produced by hundreds of individual stressors accumulated over the course of years, as opposed to PTSD caused by rape, which is typically the result of a single event. For all forms of PTSD, Pitman told me, Prolonged Exposure is "not as beneficial as advertised," adding that "the complications associated with it are under-reported and under-represented in the literature."

Toward the end of our conversation, I confessed to Pitman that I was anxious about criticizing what is, by many accounts, an effective therapy for PTSD, and I explained to him that another highly respected researcher had advised against it, lest I be seen as a "difficult" patient. Pitman was unswayed. "This is important. This is a gap in the research that needs to be addressed."

Two days after the knife incident, I returned to VA San Diego for my regular Thursday afternoon appointment with Scott feeling more than a little ill at ease. I was angry. Angry at the drivers ahead of me, angry at the VA, angry at myself for having rendered myself helpless, cut off from the world, phoneless. Angry in a stereotypically ridiculous way that I had always associated with clichéd crazy Vietnam veterans, people with anger control issues like John Goodman's character in *The Big Lebowski,* a reference that, when I thought of it, failed to make me laugh. Before the drive from my house in North Park, conscious of my state, I had, in fact, walked the length of the alley behind my house to ensure that there were no obstructions, no trucks piloted by absentminded handymen that might block me in and cause an incident.

On the drive, past the Mormon temple, past the Whole Foods on La Jolla Village and onto the UCSD campus, I debated what to say to Scott about what in my mind I was already thinking of as "the knife incident." I had, in fact, already set the knife aside, placing it in a drawer, out of view of the neighbors.

The knife at this point had ceased being a kitchen tool and was now something else altogether, having passed into the realm of symbolic objects. Objects tainted by violence. The knife was now a piece of evidence. An object needing to be removed from normal domestic circulation.

I had done all of this without actually looking at it. I had, after walking down to the dumpster to throw away what remained of the phone, picked up the knife and placed it in an unused drawer in the far corner of the kitchen. I had not thrown it away.

It had taken some concentration to make the drive, to keep my truck on the road, to keep what I thought of as "nausea" in check, though I recognized that *nausea* wasn't the right word. It wasn't that I was going to throw up, it was that I felt sick in some deeper way, as if my body was somehow at war with the world on an almost chemical level. "The force of the experience would appear to arise precisely, in other words, in the collapse of its understanding," wrote Cathy Caruth in *Trauma: Explorations in Memory.* In my journal, dated April 24, 2013, I had written, "Feeling raw and nauseous in some deeper way that defies description."

Back in the therapy room, after apologizing for the awkwardness induced by my raw emotions, I briefly outlined the details of what had happened. The knife. The phone. The loss of control, which was uncharacteristic for me, being someone with no police record, no history of violence. Being someone who had, in fact, hated the hand-to-hand combat training he'd undergone at Quantico. By all appearances, Scott was unsurprised. Had I been drinking? he asked. I told him I had drunk my usual amount, one or two beers afterward, but that I had deliberately avoided getting drunk because I didn't know what I was capable of at that point.

There was a pause.

"You were not drunk at the time?" he asked.

"No."

"Or had *any* beers?"

"No," I explained. "That came later."

I asked if we could try something else, treatment-wise. I mentioned that the imaginals were a problem. He seemed to sense that I was unhappy, and he switched metaphors again and began describing me as the driver of a figurative automobile and he as the navigator. "Now I might be a nagging navigator but we're not going forward until you're ready and your foot goes on the gas."

The problem, as I explained to Scott, had nothing to do with alcohol or metaphorical bandages being ripped off or pots being stirred or papers being blown into the wind or cars being driven or not driven, but instead a fundamental misapprehension of the nature of trauma as I experienced it in Iraq, trauma that to my way of thinking was far more about the cumulative effect of living under fear of death for months and then coming home and realizing that no one cared in the slightest about it than it was about a single close call with an IED in Saydia. In my mind, to continue the therapy after what had happened with the knife seemed "completely insane."

With this declaration, delivered through clenched teeth, I became what is known in the literature as a "noncompliant patient." A patient resisting treatment. A patient who no longer conforms to the clinical regimen being tested. A patient who, as Gary Greenberg would later explain to me at length, is oftentimes no longer considered in the results of many studies and is essentially dropped from the rolls altogether.

"It is important to emphasize that exposure may lead to serious complications." So notes Harvard professor of psychiatry Bessel van der Kolk in *Traumatic Stress: The Effects of Overwhelming Experience on Mind, Body and Society.* Van der Kolk continues, "Vaughan and Tarrier (1992) reported this technique to be useful in seven subjects; two were not helped, and in one there was an increase in both intrusion and avoidance symptoms. Pitman et al. (1991) stopped a flooding study with Vietnam veterans because a number developed serious adverse reactions." Six months later, I would listen as Roger Pitman explained these adverse reactions to me on the telephone, adverse reactions that he remembered vividly twenty years later.

There is a lot of "good" science behind PE, science that extends in a clean, unbroken chain all the way back to the nineteenth century, science that has had every opportunity to be overturned by subsequent researchers and has not been. Science that has been embraced by the powers that be on a systematic basis. Science that has, nonetheless, in some instances, been shown to have made matters worse. Much worse.

Thinking about all this over the months that followed, I began to wonder what had made such an extreme therapy seem necessary, a therapy that to the casual observer might seem cruel and unusual. And I began to wonder, what is it about post-traumatic stress that makes such sadistic methods seem reasonable? What is it about post-traumatic stress that so confounds the clinical mind that it resorts to methods that are virtually indistinguishable from torture? Could it be that there is some daemonic repetition-compulsion at work here? A desire to force a kind of mastery over it by obsessively revisiting it? Reflecting on this with a writer friend, then a PhD student at UC Irvine, she mentioned offhand that PE seemed in some ways to resemble an exorcism. Prior to undergoing PE, I had, in fact, read about some of the extreme measures taken by the British and French armies during World War I to deal with the epidemic of shell shock, measures that included the systematic use of electrocution, a therapy that, according to one historian of the subject, "seemed to work in that it could remove the symptoms."

Not long after I described to Scott my reactions, I informed him that unless we could locate another form of therapy, a therapy that did not involve repetitive imaginal flooding, this would be my last session. After debating the pros and cons of me dropping out, I described for him the other trauma survivors I had spoken to who also had adverse reactions to PE.

"I would be careful saying that PE doesn't work. We've had hundreds, even thousands of veterans go through this and it worked for them," he said.

I responded by saying that the British had electrocuted hundreds, even thousands of soldiers during World War I and that, technically speaking, it had "worked" for them as well.

He did not seem pleased by this comparison.

In his view, we were at a tipping point and were "getting into something dangerous," and that this was "to be expected." After several minutes of this back and forth—Scott insisting that PE was effective and the best possible treatment for me and me declaring it to be "insane"—we called it quits.

Before we parted, in a deliberate tone, as if to make clear to any third party listening to the audiotape of our session that I was now "noncompliant," he asked, "Would you like to terminate Prolonged Exposure treatment with me?"

"Yes."

I began to feel better almost immediately after quitting PE therapy. The anxiety I had felt, knowing that I would be forced to mindlessly relive the ambush at Saydia, dissipated in an almost mathematical fashion. Every day I was away from the therapy, my anger and fear decreased by a few percentage points. After two weeks without PE therapy, I felt almost normal again. This, I would discover after reading Roger Pitman's research and other published studies, was typical of those who suffer adverse reactions from PE—the feelings of building terror slowly evaporate, and the patient returns to the state prior to the beginning of the treatment. There are no documented cases of veterans or other PTSD survivors committing suicide as a result of PE, but I worried that as transient as my symptoms were, for a vulnerable person with fewer resources at their disposal, this downturn could prove destructive if not fatal.

A few days after terminating PE, I called the VA to see what my options were. The next step, I was told, would be to try the other major evidence-supported therapy for PTSD, known as Cognitive Processing Therapy or CPT. Normally done in a group setting of around a dozen veterans, the next group began in three weeks.

Meeting at the smaller Mission Valley clinic, across the street from the Office Depot and smack in the middle of one of the largest retail corridors in Southern California, CPT went every Thursday at noon for ninety minutes. The vibe was entry-level AA, except that instead of the usual looks of bland resignation and court-ordered contrition, there were some ten-thousand-yard stares, some guys numbed into near-statues, while other guys seemed to be tripping hard on one kind of stimulant or another. The dozen of us in the room were a study in what Judith Herman, in her classic *Trauma and Recovery,* called the "dialectic of trauma"—some of us were up, some were down, some were just . . . elsewhere. Whenever the facilitators said something about IEDs or snipers, a half-dozen legs would start jumping up and down like sewing machine needles.

There were the usual introductions. There was Fernando, the recently retired Marine who had done seven deployments to the Middle East since 9/11. There was Greg, the young father who played with his aluminum cane after limping to his seat. Tim, the Iraq vet now at San Diego State. Kyle, seated in a plaid thrift store chair to my left, his eyes patrolling the room from underneath a camouflage baseball cap. I recognized Josh, one of the veterans from my in-processing exam months before. He struck me as being almost like an invalid. He was nearly completely immobile in the waiting room as his wife sat next to him, patiently guiding him through a thick stack of intake forms, line by line. To my right was a sign that read: PLEASE REFRAIN FROM TELLING WAR STORIES. YOUR STORY COULD BE A "TRIGGER" FOR SOMEONE ELSE.

Yes, at first glance, this was what should have been a depressing scene, and yet I was secretly elated. This was a room of suffering, a room filled with enough anxiety to power a small city, filled with guys who had paid a lot for daring to sign up, probably a lot more than they'd ever expected to pay, but to me it was a room filled with a strange kind of almost poetic beauty: something we are so rarely allowed to see in this world, trauma and loss and the work of history written on the human face. It might've just been the odd buzz I got sometimes after an evening formation in the Corps, a kind of churchy feeling, but there was, it seemed to me, something noble about the scene before me, heroic in the ancient Greek sense. This room, I saw suddenly, was part of the journey, a waystation on a great odyssey: some of us were going up, some of us going down, but all of us in the room, every one of us, whether we wanted to or not, were going somewhere.

It was like the opposite of a firefight. This was the place where the saving started, even if the therapy sucked and the gesture of showing up was all that you had to hold on to; this, too, was where the dying started, or was at the very least observed, watched by the faces that filled the room.

Later, I would get angry about the sign, which for some reason I always ended up sitting next to, so that it was one of the first things I saw whenever I entered the therapy room. The sign served an important purpose no doubt, but it was just so maddening, so disheartening to know you had something in your mind that only highly trained professionals could handle, like a test tube of Ebola. I knew this already. I just didn't need to see it in writing. It was just like the CAPS and Sarah, another example of what I was starting to think of as the Quarantine Effect, a way people had of making survivors feel like they were untouchable, members of a caste whose bad karma wasn't just contagious but actually a hazard to the general public.

Our facilitators, Chloe and Heather, were both postdoctoral students in their late twenties. Chloe was an angel of understanding, sweet in that all-American way and with a deep well of patience that I have always associated with people from small Southern towns. Heather, who, as it happened, had done my initial intake seven months prior, was tougher, with a cut-the-shit East Coast demeanor that lent her a certain authority. It felt like they came as a set, one balancing the other.

The group began, oddly enough, with a question.

Her pen poised over a whiteboard, Heather asked, "What does PTSD mean to you guys?"

"Nightmares."

"Never feeling safe."

"Drinking too much."

"Feeling dead inside."

"Not being able to talk to my wife."

"Can't sleep."

"Feeling like I'm missing out on my kids."

"Isolation."

"Waiting for another terrorist attack to happen."

Knees started jumping up and down.

"Being angry all the time."

"That's good," Heather said, pausing for a moment. "That's something I hear from veterans a lot. 'Anger is the only emotion I can do.'"

It all went on the whiteboard.

To my left, Kyle said quietly, "FTW."

Leaning over, I asked him what FTW meant. Twisting his face to one side, he whispered conspiratorially, "Fuck the World."

Later, Kyle told me this was his fourth time through CPT. He would feel better for a while, then the anger would come back, so he'd drop in. It was like catechism for him. Kyle was a gearhead, a guy who connected to the world through his hands when his hands were in the guts of a car. He had the heavy-lidded intensity of someone who was on meds and hating it, and talking to him, you got the sense that the volume of his personality had been seriously turned down. Before he'd been maybe a nine. Now he came across as a five and a half.

We were handed yellow workbooks that said CPT-C PATIENT on the cover.

Homework, Chloe explained, was a big part of CPT, and there would be worksheets to complete before coming to group each week. "You will get out of it what you put into it." She managed to get this across without sounding like a nag. Chloe was so nice, so consistently genial, that it was hard to imagine that she ever said anything rude or unpleasant or ever cursed at other drivers while stuck in traffic.

The idea behind CPT, she continued, was to examine your thoughts and look at how thoughts lead to feelings and how these thoughts and feelings eventually lead to beliefs about yourself and the world.

"CPT teaches you to avoid extreme thoughts," she said.

Cognitive Processing Therapy is one of the most popular treatments for PTSD. Along with PE, it is one of the VA's "Schedule A" psychotherapies. Originally created by Patricia Resick at VA Boston to treat rape victims, CPT was adapted from a popular school of psychotherapy known as Cognitive-Behavioral Therapy. Cognitive-Behavioral Therapy, or CBT, helps patients reframe environmental stimuli, redefining the ways people respond to events in their life. The theory behind CBT is that mental health is guided by adaptive reactions to the world. According to one of the architects of CBT, "As part of our emotional nature, fear occurs as a healthy adaptive response to a perceived threat or danger to one's physical safety or security. It warns individuals of an imminent threat and the need for defensive action. Yet fear can be maladaptive when it occurs in a nonthreatening or neutral situation that is interpreted as representing a potential danger or threat." CBT was created by East Coast academics, but it has what at times can feel like a touch of Zen philosophy, specifically the notion that all events in the world are basically neutral and that it is our response to them that dictates everything that happens next. It is a psychotherapy that one of its original proponents described as a kind of "learned optimism."

The founder of CBT, Aaron Beck, is professor emeritus of psychiatry at the University of Pennsylvania and president of the Beck Institute for Cognitive Therapy and Research. Originally trained as a psychoanalyst, Beck came up with CBT for the treatment of depression. As he put it, during the 1960s, he got "caught up in the contagion of the times," times dominated psychiatrically by a campaign by the

National Institute of Mental Health to implement "systematic clini-cal and biological research." A good Freudian, Beck began looking into the dreams of depressed patients. According to Freud's theory of melancholia, what he should have found was a kind of repressed rage, but what he found instead was that "the dreams . . . contained themes of loss, defeat, rejection, and abandonment, and the dreamer was represented as defective or diseased," what he understood to be an amplification of the patient's waking life. Reflecting on this, Beck began to think that depression was caused less by unconscious con-flicts in the mind and more by pessimistic thoughts, thoughts that became habitual ways of interpreting the world.

Something was out of balance with the patient's inner life, but it wasn't the war between the id, ego, and superego that was causing it. In Beck's view, it was the schemas, the dysfunctional beliefs that or-ganized a patient's experience and gave rise to erroneous cognitions. To correct this, Beck began experimenting with what he referred to as "Socratic questioning," in stark contrast to the intense retrospec-tive probing that he had been trained in as a psychoanalyst.

Beck designed a therapy derived from behavioral therapy, fusing it with the then-emerging field of cognitive science. In cognitive therapy, he explained,

> therapist and patient work together to identify the patient's dis-torted cognitions, which are derived from his dysfunctional be-liefs. These cognitions and beliefs are subjected to empirical test-ing. In addition, through the assignment of behavioral tasks, the patient learns to master problems and situations which he previ-ously considered insuperable, and consequently, he learns to re-align his thinking with reality.

In a way, CBT is the ultimate evidence-based psychotherapy because its effectiveness is not only designed to be measured empirically, but the actual nuts and bolts of its methodology are based on what pur-ports to be an empirical view of the world. As one rather smitten writer put it, "CBT teaches objectivity."

In CPT, which applies principles of CBT to treat post-traumatic stress, the therapist begins by asking the patient to write down why they think the traumatic event occurred. Together, the patient and therapist create a "stuck point" log, cataloging the ways in which incorrect beliefs about the traumatic event prevent the patient from recovering. (In this formulation, PTSD is described not as a disease but as an instance of "nonrecovery.") Some examples of stuck points could be "I never should have left the party with Keith. Being raped was my fault" or "Losing Nate near Sangin was my fault. My patrol took a bad route back to base and walked into that IED. As assistant patrol leader, I should have said something." Like PE, there is a certain repetitive quality to CPT. The first few weeks of therapy involve working through a series of "A-B-C Worksheets" (Activating Event, Belief/Stuck Point, Consequence), which helps break down the patient's inner monologue of thoughts to understand the logical sequence behind their feelings. So, for our rape victim, the sequence might go as follows: "I never should have left the party with Keith. Being raped was my fault. I feel like a damaged person." Once the patient sees this cycle, she can begin to exert some control over the process.

From a philosophical point of view, CPT is, in a sense, a very American form of therapy. CPT focuses on the day-to-day business of life, of keeping the cognitive operating system up and running. CPT, as a therapeutic regimen, is not interested in the past, nor does it address any of the weighty metaphysical or social issues that trauma raises. CPT is a short-term therapy with fixed goals and limitations, a form of psychological first aid. CPT takes no moral position. It solves nothing. It helps get you out of bed in the morning.

CPT has been extensively studied and has come to represent a standard of care in the United States that insurance companies are willing to pay for. It seems to have a significant effect on PTSD. A 2002 study by Resick, using a large sample of sexual assault victims, found that CPT worked as well as PE therapy, though CPT performed better in dealing with aspects of guilt. (I would add, however, that CPT has a distinct advantage over PE in that it is less risky to the patient's immediate mental health and safety, an important consideration for veterans, a population known to exhibit aggressive behavior and alcoholism and to have an unusually high suicide rate.)

Another study, published in *Behavior Therapy* in 2004, conducted a five-year followup of patients who underwent PE and CPT; 29 percent of the patients who had undergone PE experienced a relapse of PTSD symptoms, while none of the CPT patients had.

The major problem with discussing both CPT and PE as therapies is that they are both, more or less, explicitly designed to be studied by researchers, and as "manualized" therapies, they intentionally minimize the individual role of the therapist. A number of critics, including Gary Greenberg and B. E. Wampold, have pointed this out and believe it to be the major shortcoming of both therapies. Their position is, roughly, that the rapport, the "therapeutic alliance," established between patient and client is the most important thing about any therapy, and that such an alliance is, in fact, more important than the therapeutic protocol being used, an argument supported by several studies. As one rape survivor put it, "Good therapists were those who really validated my experience and helped me to control my behavior rather than trying to control me." My friend Elise, who was raped, was blunter: "A lot of therapists lack empathy and don't really know what they're doing. It's harsh to say, but ideally, they should have experienced trauma themselves."

One stunningly illuminating study conducted by Hans Strupp at George Washington University in 1979 proves the critics' point: Strupp took professional therapists from a variety of theoretical backgrounds and pitted them against a group of English professors, telling them to use basic therapeutic techniques and to establish an empathetic, understanding relationship with their patients. The English professors performed as well as the experienced psychotherapists.

For our second session, Heather began by describing what she called "just-world theory." A belief system that many people adhere to even if they don't realize it, just-world theory says roughly that "good things happen to good people, and bad things happen to bad people. Bad things have happened to me. Therefore, I must be bad."

While I certainly didn't feel that the war or Saydia had made me into a bad person, the theory resonated with me. People join the

Marine Corps for a million different reasons, but from my earliest days in the service, and especially after choosing the infantry, I felt driven by a kind of self-destructive impulse, a desire to experience what I thought of as the extremes of existence, to experience life at the brink. My decision to go to Iraq as a writer was an extension of this desire and had left me feeling that there was something both ennobling and degrading about war: ennobling because it taught you about the joys of survival and brotherhood, degrading because it showed you how war turned men into dogs.

Joseph Conrad, in *Heart of Darkness,* described what he called "the fascination of the abomination," the powerful need to "live in the midst of the incomprehensible." To truly see it, you had to be touched by it, take on some of the darkness.

Or so I thought.

As I pondered what Heather had said, I began to realize just how much this fascination of the abomination had come to color my life. Like many of my Marine buddies who had served in the Gulf War and Somalia, I returned from Iraq feeling marked, changed in some way beyond expression, and that because I had been touched by death, I no longer belonged to the normal world. It wasn't simply that I had loved the excitement of the war and that stateside life felt boring, but that the things I had seen in Iraq made it impossible for me to believe in the normal fictions that most people cling to in their daily lives: the lie that the world is safe, the lie that society is just, the lie that the government can be trusted, the lie that good works are rewarded, the lie that bad people are punished. T. E. Lawrence, who saw his cause betrayed by the British government after World War I, seemed to feel something similar, saying, "If ever there was a man squeezed right out dry by over-experience, then it's me. I don't think I'll be fit for anything ever again."

From my earliest days as an officer candidate at Quantico, I had been told that leaders are held accountable for their actions. In my mind, the Bush administration and senior officers within the military were never held accountable for their actions. The sequence of events that culminated in 2004 with Bush's reelection after the debacle of the first battle of Fallujah and Abu Ghraib shook me to the core, controverting the lessons that as a Marine I had been raised on—that actions had consequences and that committing troops to battle was a sacred undertaking—and in the process severely damaging whatever version of the just-world theory that I had held up to that point.

About these sorts of elemental questions, questions which many survivors struggle with, questions that the ancient Greeks looked at as a violation of *themis,* or justice, CPT has curiously little to say. More to the point, therapists using the CPT protocol tend to ask about important, weighty issues, issues that have defined history in some instances, and then when they hear your answer, they tell you that perhaps you are being a little pessimistic about it all.

When, in one of my first "A-B-C" sheets, I wrote that "A. The government lies. B. People in power are liars and their lies killed friends of mine. C. I feel sick and helpless about it," I was urged in the corresponding example "A-B-C" worksheet and then, innocently, even sweetly, by Chloe to investigate whether my "B" belief was, in fact, "100 percent realistic."

100 percent realistic. The government that lied to get the country to go to war. The government that lied to cover up the worst friendly fire incident since the Vietnam War, in which eighteen Marines were killed by U.S. Air Force A-10s. The government that sent too few troops to secure Iraq. The government that overruled the judgment of commanders on the ground and ordered four Marine battalions into Fallujah and then pulled them out when Iraqi legislators complained, as reported in *Salon* and the *Los Angeles Times* and later explored at length in an Oxford University study. The government that continued to insist that the Sunni insurgency was "in its last throes" even as casualties were peaking in Anbar province. The government and its successors that have continued to insist that the 2007 surge of American troops "worked" when in fact the majority of the Iraqi Army units trained by the United States crumbled in the face of an Al Qaeda assault in 2014.

Was this a case of my being a noncompliant patient again? A case of my resisting treatment on philosophical grounds? Was I being needlessly argumentative? Perhaps. Though I think the better question to be asked is if the sort of alienation and mistrust of society I experienced after Iraq wasn't extreme or "unrealistic" at all but was, in fact, entirely appropriate, appropriate for the same reasons that it was appropriate for Siegfried Sassoon to be disgusted with British society after World War I, saying, "In the name of civilization these soldiers had been martyred, and it remained for civilization to prove that their martyrdom wasn't a dirty swindle." Was it not possible that "civilization" was being unrealistic, expecting veterans to forgive and forget? Wasn't my disillusionment the more empirically accurate response, given the lies about the use of military force that continue to inform American policy?

Another, slightly more paranoid argument that could be made here is that therapies like CPT silence trauma survivors, telling them to buck up and forget about all those regrettable events they went through, regrettable events that often resulted from abuses of power. As part of a larger argument about the need to view survivors of trauma as messengers from a kind of underground, Judith Herman asserted that "like traumatized people, we [as a society] need to understand the past in order to reclaim the present and the future."

In all fairness, it was stimulating and useful for me to consider the myriad questions of the just-world theory. It was also useful to examine how my trust in society changed after Iraq. And it's possible that Chloe and Heather and Patricia Resick and Aaron Beck all have a point. Maybe with traumatic events, the best way to get over them is to try to see them as truly exceptional, isolated, one-off incidents, and the lessons are best examined on a case-by-case basis rather than used to judge the entire world.

But the historian in me wonders what would have happened if the VVAW agitators who fought to have PTSD recognized had come to see the Vietnam War as a truly exceptional, isolated event. A one-off. And I wonder about the direction that PTSD has taken since 1980. I wonder if by treating it with the punitive reconditioning of Prolonged Exposure and the Yankee optimism of cognitive therapy, clinicians haven't reduced the moral questions at the heart of PTSD—the proper use of military force, the safety of women in society, the efficacy of torture—to distant also-rans, asterisks in the clinician's handbook. I wonder if in the process they haven't served to reduce one of the most powerful humanistic concepts in history to a strictly technical matter. And, coincidentally, if they haven't served to realize the worst fears of the founders of PTSD, people like Robert Lifton and Arthur Egendorf, who worried that the diagnosis would be morally neutered by psychiatry.

As the group sessions went on, we were asked to transfer the contents of our A-B-C sheets into "Challenging Questions Worksheets," where we were encouraged to investigate our various stuck points on the basis of a number of questions. *Is your belief based on facts? Are you thinking in all-or-none terms? Is your source of information reliable? Are you taking the situation out of context and focusing on one aspect of the event? Are your judgments based on feeling rather than facts?*

Interestingly, while a couple other veterans had concerns similar to mine, concerns that were labeled as revolving around "social trust," a larger number were concerned with issues of "safety and security." One of the recurring themes of the group involved what Tim described as his dislike of "people of different races," specifically "Middle Easterners," a group that seemed to include anyone wearing non-Western headgear. Tim would later recount a recent incident in which he'd assaulted a local Iraqi pawnshop owner after getting into an argument with him. Being yelled at in Arabic, he said, had set him off. His leg doing the sewing machine needle, he explained that he had recently gone off his meds and that on the day of the altercation he had been wearing a memorial T-shirt with the words INSURGENT HUNTER printed on it along with the name of a dead buddy.

In response to all of this, Tim was asked to consider whether his response to hearing Arabic wasn't a case of inappropriately applying knowledge specific to Iraq to the environment of the United States. Was it not also possible, Chloe asked, that behaviors that were possibly appropriate eight years ago in Iraq were not appropriate in present-day America? Continuing, she asked if he wasn't taking the "situation out of context," seeing a pattern that wasn't exactly there, a phrasing that to me sounded suspiciously like apophenia.

Fernando then told us how he'd stopped going to movies after seeing a group of "Middle Eastern" people gathered inside a theater. He was, he said, always "waiting for the other shoe to drop," "waiting for another attack to come."

Later, toward the end of the twelve-week group, I talked with Fernando while we sat in the clinic's waiting room. He told me that going to the group had helped him, and that he really appreciated being able to talk to Chloe and Heather, though he was upset that Heather had left the group at the midway point (her fellowship at VA San Diego had ended, and she had moved on to a new assignment within the VA), a reassignment that he called "fucked up" and that had upset everyone and corresponded with a sharp drop in attendance. He still seemed tentative, frustrated by his perceived lack of safety, and he still got upset when he saw women in what he called "full-on burkas" in Target, but he did seem more relaxed, less agitated.

Like Fernando, I found CPT to be useful. It provided a set of skills and, for lack of a better phrase, a useful set of perceptual tools. And like him, I found the idea of filling out A-B-C sheets and thinking through my stuck point logs and connecting them up via a Challenging Beliefs matrix to be impractical and somewhat ridiculous. Would I need to reexamine every moment of my past in this way to achieve a kind of balance? Worksheet by worksheet? If by accident I remembered the Marine from 1/1 who'd told me about his need to tell his wife everything, the Marine who subsequently caught two legs full of shrapnel, was there an appropriate worksheet available for such a memory? A worksheet to describe the connection I'd made that day, that you needed to be careful who you told what? Was there an appropriate worksheet for all the things I tried to tell Erica but couldn't? A worksheet to contain, to "reality test," all the words I needed to say to her but didn't?

It struck me, as we sat talking amid the odd, junk drawer clutter of the waiting room, that CPT, whatever else it was, was an attempt to arrest the flow of time, to slow down the moments that had happened too fast, to impose an order and a rational meaning on them. To, in other words, strip them of their mystery, their capacity to haunt. (In my journal, I wrote, "If PE is like emotional chemo, then CPT is like a form of emotional tai chi.") And I wondered how much of my resistance to it was simply my unwillingness to let go of the memories, to let go of the war's mystery, its specialness. If I let it all go, if it became an experience just like any other, an isolated event, what was left? Who was I then? If the war was of no enduring moral concern, why was I still haunted by it?

Fernando, a more practical man than me, asked before we broke for our final session, "So I am going to have to carry these worksheets around with me for the rest of my life?"

Psychodynamic therapy, the therapeutic school that grew out of Freudian psychoanalysis, while never in vogue for the treatment of PTSD, has a respectable track record for treatment. Equally important, psychodynamic thinkers, many of whom practice outside of any major institution, continue to generate some of the most lucid and powerful ideas about human trauma. While the consensus among trauma workers today is that psychodynamic therapy is an anachronism, a historical curiosity not on par with evidence-supported treatments like PE and CPT, it's worth remembering that the original psychiatrists who theorized PTSD—Chaim Shatan and Robert Lifton—were both working within the larger psychoanalytic tradition. Additionally, many of Freud's original insights about adult trauma have stood the test of time, including his idea of the repetition-compulsion, which remains one of the most powerful concepts within the field of trauma studies. Nevertheless, the problem with the psychodynamic school with respect to PTSD has always been its overemphasis on childhood development and its reluctance to focus on adult-onset trauma. As Ghislaine Boulanger, a Columbia University psychologist and psychoanalyst, has written, "For most of the 20th century, psychoanalytic theory paid scant attention to those who had been wounded by reality." Boulanger, who has worked with political refugees for decades, is one of a handful of theorists pushing the development of a psychodynamic understanding of PTSD, which she refers to as "adult-onset trauma."

The VA, which sets the tone for PTSD treatment worldwide, has long emphasized strictly empirical therapies, like PE and CPT, and gives short-term psychodynamic therapy a "C" rating for efficacy, its lowest ranking and a stark reminder of the intellectual divide in psychiatry that pits the Freudians and the quasi-Freudians against the biological psychiatrists, pits the biological psychiatrists against those with a more cognitive-behavioral bent, and so on.

As I quickly learned when I began interviewing clinicians for this book, the mental health field is a staggeringly Balkanized one where broad consensus on any major issue is almost nonexistent and where hard science increasingly has the upper hand. Freud and his acolytes may have articulated some of the basic concepts that led to PTSD, but one is unlikely to hear him credited or quoted at a trauma conference. One senior VA administrator I spoke to sees the current emphasis on biology and narrowly defined empiricism as essentially a self-fulfilling prophecy, arguing, "Biological research is where the money is, so that's where the discoveries, if you want to call them that, tend to come from." Though he was trained in psychoanalysis, he explained, "I don't usually describe myself as having a psychodynamic background because it usually makes for an unproductive conversation."

The major complaint leveled at psychodynamic psychotherapy is that it is not evidence based. Columbia psychiatrist and Nobel laureate Eric Kandel, who grew disillusioned with psychoanalysis shortly after beginning his clinical training, wrote, "Sixty years after its introduction . . . psychoanalysis had exhausted much of its novel investigative power. By 1960 it was clear, even to me, that little in the way of new knowledge or insights remained to be learned by observing individual patients and listening carefully to them. Although psychoanalysis had historically been scientific in its ambitions — it had always wanted to develop an empirical, testable science of mind — it was rarely scientific in its methods. It had failed over the years to submit its assumptions to replicable experimentation. Indeed, it was traditionally far better at generating ideas than at testing them."

Despite the lack of a distinguished scientific pedigree, psychodynamic psychotherapy remains a wellspring of ideas and a viable option for treating people with PTSD, especially people who suffer from trauma-induced guilt and shame and what is sometimes referred to as "complex" PTSD, or PTSD caused by years of extended trauma. Russell Carr, a navy psychiatrist at Bethesda–Walter Reed in Washington, has developed a promising short-term PTSD treatment based on a contemporary psychodynamic therapy known as "intersubjective systems theory." Carr, who spent a year deployed to Baghdad, pointed out in a 2011 article that while psychodynamic therapies lag behind PE and CPT in development and acceptance, there remains a powerful need to develop other types of therapies, if for no other reason than because many PTSD "therapies with the most empirical support have dropout rates as high as 54%."

Intersubjectivity theory, the school of thought that Carr employs, is derived from the work of Robert Stolorow, a Santa Monica–based psychoanalyst and philosopher. According to Stolorow, a person who survives a traumatic event often perceives life in a fundamentally different way than the rest of the world—a world populated by people Stolorow calls the "normals." A traumatized person, in his view, no longer believes, or has an intellectual understanding, that the world is a dangerous place, but instead feels its danger and menace in a profound way. Over time, such people find themselves deeply at odds with the rest of the world. The survivor may feel trapped inside the moment of maximum danger, unable to escape its force. The present has ceased to exist. The "normals," who are still living in a coherent world of past, present, and future, can never understand the dissociated moment that the survivor still lives within. As Stolorow sees it, everyone wants to be understood, so much so that traumatized people are inexorably drawn toward others who had similar experiences, what he refers to as "siblings of the same darkness."

In his military practice, Carr treats some of the most chronic and complex PTSD cases in the country, including snipers, forward air controllers, and special operations personnel who have killed Iraqis and Afghans in the line of duty and struggle with the guilt and shame associated with killing another human being. Carr argues that intersubjectivity, with its focus on empathy, the unique emotional life of the patient, and helping the patient find a "relational home," is an extraordinarily powerful therapy. Having spoken to both Carr and Stolorow at length, I can attest to the fact that while intersubjectivity lacks an extensive empirical grounding, the basic ideas behind it offer a refreshing contrast to the robotic, one-size-fits-all protocols of PE and CBT.

The problem is, of course, that intersubjectivity, like classical psychoanalysis, is more philosophically dense than PE and CPT, a fact that presents some challenges for its widespread use. Nevertheless, Carr, who was forced to truncate and condense many of Stolorow's ideas while in Iraq, has found tremendous success with it. Like all psychodynamic therapies, intersubjectivity relies more on the art of therapy than the science, which forces the therapist to focus more energy on developing a connection with the patient. All of which seems to have worked for Carr, who, while in Iraq, had several soldiers tell him, "Doc, you get this more than anyone I've talked to about it."

I can see the point of people, like Eric Kandel, who argue that psychoanalysis isn't based on science. The thought of putting a young Marine lance corporal on the couch is ridiculous. Still, talking for a few hours to practitioners like Carr, Stolorow, and Boulanger while researching this book helped me about as much as twelve weeks of CBT. The main thing I got from the psychodynamic psychotherapists I talked with was a deeper sense of the psychic cost of trauma, a humanist sensibility, as well as a refreshing willingness to think through issues relating to trauma in more than the rote terms of the manualized therapies. Carr, Stolorow, and Boulanger all got excited and emoted while in conversation, whereas the CPT and PE advocates I interviewed seemed to talk about trauma from a cool remove, as if by not engaging their own emotions they could somehow remain above the fray. Now, I'm a writer, and I experienced the war through the lens of an infantry officer turned journalist, so I'm hardly your average survivor, but I really benefited from talking about how trauma has altered my sense of time and hearing what Martin Heidegger thought about it.

And while almost no one within the VA will admit it, these sorts of "nonspecific" effects of therapy, all the benefits a patient gets from connecting and developing a rapport with a therapist—even if they're just English professors who've been briefed on a few therapeutic techniques—has a lot of empirical support. But from what I can tell, the VA and the Department of Defense, the eight-hundred-pound gorillas of PTSD treatment, aren't terribly interested in that sort of thing. What they seem to want instead is mass-produced, scalable, scripted therapies that make for compelling PowerPoint slides. In a way, it's a lot like what you see in the national debates over education. Every parent knows that it's the passionate, sometimes eccentric teacher-artists who really make the difference in their children's lives, but it's incredibly difficult to institutionalize that kind of quality teaching, and educational administrators in the United States frequently view those brilliant *Dead Poets Society*–style teachers with suspicion because they fear the unknown.

Still, there are signs of hope. The VA has begun training some veterans as patient advocates who sit in on group therapy sessions. In 2010, the Marine Corps began fielding a peer counseling–type program that trained noncommissioned officers in basic techniques of combating operational stress. There are also the roughly two hundred "retail"-style Vet Centers run by the VA, located in strip malls across the country, which offer what is sometimes dismissively referred to by VA researchers as "supportive" counseling. Several veterans I interviewed found the Vet Centers to be the better option because they are smaller and the waiting list is far shorter than at your average VA hospital.

Most people cannot emerge from post-traumatic stress by simply gutting it out. Chronic PTSD is a life-threatening event and has to be treated or intensively managed by loved ones. During treatment, you must continue to fight, continue to seek insights into your experience, continue to read and to introspect, continue to seek out the company and advice of others. The community of survivors is a real thing. Researching this book has brought me closer to friends who have survived rape, just as it has brought me closer to other veterans and family members who have survived accidents in the wilderness. As I have attempted to demonstrate in these pages, going to therapy is not a sign of weakness, any more than going to a battalion aid station or an emergency room to have a broken bone set is a sign of weakness. Many of my heroes have struggled with post-traumatic stress: grizzled master sergeants, Medal of Honor winners, acclaimed mountaineers, poets, novelists, and artists of every stripe. Therapy saves lives, and the simple fact is, if you're embarrassed about it, you don't even have to tell anyone: just go. Just seeking out therapy has a proven salutary effect: researchers refer to this as the "expectancy" phenomenon. It's a surprising thing to say, but even sitting in a waiting room can make you feel better because you've already taken one step away from the pain.

One of the odd paradoxes of trauma is that it happens in a moment, but it can consume a lifetime. The choice as to how much time it is permitted to consume is usually in the hands of the survivor. I have interviewed a number of trauma survivors who speak of the time after being raped, or their time addicted to crystal meth after the war, as their "lost years," as time that they pine for, time that they want back. I consider myself something of an enlightened stoic, someone who has found deep meaning in struggle, pain, and exertion. Some of my happiest moments in life have come after almost dying. Winston Churchill said, "Nothing is so exciting as being shot at without result." Life is meaningless without suffering, but there comes a time when you have to accept the fact that not all pain is purifying or ennobling and that numbing out and isolating yourself from the world is counterproductive and destructive to yourself and your loved ones.

As a former Marine and someone who has reported on war for years, I see that we have come to the end of over a decade of seemingly never-ending bloodshed. With the end of horror comes the hope for insight. Ernest Hemingway, writing in 1946, the year after World War II ended, said, "We have come out of the time when obedience, intelligent courage, resolution and the acceptance of discipline were most important, into that more difficult time when it is a man's duty to understand his world rather than to simply fight for it."

7

DRUGS

J IM MCGAUGH IS used to seeing his name on the sides of buildings, being feted, and seeing his portrait hanging in long hall-
ways. But Jim McGaugh is no titan of industry, nor is he a star athlete or a financial wizard with a taste for philanthropy. Jim McGaugh
is a neuroscientist. Into his eighties now, when he leaves his office at
the University of California, Irvine's Center for the Neurobiology of
Learning and Memory (which he founded in 1981) on his way to the
science library, he walks by James L. McGaugh Hall, a four-story lecture building completed in 2002. One of the first professors hired at
UC Irvine when the campus opened in 1964 and a perennial Nobel
favorite, McGaugh has devoted his entire sixty-year career to understanding the biological nuts and bolts of human memory.

An archetypal Man of Science, McGaugh looks a bit like a retired
news anchor, a man who has lived inside the fort of his own gravitas
for so long that it is hard to imagine that he was ever a gawky teenager, a boy with only a bike and a baseball glove to his name. Speaking in a kind of restrained stentorian tone that is reminiscent of the
Midwest but is, in fact, native to the lost continent of pre-1970s
California, McGaugh is strictly business. A mop of gray hair rises
over the metal-framed glasses on his nose. Educated at Berkeley at
the height of the Cold War, he works in a corner office overlooking
the road that rings the campus. It's an open space, the white walls
continually washed in California sunlight; two broad desks are stationed in the corners. Access to the sanctuary is granted by a secre-

tary whose mastery of his schedule and daily routine makes her seem less like an assistant than a third arm.

In the world of memory science, McGaugh is a living legend, having seemingly from day one dispensed with the timeworn idea that human memory is a static, frozen entity, a tape recorder forever running, seeing it instead as a living, inherently irrational, moody thing, a thing deeply prone to revision and manipulation.

If McGaugh's work has a governing principle, it is this: unlike men, memories are not created equal. Early in his career, he saw that emotion, as much as any other factor, influences the way memories are formed in mammals. While this fact was not acknowledged by science until relatively recently, humans have intuited this for centuries. As McGaugh wrote in the preface to his book *Memory and Emotion,* "In medieval times, before writing was used to keep historical records, other means had to be found to maintain records of important events, such as the granting of land to a township, an important wedding or negotiations between powerful families. To accomplish this, a young child about seven years old was selected, instructed to observe the proceedings carefully, and then thrown into a river. In this way, it was said, the memory of the event would be impressed on the child and the record of the event maintained for the child's lifetime." This odd story of how fear can influence memory has come to dominate McGaugh's work and will, in all likelihood, define his legacy.

Scientists have known for a long time that certain drugs enhance memory. One study published in 1917 by psychologist Karl Lashley showed that rats given very low doses of strychnine were able to memorize mazes much faster than rats given a dose of a saline solution. (In small amounts, strychnine, often used as a rat poison, acts as a stimulant.) McGaugh stumbled across Lashley's research in the fifties when he was a graduate student at Berkeley and began thinking about what this might mean for the long-term storage of memory. He knew, for instance, that you could disrupt the learning process in rats by delivering an electrical shock about an hour after they had been trained in a laboratory task, a fact that suggested that something continued to happen inside a rat's brain after a learning event occurred. Put another way, long-term memories are not made in an instant. It takes time for the "concrete" of memory to set. Neuroscientists refer to this process as "memory consolidation." Keeping this in mind, McGaugh speculated that he might be able to enhance memory in rats by injecting them with a stimulant soon *after* learning a task, in essence throwing the rat into a river, as in his example from early Medieval history.

His graduate advisor thought it was a terrible idea when he brought it up to him. "It was a short discussion," McGaugh wrote mordantly forty years later.

Frustrated by his advisor's reaction, McGaugh waited for him to go on sabbatical in Europe and then began his experiment, injecting rats with strychnine shortly after training them. To his delight and astonishment, he discovered that his intuition had been right. Given a strategically timed dose of strychnine, rats made fewer errors and were able to navigate the mazes in the lab more efficiently. This idea that drugs administered after an event would enhance the memory of it has since been replicated in dozens of experiments throughout the world.

Soon after getting his PhD, McGaugh began experimenting using a number of other drugs to enhance memory, including amphetamines, picrotoxin, and morphine. After a series of dead ends in their work, McGaugh and Larry Cahill, one of his Irvine colleagues, began studying the effects of naturally occurring stimulants on memory. They soon discovered that adrenaline, the chemical released when a mammal is excited, enhanced the memory of a given event in a way similar to strychnine, and they could radically improve the ability of rats to remember experiences by injecting them with adrenaline.

But what if, McGaugh wondered, the reverse was true? What if you could inject rats (or people) with a substance that undermined the influence of adrenaline on the process of memory? What if you could make someone forget or at least dampen the power of a particular memory?

When I met McGaugh in his office on campus, he began by explaining the underlying neuroscience behind his work, concluding his minilecture with a blockbuster: there was a drug that could, from a neurological standpoint, prevent PTSD.

This drug—propranolol, a beta-blocker developed to prevent heart attacks in 1964—blocks the action of adrenaline within humans. As he explained, if you were to administer propranolol to a person a few hours after a traumatic event, you would block the neurological process that would otherwise cause that memory to become traumatic. In the language of neuroscience, you would prevent its "overconsolidation" within the brain and prevent the event from being permanently etched into the amygdala, one of the brain's fear centers. You would prevent the patient from being "thrown into the river." The experience would be remembered much like any other event was remembered—without the elevated heart rate, without the shortness of breath, and without the amygdala being unduly impacted. A serious car crash would be rendered identical to a trip to the coffee shop, neurologically speaking.

Further, he explained, propranolol was completely safe, could be taken orally, had few side effects, had been in wide use for decades, and was off-patent, which means that, like a number of older drugs (such as penicillin), it wasn't controlled by a particular drug company.

The only catch was the timing. For propranolol to work, you had to administer it to the traumatized person within six hours of the "emotionally significant" event, and the sooner the better ideally. As I would learn later, the other not-small problem, at least for soldiers in a war zone or for refugees living in displaced persons camps and the like, is that for as long as the person is on propranolol, they are going to have to live without the benefit of adrenaline and the normal fight-or-flight response that would allow them to deal with danger. They would, in other words, be defenseless—tiger meat, from a Darwinian perspective.

An hour later, I left McGaugh's office bewildered. While I'd gleaned a few nuggets of basic neuroscience, some things were far less clear to me than when I'd arrived. As I made my way across the sleek UCI campus, I wondered if I'd had it wrong all this time. All along, I had been thinking of trauma and PTSD as a profound, almost existential condition, a way of being in the world as much as a discrete diagnosis. Could trauma—the nightmares, the daemons, the vanished hopes, the impacted grief, the lost time, the great over-turned jigsaw puzzle that used to be a person's life—simply be the product of an ill-timed surge of adrenaline? An overrelease of epi-nephrine (the proper name for adrenaline) that resulted in a corre-sponding overrelease of norepinephrine (a neurotransmitter released during times of stress) in the amygdala? An overrelease that resulted in an overconsolidated memory trace in the fear center of the brain? Was this to be the historical conclusion to the odyssey begun by Lif-ton and Shatan four decades before?

The idea that our memories, the fund of information that makes us who we are, could be manipulated so easily flew in the face of nearly everything I wanted to believe about post-traumatic stress. It flew in the face of everything I wanted to believe about human nature. The world is so big, so complex, so replete with surprise and disillusionment and sublime loss, and the idea that they could all be banished by a heart pill invented six years before Lifton had even set foot inside the VVAW office was more than I was prepared to accept.

In my own way, I felt a little like John Keats in 1816, pondering the new world being ushered in by Isaac Newton. The natural sci-ences, he wrote,

> . . . will clip an Angel's wings,
> Conquer all mysteries by rule and line,
> Empty the haunted air, and gnomed mine—
> Unweave a rainbow.

Nevertheless, there remained the not-insignificant problem of timing, of administering the propranolol within the requisite six-hour window after the traumatic event. As a lifelong student of war and disaster, I understood this to be a tall order indeed. The idea that you could expect to pull thousands of troops off the line during a war, or round up tens of thousands of hurricane victims, and admin-ister them a drug that would render them helpless as sheep for ten to twelve days seemed like a classic case of science failing to live in the real world. In the case of infantry and special operations troops, you would in essence be rendering them combat-ineffective, denying them the use of the biological hardware fine-tuned over millions of years of evolution.

But, as I would learn after returning home and Googling around, researchers have been hard at work trying to solve the timing problem ever since McGaugh and Cahill made their initial discoveries. In 2008, Roger Pitman at Harvard, along with some of his colleagues, published a preliminary study in the *Journal of Psychiatric Research* that tackled the timing dilemma head on. While the number of research subjects involved was relatively small, the results were promising. Pitman took a group of patients diagnosed with PTSD, and after selectively exposing them to emotionally disturbing slide imagery, gave them doses of propranolol. What they found was astonishing: reactivating their memories with the slides coupled with the administration of propranolol reduced their symptoms by nearly 50 percent. (A similar experiment, conducted in 2001 by Pitman with McGaugh's input, administered a ten-day course of propranolol to forty-one emergency room patients within six hours of a traumatic event, and it had a slightly better outcome.) Pitman's results were encouraging enough that the Department of Defense awarded his team seven million dollars to develop a drug therapy to block this sort of traumatic memory reconsolidation in PTSD patients.

In January 2014, Pitman told me he was putting the final touches on a study that used "imaginals" similar to those used in PE therapy to activate patients' symptoms several months *after* a traumatic event and treating them with propranolol, and that they're finding the same pattern of reduced post-traumatic symptoms. In other words, the timing problem with propranolol may have been solved.

In *Eternal Sunshine of the Spotless Mind,* the 2004 film directed by Michel Gondry, a reclusive artist named Joel Barish (played by Jim Carrey) discovers that his exgirlfriend has had her memories of their relationship erased through an innovative procedure developed by a psychiatrist. Devastated and angry, Barish decides to have the same operation done to have his brain expunged of any trace of his ex.

When he asks if there is any risk of brain damage, the psychiatrist, Dr. Mierzwiak, responds, "Well, technically speaking, the operation is brain damage, but it's on par with a night of heavy drinking, nothing you'll miss." In time, Barish comes to regret his decision, and for the bulk of the film, we see the star-crossed lovers chasing one another through Barish's various memories before they are vaporized by Mierzwiak and his technicians.

The film, written by Charlie Kaufman, hit theaters before propranolol's medical potential had been widely reported (a 60 *Minutes* story on propranolol aired two years later, in November 2006), but the procedure depicted in the film resembles propranolol in enough respects that we have to credit Kaufman for creating a work of art that life has seen fit to imitate. In Kaufman's story, the effect of this technologically induced amnesia is almost entirely negative, creating a kind of moral chaos. Characters, unconcerned about the consequences of their actions, actions that no one will remember, betray one another as a matter of course. The romance at the center of the film is nearly destroyed by the ability to erase memories on a whim. All sense of an objective, stable reality is lost. As the plot unfolds, we learn that the seemingly benevolent Dr. Mierzwiak has, in fact, used the procedure several times to delete an affair he'd had with his attractive young receptionist, played by Kirsten Dunst. The movie ends with Dunst's character stealing all of Mierzwiak's files and mailing them to his roster of patients in an effort to undo the damage wreaked by this neurological Frankenstein. Society, it seems, is not ready for wholesale memory erasure.

Kaufman's screenplay, heavily influenced by the work of science fiction novelist Philip K. Dick, presages much of the criticism that has followed the advent of propranolol. In October 2003, before the most promising experiments by Pitman had even been published, President Bush's Council on Bioethics released a lengthy monograph titled *Beyond Therapy: Biotechnology and the Pursuit of Happiness,* in which the authors, addressing the potential of propranolol, asked "Would dulling our memory of terrible things make us too comfortable with the world, unmoved by suffering, wrongdoing, or cruelty? Does not the experience of hard truths—of the unchosen, the inexplicable, the tragic — remind us that we can never be fully at home in the world, especially if we are to take seriously the reality of human evil? Further, by blunting our experience and awareness of shameful, fearful, and hateful things, might we not also risk deadening our response to what is admirable, inspiring, and lovable?"

The Council's report, which was regrettably loaded with early War on Terror–style references to "evil" and "evildoers," still manages to get its basic point across: propranolol is one of the most morally challenging drugs to emerge in a very long time and could radically alter how society deals with trauma and moral terror. As numerous bioethicists have observed, the moral problems it introduces are virtually limitless. As Chuck Klosterman, an author and *Esquire* columnist, argued, "Propranolol might be the most philosophically vexing pharmaceutical since Prozac. It openly questions the significance of reality."

Klosterman, an avid student of pop culture, goes on to ask, "How big is your life? That is neither a rhetorical nor impossible question. The answer is easy: your life is as big as your memory. Forgotten actions still have an impact on other people, but they don't have an impact on you; this is the entire point of *Memento*. Reality is defined by what we know, and we (obviously) can't know what we can't remember. What this means is that propranolol provides an opportunity to shrink reality. It doesn't make past events wholly disappear from the mind, but it warps their meaning and context. So if people's personalities are simply the aggregation of their realities (and if reality is just an aggregation of memories), it can be argued that propranolol is a drug that makes people's lives artificially smaller."

Klosterman and other critics assert that by tinkering with the rudiments of human memory, we might unwittingly change human nature itself, rendering terror, atrocity, rape, and every manner of depredation a banal occurrence. As Paul Outka, an English professor at Florida State University, inveighs, "To be denied a 'normal psychopathology,' to be remade into an entity that can witness any horror and survive without permanent damage, is to be a fundamentally different sort of human."

Outka makes a good point. While it is too early to say exactly how powerful propranolol will be in diluting the power of traumatic memories, one of the foundational principles of recognizing trauma among humans is that it serves a greater moral purpose. PTSD is, in a manner of speaking, a way of institutionalizing moral outrage. As Robert Lifton and others have argued, to treat trauma on a strictly technical basis, like any other psychic ailment, is to miss the point entirely. To them, trauma transcends the individual. Trauma is symbolic. Trauma is history made manifest in the flesh. Trauma, when heard by society, is a form of testimony.

It is no coincidence that since the Vietnam War and the advent of PTSD, the casualty totals of American wars have fallen dramatically. Among the many things that PTSD has done is given victims of violence a status they lacked before. Society today is far more sensitive to the concerns of the victimized than it was in the first half of the twentieth century, and this is, in no small measure, due to the advocacy work of the Vietnam generation. If through the miracles of modern neuroscience we end up significantly diluting the moral force of trauma, we risk creating a far more violent and cruel society than the one we currently live in.

Nevertheless, not everyone is convinced that propranolol represents a threat to the social order. Adam Kolber, a law professor at the University of San Diego and the author of a widely read neuroethics blog, has, with respect to propranolol, advocated for what he calls "freedom of memory." Kolber quotes one survivor, who said, "I have severe [PTSD] and would sell my soul to the devil himself to be rid of my 24/7 hellish flashbacks and night terrors." His extensive sixty-six-page legal review of the possible impacts of propranolol concludes by saying, "Concerns over memory dampening are insufficient to justify broad restrictions on the therapy. Furthermore, having the choice to dampen memories supports our interests in self-determination and in avoiding mental illness and upset enables us to identify more strongly with memories that we decide to keep. Given the potential that memory dampening has to ease the pain of so many people, and that, at a minimum, memory dampening ought not be entirely prohibited, it follows that we should have some right to dampen our memories."

Despite the controversy surrounding its use, the therapeutic potential of propranolol and beta-blockers is still largely unknown. The drug, in its current form, can diminish the potency of certain types of memories under certain conditions, but it is by no means a memory wipe–type drug of the sort depicted in science fiction movies like *Men in Black*. As Pitman has argued, "The original memory is indeed still there, deep inside the brain." And as I discovered firsthand undergoing imaginal therapy with the VA, post-traumatic stress is frequently caused by a whole series of stressful events, a large swath of time spent under stress, rather than a single, discrete event that can be easily isolated and treated with beta-blockers.

In this way, propranolol raises still more vexing issues with respect to the PTSD diagnosis as a whole because in no clinical trial have post-traumatic stress symptoms been eliminated completely by administering either a beta-blocker or another similar drug. Virtually every experiment published so far shows that disrupting memory consolidation and/or reconsolidation results in the PTSD rate being cut roughly in half. What then are we to make of this other half, the patients who despite being given propranolol or a similar drug go on to develop post-traumatic symptoms? Are they the result of a flawed experimental design? Are they noncompliant patients? Are they misrepresenting their symptoms to the assessors who give them the CAPS? Or is it possible that part of what we call PTSD exists outside of the realm of neuroscience as it is understood today? Is it possible that some aspect of trauma exists in the moral sphere, a sense not merely of being haunted by horror but in some way feeling tainted by it?

Regardless of the technical specifics, the dearth of knowledge about the long-term consequences of mixing beta-blockers and trauma remains a serious concern. Although millions of people have taken propranolol over the years, only a relative few have taken it in the manner being advocated by scientists. And tinkering with the human nervous system and the fight-or-flight response, which has kept humans alive on earth for millions of years, is not without risk. The heightened perception of danger and the exaggerated startle response we see in post-traumatic stress is something that evolution has preserved and has undoubtedly helped to keep humans biologically competitive for millennia. As with so many things in science, we have only the slightest idea of what will happen after a new technology is introduced into society. The problem, really, is that while humanity continues to experience huge leaps in technology, we experience no equivalent leaps in our ethical capacity. In the never-ending arms race between technology and ethics, technology always wins. Researchers who tally the results of this immortal race have a name for it: history.

As I've argued elsewhere in this book, technology is the great transformer of trauma. With the advent of propranolol and our ability to manipulate memory to an unprecedented degree, we will likely see a radically different set of human responses to trauma in the years to come. Because propranolol was approved by the FDA decades ago, it is already being prescribed on an off-label basis in emergency rooms and by psychiatrists across the United States, with some success from what I've been told.

Interestingly, the researchers most closely associated with this new procedure have been largely silent on its potential ethical implications. I asked both Pitman and McGaugh about the potential negative social impacts of propranolol, and both declined to respond.

Thankfully, there are a number of other drugs useful for treating post-traumatic stress that are less controversial than propranolol. Prazosin, a drug first used to reduce high blood pressure, has been found to be effective in reducing nightmares in traumatized people, and knowledge of its properties predates the advent of PTSD. Prazosin works by limiting the action of noradrenaline in a part of the brain known as the locus coeruleus, an area heavily associated with arousal and wakefulness. Prazosin doesn't knock you out. It's not a sedative. It extends sleep once you doze off, and its effects last around eight hours. One 2003 study conducted by Murray Raskin on ten

Vietnam veterans found that taking a small dose of Prazosin before bedtime dramatically reduced their nightmares and other sleep disturbances. A subsequent study using civilian PTSD patients found that subjects slept on average ninety-four minutes longer than those who were not taking the drug. Many of those who take Prazosin describe their traumatic, often repetitive nightmares being replaced by regular dreams devoid of traumatic content.

Some of the most experienced psychiatrists who treat PTSD believe that quality, restful sleep is the *sine qua non* of PTSD recovery and that its absence serves to exacerbate other symptoms of anger, impulse control, and general irritability. So Prazosin holds tremendous potential, and it is unusual among PTSD drugs in that it directly addresses one of PTSD's core symptoms. Some clinicians have even noticed that their patients drink less while on Prazosin because they're not using alcohol to help them get to sleep or as a means to escape from the pain of their symptoms.

The most popular class of drugs prescribed for PTSD are the Selective Serotonin Reuptake Inhibitors, or SSRIs, which bring about higher levels of serotonin in the brain. Prozac, Zoloft, Paxil, and Celexa are all SSRIs. One 2004 survey that looked at 220,000 VA patients found that SSRIs were far and away the most prescribed drugs for PTSD; 85 percent of those studied, if they were on psychotropic medication, were on an SSRI. (Given the VA's leadership role in PTSD research, it is likely that this pattern holds true for the general population.) Among the SSRIs, Zoloft is the most commonly prescribed for PTSD. SSRIs do not address the underlying pathology of PTSD, but they do help patients manage their symptoms.

Jenny G., an air force veteran who saw combat in one of the deadliest provinces in Iraq, began taking Zoloft for her PTSD after Prolonged Exposure therapy brought her nightmares back, and she told me, "Medication has really changed my life. Before I went on meds I would obsessively remember and worry about the littlest things. On Zoloft, I don't worry as much. I don't obsess as much. I'm less angry. I got to a point where I would not be able to eat or sleep because I would be worrying about something, and it would make me sick. At one point, my ex-husband threatened to take custody of my daughter. That was probably my breaking point. My doctor told me, 'I'm afraid you might have a stroke or something.' So I went on Zoloft. I couldn't fly anymore after that because I was on meds, but it was worth it."

Once out of the air force, Jenny briefly went off Zoloft in order to take part in a VA study with another drug and found that her symptoms reappeared almost immediately. "I went right back to the way I was before. I was in such bad shape. If I hadn't gone back on Zoloft I think I probably would have been arrested for assaulting someone. My personal hell is Walmart. There are just so many people in there, people all over the place. People just get right up next to you, no matter where you go. Unmedicated, I would just go crazy if I had to go in there and end up having huge inner arguments with myself. For some other veterans I've talked to, Zoloft hasn't worked at all. But it's been a miracle for me. It seems to work with my brain chemistry. It has definitely brought back a little bit of who I used to be. I still feel like an alien, not the old pre-Iraq version of me, but it's better than before."

Zoloft and other SSRIs have a decent track record with PTSD, but their use with the disorder is essentially accidental, as SSRIs were originally designed to treat depression, not PTSD. Shortly after Prozac, the first SSRI, was marketed in 1987, VA psychiatrists, hearing about the great successes their colleagues were having with it, began prescribing it for PTSD patients, even though the research didn't yet exist to support its effectiveness with the condition. While the results of SSRIs on PTSD patients were positive, they have never been on the order of the transformative, revolutionary changes seen in some depressives, changes that came to dominate the American imagination in the mid-1990s with widespread reports of Prozac's ability to make some people "better than well." Instead, what doctors found was that SSRIs relieved some of the depression and anger associated with PTSD and alleviated the suffering of the most anxiety-ridden sufferers, like Jenny G. That Prozac, Zoloft, and Paxil are all considered by most physicians to be safe drugs, easy to prescribe, and with a very limited side-effect profile has made this development easy to accept, especially when they are compared to some antipsychotics, like Seroquel, which have proven to be controversial. As one scientist at Eli Lilly put it, "Prozac is a very forgiving drug."

One widely held belief among psychiatrists is that mental health disorders are best treated with a combination of medication and psychotherapy, and this seemed to be the case with PTSD, but by the end of the twentieth century, there was no still no science to support giving SSRIs to PTSD patients. They certainly didn't seem to be hurting patients, and they helped lift them out of the deep funks and ruminative purgatories that so many trauma survivors are prone to. But it wasn't until 2002, some fifteen years after Prozac's introduction, that the results of the first two randomized clinical trials on Zoloft as a treatment for PTSD patients were published.

These studies mostly confirmed what practitioners in the field had been seeing for years. Both experiments saw modest improvements in CAPS scores for hyperarousal and emotional numbing, but the drugs did virtually nothing to reduce the flashbacks and nightmares that are the hallmark of PTSD. The other major problem that the clinical trials revealed was that while Zoloft had a marked effect on civilian women who had been sexually traumatized, it had virtually no effect on a group of male Vietnam veterans recruited for a series of studies. (Since 2002, other studies have been published on non-American veterans using SSRIs with slightly improved results.) SSRIs seem to perform best on certain types of PTSD patients, with female victims of sexual assault being the most responsive to medication. Additionally, there is almost no evidence that those suffering from PTSD caused by single, onetime events, like car crashes, natural disasters, and terrorist attacks, benefit from SSRIs.

Despite these shortcomings, the trials published in 2002 and others were enough to persuade the Food and Drug Administration to approve Zoloft and Paxil for treating PTSD. In 2004, the American Psychiatric Association followed suit, recommending SSRIs for the treatment of PTSD with "substantial clinical confidence." There was now a curious duality to drug therapies and PTSD. On the one hand,

there was a class of drugs that were safe, popular (both among doctors and in the public mind), and seemed to address a few of the major symptoms associated with PTSD. On the other hand, none of the
clinical trials on long-term chronic Vietnam veteran PTSD sufferers,
a group that had long served as the nucleus for PTSD studies, had
shown an improvement in symptoms. Indeed, in one study using
Vietnam veterans, the placebo group outperformed the group given
SSRIs. Seeming to recognize these inconsistencies, in 2008 the Institute of Medicine, the most prestigious medical practice review body
in the United States, released a report that officially recognized what
many researchers already knew: there was no evidence that any drug
actually treated PTSD across the board, SSRIs included. In the lexicon of the VA, there remains no "gold standard" pharmacotherapy
for PTSD, and in the VA's clinical literature, the various pharmaco-
therapies are described as merely "an important adjunct to the evidence-based psychotherapies for PTSD." This lack of drug success no
doubt played a role in the VA's decision to support the broad rollout
of Prolonged Exposure and Cognitive Processing Therapy beginning
in 2006.

One of the major roadblocks to substantial drug breakthroughs
with PTSD is that unlike ailments such as clinical depression and
attention deficit disorder, PTSD has never garnered the attention
of the pharmaceutical industry, which traditionally underwrites the
lion's share of drug research. As Dewleen Baker, one of the investigators on the original 2002 Zoloft clinical trial, explained, "PTSD
was defined much later than depression and most drug companies go
after depression first, then only develop drugs for PTSD as an after-
thought. Many within the industry don't understand the relatively
high prevalence of PTSD, and I think some have been scared off by
the crazy Vietnam veteran myths. Sertraline [Zoloft] was studied in
part because the research was driven by someone who had a relative
with PTSD, a Korean War veteran, and knew about the disorder and
the need for treatments. Companies only make money if they study
and get drugs to market which can be patented, thus potentially
non-patentable compounds are not in contention."

This frustrating lack of progress with drug research also reveals one of the lingering problems with PTSD: the utter lack of a coherent neurobiological model.* Simply put, neuroscientists, despite their claims to the contrary, have only the most rudimentary knowledge of what's going on inside the brain of a traumatized person. The PTSD diagnosis, from its earliest days, was criticized as being too nebulous, too heterogeneous, too diverse in etiology, too full of gauzy philosophical ideas to earn a clear position within the psychiatric nosology. Many of these criticisms, evident to researchers in the late 1970s, remain unresolved forty years later. Powerful treatments for mental health disorders arise from a deep understanding of the causes of those disorders. Identifying the altered adrenergic mechanisms seen in PTSD is only the first step toward that understanding. Unfortunately, it's questionable whether that step will be taken; as off-patent drugs, there is little economic incentive to research and market either propranolol or Prazosin. To mount a successful treatment campaign against PTSD, you don't just have to know what it is and where it comes from, you have to understand what it does, an understanding that is so far lacking.

To be fair, researchers don't completely understand why SSRIs work for depression either, but depression is a much older and more common ailment than PTSD, and the major pharmaceutical companies have had far more time and financial incentive to develop drugs to treat it. The development of Prozac, for instance, reaches all the way back to the 1960s, when a handful of organic chemists working for Eli Lilly began thinking about the role of serotonin in the brain. Matthew Friedman, the first and longest-serving executive director of the National Center for PTSD, has even suggested that in the future a radical "paradigm shift" for PTSD might be in order, whereby the diagnosis is sliced up and reconceptualized as a cluster of related disorders, in which "several distinct, pathological post-traumatic disorders are operationalized." In Friedman's view, this

---

* As Immanuel Kant famously put it in his philosophy of morals and mind, "We can never, even by the strictest examination, get completely behind the secret springs of action."

could mean dividing it into a group of disorders based upon how it alters the adrenergic mechanism, the glutamatergic mechanism, the hippocampal-pituitary axis, and so on.

As a society, we now find ourselves at a curious crossroads with PTSD. The disorder has never been closer to the center of the national conversation, and yet its relationship to pharmacology remains as uncertain as ever. Unlike depression, which has long been recognized as a fundamental part of the human condition, PTSD remains to a surprising degree a cultural and existential phenomenon, a condition with no cure and little solid biological grounding. What does this mean for its future as a vein of human experience? As a diagnostic category? Given our current love of pharmaceuticals, the fact that PTSD isn't powerfully treatable with any class of drugs would almost seem to doom it from a medical perspective, and yet the diagnosis has continued to grow in popularity, a situation that raises several thorny questions: If our biological grasp of PTSD is so weak, if it can't be effectively treated with drugs, then what sort of disorder is it exactly? Can something exist as a psychiatric disorder if no dedicated drugs exist to treat it? Is it truly a psychiatric disorder, as we understand them today, or is it perhaps something akin to a "moral injury," as some theorists, like Jonanthan Shay and Brett Litz, have suggested?

My own view of the relationship between drugs and PTSD is reminiscent of what Frank Sinatra said when a reporter asked him about his philosophy of life—"Basically, I'm for anything that gets you through the night—be it prayer, tranquilizers, or a bottle of Jack Daniel's." I think you should judge pharmaceuticals based on how useful they are to you and balance their side effects with how you want to live your life. (I personally think that alcohol, taken in moderation, is one of the best PTSD drugs ever invented, a view held by several other trauma survivors I know.) Modern pharmaceuticals raise a host of vexing philosophical questions about human agency and identity, but with respect to PTSD, I am inclined to say that if a particular drug works for you and helps you control your symptoms, helps get you through the night, then that is almost certainly a good thing.

I have never taken Zoloft or any other SSRI (although I nearly did as part of a VA experiment), but I understand that in many cases, Zoloft and other similar drugs have been one of the only things that have kept some trauma survivors from killing themselves. PTSD represents so many things to so many people, is so closely tied to our complex cultural narratives about death and aftermath, and is so off-putting to Big Pharma that I think it's unlikely (with the possible exception of propranolol) that a defining drug will emerge any time soon.

8

ALTERNATIVES

TALL, BLONDE, AND with a gait that makes her look as if she is forever making her way onstage to accept an award, Elise Colton had always been impossible to ignore. Opinionated, profane, and blunt, she is not someone who tends to bring out the dispassionate side of people. When, after I'd known her for years, it came out that she'd been an actress in her youth, I said to myself, "Yes, of course."

Originally from New York, by the time I met her, Elise had embraced the gospel of California: she was eating well, drinking less, and living better than she'd previously thought possible. Her voice still had an East Coast edge that got sharper once you learned to listen for it. Beneath it all there was the wit, that tincture of the streets that as a rule doesn't happen west of the Mississippi, the wit that could guide and nurture an entire evening, take you from the usual small talk off to that distant, rumored land where no one ever said anything stupid or false or cheap.

Her moment in trauma's black spotlight came early, too early. Yet who, when their life's breaking point arrives, could ever say that it came right on time, just when it should have? It was the summer of 1996. She was nineteen and living in a tiny apartment in the city. She had been invited to a party out in the Hamptons being thrown by some TV people. A guy she knew from around the industry named Michael had offered to give her a ride. Elise was, as she put it years later, "a bit of a wild child," and she liked a good party.

At the party and with a drink in her, a friend pulled her aside. "Elise, you should know, Michael is not a very nice guy and I just want you to be careful because I don't think he has good intentions."

"That's honestly the last thing I remember," she told me.

Later, when whatever drug that Michael had put in her drink kicked in and he took her back to his house and raped her, there would be a sense not just of losing consciousness, of slipping into darkness, but of dying or something close to dying.

"I kept passing out," she explained. "I have no idea how long it went on." Between the long stretches of darkness, there would be flashes of clarity. "I would wake up for a moment and then feel my head being smashed into a wall and then I would go under again. I knew he was going to kill me. I'm surprised I lived. I honestly don't know why he didn't kill me. And I honestly have no idea why after he raped me, he dropped me off at home the next morning. These are things that make no sense to me."

Afterward, when Michael, whose last name she could never recall, dropped her off curbside, as if the whole thing had been a date, she went straight upstairs and crawled into bed, not telling anyone about her ordeal. What could she say? It was still early in the morning, predawn, and the darkness hid her bruises, her concussion, her broken ribs. Even she didn't know how bad off she was. The next day, when she woke up, her roommate got a look at her in the light and "pretty much freaked out." Her roommate managed to collect herself, and together they went to the hospital, where Elise stayed for a few days.

She had never been close to her family. There are those truly awful families that resemble warring tribes and there are those other families that fill the world with their light, make the universe seem like a safe, nurturing place. Elise's family was somewhere in the middle, but her rape seemed to her to be more than they could handle.

"My mother was completely crazy," she explained. "Telling her would've made things so much worse for me, so I never told my family. I kept it within my circle of friends in the city. I was so ashamed about it. I thought being raped was my fault. I knew I had been partying too much and for years I thought I had somehow brought it on myself." Along with her friends and the policemen who took her statement, a plan began to take shape in Elise's mind, a plan to prosecute Michael, to bring him in, make a case. The police were encouraging and told her, based on what they had, that the chances of getting him were good.

Around this time, Elise's father fell ill and was hospitalized with a lung infection. When he died a few weeks later, it was like a world ending. It was a one-two punch. "I'm pretty sure I had PTSD already but when my dad died, it just spun me. My whole concept of reality just stopped. I don't want to say that I should've been institutionalized but I needed to be in some kind of facility."

After her father passed away, Elise began to lose track of time. She was alive, technically speaking, but she was mostly just going through the motions, each day a photocopy of the one before. She would get up, put on layers of makeup to cover the bruises, go to work, come home, and then immediately crawl back into bed. Eventually, the bruises went away, but the routine remained. Wake, work, sleep, repeat. Months went by. She quit acting and took a job at a cosmetics counter in a department store. "Sleeping my life away was just my way of not facing what had happened. I just couldn't deal with the world any longer. To me, the entire world was a dangerous and frightening place and I couldn't handle even the slightest bit of attention. In social situations, people would look at me and expect me to say something and I would just get beet red. Somehow I got by but I was so hypervigilant, so locked into fight-or-flight mode that I can only remember parts of my life, bits and pieces. The entire world was a trigger for me, but my number one trigger was men. I was completely unable to handle attention from any male in any capacity."

About the only man she could handle was her childhood friend, Martin. One day, out of the blue, Martin asked if she wanted to drop some acid. Sure, she said. "I figured I was probably gonna have a bad trip. So I told him, 'I honestly don't think my life could get much worse than it is right now.' I think I just needed some chemical to rock my world. There was no reaching me. I saw a therapist at one point but it was useless. I would just shut down. So I dropped acid and it was just a classic hippie experience," she said, laughing. "We were frolicking outdoors like children, becoming completely obsessed with individual blades of grass, wandering through the park and thinking it was a cow pasture. It was stupid and I don't really recommend it, but dropping acid helped knock me out of my depression and woke me up a little bit. I remember saying to Martin, 'It reminded me that there are small things that you can still enjoy. I had just been so preoccupied with these huge questions, like why did this happen to me?"

Elise had been very unlucky in some ways, but in another way, she was very lucky: she had a solid group of friends who knew her and understood that something needed to change in her life. When Martin and some of her friends decided to go to Europe for a few months, even though she didn't really want to, she decided to tag along. Even in Europe, though, it was like she was a ghost inhabiting her former self. "My memories of the continent are so disjointed. People ask me about Germany and England and I know intellectually that I was there for months but I can remember almost nothing about my time there. And my sense of direction was completely messed up. I was in Galway, this really charming town in western Ireland with my friends for a few months and they would tell me to meet them somewhere in town and I would just get completely turned around. They all seemed to be able to navigate the town pretty easily but I was just hopeless."

The trip was originally intended to be for just a few months, but she ended up staying in Europe for close to three years. At one point, she found herself helping to manage a bed and breakfast in a small village in Belgium. Being in a completely different place helped her put some distance between her and her past. It was almost as if there was a healing power in the new geography, a way of drawing a line behind you, and even if you were the same person, you were in a new place, which made you feel new in a way.

When she finally returned to New York, Elise felt a little bit better, but she was still at odds with herself. "I kept obsessing over what had happened. The trauma continued to ring through my head and I just couldn't get it to quiet down. I knew I needed to get well and start taking care of myself and so I started going to the gym. In Europe I had been drinking a lot and smoking a ton of hash and with the gym, it was like I just traded addictions. I was working out three hours a day every single day, just in there sweating out my anxiety. And the stronger I became, the more confident I became. For a while, I took self-defense classes with a guy who used to train the Green Berets."

Good things were happening now. Every day, Elise was more in control of herself, more alive, more comfortable in her body. But the real game changer was yoga. "I know I sound like such a hippie but I remember one day after a really good session, the instructor had us just lie there completely still for like fifteen minutes, focusing on our breathing. It just really calmed me down, and it was honestly the first time in six years where I felt genuinely calmed down and in some way, almost . . . nurtured. Ever since the rape, I had just been running, running, running even when I came back from Europe. My entire life had become a treadmill, go, go, go. I just didn't want to face it."

Yoga worked, walking her off the knife-edge of hypervigilance she had been on for six years. After a couple weeks of classes, she could feel herself beginning to inhabit her body again. She began to bond with her yoga instructor, Susan, the only one she'd had up to that point. "I just recognized that she had something that I wanted. She had a confidence. She was calm and assuring and centered and welcoming and open. I was the complete opposite. I was closed and terrified and defensive and avoiding eye contact. I ended up going to her for a solid year." Eventually, the two became good friends outside of class, occasionally having dinner, which only served to underscore the differences between the two, how much time she'd lost. Susan, it turned out, was actually a few years younger than Elise, but Elise saw a strength of character in her that she envied.

After attending classes for a year, she was ready to take the next step, and after talking it over with Susan, Elise quit her job in the city and moved to a yoga ashram in rural Quebec. "There's just fucking nothing up there, man. Just emptiness followed by more emptiness." Inside the ashram, things worked on an almost military routine. Yes, you could make friends and chat over lunch with the other people inside, but mostly what you did was get up early, chant, practice yoga, and do chores. "I pretty much did nothing but yoga and meditation from six o'clock in the morning till ten o'clock at night for two months." She noticed that there were other people there working through various crises. A rumor going around was that one of the cooks at the ashram was an Iraq veteran.

The ashram was designed around a thirty-day certification course in Sivananda yoga. The idea was you showed up, put in a month, took a couple of exams at the end, and then returned to the outside world as a bona fide yogini. But at the end of her month, Elise wasn't ready to go back yet. It was one of a series of active choices she took to get her life back. "I didn't want to leave until I knew I had my life under control, so after I got my cert I stayed on for another month." About her time at the ashram, she said, "It was the single most impactful thing I've ever done. I say sometimes that it returned me to myself, which isn't entirely true because I was nineteen when I was raped, but it returned me to a place where I could deal with life for the first time."

Once she went back to New York, things started happening fast. After being back for a couple weeks and dealing with the reverse culture shock of living in a big American city, she knew she needed to escape and start over somewhere. One day, she was sitting in a café with her friend Martin, talking about moving to California, when she saw this hippie-looking guy with a gray ponytail and an odd look about him. As this stranger turned and walked out of the café, she saw two words printed on the back of his T-shirt: HEAD WEST.

"So it was pretty much decided at that point," she said.

When I first met Elise, she was teaching yoga in Long Beach, sometimes leading sessions down at the end of a peninsula where enormous yachts passed a small grassy park right on the water. "Coming to California was like hitting the start button for me. I was like, okay, Elise, who are you now? I knew I needed to be somewhere warm, somewhere with a healing energy that I could tap into, where

I could just live a simple life and do a couple things. I figured I would just get an apartment on the beach and work as a waitress."

After heading west in 2002, Elise ended up getting her bachelor's degree in psychology from UCLA and marrying an architectural engineer, who sits in on her morning yoga classes sometimes.

When I asked her why yoga was so powerful for her, she said, "Western therapy just didn't work for me. Sitting there, talking with a therapist who's like 'Hey, let's sit down and relive the thing A to Z, and go over it again and again and again in your mind' didn't help me. I just became a sobbing hysterical mess. I couldn't get through it. I refused to take medications. I had a strong desire to be clean, even though I ended up drinking a lot. I was trying to feel my way out, and yoga made me feel better, so I went with it. It worked."

Elise's story is not unusual. The fact is that for many people, Western talk therapies do not work for post-traumatic stress. Modern psychotherapy, partially inspired by the Freudian ideal of catharsis via verbiage, is in some ways the last thing some people need. As anyone who's experienced true terror will tell you, the essence of the experience defies words, a fact that only serves to irritate some therapists, many of whom cling to a sort of crackpot wisdom that says that disclosure is the only way out. Jonathan Shay, a VA psychiatrist, describes in *Achilles in Vietnam* a situation similar to what Elise saw. "During the early days of the current era of PTSD treatment, mental health professionals shared a folk belief that simply 'getting it all out' would result in safety, sobriety, and self-care. The consequences of these well-intended 'combat debriefings' were catastrophic, resulting in many suicides."

As an alternative to mainstream talk therapy, yoga stands out as a uniquely effective treatment, precisely because it insists that people shut up and start listening to their bodies. Yoga works to correct the central lie of Western philosophy, which goes all the way back to Descartes, who said that the body and the mind are distinct entities that exist independent of each other.

It is almost as if researchers have been talking to Elise: a number of recently completed studies, including one conducted by David

Emerson and Bessel van der Kolk at Harvard Medical School, have shown that yoga is very effective at reducing the hypervigilance and hyperarousal associated with PTSD. If you're familiar at all with yoga practice, it's not hard to imagine why. Yoga teaches mindfulness of breath, calmness, and connection to the rhythms of your body, allowing you to feel "at home" in it. All of these core practices serve to repair the damage done by trauma. As van der Kolk points out, "Neither CBT protocols nor psychodynamic therapeutic techniques pay sufficient attention to the experience and interpretation of disturbed physical sensations and preprogrammed physical action patterns."

One of the major long-term goals of any trauma therapy is to get survivors to change their perception of time, to focus less on the past and focus more on the present. Yoga seems to do this by encouraging you to focus on the "now" of your physical self, a form of nonthinking that might seem counterintuitive at first. Psychologist Mihaly Csikszentmihalyi describes this state as one of *flow,* arguing that "after an episode of flow is over, we generally emerge from it with a stronger self-concept . . . The musician feels at one with the harmony of the cosmos, the athlete moves at one with the team, the reader of the novel lives for a few hours in a different reality. Paradoxically, the self expands through acts of self-forgetfulness." (Several trauma survivors have told me that they found the focus on "being present," as described in Eckhart Tolle's *The Power of Now,* to be strikingly powerful for them. As Tolle argues in his book, "To be identified with your mind is to be trapped in time: the compulsion to live almost exclusively through memory and anticipation. This creates an endless preoccupation with past and future and an unwillingness to honor and acknowledge the present moment and *allow it to be.*")

Yoga is also, as Elise readily admits, ridiculous. There is nothing sillier than seeing a bunch of people standing around in a park twisted into enlightened pretzels, repeating words from a long-dead language. Yoga is moronic, which is part of what makes it so great. In the Marine Corps, we had a saying: "If it's stupid but it works, then it isn't stupid."

Personally, I plan on doing stupid, functional things like yoga for the rest of my life.

Anton Chekhov, who was a doctor as well as a writer, once observed that "if many remedies are prescribed for an illness you may be certain that the illness has no cure." There are many remedies recommended for post-traumatic stress, a truly bewildering variety of choices that can seem at times like a psychological supermarket. Some of these alternatives seem at first like applied common sense, while others seem more like applied hobbies, ideas that took root after someone found comfort in them and began recommending them to friends. Some of them sound suspiciously like religious cults. Many of these therapies exist on the margins of modern science and are only now being explored by researchers. One review of alternative therapies published in the VA's *PTSD Research Quarterly* in 2012 concluded that "the most striking finding overall is the relative lack of empirical evidence for CAM [Complementary and Alternative Medicines] for PTSD." Very few of these alternatives seem genuinely harmful or dangerous, except possibly to your bank account. The sheer number of them speaks to the magnitude of the problem, the inherent complexity of PTSD, and the extremes to which people will go to seek relief from their symptoms. With the growth in popularity of the PTSD diagnosis and mounting concern about the welfare of Iraq and Afghanistan veterans, alternative therapies are showing up everywhere these days.

One crowdsourced website I consulted, which maintains a regularly updated database of therapies for PTSD, lists seventy-nine such remedies, including acupuncture, art therapy, biofeedback, fish oil, gardening, hiking, hot tea, journaling, marijuana, MDMA, meditation, moving to a new city, Reiki, "using a clear shower curtain," vitamin C, vitamin D, walking, white noise, yoga, and zinc. Mingled with these curatives are a host of general lifestyle choices, such as getting exercise, eating well, enjoying nature, playing sports, going to church, and spending time with friends. In the course of researching this book, I crossed paths with advocates for boxing, cycling, horseback riding, in-line skating, mountaineering, Native American sweat lodges, rifle marksmanship, tai chi, and warm water therapy as post-trauma treatments. In 2011, a journalist friend of mine spent several weeks in Georgia interviewing members of a Christian group that performs exorcisms on traumatized people.

In Southern California, where the military and the West Coast self-improvement culture often overlap, a cottage industry of PTSD curatives has cropped up, with yoga practitioners, tai chi devotees, fitness professionals, and virtual reality researchers all advertising help for the traumatized. One mixed martial arts gym a few blocks from my house has a vets-only team whose organizers promoted its benefits for veterans with PTSD. At the beginning of my research, I ran into a retired couple in the mountains north of San Diego who were putting together a horse ranch for traumatized veterans. Perhaps the most entertaining remedy came from a man from Texas who touted the benefits of *Tetris,* claiming the classic video game helped him with his PTSD. In short, there is no shortage of ideas for PTSD therapies, nor is there a shortage of concerned citizens with advice for those who struggle with the condition.

In *Once a Warrior, Always a Warrior,* Charles Hoge, a retired army psychiatrist and the author of an influential PTSD study in the *New England Journal of Medicine,* writes, "There are numerous new modalities of treatment being promoted for PTSD, and treatments *du jour* seem to be constantly springing up as the latest 'answer' to the PTSD problem. A lot of interest has been generated by increased government funding for research for both these conditions since the start of the wars in Iraq and Afghanistan . . . Some of these have been promoted in news stories, and many veterans have questioned why the DoD and VA have not adopted them for regular use. The reason is that these modalities have not been proven to be effective in rigorous research studies." He concludes by saying, "The bottom line is that there is no 'magic bullet' for PTSD, and claims to the contrary should be taken with more than a grain of salt."

While I agree with Hoge about the absence of a magic bullet, my experience suggests that many nonstandard therapies have value, in part because they create what researchers call an expectancy effect, where the simple expectation of improvement communicated through the practitioner brings about healing. A guiding principle when shopping for therapies is that PTSD is an incredibly complex condition, and it manifests itself in people in a dizzying variety of ways. As the philosopher Roland Barthes wrote, "Each of us has his own rhythm of suffering." In addressing one's particular rhythm of suffering, one often must undergo a process similar to the one that Elise underwent, experimenting with different therapies, while paying close attention to your individual symptoms, eventually settling on the therapy (or therapies) that feels right for you.

Another reason to consider one of the many alternative therapies out there is that they often offer a host of positive, difficult-to-quantify social effects that are hard to find with traditional manualized therapies. For example, the idea of training people with PTSD to be cage fighters, as Iraq veteran Todd Vance is doing at the Undisputed gym in San Diego, seems ludicrous at first and potentially even damaging. What exactly, one might reasonably ask, is the point of exposing traumatized people to even more violence? For my part, I hated the hand-to-hand combat training I did in the Marine Corps and have long found the mixed martial arts subculture to be a parody of American hyperaggressive masculinity. But when I sat in on one of Vance's classes upstairs at Undisputed, I found my mind changing.

Watching a group of sweaty young vets working on various holds and groundfighting techniques, I saw that MMA does provide a structured social environment for young men (and women) and a way to achieve a state of flow where they can get out of their heads and focus on mastering a regimen of techniques, not entirely unlike yoga. Like yoga, MMA seems to offer a wealth of hard-to-quantify nonspecific therapeutic benefits of the sort that frequently drives researchers crazy when they compare PTSD treatment protocols. More to the point, yoga and MMA, as disparate as they might seem at first, both offer an opportunity to escape "the PTSD bubble," a chance to get out of the house and interact with people, while doing something that helps them create a greater knowledge about their bodies, a process that psychologists refer to as interoceptive learning.

In 2012, after finishing CPT, I took part in a VA study that examined mantram repetition as a PTSD therapy. The experiment, led by a nursing researcher, applied the teachings of Eknath Easwaran to the problems of post-traumatic stress. Easwaran, who was an English professor in India before he came to the United States in 1959 on a Fulbright scholarship, teaches that we all have inner resources for dealing with crises, and that by developing skills to cultivate an inner calm, we can transcend "the storms of life." The study used group therapy to introduce Easwaran's principles and took place in one of the outbuildings at VA La Jolla. For the first session, the six of us were given workbooks and copies of Easwaran's book *Strength in the Storm* and told to read a few chapters for the following week. Much like CPT (and Buddhist teachings), Easwaran's philosophy revolves around the idea that the world is a largely neutral place, and it is the human reaction to events that determines the outcome. As Easwaran wrote, "We can't control life, but we can control how we respond to life's challenges. The answer lies in stabilizing the mind."

For our next session, our leader, a kindly retired psychiatric nurse named Kathy, had us select a mantram from a list of ecumenical phrases ("mantram" is the correct conjugation of the Sanskrit, meaning "an instrument of thought"). I chose "Om Shanti," a Sanskrit invocation for peace. The idea, Kathy explained, was to repeat our mantram as many times as possible each day, especially during relaxing times at first. As time went by, the mantram would become a personal codeword for inner calm and could be used in times of stress or fear to disrupt the fight-or-flight response.

One of our group was a Marine I recognized from Iraq named Andy. Andy had, like Fernando, done seven overseas deployments since 9/11. "Forty-nine months I've been away from my family," he explained. As the group progressed, I found out that Andy and I had another thing in common: we were both members of an elite, little-known fraternity within U.S. military circles. We were both former Marines who surfed. Andy, however, was no chilled-out surf bro who'd worn a uniform between paddle outs (which was how an old company commander once described me). One look at him and you could tell he'd been down some bad roads. I had run into Andy at a small base west of Fallujah six years before, and I remembered him even then as unusually angry and short-fused. Toward the end of the eight-week study, he was surfing again and thinking about quitting his job, a job he didn't entirely need, and moving to a smaller house to shrink his mortgage.

The group ended a couple weeks later. The consensus was that while it was not a miracle, mantram repetition was helpful. For a variety of reasons, mantram repetition didn't really do it for me. I've always been restless and distractible by nature, and the idea of sitting in place and repeating the same three syllables over and over again for hours was, well, boring as shit. Reading for me is practically a biological function, and after about ninety seconds of saying "Om Shanti, Om Shanti, Om Shanti" in my apartment during my designated mantram times, my eyes would wander like heartsick lovers over to the nearest bookshelf, and before I knew it, my mind would be consumed by the plot of the latest Thomas Pynchon novel, not my mantram. Nevertheless, I was the only one in the group who didn't find mantram repetition helpful. Andy, in particular, said that it had helped him a lot. I'm inclined to believe his testimonial, since it's supported by the evidence of my observation. I'd seen him in Iraq, and he did seem slightly more at peace by the end of the eight-week study.

With a few notable exceptions, alternative therapies are informed by premodern, prescientific traditions. Yoga and mantram repetition are arguably even antiscientific, being mostly unconcerned with the mind-body divide, instead focusing on ways to connect these realms. If one starts with the idea that modern trauma begins with the railroad, electricity, and industrialization, it's not hard to see how these alternative therapies might work by putting us in touch with cultures and traditions that predate modern civilization. In that way, the charge leveled by Hoge and the VA is exactly correct, as alternative therapies tend to be more philosophy than science, standing in stark contrast to science, which works by isolating individual components in nature and subjecting them to experimentation. Elise's story is instructive: while I know that she's familiar with the workings of the amygdala and the hippocampus, the process that took her from being a haunted, hypervigilant young woman to who she is today had nothing to do with the miracles of modern neuroscience and was primarily concerned with reacquainting her with her breath and emotional processes, which have thus far eluded scientific scrutiny. Of course, simply because these healing and consciousness-centering traditions are older than the scientific method doesn't mean that they can't be tested by reasonably objective means.

Which, it turns out, is exactly what Jill Bormann, the organizer of the mantram repetition study, did. All of us were given a CAPS before and after the study. Bormann, whose results were published in April 2012, found that of the 146 veterans studied, 30 percent "no longer met the diagnostic criteria for PTSD, compared to only 14 percent in the standard care group." Now, admittedly, as a self-reported measure the CAPS is a very limited tool, but if Andy was any indication, mantram repetition appears to work. Importantly, unlike PE (and the new virtual reality exposure therapy, which uses video technology to achieve the same end state), mantram repetition and yoga are cheap, risk-free, and portable.

One therapy that has bridged the divide between alternative and mainstream is eye movement desensitization and reprocessing, or EMDR. EMDR was developed, or more accurately discovered, in 1987 by Francine Shapiro, a researcher in Palo Alto, and it works by stimulating both sides of the brain while activating memories of the trauma. The conceit behind EMDR is that trauma happens because the brain is so overloaded with information during the moment of maximum horror that it stops making memories in the normal way.

As Shapiro describes in her 1997 book, "The seed of EMDR sprouted one sunny afternoon in 1987, when I took a break to ramble around a small lake. It was spring. Ducks were paddling by, and bright blankets full of mothers and babies were laid out on wide green lawns. As I walked along, an odd thing happened. I had been thinking about something disturbing; I don't even remember what it was, just one of those nagging negative thoughts that the mind keeps chewing over (without digesting) until we forcibly stop it. The odd thing is that my nagging thought disappeared. On its own . . . I started to pay careful attention as I walked along. I noticed that when a disturbing thought entered my mind, my eyes spontaneously started moving back and forth. They were making rapid repetitive movements on a diagonal from lower left to upper right. At the same time, I noticed my disturbing thought had shifted from consciousness, and when I brought it back to mind, it no longer bothered me as much."

The therapy, which Shapiro has continued to articulate and develop since her day at the lake, is built on this basic principle of engaging disturbing memories while attempting to stimulate the different halves of the brain. Recent additions to the EMDR playbook include using other stimuli, like flashing lights, alternating sounds, and directed hand taps, all of which aim to aid the brain in information processing. From Hoge's perspective, EMDR and much of Shapiro's work suffer from what might be called the "magic bullet" fallacy, in that she consistently and often breathlessly describes it as "the breakthrough therapy" for a whole host of ills, claiming at one point that "84 to 90 percent of the people using EMDR—victims of rape, natural disaster, loss of a child, catastrophic illness or other traumas—have recovered from posttraumatic stress in only three sessions." This tincture of snake oil hasn't escaped the attention of VA-aligned researchers, and many of Shapiro's assertions remain disputed by neuroscientists, particularly the idea that eye movements help reprocess traumatic memories. Despite these criticisms and complaints about how EMDR is being marketed to the public, a number of studies have found that EMDR is effective for PTSD. Some studies that have tried to isolate the active ingredients in EMDR suggest that its effectiveness has little to do with eye movements and more to do with the fact that EMDR is generally "client-centered," allowing the patient to choose the manner and pace of the therapy.

Clint van Winkle, an Iraq vet who underwent EMDR in 2007, wrote in his memoir *Soft Spots* that "the therapist lets you control your thoughts, and only steps in if it gets too rough in your head. We're taking it slow, working our way into full-on war memories. When we get to that point, my neurotransmitters will be firing at the cyclic rate of a .50 cal . . . Why EMDR works, nobody really knows. Even practitioners have problems explaining the results they see in their patients. It's possible that the process of watching fingers move side to side evokes some sort of placebo effect where patients just think things are getting better, wishing so hard for positive results that they actually feel they have found one in EMDR. Placebo, wishful thinking, whatever. I'll take the help where I can get it."

EMDR exemplifies a recent trend in alternative therapies in taking a nugget of neuroscience and joining it with an anecdotal observation from real life to create something akin to a revolutionary cure. (Though a great deal of this inflation problem is the fault of the media, which has an awful habit of reporting virtually any emerging PTSD therapy as if it is the ultimate cure that will signal the end of human trauma as we know it. The *New York Post,* for example, in the days after 9/11 hailed EMDR as a "miracle cure." *Salon* and other media outlets ran similar coverage.) EMDR occupies a unique position in the world of PTSD in that while many leaders in the medical establishment find its theories kitschy and even silly, it has also been designated by the VA as an evidence-supported treatment, making it nominally on par with PE and CPT. Nevertheless, there remains a detectable skepticism toward EMDR within the VA and the research it sponsors. Tellingly, when I asked around the VA system in Southern California (I called VA San Diego and VA Long Beach), I was told that EMDR was not available, nor were there plans to make it available any time soon.

Obviously, we have much more to learn about the relationship of trauma to the brain, body, and spirit, and it would be a mistake to lean too heavily on any one type of therapy or on any one type of study. It would also be a mistake to assume that hearing the phrase "evidence-supported" before a given therapy means that it will work for you. "Evidence-supported" and "evidence-based" mostly mean that a lot of doctors happen to like it, oftentimes for reasons that have less to do with the actual value of a therapeutic protocol than with trendiness. And it's worth remembering that, for a period of time, a lot of doctors liked the lobotomy as a post-traumatic treatment and inflicted that procedure on thousands of veterans during the 1940s. Indeed, the technique was so well liked that its inventor, Egaz Moniz, was awarded the Nobel Prize in medicine in 1949.

What is most striking about how therapies are developed and

implemented in PTSD-land today is how rarely one actually hears what patients think about it all. Perusing the technical literature of trauma, one almost never reads a patient's individual account of a protocol they're undergoing. If they're mentioned at all, they're spoken of as "subjects" or "female sexual assault victims" or, most often, merely as numbers, as $n=246$.

To be fair, this is how science is done — that is to say, impartially and clinically — and one can quite easily find testimonials for PE and CPT on the VA website and on YouTube, but they are just that: testimonials delivered by, you'll forgive me, shills for the VA. There doesn't seem to be any conspiracy at work here, just an assumption on the part of the psychiatric establishment that they know what's best for their patients. In fact, the only consumer-type ratings of PTSD therapies by patients I've ever found were unscientific surveys conducted by third-party groups with their own goods to market at me.

The abuse of power by psychiatrists is a fraught subject, ground that has been well tilled by the likes of Michel Foucault, Edward Szasz, R. D. Laing, and many others. I won't attempt to rework that soil here except to say that it is exceedingly odd that virtually all the post-trauma therapies in use today were invented, refined, and implemented by American academics, far removed from the battlefield, far removed from the streets of Detroit or Mogadishu. Whenever survivors' views are included in the policymaking process, it is inevitably well after the major decisions have been made and the clinical die cast. In shamanic societies, which represent some of the world's oldest healing traditions, healers were often trauma survivors themselves. Wisdom was presumed to flow from the experience of surviving into the healer's thought process. In the West today, the opposite is true. It is the most protected, the most insulated, the most innocent who are presumed to be the most knowledgeable about loss, terror, and moral chaos. Trauma workers today are schooled to look at survivors through the cold lens of modern medical pathology, adopting the same moral framework and the same lexicon that are used to treat malaria and measles.

Chatting with Elise one day about this, she told me that she had seriously considered becoming a psychologist, but she abandoned that prospect because "clinical psychologists are just that. *Clinical.*"

Many people have asked me if writing this book has helped me with my own post-traumatic stress. Generally speaking, I hate the idea of turning writing into therapy, and I did not conceive of this book as a therapeutic project, but delving into the history and literature of PTSD has, in fact, been extraordinarily useful. Writing about it has been difficult at times, but it has shown me unexpected facets of my own past. Using writing as therapy is a tricky business because it can so easily turn into an orgy of self-pity and navel-gazing. As Alice Sebold said, "My feeling is that therapy is for therapy and that writing can be therapeutic, but therapeutic writing should not be published." Still, the process of writing, of trying to capture your experiences on the page, however skilled or unskilled you may be, can be extremely helpful, allowing you to see patterns in your life that were invisible before. It can also be incredibly cathartic.

It was Ford Madox Ford who wrote, "You may well ask why I write. And yet my reasons are quite many. For it is not unusual in human beings who have witnessed the sack of a city or the falling to pieces of a people to desire to set down what they have witnessed for the benefit of unknown heirs or of generations infinitely remote; or, if you please, just to get the sight out of their heads."

Trauma destroys the normal narrative of life, and trying to put the pieces together into a story is, in many ways, the ultimate act of healing, the way we know that a certain perspective has been achieved. Some artificial intelligence researchers even think that this ability to create and learn from stories is what ultimately divides us from machines. One Iraq veteran I spoke to, who refuses to do traditional talk therapy but maintains an online blog, told me, "EMDR helped a little bit but there was a phase I went through where I just didn't want to let go of the memories, I didn't know how to describe it, really, but I was afraid I would forget, so I tried to write it down. Writing has been great because I'm not saying it, I'm writing it and by writing it out, I've been able to say things in the blog that I've never said out loud to people. It's easier because it's a bunch of people that

I can't see. I don't have to see them every day. I just said to myself, 'I'm gonna get it up, and then it'll be out of my head.'"

I can't say that writing has ever helped me put something out of my head, in the way it did for Ford Madox Ford, but it has helped me to better understand my life. Writing is a form of concentrated thinking, a type of directed meditation, and it can serve as a powerful way of reclaiming and asserting control over one's past, of locating and processing emotions in a way that risks no embarrassment or shame. The act of writing, especially of putting pen to paper, has always had a sacred quality. The process by which one creates a paragraph—of conceptualizing, framing, and sequencing a moment in time—is the same process that governs some of the most sophisticated psychotherapies.

Timothy Wilson, a psychologist at the University of Virginia, argues for something similar to this in his book *Strangers to Ourselves.* Wilson thinks emotional learning takes place when we step back and look at our lives almost as a literary critic might, placing each incident in the larger sweep of narrative. Wilson writes that "the point is that we should not analyze the information [about our feelings] in an overly deliberate, conscious manner, constantly making explicit lists of pluses and minuses. We should let our adaptive unconscious do the job of finding reliable feelings and then trust those feelings, even if we cannot explain them entirely."

One of my personal favorite therapies for combat PTSD comes from New Zealand. An ancient tradition within Polynesian cultures, the *haka* was originally an ancestral war cry performed before battle. Designed to intimidate the enemy, in recent times the rite has been adopted by Kiwi sports teams like the "All Blacks" rugby squad as well as by the Royal New Zealand Infantry Regiment. The regimental *haka* is performed at a number of ceremonial occasions, including funeral services, sometimes beginning as the casket of a fallen soldier is borne toward the gravesite. The dance, as it is typically interpreted, involves making a set of intense facial gestures, slapping the thighs, and stomping the feet, all while yelling a fierce Maori war cry. Sometimes, a new chant will be written by a member of the regiment to commemorate the end of a long deployment or the return of a unit from combat.

As a tool to aid the work of mourning, the *haka* seems incredibly powerful and cathartic to me. The footage I've seen of the regimental *haka* is beautiful and moving. I have never been to New Zealand, but the literature on the ritual suggests that it allows people to honor the dead in a dramatic and emotionally resonant manner that provides a kind of closure and marks the passage from the realm of war to the realm of peace. In North America, we have no rituals governing the return of warriors from battle, nor do we have any traditions to guide survivors of trauma back into society. Instead, we leave them in a state of liminality, home from the horror but in body only, and sometimes not even that. This perhaps helps explain why the PTSD diagnosis is so popular—it's a medical concept that serves (however crudely) a deeper mythic need.

Rituals are difficult to invent, and invented rituals are nearly impossible to pull off with any kind of authenticity. Still, it can be done. In the mid-nineties, a group of clinicians at the VA in West Haven, Connecticut, led by David Read Johnson, began experimenting with rituals as therapy. The technique involved a symbolic reenactment of the departure of the veterans from the family with a series of church-like call-and-response readings. A subsequent ceremony to honor the dead involved the veterans, families, and the VA staff. According to a paper published by Johnson in the *Journal of Traumatic Stress,* the response by veterans and their families was very positive, with all of the family members who attended rating it as "extremely helpful."

Sometimes I think that half of combat PTSD in America would disappear overnight if we required citizens to take a more active role in both war-making and welcoming warriors home. If there's a national security measure we need to pass, maybe it's one that forces citizens to be directly involved in the war effort, either by reinstating the draft or by making VA employment a form of national service. I firmly believe that the lack of ritual and authentic public engagement in the war-making process is a major cause of PTSD and, paradoxically, a justification for it as a diagnostic category. One unusually thoughtful therapist I interviewed went so far as to describe the advent of PTSD as a kind of *mitzvah* by Americans for veterans, a way of making amends for all the wars we send them to.

The industrialization of war is a relatively new phenomenon, and no other country sends as many men and women overseas to kill as we do. No other people in history has sent as many as far away with as little sacrifice demanded of the average citizen as we do. No other people in history is as disconnected from the brutality of war as the United States today. Were the truth of war to become apparent to Americans, we wouldn't continue to train, equip, and deploy warriors the way we do. Nor would we ask them when they came home if they killed anyone.

9

GROWTH

THE CLOSEST Steve House has come to the other side, the time when death was most imminent, wasn't the time he climbed K7, a fearsome 22,770-foot peak in Pakistan's Karakoram Range, alone with a pack that weighed just seven pounds, nor was it the time when he and two other climbers got lost halfway up Denali with no tent, sleeping bags, or other overnight gear. Rather, it was on the north face of Mount Temple, a minor peak in Canada's Banff National Park that is regularly climbed by tourists using a popular foot trail. In 2010, House was leading a route up the 11,627-foot mountain when a piece of rock came loose beneath him. "As I fell, I was relaxed at first. A flake had broken, not all that unexpected considering the incredibly bad rock quality on Mount Temple. Then the [protective] gear started pinging out of the partially decomposed limestone. One . . . two . . . three . . . four . . . the fifth piece, a large cam in a solid, but flaring, pocket of rock almost held me. But it too ripped as the rope started to slow my descent. The sudden jolting free-fall flipped me upside down and I crashed my right side into something hard, something painful, and was spun around again when I finally came to a stop half-sideways eighty feet lower than where I'd started."

As House later explained, "I was on a sloping snow ledge with Bruce [his partner, Bruce Miller] just twenty-five feet to my right. What probably held me was a groove in a snow-mushroom that I'd stamped out with a boot."

One of the world's premier alpinists, House knew better than most that the mountains possess a unique ability to foil even the best-laid plans, transforming the most casual outing into a catalogue of horrors, but to die like this would be absurd. Assessing the situation, he quickly discovered that he'd broken several ribs, his pelvis, and was having trouble breathing. Between clenched breaths, he called over to Miller and told him to get out his cell phone and see if he could call 911. Deep down, House knew that he was in trouble. He figured that a rescue helicopter could probably get close to where he was, but the clock was ticking. "My chest hurt like hell and I knew I didn't have all day. I couldn't really move, so if the pilot came in and wasn't able to get to me, I knew that I was going to die."

As it happens, Steve House is my cousin. Growing up, our families spent summers backpacking together in the mountains of Eastern Oregon. My cousin "Stevie" had always been strong and a committed athlete, but something seemed to happen after he graduated from high school and went off to college. His junior year at Evergreen State, he decided to study abroad in Slovenia, immersing himself in the vibrant climbing club culture there, eventually taking part in several major climbs, including an ascent of Triglav, Slovenia's highest peak.

When I finally caught up with him years later, it was like the story they used to tell about bluesman Robert Johnson going out to the crossroads and making a deal with the devil, trading his soul for mastery of the guitar. Steve wasn't "Stevie" anymore, nor was he a mere mortal once his feet touched granite. During the years I was sweating my way up the hills of Camp Pendleton, Steve was working his way up the loftiest peaks of the Himalayas and steadily rising in mountaineering's ranks as a leading proponent of a "fast and light" school of climbing, a philosophy that held that the less gear carried, the better. A man held in awe by the best in the sport, during the 1990s, other climbers began half-jokingly referring to him as the "Great White Hope" of North American alpinism.

House's crowning achievement came in September 2005, when he and his partner Vince Anderson scaled Nanga Parbat, the world's ninth highest mountain, via the Rupal Face, an imposing and famously deadly formation considered to be the largest mountain wall in the world. Unencumbered by the heavy loads most climbers carry, the two battled up the mountain's snowy face in a little over six days. The ascent, completed without the aid of a support crew or supplemental oxygen, won the pair the Piolet d'Or, mountaineering's highest honor. Describing his time on the summit, House said, "The only thing I can compare it to is being on the moon. You look out and the sky isn't blue anymore, it's black because you're so high up. You can see the curve of the earth. You look down and you can see thunderstorms happening ten thousand feet *below* you. We hadn't spoken to anyone else in almost a week. It felt like we were the only two people in the world."

While House considers the ascent of Nanga Parbat to be his greatest accomplishment, it was his accident on Mount Temple that would prove to be the greater turning point in his life. Talking about it years later, it was as if the peaks represented the two crucibles of his life: one was a pinnacle of outward achievement and social recognition, the other a dark buttress of fear and regret.

Trapped on the flank of Mount Temple and in great pain, House began to take stock of his situation. He could tell he'd broken some ribs. Breathing was difficult. It was all he could do to take "tiny, shallow baby breaths." He couldn't move. After yelling at Miller to call 911, House spent the next ten minutes trying to crawl toward him. Eventually, he was able to reach his partner but not before his right lung collapsed. Fortunately, help was on the way: a helicopter was being dispatched from nearby Canmore, though it would be a while before the rescue wardens, who were located in the town of Banff, were assembled and loaded onto the aircraft. As he explained to me years later, "The most traumatic thing, the thing I think about the most is lying there, waiting on that ledge for the helicopter."

As W. H. R. Rivers noted shortly after World War I, immobility, powerlessness in the face of death, is often what most vexes the psyche. House was on the ledge for a long time. Looking back on it, he recalls the hours trapped on that tiny shelf of snow and ice as a time of life-altering insight. Mulling the prospect of his own demise, he began to take stock of his life, noting patterns that had seemingly been invisible before, hidden by the daily rush of events.

For most of his adult life, he had lived by the simplest of codes: to climb the greatest mountains in the world with as little baggage as possible, stripping everything away until only the absolute essentials remained—the climber, the mountain, and a few pieces of gear. It was an ethos, he saw, that had come to dominate his personal life as well, a simple unwillingness to allow either his own feelings or other "flatland" concerns to get in the way of the summit. In his zeal to climb, to explore the radical topography of the heights, to take part in what British mountaineer George Mallory called the "struggle of life itself upward and forever upward," he had neglected the life below. "On the ledge, when I thought back on my life and all the climbing I'd done, I felt really good about that. I hadn't done everything I wanted to, certainly, but I realized that I had done a lot and I was pretty happy about that. But there were other parts of my life where I saw that I hadn't done everything I wanted to. I realized that the relationship I was in was not what I wanted. I knew it wasn't healthy. And I thought about my sister and my family and I realized that I never really felt like I had been part of a family since I left home to go to college. So I was like, yeah, I want to have that, I want to be a part of nurturing a family of my own and seeing it through."

On the ledge, House began thinking about his climbing career as well. "After Nanga Parbat, part of me was just *done.* And it's hard because climbing as a sport doesn't really have a way to retire. It doesn't have that model. It's not competitive like cycling or other sports, so most climbers, as they get older, don't really retire, they just climb until they can't walk anymore and that's partly what's beautiful about it but I realized that I had been banging my head against the wall trying to recapture the feeling I had gotten from Nanga and no climb was going to give me that."

Finally, after two hours on the side of the mountain, the rescue helicopter arrived. After a quick survey of the scene, the helicopter drew closer and lowered a rescue warden. Dangling at the end of a line was a mountaineer House had climbed with a few years before. "Hey, Steve, it's Steve Holeczi, everything's gonna be okay," he said.

"When he called out to me like that, I felt this huge wave of relief. I knew I was going to be okay." A few hours later, House was in a hospital in Banff. A week after that, he was flown to a hospital near his home in Central Oregon. It would take months of physical therapy, but eventually he would begin climbing again. During his recovery, he kept a journal, as he did on all of his expeditions, trying to make sense out of what had happened. "It was hard when I was on painkillers and most of my journal entries were like two and a half sentences long."

Ruminating for months, House saw that his life had been changed. "The accident basically recalibrated everything about my life," he told me. "It recalibrated my value system. I felt like, 'Okay, this huge thing happened and rather than fight it, I'm gonna let it change my life, in fact, I'm gonna *help* it change my life. I'm gonna use the momentum of this event to fix things that I think are wrong and try to create things that will take me in a better direction.'"

In the wake of the accident, Steve House embarked on what amounted to a new life. After a long, painful process, he ended his relationship with his long-time girlfriend and relocated to Colorado, a move his climbing partner Vince Anderson had been urging for years. Shortly after arriving in Colorado, he met and fell in love with an Austrian woman. "That was one thing that took me by surprise," he confessed. "Eva was the perfect thing to come into my life, but I didn't expect her so quickly! I felt like I made the space for that inside, I understood what it was that I wanted and needed and she appeared almost instantly, within weeks. That was very reaffirming. I felt like okay, I made the right choice."

In 2011, the two were married on a gorgeous stretch of the Oregon coast. A year later, he and Eva founded Alpine Mentors, a nonprofit organization that helps train aspiring alpinists, based on the European apprenticeship model that House had experienced in Slovenia. Inspired by the alpine club culture he'd seen and the older climbers who took notice of him when he was an up-and-coming alpinist, he looks at the group as his way of giving back to the climbing community. "It's less about the trips that we take than about the relationships we help create," he explains. Climbing remains the organizing principle of his life—as he puts it, "I still believe in climbing. I still believe that mountaineering is an incredible way to know yourself"—but House's career has more of a service orientation to it now, in marked contrast to his earlier years as a climber, almost as if he has reached the end of one ambition and taken on another.

The idea that positive change can come from suffering is not new. Humans have long been inspired by the notion that greater perspective, even transcendence, can result from loss and privation. The Caribou shaman Igjugarjuk once said, "All true wisdom is only to be learned far from the dwellings of men, out in the great solitudes; and is only to be attained through suffering. Privation and suffering are the only things that can open the mind of man to those things which are hidden from others." A number of world religions are built upon this idea. The core principle of Buddhism is that suffering is at the heart of human existence, a fact embodied by its founder, Siddhartha Gautama, a Nepalese prince who renounced wealth and comfort in order to seek enlightenment. Could he have found enlightenment by some other, less painful method? Perhaps. But there is something about intense suffering and rising above, even repudiating, the needs of the body that can lead to a heightened state of awareness. The philosophy of the ancient world is similarly rife with thinkers who saw misfortune as one of nature's great teachers. Epictetus, the first-century Stoic philosopher and onetime slave, advised, "On the occasion of every accident that befalls you, remember to turn to yourself and inquire what power you have for turning it to use."

Across the ages, societies have looked to the mystic wanderer or the prophetic martyr who emerges from the desert or the prison cell for their deepest moral insights. The list of wisdom-bearing sufferers is so long and consistent across time as to constitute an archetype. The life stories of Moses, Jesus, Mohammed, Gandhi, T. E. Lawrence, Martin Luther King Jr., and Nelson Mandela are all built around this theme. Joseph Campbell, in his influential tome *The Hero with a Thousand Faces,* created a vast world-encompassing theory of human myth based on this idea of a hero being drawn into the wilderness, stripped of his worldly accoutrements, transformed, and then, finally, returned to society as a wise champion. More recently, novelist Ha Jin, reflecting on this daunting theme of wisdom wrought by pain, wrote, "Some great men and women are fortified and redeemed through their suffering, and they even seek sadness instead of happiness, just as Van Gogh asserted, 'Sorrow is better than joy,' and Balzac declared, 'Suffering is one's teacher.' But these dicta are suitable only for extraordinary souls, the select few. For ordinary people like us, too much suffering can only make us meaner, crazier, pettier, and more wretched."

Of course, there are as many different responses to suffering as there are people in the world, but as the PTSD diagnosis has continued to grow in popularity, researchers have started searching for new ways to look at trauma apart from the simplistic "you have been scarred for life" mindset that seemed to be the prevailing sentiment of the Vietnam era. Indeed, some Vietnam vets have complained to me about this phenomenon, saying that they resent the presumption of psychological damage being connected with their military service. Elliott Woods, an Iraq veteran turned reporter, echoed this sentiment, saying, "It feels to me as if the U.S. civilian population has pathologized the veteran experience." In a 2014 speech, James Mattis, an outspoken retired four-star general who is something of a cult figure among Marines, went so far as to say that "there is a misperception of our veterans out there, that they are somehow damaged goods." Mattis said, "I don't buy it."

Perhaps the most radical of these reformulators is Richard Tedeschi, a psychologist at the University of North Carolina, Charlotte. In the early nineties, Tedeschi was looking for a new line of research. "I thought, who do I want to know the most about, distressed or violent or crazy people?" he explained. "Instead, I think I want to know the most about wise people. Perhaps I'll learn something myself." Along with his research partner at UNC Charlotte, Lawrence Calhoun, he began interviewing people who had suffered from severe physical injuries, including a number of people who had been paralyzed in car accidents. After that, the two interviewed senior citizens who had lost their spouses. In case after case, they found that while the person regretted the loss of their mobility or their spouse, the experience had altered them for the better and given them a fresh perspective on life.

After a follow-up study of hundreds of trauma survivors, Tedeschi was able to boil these positive developments down to three general "domains": a changed perception of the self, a changed sense of one's social relations, and a changed philosophy of life. As Tedeschi wrote, "It is in the realm of existential, and for some persons, of spiritual or religious matters that the most significant post-traumatic growth may be experienced." In 1995, Tedeschi and Calhoun published their first book on the subject, titled *Trauma and Transformation*, coining the term for which they are now synonymous: post-traumatic growth. The following year, they published what amounts to a sunnier, more upbeat twin of the CAPS, the post-traumatic growth inventory. Tedeschi's research has led him to a stunning conclusion: post-traumatic growth is far more common than post-traumatic stress.

Perhaps unsurprisingly, Tedeschi's research has not been embraced by the PTSD community. One senior VA psychiatrist I spoke to scoffed at the idea of post-traumatic growth, calling it an insult to people who have suffered. Some researchers question whether post-traumatic growth is a real, observable phenomenon. "I have no doubt that there are people, perhaps many people, who do change in positive ways, but we are not able to measure it," said Howard Tennen, a professor of community medicine and health care at the University of Connecticut.

The fact that some of the most experienced trauma workers are skeptical of post-traumatic growth as a clinical concept isn't terribly shocking. Part of the undisguised disgust I encountered was no doubt due to the fact that the idea of telling someone that trauma might actually be *good* for them seems morally outrageous. The term itself, post-traumatic growth, is problematic; replacing "stress disorder" with "growth" makes it almost seem that it is being offered as a kind of alternative to PTSD, as if there were some sort of choice to be made. These questions of framing all highlight the degree to which psychiatry and the Western scientific mindset are limited by their own preconceptions. Science and psychiatry like to market themselves as being open to any proposition, but ultimately, the ideas that are the most likely to gain currency are those that can be easily isolated and measured. In that environment, the idea of testing for something as nebulous as personal "growth" would seem to be a fool's errand.

The other reality that virtually no one within the VA likes to talk about is that the PTSD community today is essentially a special interest group within medicine and the federal government. Every year, billions of dollars are earmarked for PTSD research, treatment, and disability payments, and the idea that people stand to benefit from being blown up, shot at, or raped threatens to undermine the entire moral argument—and financial support—for PTSD. For its part, the VA and the military seem to have adopted a wait-and-see approach to the idea of post-traumatic growth. Tedeschi is one of a handful of researchers looking into post-traumatic growth, and the body of research relating to it is puny compared to PTSD. But the VA isn't exactly closed off to the concept, either. As Matthew Friedman, the recently retired executive director of the National Center for PTSD, told me, "PTSD and post-traumatic growth aren't mutually exclusive. They can both happen at the same time."

Recent research confirms Friedman's contention. In 2007, Zahava Solomon, an Israeli psychiatrist, surveyed 103 former POWs from the Yom Kippur War and found that while 23 percent of them still met the criteria for PTSD thirty-four years later, virtually all of them reported significant growth using Tedeschi's scale. According to Solomon, "Posttraumatic stress disorder is not necessarily indicative of an absence of psychological growth and maturation. These two different types of outcome cannot, therefore, be conceptualized as two ends of the same continuum; they are not necessarily characteristic of two different types of individuals."

Steve House is a good example of Solomon's point. When I asked him what he thought about PTSD, he admitted that he had no idea what it was exactly. But he also told me that he continued to have distressing dreams about waiting on the ledge for the rescue helicopter to arrive, so it's possible that by the standard definition, he might have been diagnosable, but overall, he seemed far more interested in learning and physically recovering from his accident than dwelling on the symptoms of PTSD. In that way, House seems to serve as an exemplar of recovery. What saved him was his willingness to engage his inner resources, to stop and consider the fundamentals of his life, and then, perhaps most importantly, to take action. As Ben Shephard, a British historian of psychiatry and sometime critic of PTSD, wrote, "A job and a relationship can work wonders."

Paradoxically, Solomon and other researchers have also discovered that the more severe the trauma, the more likely the survivor is to report that they have benefited from the experience. In study after study, former long-term political prisoners and prisoners of war, when compared against regular combat veterans or single-event trauma survivors, reported more positive outcomes from their experience. In one study of U.S. Air Force POWs from the Vietnam War conducted by researchers at Yale, fully 61 percent of those surveyed felt the experience had been in some way beneficial. The Yale researchers were "impressed by the number of prisoners of war of the Vietnam war who explicitly claimed that although their captivity was extraordinarily stressful — filled with torture, disease, malnutrition, and solitary confinement — they nevertheless . . . benefitted from the captivity experience, seeing it as a growth experience."

Dennis Charney, a professor of psychiatry and neuroscience at Mount Sinai, studied American prisoners of war who did not, despite the traumas they endured, develop PTSD, and he identified a number of critical psychological elements that led to their resilience: altruism, having a solid moral compass, spiritual faith, having a role model, social support, confronting one's fears, and seeing oneself as having a mission in life. The key predictor of who would bounce back from the ordeal and who would not was a sense of optimism. One study of Vietnam War ex-POWs even found that optimism or the lack thereof was more important than the nature of the trauma itself. Holocaust survivor Viktor Frankl, in his classic book *Man's Search for Meaning,* argues for something similar, for what he calls a kind of "tragic optimism" based on a determination to "say yes to life in spite of everything," arguing that "life is potentially meaningful under any circumstances, even those which are the most miserable."*

The problem with all of these examples is that they are extreme cases: House is an elite mountaineer and arguably one of the more resilient people on the planet, while most of the Vietnam War POWs were highly trained, college-educated aviators. Likewise, Viktor Frankl was a highly unusual man who, after the Nazis occupied Austria, refused an American visa in order to remain with his parents in Vienna. (As one psychiatrist I spoke to pointed out, Frankl also took his doctoral dissertation with him to Auschwitz in order to work on it during his imprisonment, an unusual choice by any standard.) In fact, a substantial portion of the post-traumatic growth literature is derived from studies of exceptional populations, like the American POWs from Vietnam and other POW cohorts.

And, in truth, the literature on post-traumatic growth seems to suffer from a kind of inspirational "magic bullet" fallacy, a selection bias in choosing the most transcendent anecdotes from the hundreds of interviews conducted. Tedeschi, for instance, was quoted in a *New York Times Magazine* article describing a patient whose helicopter was shot down in Vietnam. "As he fell from the sky in the midst of gunfire and explosions, a peace came over him. He saw the jungle around him, and it was beautiful. He felt connected to everyone, even enemy soldiers."

What is this other than a kind of religious experience, an epiphany?

Later in the article, Tedeschi seems to concede this. "Maybe that was all an illusion," he said. "But that became a guideline for his life, so I don't think you can dismiss it."

Like a lot of old-school PTSD types, I was deeply skeptical when I first heard the term "post-traumatic growth." It seemed like a classic example of what Europeans often say about American culture—that

---

* Some research has suggested that these survivors' success in the face of trauma is related to the abundance of a brain chemical known as neuropeptide Y, though the cause-and-effect relationship remains unclear: does neuropeptide Y lead to resilience or do resilient people simply have more of it?

over and over again, we are commanded to smile, to be happy and optimistic, no matter the circumstances. As a rule, I am suspicious of people who think a positive mental attitude is the cure for all ills. It was a similar unrealistic optimism that led many to think Jeffersonian democracy would flourish in Iraq after the American "liberation." But thinking about House's response to his accident, I wonder if we often fail to consider the opportunities for positive change and wisdom-making that trauma grants us. I wonder if, on a certain level, post-traumatic stress suffers from a kind of storytelling problem within the culture. If society expects veterans, rape victims, and other survivors to be broken, doesn't PTSD become a kind of self-fulfilling prophecy? Is it possible that the mythology of the condition is still too heavily influenced by the memory of the Vietnam War, a war whose veterans were often looked upon as being somehow morally compromised?

Looking back on my experiences in the VA, there were only a very few occasions where any sort of growth-oriented thinking was encouraged. Never was I invited to think of how my experiences might be converted into a kind of wisdom or moral insight. When I did so on my own initiative, I was admonished for "intellectualizing" and for straying from the strictures of the therapeutic regime. Instead, I was encouraged to focus on my symptoms, to think about how to correct my various misperceptions so as to become more normal.

Whatever the shortcomings of his research, Tedeschi makes a good point. If we, as people, can't find something redeeming in war and other disasters, where can we find it? The problem might, in fact, relate to how the academic disciplines are organized today. Psychiatry and clinical psychology are simply not equipped to explore the kinds of questions Tedeschi raises. Psychiatry, clinical psychology, and the neurosciences focus on disease, not personal growth. It was this limitation that drove psychologists like Martin Seligman and Mihaly Csikszentmihalyi to begin exploring the more positive aspects of human psychology, like the psychology of creativity and what Csikszentmihalyi called "flow," or the *autotelic* state, which it turns out fits quite nicely into a number of alternative trauma therapies. As it stands now, however, far more resources are directed at addressing the negative aspects of trauma than exploring the possible opportunities for insight. As Tedeschi himself admits, most post-traumatic growth seems to be spiritual and philosophical in nature.

Despite all this, I think survivors like House and the Hanoi Hilton POWs can offer practical, secular lessons on managing post-traumatic stress. Talking to Steve, I was struck by his impulse to embrace the accident as an opportunity to change his life. As he put it, he didn't just *let* it change his life, he *helped* it change his life. He took advantage of its momentum to take him to a different place, as Epictetus might have suggested. There was also an element of being prepared to see the need for change as well. Like a lot of mountaineers, House is an unusually thoughtful and circumspect person who has been forced by the exigencies of long expeditions to pay close attention to his emotions. In other words, he knew himself, even before the accident happened. He always took a stack of books and a journal with him on expeditions for the inevitable tentbound days at base camp, which helped expand his store of self-knowledge. After his fall, he took an active role in his own recovery, deciding to go off painkillers to assess the extent of his injuries and then, when he was ready, to begin climbing again. He sought—and found—patterns in his life.

Similarly, the POWs that Zahava Solomon and others studied showed a capacity to adjust their internal emotional state and coping skills to different situations. They learned to look for things they could control within their environment. When they found those things, they exploited them. James Stockdale, one of the ranking POWs at the Hanoi Hilton, recalled the wisdom of Epictetus while he was in captivity, writing that "I remembered the basic truth of subjective consciousness as the ability to distinguish what is in my power from that which is not."

Did I grow because of Iraq? I grew and I shrank. Parts of my mind that I didn't know existed before appeared. It was like waking up and noticing that someone has built a new addition onto your house during the night. I stepped into it and enjoyed the new space. But the other, older parts of the house looked different than they had before. Changed. With a darker coat of paint. I had to learn the new layout.

The war was awful, but it was like a refuge from real life in a lot of ways. Certain things were harder over there, but certain things were easier. In death's lengthening shadow, your life shrinks down to a few, very important concerns. Like a leaf held up to the light, you see life as a series of branching veins. A lot of ridiculous demands and expectations that drive people crazy stateside don't exist in a war. You don't have to worry about how you look, for instance. Fretting over the kind of car you drive seems like the height of folly. In a strange way, you are free. The only thing you can lose is your life.

Living out of a backpack for months, I learned that I didn't need very much to be happy. I learned that most people waste their lives obsessing over consumer items that serve no real purpose. Once I was back in the world, this focus, this streamlining of life's priorities, gave me a new confidence. I carried myself differently, more assertively. There was a new faith, derived from a simple declarative statement that echoed in moments of pain and crisis: *Well, this sucks, but it's better than Ramadi.* I also learned how to ignore things that were beyond my control, like death.

But the war also gave me knowledge that I don't know how to live with. It taught me that the world is a dangerous place. That death is random. That governments lie as a matter of course. That time is elastic. That terror is relative. That truth is local, tribal even. That what is true in Baghdad isn't necessarily true in Ramadi. That what is true in Basra is almost never true in Ramadi. That things only seem absolutely true in Washington. That the closer you get to death, the harder it is to know anything for sure. The war was another world. A lot of things that happened there only made sense there. A lot of things that happened there made no sense at all, but they happened anyway.

Was this growth or just too much information?

The war gave me a kind of maturity, but it made me a child again. When I got back, there were simple human moments that I realized the war had taught me how to see again. Basic sights overlooked by people who had never almost died or walked through a destroyed city. My eyes seemed to work differently. They were hungrier, more sensitive to beauty. Flying over Greenland on my way back in 2004, I saw the glaciers, melting and wondrous and reflecting seven kinds of white, and cried. Before the war, I would have told myself it was only scenery. I became a watcher of night skies, of cloud formations, of shooting stars. The world had a music I'd forgotten how to hear. Whatever secret harbor of wonder, of childlike yearning for the sights of the world, that drains away as we grow up, had been filled again.

Then, just like that, the whole thing would flip, somebody would say something callous or ignorant, and I'd be angry again. Angry at the direction the world had taken. Angry at how stupid people were. How everyone seemed to have accepted the war, the wasteful, mammoth injustice of it, with a shrug.

Did being made crazy by this fact mean that I was actually going crazy?

I stewed on this for months. Was I mad or wise? Was this loss or insight? Stress or growth? In 2004, these were difficult questions to answer. Ten years later, I still don't have the answers.

Years before, in my youth, a friend asked me a question that I've never been able to shake. It was on Okinawa when we were lieutenants, full of ourselves, confident and feral. We were all so strong, and we knew nothing could kill us. At most of the parties on-island, I was among the quietest and most aloof. Others would be drinking and dancing, shouting nicknames at each other. I would be off in a corner, dabbling in unauthorized ideas with a friend who'd gone to Penn State. One night at the Kadena officers club, a classmate whom I hadn't seen in years appeared beside me.

At Texas A&M, Jon had been a model cadet and was my perfect foil: a leader where I had always been a misfit. He and I had both been on the freshman drill team, a unit that began every practice with everyone doing a thousand sit-ups in sets of a hundred beneath an upperclassmen's dorm window. At the end of fall semester, I quit the team and Jon had gone on and distinguished himself, eventually being invited back as a coach his sophomore year. Our senior year, he had commanded the honor guard for the governor, a position that came with privileges and a stipend. He was one of a pack of young men who held all the top billets in the Corps of Cadets, guys who ran around campus from activity to activity, already fully vested in life at nineteen. Fated to run the world, or at least a sizeable chunk of it, his luck had changed at Quantico.

During a live-fire exercise in the woods, there had been some confusion, and another lieutenant had shot him by accident between the shoulder blades. The bullet, on its journey through his body, a journey that I think of sometimes as a kind of odyssey, had taken a nasty turn, ricocheting off his collar bone, zigzagging through his neck, eventually exiting his cheek, leaving a long, brutal scar across his face. I hadn't seen him in years and assumed that after the accident he'd left the Corps.

Needless to say, Jon had changed. At A&M, he'd been top of the heap, and he knew it. Cocky and with a hint of cruelty that is often the mark of the professional military man, he had never been a close friend. The man before me now seemed softened, chastened. After catching up for a few minutes, he asked me in a quiet voice, "Why are you here?"

"Here, what do you mean *here?* Like Kadena?"

"The Marine Corps."

I gave him a look of disbelief and made some evasive reply, but the question chilled me. He knew the truth. He knew that on a certain level the Corps was just a pose for me, that I was watching the drama of it from a distance, not letting it touch me. That it wasn't fully real to me yet, that it was play.

He had spoken to me as a seer, a man who had crossed a certain kind of threshold. When I think of him, I imagine him looking back over his shoulder from a distance, wondering when the rest of us will catch up. Among my college classmates, he had been dealt the worst hand by far. What had happened was wrong and grotesquely unfair, but it had happened just the same. And yet through some alchemy, Jon had been made better, more thoughtful, more perceptive. The bullet—his bullet—had taken things away, but it had given him things, too.

Epilogue: Counterfactuals

I am often asked if I regret going to Iraq or if I regret going into the Marine Corps. And it's odd, because I can without too much effort imagine alternative universes for practically every historical scenario in the world—a world where the United States never enters World War I, a world where Saddam has the WMDs, a world where the battle of Fallujah never happens—but I have never been able to build a counterfactual world where I do not go into the Corps, a world where I don't get the letters USMC tattooed across my back, a world where I don't get on a plane and go to Iraq. I can even imagine a world where Erica doesn't disappear to Vegas and we stay together and get married, but I cannot see the me who doesn't go in, who doesn't go over and get blown up and almost shot down.

I'm a writer. I have studied the mechanics of fiction at the graduate level, learned how to create and nurture alternate worlds in my own head. But there's no alternate nonwar world of me.

In short, there's no counterfactual of me.

It's somehow too much to ask, to make a life without a war in the middle of it. It's a little bit like what Freud said about trying to imagine your own death: it's beyond my ken. It's like a death in that it's the absolute unknown, it opens a window to the world and lets every possibility in. It's too much. When I start to think about it, my brain just goes to static, like a radio turned to a dead station. In every inner universe I make, I do go in, I do go over.

But let's call this what it is: a failure of imagination on my part.

I know I am not normal in this way. I know some people who can't stop their brains from tackling all the possibilities, who are terrorized by their counterfactuals, guys who after one bad episode or another see their insides turned into tape loops, tape loops with questions on them. Questions like *What if? What if? What if? What if?* or, worse yet, *Why didn't I? Why didn't I? Why didn't I? Why didn't I?* playing over and over in their heads. In between the questions, there are worlds. Worlds where they aren't so afraid. Worlds where they aren't so tired and falling asleep during security halts that they take the longer, more tedious, safer way back to their patrol base. Worlds where their best friend lives. Where he walks past the IED buried in the side of an irrigation ditch. A world where he goes back to the barracks at San Mateo, where he gets out of the Corps, takes a job at a coffee shop in Tucson, goes to Pima Community College on the G.I. Bill, eventually gets into U of A down the road. Or a world where the IED hits another guy in the patrol. Or where they take a long security halt at the turnaround point, take a breather, and everybody lives because they're not so wasted.

Everyone does this. We all build counterfactuals out of our lives, even when we don't realize it. What if I didn't have that last drink? What if I'd taken that job in Baltimore? It is possibility that kills us in the end, sheer chance, a kind of optimism that tells us that anything is possible. Life doesn't work this way, but we wish it did. We wish that life could be lived with the benefit of hindsight, with wisdom coming when it should. We wish we could go back and marry the right girl. We wish we could go back and take that test again.

I would not go through another war again. Yet I know that another one is coming. Another war is coming, and no one can do anything about it. In every world my mind makes, a war comes. Even now, it is making itself ready. Thinking about this, I recall what Heraclitus said:

> *Justice in our minds is strife*
> *We cannot help but see*
> *War makes us as we are.*

War has made me as I am.

And there's a kind of beauty in that, or at least a kind of order, something that helps me make sense of the world.

To me, asking *Do you regret going to Iraq?* or *Do you regret going into the Corps?* is almost like asking *Do you believe in God?* It's a really big question, a question that many people can answer with ease but one that tells you a lot about that person, how they see the world, how they see the role that fate plays in human life. But when I think about it, what I usually say is this: I believe in nature. I believe in brokenness. I believe in wholeness. I believe in whatever it is that connects the one to the other. I believe in it in the way that a geologist believes in the mutability of hills, of waterfalls, of beaches. It just is. I went in and went over because the situation seemed to demand it. It was a similar attitude that some playwrights in ancient Greece took, a kind of tragic realism, of staring into the abyss of terror and suffering as a way of affirming life. To fully appreciate the joys of this world, one must understand how temporary they are, how fragile human existence is.

"Beneath those stars," Melville wrote, "is a universe of gliding monsters."

On the way back from my first trip to Iraq, I was chatting on the tarmac of an airfield near Fallujah with an old Marine buddy I'd chanced into. He'd left the infantry and become a helicopter pilot, and it was like he was a different person now. He was a guy who knew how to do all that incredible stuff up in the air, miracles really. I was trying to imagine him in the cockpit when we got the word that some "angels" were arriving and for everyone to get in line. I stood beside my friend while he saluted. Then I learned what they meant by "angels."

Two aluminum coffins with American flags stretched over them were being hoisted into the back of a C-130 by a forklift.

"Angels" were corpses.

A few minutes later, when we were about to load up on the plane, the crew chief stopped me and said, "Sir, I'm gonna need to get your camera from you." He was the first of three guys to tell me that photographs weren't allowed on the flight, including a major who, when we were halfway to Kuwait, unstrapped and walked the length of the plane to deliver the news.

I can see now that this tarmac was a kind of dividing line, a demarcation between one world and the next. On one side of the line, real people got blown up and shot in the face. Real people got mortared in the shitter and drowned in filthy canal water inside overturned Humvees. On the other side of the line, people referred to the dead as "angels" and made sure that no one took photos of them. Here was where the language changed. Here was where certain facts became unspeakable. Here, then, was where a certain kind of alchemy began, an alchemy that changed the facts of life and death, the horror of daily life in Iraq, into a kind of Sunday-school story.

What became of that world on the other side of the line? What became of that way of being, that way of feeling, that time, that history? What became of the Marines whom I sang the theme from *Aladdin* with on the way to the ambush site in Saqliwiyah? What became of the sergeant from 1/1 who cursed me in the hotel? What became of Reaper, the philosopher of Saydia? What became of the soldiers who jinxed me? Called out my fate like it was a common fact?

America didn't look the same when I came back to it that first time. The houses were closed to me now, shuttered, the people foreign. I had only been gone three months, but it felt like years had passed. A silence came over my life, one I didn't know how to break.

Later, after I was back from the war for a few years, I read a poem Siegfried Sassoon wrote called "Fight to a Finish." Toward the end of the poem, Sassoon imagines leading a bayonet charge into a crowd of smug, patriotic civilians after a victory parade in London. The poem ends with an assault on Parliament, payback for a stupid war. It is a fantastical poem, written in a tone that seems intended to shock, but I wasn't surprised when I read it. I didn't serve in a war like Sassoon, but I recognized the anger, the feelings beneath it, feelings so potent that you never spoke of them, even to friends. Even to lovers. Even to yourself most of the time.

Sometimes when I get depressed or worried that my memories of the war are slipping, I get into my truck and make the trek up to La Jolla, that beautiful place that hovers over the dark Pacific like a hallucination, that place with the hills covered in what looks like mohair. I drive up past the Mormon temple, past the organic market and the pharmacy school, and I park, and I walk through the sliding doors of the VA and take the elevator up to Same-Day Psychiatric on Two North.

When I get there, I just sit and listen for a while, taking in the waiting room while they call out the names of those who are next. I spent hours waiting here for my name to be called. I used to hate waiting here, but now I don't mind it so much, and I know my name won't be called, at least not today. To my right is a man pouring his life into a cell phone, telling a friend that he's so sorry, that he needs him to go into his bedroom and throw away all the coke in his backpack because he's so sorry, but he can't be trusted anymore. To my left is a man whose leg is going up and down like a jackhammer. Everywhere are the faces, each like a page from a book that never ends. Looking out over the room, which was full yesterday and will be full tomorrow, I sit thinking as the names of the chosen float through the air, and I wonder which one of them was in Danang, which one of them was in Fallujah, which one of them was in some godawful place in Afghanistan that I've never even heard of, which one has a heroin habit that will kill them, a wife who is going to leave them, which one has lost more than they ever knew they had, has paid more for their dreams than I ever paid for mine, and to all of them I say it's okay, it's okay, it's okay.

Acknowledgments

Thank you to Mike, Kay, and Bev. Thank you to Ryan and Lisa Sims, Joe Garza, Michelle Latiolais, Ron Carlson, Geoffrey Wolf, Elliott Woods, Ted Genoways, Ramona Ausubel, Ismet Prcic, Nathan Phelps, Mitchel Zafer, Steve House, Steve Schall, Alex Gilvarry, Joel Kiker, Elizabeth Wyatt, Christine Eubank, Beverly Prange, Jesse Weiner, Margaux Wexberg-Sanchez, Rey Leal, Annessa Stagner, Jo Dery, Matt Sumell, Ryan Ridge, Jon Wiener, Tom Ricks, Ghislaine Boulanger, Gerald Nicosia, Marc Walker, Mike Bryant, Maggie Shipstead, Jen Percy, Derek Keller, Dewleen Baker, Leila Mansouri, Dan Morris, and Angie Wolf.

Thank you to Seth Fishman and Andy Kifer at the The Gernert Company. Thank you to Eamon Dolan and Ben Hyman and everyone at Houghton Mifflin Harcourt. Thank you to Bryan Russell.

Thank you to Field Test Film Corps, Bob Sims, Edward Woods, Lisa Kenney, Bridgid MacSeoin, Leon Higley, Jacob Snyder, Jessica Halpin, Kees Marijs, Mary Jane Nealon, Patrick Austin, Matthew Philip Wee, Seth Tucker, Jill Britton, James Lemke, Evan McGee, Joshua Lewis, Matthew Desautel, Cheryl J. Taylor, Lorene Delany-Ullman, Patrick Coleman, Rob Kunzler, Brittni Waldow, Cindy Boyer, Mary Duran, Caroline Davies, Gunveen Kaur, Jane Satterfield, and Michael Pavlichek.

Thank you to the National Endowment for the Arts, to the Mac-Dowell Colony, to the Norman Mailer Writers Colony, to the staff at the Dolph Briscoe Center for American History, to the staff of the Richard Nixon Presidential Library, and to the U.S. Navy Seabee Museum in Port Hueneme, California.

Notes

While much of this book is based on my own life experience and firsthand reporting, I also relied on the hard work of a number of other researchers and writers. In these notes, I have tried not only to identify my sources but also to briefly explain how I arrived at certain conclusions. Research is a detective story. What follows is the trail of clues, some found in the library and in archives, some found on the internet, and others at conferences and lectures I attended. The story of PTSD is one with a poor signal-to-noise ratio—there are a lot of people saying a lot of things about it, many of them contradictory. Writing this book has taught me to be a better critical listener as well as a better critical thinker. I have also learned the value of peer-reviewed science, as well as the value of reaching out to thinkers who have been banished to the intellectual wilderness by the popular trends of the day. I have also come to appreciate anew the empirical value of poetry and fiction, the forms of inquiry that originally informed and inspired this book.

I also wish to honor the writers upon whose shoulders I stand. Judith Herman's *Trauma and Recovery* (New York: Basic Books, 1992) remains a foundational text and provides a superlative overview of the field of trauma studies from a psychiatric standpoint. Alice Sebold's *Lucky* is a one-of-a-kind book: powerful and well written. It helped me immeasurably. Gerald Nicosia's *Home to War: A History of the Vietnam Veterans' Movement* (New York: Three Rivers, 2001) is an excellent history of the movement to have PTSD recognized in the 1970s. Jonathan Shay's *Achilles in Vietnam* (New York: Scribner, 1994) and *Odysseus in America* (New York: Scribner, 2002) both give a sense of how trauma was conceptualized in the ancient world and how Greek mythology can illuminate our understanding of trauma today. Ben Shephard's *A War of Nerves: Soldiers and Psychiatrists in the Twentieth Century* (Cambridge, MA: Harvard University Press, 2001) is an excellent survey, though it occasionally suffers from a curious ethnocentrism. Shephard's treatment of the world wars is superb. His treatment of the American experience in Vietnam is less than superb. Paul Fussell's *The Great War and Modern Memory* (New York: Oxford University Press, 1975) is an enduring masterpiece and captures the cataclysm of World War I and how that conflict continues to influence our world today. An overlooked work of scholarship is Eric Leed's *No Man's Land: Combat and Identity in World War I* (Cambridge: Cambridge University Press, 1979). Leed's discussion of liminality and war neuroses is illuminating and informed much of my thinking. Laurence Gonzales's *Surviving Survival: The Art and Science of Resilience* (New York: W. W. Norton, 2013) thoughtfully examines the science behind trauma and resilience. From an organizational standpoint, I gleaned much from Siddhartha Mukherjee's *The Emperor of All Maladies: A Biography of Cancer* (to which I owe the literary conceit of a clinical "biography") and Andrew Solomon's *The Noonday Demon: An Atlas of Depression.* Finally, I am indebted to William Gibson for teaching me about the concept of apophenia, which I first discovered in his novel *Pattern Recognition.*

Prologue: The Warning

page

xi *Apophenia: finding patterns:* Sophie Fyfe of University College London, in her article "Apophenia, Theory of Mind and Schizotypy: Perceiving Meaning and Intentionality in Randomness" (*Cortex 44,* Nov-Dec 2008: 1316–1325), defines apophenia as "the perception of connections or meaning in unrelated events." As William Gibson explained in a 2003 article in *The Telegraph,* "It's probably projection, but I'm inclined to think that everyone experiences it, to some extent . . . It seems to me that it is the thing we do which distinguishes us from other species. We seem to be so evolved to do it that we're prone to seeing faces in clouds. I bet birds don't see birds in clouds, right?"

xii *a prominent psychoanalyst:* The psychoanalyst I spoke to was Robert Stolorow of the Institute of Contemporary Psychoanalysis, Los Angeles.

Introduction

1 *a handful of disgruntled Vietnam veterans:* The best resource for those interested in the Vietnam Veterans Against the War "rap" groups is *Home to War: A History of the Vietnam Veterans' Movement* by Gerald Nicosia. Nicosia collected six hundred oral histories from VVAW members, the transcripts of which are stored at the Dolphe Briscoe Center for American History in Austin, Texas. The importance of Nicosia's contribution to the history of PTSD is hard to overestimate.

psychiatric Esperanto: Ethan Watters, "Suffering Differently." *New York Times Magazine,* August 12, 2007. This quote comes from Allan Young, a historian of PTSD and medical anthropologist at McGill University. On page 29 of *Crazy Like Us,* Watters writes: "In the spring of 1881 one popular French journalist wrote, 'The illness of our age is hysteria. One encounters it everywhere. Everywhere one rubs elbows with it ... Studying hysteria, Monsieur Lasegue, the illustrious master, and Monsieur Charcot have put their finger on the wound of the day ... This singular neurosis with its astonishing effects ... travels the streets and the world.'"

the fourth most common psychiatric disorder: Rachel Yehuda, "Post-Traumatic Stress Disorder." *New England Journal of Medicine* 346 (2002): 108–114, p. 108.

In 2012, the federal government spent: IOM (Institute of Medicine). *Treatment of Posttraumatic Stress Disorder.* See also Finley, *Fields of Combat,* 128. Finley provides an excellent insider account of the workings of VA San Antonio, which paralleled my experiences at VA San Diego. It is important to emphasize when discussing the VA what a vast system it is and how each site varies in the quality of care provided. The VA centers at San Diego and San Antonio are unusual and instructive because of the large military/veteran populations in both cities. In 2004, the VA reported that it spent 4.3 billion dollars on PTSD disability payments to veterans. This earlier figure is cited in Finley.

Since the attacks of 9/11: Watters, on page 71 of his book *Crazy Like Us,* describes the international response to the tsunami in Sri Lanka, saying, "By 2004 PTSD was on the cusp of becoming the international lingua franca of human suffering."

2 *Consumers who are so inclined:* www.patchstop.com, SKU: P3216.

There remains a small but vocal cadre of researchers: Allan Young, in *Harmony of Illusions,* argues that the condition we know as PTSD was not discovered but was "glued together" by "the practices, technology and narratives with which it is diagnosed, studied, treated and represented." Two leading historians of psychiatry, Edward Shorter at the University of Toronto and Ben Shephard, the author of *War of Nerves,* have both argued that the PTSD diagnosis and the science behind it are dubious. An illuminating collection of dissenting voices can be found in *Posttraumatic Stress Disorder: Issues and Controversies,* edited by Gerald Rosen.

Pierre Janet, a French neurologist writing in 1925: Herman, *Trauma and Recovery*, 35.
Over time, PTSD has changed not only: See Don DeLillo's post-9/11 novel *Falling Man* (New York: Scribner, 2008), where a character says, "These are the days after. Everything now is measured by after." Roger Luckhurst of the University of London makes a similar argument in his excellent scholarly work *The Trauma Question*.

both as a mental condition and as a metaphor: For a fascinating discussion of this, see Seeley, *Therapy after Terror*, 147–167. See also Susan Sontag's classic *Illness as Metaphor* (New York: Vintage, 1979). In the chapter titled "Trauma as Metaphor," Seeley argues, "Cultural conceptions of insanity, normality, morality, and reality are constantly in flux. Indeed Sontag's claim that physical illnesses are metaphors, in that they stand for, call up, and play out dominant social themes, anxieties, and inequalities applies to mental disorders as well. Like labels for physical diseases, labels for mental disorders designate the ills and ill fortunes of others" (150).

The ancient Greeks staged plays: Jonathan Shay, in his pioneering *Achilles in Vietnam*, says, "The ancient Greeks had a distinctive therapy of purification, healing and reintegration that was undertaken as a community. We know it as Athenian theater . . . the distinctive character of Athenian theater came from the requirements of a democratic polity made up entirely of present or former soldiers to provide communalization for combat veterans . . . The Athenians communally reintegrated their returning warriors in recurring participation in rituals of the theater" (230).

3   *Like Nick Carraway returning from:* Fitzgerald, *Great Gatsby*, 2.
5   *"The war itself was a mystery":* O'Brien, *In the Lake of the Woods*, 76.
6   *One British World War I veteran:* Eric Leed, "Fateful Memories: Industrialized War and Traumatic Neuroses." *Journal of Contemporary History* 35 (2000): 87. Leed is quoting Charles Edmund Carrington, who said, "The 1916 fixation had caught me and stunted my mental growth, so that even ten years later I was retarded and adolescent. I could not escape from the comradeship of the trenches which had become a mental internment camp."
Alice Sebold, in her bestselling: Sebold, *Lucky*, 27.
This palpable sense of not belonging: I owe a great debt to Karen Samuels at Memorial University of Newfoundland, who introduced me to the idea of PTSD as a state of liminality. Her article "Posttraumatic Stress Disorder as a State of Liminality," published in the Spring 2006 issue of the *Journal of Military and Strategic Studies*, was extremely helpful and opened up a whole new way of thinking about the issue. Eric Leed's discussion of liminality and war trauma in *No Man's Land* is likewise excellent.
Arnold van Gennep coined the term: van Gennep, *Rites of Passage*, 11.

7   *Yet as Victor Turner, an influential anthropologist:* Turner, *Betwixt and Between*, 5.
9   *Women have always played a pivotal role:* Shay, *Odysseus in America*, 131–134. Mythology is filled with this theme of balance being achieved only through an interplay of the sexes. Paul Fussell, in *The Great War and Modern Memory*, wrote that

"after considering the matter for centuries, the ancients concluded that one of the lovers of Venus is Mars. And Eros, some held, is their offspring. Since antiquity everyone who has experienced both war and love has known that there is a curious intercourse between them" (339). See also Campbell, *Power of Myth,* 64–65.

12 *Looking back on this post-Iraq:* Hemingway, *Complete Short Stories,* 109–117.

13 *It reminded me of something a veteran:* This comment is drawn from an interview I did with a Marine who fought at Observation Post 4 along the Saudi-Kuwait border in January 1991. See my 2004 book *Storm on the Horizon* (New York: Free Press, 2004), 73–79.

PTSD may well be the Esperanto: This impression of the literature being fragmented and "silo'd" was reinforced by my discussions with Jonathan Shay, whose groundbreaking work combined mythology, classical studies, and psychiatry. Shay, talking about his willingness to ignore the traditional boundaries between academic disciplines, at one point described himself as an "intellectual slut." He gestures toward this in *Odysseus in America,* at one point arguing, "At best, the distinctions among brain, mind, society, and culture are throwaways — temporary guides to perception and communication, temporary artifacts of the philosophical, institutional, and methodological history of the West" (248).

Other observers, such as Stossel in *My Age of Anxiety* (2013), have chalked this lack of coherence up to the longstanding intellectual discord in medicine and the sciences: "The conflicts between these different perspectives — and between the psychiatrists (MDs) and the psychologists (PhDs), between the drug proponents and the drug critics, between the cognitive-behaviorists and the psychoanalysts, between Freudians and Jungians, between the molecular neuroscientists and the holistic therapists — can sometimes be bitter. The stakes are high — the future stability of large professional infrastructures rides on one theory or another predominating" (53).

14 *"trauma impacts the whole critter":* Interview with Jonathan Shay.

One leading VA researcher: This extremely knowledgeable researcher had studied PTSD for over two decades and had published dozens of scientific papers on the subject. Curiously, her grasp of the nuts and bolts of military life and the basics of the Iraq War seemed almost nonexistent. This proved to be a common experience in my dealings with VA clinicians, which like the entire American medical establishment breeds an exceedingly narrow and parochial species of professionalism and does little to reward interdisciplinary learning. This overspecialization results in, among other things, a research literature that is virtually incoherent to anyone working in another field. As one British historian opined recently, "Researchers today no longer write in English." At the risk of sounding shrill, virtually all of the leading minds on the subject of trauma have been committed *generalists,* thinkers well versed in philosophy, biology, sociology, history, psychology, and literature, W. H. R. Rivers, Robert Lifton, Chaim Shatan, and Jonathan Shay being but a few handy examples.

One British author of an influential: Ben Shephard, 15th Maudsley Debate, King's

College London, "Post-Traumatic Stress Disorder," May 2002 (http://www.kcl
.ac.uk/iop/news/debates/podcast-archive.aspx).

14 *As Otto Fenichel, one of Freud's:* Seeley, *Therapy after Terror,* 150.

15 *It would be foolish to diagnose:* Faludi, *Terror Dream,* 2–15. Faludi writes "Virtually no film, television drama, play or novel on 9/11 had begun to plumb what the
trauma meant for our national psyche. Slavishly literal reenactments of the physical attack — preapproved and presanitized by the new Production Code committee known as 'The 9/11 Families' — or unrepresentative tales of triumphal rescue
at ground zero seemed all the national imagination could handle. *United 93,* Paul
Greengrass's almost real-time chronology of the events on the last hijacked plane,
released in April 2006, seemed to have no purpose other than to repeat what we
already knew" (2). Over the course of the book, Faludi goes on to describe the
various ways in which post-9/11 America has tended to celebrate "manly men,"
while looking to recapture a kind of "Greatest Generation patriotism." See also
Andrew J. Bacevich's superb *The New American Militarism: How Americans Are
Seduced by War* (New York: Oxford University Press, 2013). While Bacevich, a
retired army officer, focuses primarily on American foreign policy, he describes
how American pop culture is suffused with a "romanticized view of soldiers" and
"the fostering of (and nostalgia for) military ideals" (2).

Moreover, the ongoing militarization of American culture: One is reminded here
of World War I veteran Robert Graves's observation in *Goodbye to All That* (New
York: Doubleday, 1957) when he returned home from the Western Front: "England looked strange to us returned soldiers. We could not understand the war
madness that ran around everywhere looking for a pseudo-military outlet. The
civilians talked a foreign language; and it was newspaper language."

recent helicopter parenting phenomenon: Claire McCarthy, a physician and blog-
ger, made this observation on www.intelihealth.com. See also Anita Bruzzese,
"Self-Sufficiency Is Elusive to Young Adults of Hovering Parents." *USA Today,*
August 24, 2012. See also Katie Roiphe's 2012 book *In Praise of Messy Lives.*

"These are the days after.": DeLillo, *Falling Man,* 138.

16 *If war is a kind of symbolic violence:* The author and psychotherapist Gary Greenberg first suggested to me the idea that PTSD might serve a compensatory function for the civilian populace. The word he used was "mitzvah," which is Hebrew
for "good deed." In *No Man's Land,* Eric Leed writes, "The citizen-soldier has always been a central figure in what might be called an 'economy of social guilt' and
public sacrifice. He is the holder of a blood-debt upon the society he has defended
and can demand restitution for his 'sacrifice of himself' as well as for that of his
comrades who have died . . . For this temporary loss of a private self, the soldier
can demand restitution in the form of honor, prestige, or financial rewards" (204).

how modern therapeutic culture: For a fascinating conversation exploring the thesis
that the PTSD "project" has pathologized normal human adversity, listen to the
15th Maudsley Debate from May 2002, "Post-Traumatic Stress Disorder" (http://
www.kcl.ac.uk/iop/news/debates/podcast-archive.aspx).

16 *literature has been* the *primary:* The literature of trauma is rich indeed. The concept of PTSD is unimaginable without works such as *The Odyssey,* Wilfred Owen's poetry, and Kurt Vonnegut's *Slaughterhouse-Five.* Robert Jay Lifton, one of the architects of what became PTSD, seemed to sense this and wrote, in his 1973 book *Home from the War* (published seven years before the formalization of PTSD), that "I found echoes of many things I have heard Vietnam veterans say in J. Glenn Gray's *The Warriors* and Guy Sajer's *The Forgotten Soldier,* Erich Maria Remarque's *All Quiet on the Western Front* and the poems of Wilfred Owen" (18).
    "The experience of trauma is context-dependent": Interview with Robert Stolorow.

17 *"patients tell stories to describe illness":* Mukherjee, *Emperor of All Maladies,* 390. Earlier in the book, Mukherjee writes, "To name an illness is to describe a certain condition of suffering—a literary act before it becomes a medical one. A patient, long before he becomes the subject of medical scrutiny, is, at first, simply a story-teller, a narrator of suffering—a traveler who has visited the kingdom of the ill. To relieve an illness, one must begin, then, by unburdening its story" (46).
    trauma's corrosive power lies in its ability to destroy narrative: Shay, in *Achilles in Vietnam,* writes that "severe trauma explodes the cohesion of consciousness. When a survivor creates fully realized narrative that brings together the shattered knowledge of what happened, the emotions that were aroused by the meanings of the events, and the bodily sensations that the physical events created, the survivor pieces back together the fragmentation of consciousness that trauma has caused" (188).
    "the central image of post-traumatic stress": Interview with anonymous senior VA psychiatrist.
    "PTSD" was referred to as "Post-Vietnam Syndrome": Nicosia, *Home to War,* 159. Robert Lifton is usually credited with coining the term "Post-Vietnam Syndrome," though he had an unhappy relationship with it, saying in his 1973 book *Home from the War* that "post-Vietnam syndrome is a dubious, easily-abused category, especially in its ready equation of effects of the war with a clinical condition (a 'syndrome')" (420).
    This military connection continues into the present day: In *Posttraumatic Growth: Research and Practice* (New York: Lawrence Erlbaum Associates, 2006), Rita Rosner and Steve Powell say what is immediately apparent to anyone who has looked into the current state of PTSD research: "By far the best studied group of soldiers is the U.S. military, who are probably not typical for the rest of the world's soldiers. At least in the case of U.S. soldiers in recent decades, joining the army is usually a deliberate choice, which indicates that there was some sense of control. Furthermore, U.S. soldiers have always fought abroad, which means that their families are safe and their home environment is comparably stable" (200).

20 *a sort of global lingua franca:* In *Crazy Like Us,* Watters writes that "it's only been in the past twenty years that the diagnosis of PTSD has caught the world's attention. It first gained critical momentum in the United States and then began leapfrogging the globe, being put to use after wars, genocides and natural disasters. By

2004 PTSD was on the cusp of becoming the international lingua franca of human suffering." Watters quotes Allan Young, a medical anthropologist at McGill University: "We were spreading these ideas around the globe so effectively that PTSD was becoming the way the entire world conceived of psychological trauma ... The spread of the PTSD diagnosis to every corner of the world may, in the end, be the greatest success story of globalization" (70–71). A number of skeptics, like Derek Summerfield and to a lesser extent Gaithri Fernando of CSU Los Angeles, have criticized this globalization of PTSD, saying among other things that the PTSD diagnosis, as applied today, is not culture-neutral and tends to deemphasize the powerful roles of family, community, and religion.

1. Saydia

21   *Through the small, thick Humvee window:* This chapter is based on my recollections of my time as an embedded reporter in Iraq. The unit I embedded with in Saydia was 1-18 Infantry from Schweinfurt, Germany. I was on active duty in the U.S. Marine Corps from 1994 to 1998, and after completing my training as an infantry officer at Quantico, Virginia, was assigned to Kilo Company, 3rd Battalion, Fifth Marines at Camp Pendleton, California. I did one six-month deployment with 3/5 to Okinawa, where the battalion was part of the 31st Marine Expeditionary Unit (Special Operations Capable). My final year on active duty was spent as the assistant director of the First Marine Division Schools. I made three reporting trips to Iraq: April–June 2004, June–August 2006, and July–November 2007. While I was in Iraq, I reported for *Salon,* the *Virginia Quarterly Review,* and NPR.

23   *"slow-motion ethnic cleansing":* I first heard this term from Damien Cave of the *New York Times* in August 2007.

26   *I'd just spent a month in Dora:* The unit I embedded with in Dora (sometimes spelled Doura) was 2-12 Infantry from Fort Carson, Colorado. 2-12 had recently been "reflagged," meaning they had been changed from a paratrooper unit into a light infantry unit, a redesignation that no one in the unit liked. 2-12's saga is documented in David Philipps's book *Lethal Warriors: When the New Band of Brothers Came Home* (New York: Palgrave Macmillan, 2010). After they'd returned to Fort Carson, 2-12 was found to have a PTSD rate more than three times that of an equivalent U.S. Army unit that had been deployed to a less deadly part of Iraq (Philipps, 238). The dangers they lived with for months are impossible to describe with any justice. One image that stays with me is the thing I saw when I walked into 2-12's command post for the first time: 16 framed photographs screwed onto a wall, one for each soldier killed in Dora.

30   *"All sorrows can be borne":* Hannah Arendt, *The Human Condition* (Chicago: University of Chicago Press, 1958).

      Sometimes, and particularly with respect to traumatic narratives: Aries, *Hour of Our Death,* 5–7.

      To scientists, these sorts of ideas: I first encountered the concept of apophenia in

William Gibson's novel *Pattern Recognition.* The term was coined by German neurologist Klaus Conrad in a 1958 book about schizophrenia. With respect to the "face" photographed by the Viking I spacecraft, see Carl Sagan's *The Demon-Haunted World: Science as a Candle in the Dark* (New York: Random House, 1995).

31 *I felt like the German painter Otto Dix:* Annette Becker, "The Avant-garde, Madness and the Great War." *Journal of Contemporary History* 35 (2000): 72.

Freud saw that sufferers of war neuroses: Freud, *Beyond the Pleasure Principle,* 32. Peter Gay, in *Freud,* writes that "Freud noticed one version of this monotonous, destructive replay of unpleasure in patients afflicted with a 'fate neurosis,' sufferers whose destiny it is to go through the same calamity more than once . . . Freud noted, patients who display this compulsion do their utmost to dwell on misery and injuries, and to force an interruption to the analysis before it is completed. They contrive to find evidence that they are despised . . . It is as though they have never learned that all these compulsive repetitions bring no pleasure. There is something 'demonic' about their activities. That word 'demonic' leaves no doubt about Freud's strategy. He saw the compulsion to repeat as a most primitive mental activity, displaying an 'instinctual' character 'to a high degree'" (400–401).

32 *One can see this sort of obligation:* Fussell, *Great War and Modern Memory,* 411.

This sense that the life-threatening experience: Interview with Robert Stolorow. See Stolorow, *Trauma and Human Existence,* 17–22. On page 17, he writes that "the patient explained to me that with the retelling of each traumatic episode, a piece of herself broke off and relocated at the time and place of the original trauma. By the time she reached my office, she said, she was completely dispersed along the time dimension of her crushing life history. Upon hearing this, I spoke just three words: 'Trauma destroys time.'"

In Slaughterhouse-Five, *Kurt Vonnegut's novel:* Vonnegut, *Slaughterhouse-Five,* 23.

33 *"Our own death is indeed, unimaginable":* Freud, *Collected Papers,* 304–305.

"time dilates, as if I'm dreaming": Ralston, *Between a Rock,* 23.

34 *One study conducted by the U.S. Navy:* Dimoulas et al., "Dissociation during Intense Military Stress," 66–73.

Michael Herr, in Dispatches, *his classic work:* Herr, *Dispatches,* 135.

"the rapture of the deep": Ibid., 31, 250, 256.

35 *As the popular neurologist and writer Oliver Sacks:* Sacks, *Hallucinations,* 242.

PTSD is often thought of as being a syndrome: See Caruth, *Trauma.*

As Ben Helfgott, a concentration camp survivor: Sacks, *Hallucinations,* 243.

37 *As John le Carré observed:* le Carré, *Little Drummer Girl,* 5.

The year before, I'd interviewed a navy corpsman: See my essay "The Big Suck: Notes from the Jarhead Underground" in the Winter 2007 issue of *Virginia Quarterly Review,* where I tell the corpsman's story in greater detail.

2. In Terror's Shadow

41 *Once it enters the body, it stays there forever:* Rachel Yehuda, in a 2002 article titled "Post-Traumatic Stress Disorder" in the *New England Journal of Medicine,* wrote that "studies of the biologic mechanisms of PTSD have delineated circumscribed alterations in brain regions, such as the amygdala and hippocampus, that are associated with fear and memory, as well as changes in the hormonal, neurochemical, and physiological systems involved in coordinating the body's response to stress" (113). Yehuda, a professor of psychiatry at the Mount Sinai School of Medicine, in a September 2007 article titled "The Relevance of Epigenetics to PTSD" in the *Archives of General Psychiatry* (1040–1048), found that "offspring with parental PTSD displayed lower mean cortisol levels, reflected by the circadian mesor and reduced cortisol amplitude, compared with offspring without parental PTSD and children of nonexposed parents. This effect seemed to be specifically related to the presence of maternal PTSD." While there is still some debate within the medical community about whether stress damages the brain (as Douglas Bremner of Emory University argued in his 2002 book), there is little doubt that major traumatic events change the human hormonal system and that these changes are passed along to the survivor's offspring. See also Anke Karl et al., "A Meta-analysis of Structural Brain Abnormalities in PTSD." *Neuroscience and Biobehavioral Reviews* 30 (2006): 1004–1031. See also Rachel Yehuda et al., "Transgenerational Effects of Posttraumatic Stress Disorder in Babies of Mothers Exposed to the World Trade Center Attacks during Pregnancy." *Journal of Clinical Endocrinology and Metabolism* 90 (2005): 4115; J. J. Silverman et al., "Psychological Distress and Symptoms of Posttraumatic Stress Disorder in Jewish Adolescents Following a Brief Exposure to Concentration Camps." *Journal of Child and Family Studies* 8 (1999): 71–89.

Much of the evidence for the claim that the offspring of trauma survivors are biologically different from those with untraumatized forebears has come from studying the children and grandchildren of Holocaust survivors. Scott Stossel writes, in *My Age of Anxiety,* that "researchers have found analogous evidence in the descendants of trauma victims: the children and even grandchildren of Holocaust survivors exhibit greater psychophysiological evidence of stress and anxious arousal — such as elevated levels of various stress hormones — than do ethnically similar children and grandchildren of cohorts who were not exposed to the Holocaust. When these grandchildren are shown stressful images having nothing to do with the Holocaust — for instance, of violence in Somalia — they display more extreme responses, both in behavior and physiology than do their peers. As John Livingstone, a psychiatrist who specializes in treating trauma victims, told me, 'It's as though traumatic experiences get plastered into the tissues of the body and passed along to the next generation'" (255–256).

as war correspondent Michael Herr testifies in Dispatches: Herr, *Dispatches,* 35.

42 *"Trauma is democratic":* Winter, "Shell-shock," 11.

the historian Will Durant calculated: Hedges, *War Is a Force,* 10.

42 *The numbers are staggering: a 2010 study: The National Intimate Partner and Sexual Violence Survey: 2010 Summary Report.* Atlanta: Centers for Disease Control and Prevention, 2011. "Nearly one in five women (18.3%) and 1 in 71 men (1.4%) have been raped at some point in their lives." In Yehuda's 2002 article on PTSD in the *New England Journal of Medicine,* she says, "PTSD developed in 55 percent of persons who reported being raped" (109).

The most cited research study: R. C. Kessler et al., "Posttraumatic Stress Disorder in the National Comorbidity Survey." *Archives of General Psychiatry* 52 (1995): 1048–1060.

Alice Sebold, when asked why she chose to write: This quote comes from a 2002 interview with Terry Gross that was included in a reading group guide at the back of the paperback edition of *Lucky.*

Pulitzer Prize–winning novelist Cormac McCarthy: The *Yuma Daily Sun* article reads, "Clark, who led last year's expedition to the Afar region of northern Ethiopia, and UC Berkeley colleague Tim D. White, also said that a re-examination of a 300,000-year-old fossil skull found in the same region earlier showed evidence of having been scalped."

Trauma defies description: In "Whereof We Can Speak, Thereof We Must Not Be Silent: Trauma, Political Solipsism and War," *Review of International Studies* 30.4 (2004), 472, political scientist Karin Fierke defines trauma as "a 'dislocation' accompanied by an inability to mourn or speak of the trauma." Interestingly, while trauma is thought to be nearly inexpressible by many scholars, it is thought to be more readily *representable* in the visual arts, which might help explain PTSD's deep connection to film and television.

43 *the "dose-response curve":* Herman, *Trauma and Recovery,* 57. Author interview with Matthew Friedman, 2013. Friedman, the longest-serving executive director of the National Center for PTSD, said, "One of the most interesting findings in all PTSD work is the dose-response curve. The greater the exposure to the trauma, the greater the likelihood of PTSD." Friedman went on to say that researchers have observed the dose-response curve in a number of non-Western cultures.

Was she extroverted?: I. V. E. Carlier et al., "Risk Factors for Posttraumatic Stress Symptomatology in Police Officers." *Journal of Nervous and Mental Disease,* August 1997, 498–506. See also A. C. McFarlane et al., "The Etiology of Posttraumatic Morbidity: Predisposing, Precipitating, and Perpetuating Factors." *British Journal of Psychiatry* 154: 221–228.

Was she someone who was easily hypnotized?: Herman, *Trauma and Recovery,* 124. Moreover, a 1995 study by Daniel Weiss et al. titled "Predicting Symptomatic Distress in Emergency Services Personnel" and published in the *Journal of Consulting and Clinical Psychology* showed dissociative tendencies to be strongly predictive of PTSD symptoms in emergency response workers.

44 *How did she go about:* Shay, *Achilles in Vietnam,* 191. See also Herman, *Trauma and Recovery,* 7–32.

According to the Comprehensive Textbook of Psychiatry: H. I. Kaplan, ed., *Comprehensive Textbook of Psychiatry.* 4th ed. (Baltimore: Williams & Wilkins, 2009), 918–924.

In the face of terror: See, for instance, van der Kolk et al., "Pierre Janet on Post-Traumatic Stress." *Journal of Traumatic Stress* 2, no. 4 (1989): 365–378. See also Gray, *The Warriors,* 29. Gray writes, "War as a spectacle, as something to see, ought never to be underestimated ... The eye is lustful because it requires the novel, the unusual, the spectacular."

45 *It is almost as if certain types of events:* See, for instance, LeDoux, *Emotional Brain,* 256. See also McGaugh, *Memory and Emotion.*
"PTSD is a disease of time": Young, *Harmony of Illusions,* 7.
so-called acts of God: See Sacks, *Hallucinations,* 240. See also Yehuda's January 2002 article, "Post-Traumatic Stress Disorder," in the *New England Journal of Medicine,* which includes a very helpful table depicting PTSD prevalence rates on page 110.

46 *Sonali Deraniyagala, writing about the 2004 tsunami:* On page 77 of *Wave,* Deraniyagala writes, "My journeys to Yala became less frequent after I began to harass the Dutch family. By that December, as the first anniversary of the wave approached, I had this new fixation. Strangers had moved into our home in Colombo. A Dutch family. When I was first told the house had been rented to them, I raged at Rajiv for doing it. I was desperate. I screamed. I explained: the house, it anchors me to my children. It tells me they were real. I need to curl up inside it, now and again."
Returning home from Iraq in October 2007: The fire in question, known as the Witch Creek Fire, was the second largest in California history and is described in "California Fire Siege 2007: An Overview," a pamphlet produced by the California Department of Forestry and Fire Protection.

47 *an incident of so-called friendly fire:* In an October 1998 article in the *Journal of the Royal Society of Medicine,* Martin Deahl cites an example from the Gulf War where a group of survivors of a friendly fire incident suffered a PTSD rate of 56 percent, the highest prevalence rate he cites. Researching my 2004 book *Storm on the Horizon* about the battle of Khafji, I found that the veterans most haunted by the war were those who'd had comrades killed by friendly fire.
the "Hanoi Hilton" prisoner-of-war camp: Interviews with Taylor Kiland, Francine Segovia, and Richard Tangeman, April 2013. See Kiland, *Lessons from the Hanoi Hilton.* See also Dennis Charney, "The Psychobiology of Resilience to Extreme Stress: Implications for the Treatment and Prevention of Anxiety Disorders," keynote address at ADAA conference, March 23, 2006; Francine Segovia et al., "Optimism Predicts Resilience in Repatriated Prisoners of War: A 37-Year Longitudinal Study." *Journal of Traumatic Stress* 25 (2012), 1–7; William Sledge et al., "Self-concept Changes Related to War Captivity." *Archives of General Psychiatry* 37 (1980): 430–443.

48 *Describing what he called his "transforming":* See McCain, *Faith of My Fathers,* 321.

49 *when the men of the Hanoi Hilton were finally released:* Interviews with Taylor

Kiland, Francine Segovia, and Richard Tangeman. See also Peter Davis's excellent 1974 documentary on Vietnam, *Hearts and Minds,* which shows George Coker's lavish homecoming to Linden, New Jersey.

50 *As John McCain later wrote:* McCain, *Faith of My Fathers,* 323.

One group of VA investigators: Friedman, *Handbook of PTSD,* 8. On page 13 of *Post-Traumatic Stress Disorder,* Shiromani says, "Very few studies actually include the assessment of post-trauma factors in terms of their contribution to the development and maintenance of PTSD. Social support is the one exception. Across 11 studies, Ozer et al. found that perceived social support following the trauma event was associated with PTSD symptoms."

Therapists like to talk about "small-t" traumas and "Big-T" traumas: I heard this expression used by three separate psychotherapists who treat people with PTSD. Two of them were with the VA in San Diego, while the other was in private practice in Denver.

51 *These little details, many of which go unnoticed:* LeDoux, *Emotional Brain,* 142–148. See also Kandel, *In Search of Memory,* 342–345; for a more accessible discussion of conditioning, fear, and emotion, see Gonzales, *Surviving Survival,* 20–36. His chapter "The Crocodile Within" is very helpful.

During a small-t trigger, the amygdala: See LeDoux, *Emotional Brain,* 256–258. See also Yehuda's 2002 *New England Journal of Medicine* article, "Post-Traumatic Stress Disorder," 110–112.

Outwardly, this process is often described: LeDoux, *Emotional Brain,* 45. See also Laurence Gonzales, *Deep Survival,* 35–36.

"At the sound of the first droning": Remarque, *All Quiet,* 56.

52 *Big-T traumas can destroy the soul:* In *Achilles in Vietnam,* Jonathan Shay argues that "severe trauma explodes the cohesion of consciousness" (188).

People with chronic, long-term PTSD: See Robert Scaer, *Trauma Spectrum* (New York: W. W. Norton, 2005). See also Herman, *Trauma and Recovery,* 118–122. For a brief discussion of the biological aspects of PTSD, see Yehuda's 2002 *New England Journal of Medicine* article, "Post-Traumatic Stress Disorder," 110–112.

When resistance and escape from terror: Herman, *Trauma and Recovery,* 34–35.

53 *During the 1973 Yom Kippur War:* Junger, *War,* 122.

Major traumas are both a death and a rebirth: In her memoir *Lucky,* Alice Sebold writes, shortly after her rape, that "my life was over; my life had just begun" (33). On page 53, she writes that "it was an early nuance of a realization that would take years to face. I share my life not with the girls and boys I grew up with, or the students I went to Syracuse with, or even the friends and people I've known since. I share my life with my rapist. He is the husband to my fate." On page 204, Sebold says, "I remember agreeing with my mother that I had gone through a death-and-rebirth phenomenon in the span of one year." In *We Came Home* (Toluca Lake, CA: P.O.W. Publications, 1977), Richard Tangeman, a former Hanoi Hilton POW, says, "I was deeply moved by the warmth and sincerity of all the wonderful people who welcomed us home and witnessed our 'rebirth.'"

"men spared their lives in great disasters": McCarthy, *Crossing,* 146–147.

54 *World War I veteran:* Fussell, *Great War and Modern Memory,* 139.

Reunited with his family: Tangeman, *We Came Home.*

"My life was over": Sebold, *Lucky,* 33.

One Hindu survivor of the 2004 tsunami in Sri Lanka: Interview with Gaithri Fernando, 2013. In a 2012 article in *Transcultural Psychiatry,* Fernando writes, "Early in my Fulbright visit to Sri Lanka, I met Radha, a 34-year-old Tamil woman who had been severely tortured by the Sri Lankan military. During my assessment of her I was struck by her lack of distress when describing her current condition . . . I asked her what her torture experience meant to her. 'Well,' she said, 'I am *really* looking forward to my next life. I must have done some terrible things to have deserved this horrible suffering. I know that in my next birth, I will have the most wonderful life. This knowledge makes me very happy'" (396–397).

In the increasingly interconnected PTSD community: See, for instance, the 2007 HBO documentary *Alive Day Memories: Home from Iraq,* produced by James Gandolfini.

On March 25, 2010, professional mountaineer Steve House: Interview with Steve House, 2013.

55 *One friend of mine, who was raped:* Interview with Elise Colton, 2013.

Stolorow describes how for a survivor: Interview with Robert Stolorow, 2013.

As psychiatrist Judith Herman explains: Herman, *Trauma and Recovery,* 36.

56 *Poet Robert Graves recounts how:* This quotation can be found on page 288 of Graves's 1929 memoir *Goodbye to All That,* a book he described as his "bitter leave-taking of England." Here is the full quote, which describes his experience, one reminiscent of many Iraq veterans I have known: "Not only did I have no experience of independent civilian life, having gone straight from school into the army: I was still mentally and nervously organized for war. Shells used to come bursting on my bed at midnight, even though Nancy shared it with me; strangers in daytime would assume the faces of friends who had been killed. When strong enough to climb the hill behind Harlech and revisit my favourite country, I could not help seeing it as a prospective battlefield.

"I knew it would be years before I could face anything but a quiet country life. My disabilities were many: I could not use a telephone, I felt sick every time I travelled by train, and to see more than two new people in a single day prevented me from sleeping. I felt ashamed of myself as a drag on Nancy, but had sworn on the very day of my demobilisation never to be under anyone's orders for the rest of my life."

Researchers at the University of California at Irvine: Interview with Alison Holman. See Alison Holman et al., "Getting 'Stuck' in the Past: Temporal Orientation and Coping With Trauma." *Journal of Personality and Social Psychology* 74, no. 5 (1998): 1146–1163. See also Schacter, *Seven Sins of Memory,* 175.

57 *"zombie subroutines of the brain":* Eagleman, *Incognito,* 131–132. Other neuroscientists have referred to this aspect of brain function as "alien subroutines," "zombie

agents," "zombie systems," and "System 1," all of which emphasize our lack of conscious access to them.

3. Toward a Genealogy of Trauma

60 *Most people, when they first learn about PTSD:* For an in-depth discussion of PTSD's cultural construction, see Young, *Harmony of Illusions;* Shephard, *War of Nerves,* 385–399; Rosen, *Posttraumatic Stress Disorder;* and McNally, *What Is Mental Illness?,* 146–156. The idea that PTSD is not timeless and that the diagnosis has to a certain extent evolved in response to cultural conditions is controversial and upsetting to many veterans. One Afghanistan veteran reading about PTSD's slippery conceptual basis on the *National Geographic* blog "The Frontal Cortex" wrote in the comments section, "Denying that 20–30% of all U.S. forces who have served in Iraq and Afghanistan are afflicted with PTSD is outlandish! This is like denying that the Holocaust ever occurred in Nazi Germany during WWII." As McNally put it in an article in the 2003 *Annual Review of Psychology,* "Progress and Controversy in the Study of Posttraumatic Stress Disorder," "There is never a dull moment in the field of traumatic stress studies. Discoveries are continually intermixed with explosive social controversies."

what Joan Didion called its "febrile rhythms": Didion, *We Tell Ourselves Stories,* 589. See also Wheen, *Strange Days Indeed.*

Commonly thought of as a signature symptom: Edward Jones et al., "Flashbacks and Post-traumatic Stress Disorder: The Genesis of a 20th-Century Disorder." *British Journal of Psychiatry* 182 (2003): 158–163. Bartley Frueh of the University of Hawaii at Hilo made a similar point in a June 2012 article, "Suicide, Alcoholism, and Psychiatric Illness among Union Forces," in the *Journal of Anxiety Disorders* which looked for psychiatric symptoms among American Civil War veterans: "It is interesting that descriptions of classic PTSD symptoms of reexperiencing, such as nightmares or 'flashbacks' were not found in that data reviewed." Frueh's findings with respect to nightmares are hard to understand, as the literature of the Civil War is rife with veterans who claimed to suffer from nightmares and supernatural visitations. See also Luckhurst, *Trauma Question,* 179–185. Luckhurst is very good in examining the role that cinema (and seventies cinema in particular) has played in the development of PTSD as a diagnostic concept. On page 177, Luckhurst argues that "cinema in fact helped constitute the PTSD subject in 1980, and ... has continued to interact with and shape the psychological and general cultural discourse of trauma into the present day."

61 *(Civil War veterans who suffered):* See Dean, *Shook over Hell,* 101–114. See also Gilpin Faust, *This Republic of Suffering,* 161, 196.

Adding to the confusion: See Luckhurst, *Trauma Question,* 61, 148, 183.

62 *Indeed, it is this historical slipperiness:* Young, *Harmony of Illusions,* 5.

The earliest appearance of the word: Ibid., 13.

In 1866, a London surgeon: Ibid., 14. See also Shephard, *War of Nerves,* 16; Figley, *Trauma and Its Wake,* 5–14.

63 *Compared to depression, for instance:* Solomon, *Noonday Demon,* 285–286.

The never-ending ebb and flow of war: Shepard, *War of Nerves,* xxii. Interview with Bill Nash.

64 *With a mere three pages:* American Psychiatric Association, *Diagnostic and Statistical Manual, III,* 219–221.

As sociologist Georges Vigarello argued: Vigarello, *History of Rape,* 1. Joan Didion, writing about a rape case in New York in *We Tell Ourselves Stories,* in which the victim's name was persistently left out of newspaper accounts, writes that "the convention [of leaving victims anonymous] assumes that this violation is of a nature best kept secret, that the rape victim feels, and would feel still more strongly were she identified, a shame and self-loathing unique to this form of assault, that a special contract exists between this one kind of victim and her assailant . . . that the act of male penetration involves such potent mysteries that the woman is permanently marked, 'different' . . . as in nineteenth-century stories featuring white women taken by Indians — 'ruined'" (690).

Moreover, as Susan Brownmiller indicates: Brownmiller, *Against Our Will,* 11.

The other reason for this dearth: Yehuda, "Post-Traumatic Stress Disorder," 109–110.

Despite the fact that rape is the most common: Ibid.

Most of what we know about PTSD comes from studying men: See Finley's excellent *Fields of Combat,* 73–89.

65 *"PTSD is a disease of time":* Young, *Harmony of Illusions,* 7.

One possible beginning is: Much of the material in this section is drawn from Halifax, *Shamanic Voices.* There is evidence to indicate that certain PTSD symptoms are, in fact, timeless. Jared Diamond, in his book *The World until Yesterday* (2012), notes that postwar nightmares in the traditional, prescientific societies of New Guinea are common. "Men admitted having nightmares in which they became isolated from others in their group during a fight and could see no way back" (149). Many anthropologists consider the tribes of New Guinea to be a window into prehistoric man, and it is not unreasonable to conclude that postcombat nightmares are an essential aspect of human experience. Diamond also mentions that warriors in New Guinea often boast about the men they have killed, a practice in stark contrast to how warriors in the West conduct themselves today. He posits that this fact alone might account for the relatively high rates of PTSD in the modern world, a world where the spilling of blood is a (thankfully) rare occurrence to be done "off-stage," for a limited period of time, by a distinct class of citizens.

The shaman, a figure who emerged: Halifax, *Shamanic Voices,* 3–34.

66 *The secret suspicion that survivors are somehow tainted:* In *The Moral Treatment of Returning Warriors in Early Medieval and Modern Times,* Bernard J. Verkamp of Vincennes University writes, "Among the most primitive and ancient peoples, including the Jews, the overriding sentiment behind the imposition of penances

upon returning warriors had been a *horror sanguinis*. Any contact with blood, especially the shedding of blood, was deemed a source of contamination. By virtue of having killed in battle, therefore, the warrior came to be thought of as being unclean and in need of purification before he could return home or engage in any kind of cultic activity" (26).

67 *(Epilepsy was, in fact, often):* Sacks, *Hallucinations*, 133.

As one well-spoken Iraq veteran: Personal communication with Elliott Woods, 2012.

68 *The aftermath of this event is recorded:* See Philippe J. Birmes et al., "Psychotraumatology in Antiquity." *Stress and Health* 26 (2010): 21–31. See also Menachem Ben-Ezra, "Traumatic Reactions from Antiquity to the 16th Century: Was There a Common Denominator?" *Stress and Health* 27 (2011): 223–240; Menachem Ben-Ezra, "The Earliest Evidence of Post Traumatic Stress?" *British Journal of Psychiatry* 179 (2001): 467.

69 *As one VA psychologist:* Comments by Abigail Angkaw, PhD, staff psychologist, VA San Diego, 2013. In his 2011 article in *Stress and Health,* Ben-Ezra asserts, "Some aspects of the reactions to traumatic events seem to have a common denominator. This set of symptoms basically includes sleep disturbances that have a salient somatic component. Sleep disturbances are at the core of psychological trauma and PTSD symptoms" (236). Jared Diamond's anecdotal evidence from the tribes of New Guinea gives further weight to Ben-Ezra's argument.

The Greeks, by contrast, took a notably unclinical approach: Ben-Ezra, "Traumatic Reactions," 228. Ben-Ezra argues that "Homer's observations and experiences led him to understand the core human reactions to traumatic events. However, this understanding remained at the level of *epos* [i.e., that of an epic poem] rather than as part of the medical corpus, as we observed in Sumer and Babylon. This may explain why the concept of trauma was late to develop in the medical world in comparison to other mental disorders."

retired VA psychiatrist Jonathan Shay argues: Shay, *Achilles in Vietnam,* xiii.

70 *"As the legendary Oxford classicist C. M. Bowra put it":* Bowra, *Classical Greece,* 43.

The poet Heraclitus described: Haxton, trans., *Fragments,* 41.

The ancient physician Empedocles: Solomon, *The Noonday Demon,* 286.

71 *We see this in the Roman poet Ovid's* Metamorphoses: Ben-Ezra, "Traumatic Reactions," 229–230.

72 *His best friend, aide-de-camp, and comrade:* Shay, *Achilles in Vietnam,* 39–54.

Whenever I read lines like this from Homer: Interview with Kevin W., 2012.

73 *Perhaps unsurprisingly, Homer anticipates other ideas:* See Ben-Ezra, "Traumatic Reactions," 227. See also Birmes et al., "Psychotraumatology," 25.

74 *As Odysseus faces a deadly storm:* Ben-Ezra, "Traumatic Reactions," 227.

(In The Epic of Gilgamesh*):* Ibid., 226.

75 *Alice Sebold, describing her postrape roamings:* Sebold, *Lucky,* 232.

After the Civil War, the number of veterans: Dean notes, in *Shook over Hell,* that "sleepless and disturbed by memories of the war, some veterans simply left home and went off 'tramping,' walking or riding on railroad cars to wander the country-side" (168).

Closer to home, a dear friend: Interview with Elise Colton, 2012; interview with Clint Van Winkle, 2012.

The urge to reinvent one's moral and physical universe: Gonzales, *Surviving Survival,* 149.

76 *Homer died some four hundred years before Hippocrates:* The consensus among scholars is that "Homer" was not an actual historical person and that a conglomeration of bards is likely responsible for the composition of *The Iliad* and *The Odyssey.* However, following in the footsteps of a number of writers, I have used "Homer" to indicate these poets for simplicity's sake.

Some students of depression: Solomon, *The Noonday Demon,* 287.

In Denis Johnson's epic Vietnam novel: Johnson, *Tree of Smoke,* 61.

77 *If, as Siddhartha Mukherjee argues:* Mukherjee, *Emperor of All Maladies,* 575.

Keeping this in mind, leaders in the early Christian church assumed: Verkamp, *Moral Treatment,* 11.

As Pope Gregory VII put it: Ibid., 33.

78 *Apart from the theological concerns with killing:* On page 27 of *Moral Treatment,* Verkamp argues that "among ancient and more primitive peoples, the *horror sanguinis* at first reflected merely the primeval aversion for anything uncanny. By virtue of its association with the life forces, blood was viewed as being both holy and accursed, and therefore as something incalculably dangerous to both the individual and the community to which he belonged. The contaminated victim could spread a *miasma* to the whole community and sap it of its vital energies." See also Shay, *Odysseus in America,* 152.

The Archbishop of Canterbury: Shay, *Odysseus in America,* 18.

Throughout the Middle Ages, religious authorities: Egendorf, *Healing from the War,* 133.

These edicts, which came down: Verkamp, *Moral Treatment,* 20.

One church document from the tenth century: Ibid., 20.

79 *Church records from the Middle Ages are rife:* Ibid., 21. See also Egendorf, *Healing from the War,* 133.

80 *Studies of soldiers throughout history:* Grossman, *On Killing,* xvii.

As Ernest Hemingway wrote: Quoted in Egendorf, *Healing from the War,* 134.

As one army sniper, who had killed dozens: Interview with navy psychiatrist, 2013.

As Jonathan Shay argues at length: For more on the communalization of trauma, see Shay, *Achilles in Vietnam,* 188–192.

81 *Arthur Egendorf, a Vietnam veteran:* Egendorf, *Healing from the War,* 133–134.

In historical terms, technology is the great transformer of trauma: For a discussion of technology's impact on history and warfare, see Marshall McLuhan, *Understanding Media: The Extensions of Man* (Boston: MIT Press, 1994), 338–345.

As one South Carolinian declared in 1863: Gilpin Faust, *This Republic of Suffering,* 3.

82 *While visiting Union hospital ships moored:* Ibid., xiii.

82 *The major technologies that made such a cataclysm:* See McPherson, *Battle Cry of Freedom*, 287, 294, 474–477.
As Arnold Toynbee observed: Gilpin Faust, *This Republic of Suffering*, xi.
For many men, the shock of: McPherson, *Battle Cry of Freedom*, 409.
The opening engagement of the battle of Shiloh: Dean, *Shook over Hell*, 130.
One observer at Shiloh noted: Shelby Foote, *The Civil War: A Narrative — Fort Sumter to Perryville* (New York: Random House, 1958), 344.

83 *One historian, describing Sherman's tortured recollections:* Lewis, *Sherman*, 223.
Noting this, one researcher writing in 2012: Frueh et al., "Suicide, Alcoholism, and Psychiatric Illness among Union Forces." *Journal of Anxiety* 26 (2012): 769–775.
Characterizing the state of medicine as a whole: Gilpin Faust, *This Republic of Suffering*, 4.
A proper ambulance service was only established: See pages 118–123 in Eric Dean's *Shook over Hell* for a description of the Union Army's psychiatric casualty evacuation procedures and for a description of the Government Hospital for the Insane in Washington.

84 *In the mid-nineteenth century, before any formal:* Ibid., 115–116.
Another subgenre of these descriptors had a cardiac component: Friedman, ed., *Handbook of PTSD*, 20.
In 1871, six years after Appomattox: DaCosta, "On Irritable Heart," 2–52. See also Shephard, *War of Nerves*, 65, 123; Dean, *Shook over Hell*, 131; and Friedman, *Handbook of PTSD*, 20. Interestingly, some historians of psychiatry consider DaCosta's article to be the first to describe the condition that today we would call PTSD. One of the patients DaCosta described — a "William Henry" of the Sixty-Eighth Pennsylvania Volunteers — complained of horrible stomach pains and diarrhea. As Scott Stossel writes in *My Age of Anxiety* (Knopf, 2014), "Deemed by his doctors to be in otherwise good health, Henry was the first person to be formally diagnosed with 'soldier's heart,' a syndrome brought on by the stress of combat" (351).

85 *A word that has taken on different meanings:* Dean, *Shook over Hell*, 116, 128–130.
The Union Army recognized nostalgia: Ibid., 129.
By war's end, the Union's surgical rolls: Ibid, 130, 284.

86 *Hundreds of thousands of soldiers from both sides:* See Dora L. Costa et al., "Cowards and Heroes: Group Loyalty in the American Civil War." *Quarterly Journal of Economics* 118 (2003): 528. Costa estimates that at least two hundred thousand troops deserted on the Union side over the course of the war. See also McPherson, *Battle Cry of Freedom*, 820–821.
William Tecumseh Sherman, who later earned: Fellman, "Sherman's Demons."

87 *A number of states operated asylums, such as Indiana:* Dean, *Shook over Hell*, 229–231.
Stephen Crane, as an up-and-coming newspaper reporter: Crane, *Red Badge of Courage*.
In fact, the violence loosed by the Civil War: On page 98 of *Shook over Hell*, Dean writes that "during the war, soldiers had been trained to kill and thereby threw off

the restraints of civil society and accepted a life of violence; there was no immediate way to put an end to the habit of violence and reintroduce all of these men to the industrious and peaceful vocations of life. In both the North and the South a period of turmoil followed the end of the war." Dean goes on to describe the startling numbers of Civil War veterans who turned to a life of crime. See also Gilpin Faust, *This Republic of Suffering*, 142.

88 *As researchers at the University of California, Santa Cruz:* Archer et al., "Violent Acts," 937.

The U.S. Navy's Health Research Center: Booth-Kewley et al., "Factors Associated with Antisocial Behavior," 330.

89 *In many ways, the catastrophe of the American Civil War:* See Gilpin Faust, *This Republic of Suffering*, xi. See also Fussell, *Great War and Modern Memory*, 195.

As Paul Fussell, one of the war's: Fussell, *Great War and Modern Memory*, 7.

Partly because of its catchiness as a phrase: Winter, "Shell-shock," 7–11. On page 7, Winter asserts, "'Shell-shock' was a term which took on a notation which moved from the medical to the metaphysical ... My central argument is that the term 'shell-shock' was a specifically Anglo-Saxon representation not solely of damaged soldiers, but more generally of central facets of the war itself." Winter concludes his essay by saying that "the history of shell-shock, properly configured, is not the history of the officer corps, but the history of the war itself."

90 *One of the primary means for wounded minds:* Ibid., 10.

As Pat Barker, the author of a Booker-winning: See John Ezard, "Warring Fictions." *The Guardian,* September 11, 1993.

91 *Owen and, to a lesser extent, Sassoon:* Lifton, *Home from the War,* 131. On page 19 of *Home from the War,* Lifton writes that "not surprisingly, World War I writings came closest [to the feelings of Vietnam veterans], especially battlefield recollections by Europeans of their responses to that war's dreadful combination of slaughter and meaninglessness."

The first hints that the war was impacting soldiers' minds: See Lerner, *Hysterical Men,* 1; Shephard, *War of Nerves,* 1–3.

The German offensive, intended to take: See Fussell, *Great War and Modern Memory,* 43.

92 *"Watching, we hear the mad gusts tugging on the wire":* See Owen, *Collected Poems,* 34.

Charles Myers, a Cambridge psychologist: Shephard, *War of Nerves,* 1; Herman, *Trauma and Recovery,* 20; Friedman, *Handbook of PTSD,* 20–21. See also Jay Winter, "Shell-shock and the Cultural History of the Great War," *Journal of Contemporary History* 35 (2000), 10.

93 *Qualified as a physician, Myers was an example:* See Shephard, *War of Nerves,* 21–27.

On one side of the debate were the army's hardliners: Ibid., 25.

During World War I, more than 2,200 British soldiers: Friedman, *Handbook of PTSD,* 21.

94 *According to one estimate, at least two hundred thousand British soldiers:* See Kelly, *Treating Young Veterans,* 263. See also Shephard, *War of Nerves,* 109.
   A distinguished neurologist, F. W. Mott: Shephard, *War of Nerves,* 30.
   Freud's ideas on hysteria: Ibid., 104.

95 *Some contemporary trauma workers:* Interview with Bill Nash, 2012.
   This new policy, enacted by the Army Council in London: Shephard, *War of Nerves,* 32.
   Confusion about how to treat war neuroses: Ibid., 74–75. Also see Leed, *No Man's Land,* 170–180.

96 *Unsurprisingly, the use of electricity on soldiers was controversial:* See Winter, *Great War.* See also Laurent Tatu et al., "The 'Torpillage' Neurologists of World War I: Electric Therapy to Send Hysterics Back to the Front." *Historical Neurology* 75 (2010): 279–283. Tatu describes in greater detail the controversy that followed the Deschamps case.
   One doctor who championed a more liberal approach: Egremont, *Siegfried Sassoon,* 160–164; Fussell, *Great War and Modern Memory,* 121–127; Shephard, *War of Nerves,* 83–90; Leed, *No Man's Land,* 18–19.

97 *After the war, Rivers would conduct a study:* Leed, *No Man's Land,* 182.
   Rivers was fifty-one and serving as an army physician at Craiglockhart: Fussell, *Great War and Modern Memory,* 121. For more on Sassoon's state of mind during this time, see Egremont, *Siegfried Sassoon,* 159–182.

98 *Whether or not Sassoon was technically suffering:* Shephard, *War of Nerves,* 89–90; Egremont, *Siegfried Sassoon,* 174, 176, 401; See also Fussell, *Great War and Modern Memory,* 111, where he talks about Sassoon's postwar nightmares.
   As Sassoon would later write in his heavily: Sassoon, *Sherston's Progress,* 7.

99 *Rivers had been influenced by Freud:* Egremont, *Siegfried Sassoon,* 161; Shephard, *War of Nerves,* 85.
   As Sassoon saw it, the place was divided into two spheres: Shephard, *War of Nerves,* 85.
   Also at Craiglockhart was another troubled infantry officer: Egremont, *Siegfried Sassoon,* 165–171; Fussell, *Great War and Modern Memory,* 124; Shephard, *War of Nerves,* 93–95.

100 *By May, Sassoon was back in France:* See Egremont, *Siegfried Sassoon,* 203.
   The war was never far from his mind: Ferguson, *Pity of War,* 365; Fussell, *Great War and Modern Memory,* 86. In *The Great War and Modern Memory,* Fussell wrote about Sassoon, "By the time of the Armistice he was exhausted and trembly, sleepless and overwrought, fit for no literary work. He found peace and quiet again in Kent, but nightmares kept intruding. By 1926, however, he had recovered sufficiently to begin work on the obsessive enterprise which occupied most of the rest of his life, the re-visiting of the war and the contrasting world before the war in a series of six volumes of artful memoirs. The writing took him from one war to another: he finished the job in 1945. Exactly half his life he had spent plowing and re-plowing the earlier half, motivated by what — dichotomizing to the end — he

calls 'my queer craving to revisit the past and give the modern world the slip'" (111–112).

In Britain alone, there were twenty shell-shock hospitals: Shephard, *War of Nerves,* 110.

Oddly, no veterans movement ever coalesced in Great Britain: See Jay Winter, "Shell-shock," 8.

102 *The one exception to this vast amnesia:* Shephard, *War of Nerves,* 154–157; Herman, *Trauma and Recovery,* 23–24.

The book would be almost completely ignored: Shephard, *War of Nerves,* 396.

4. The Haunted Mind

103 *While people suffering post-traumatic symptoms:* On the abnormal states of consciousness that sometimes result post-trauma, see Herman, *Trauma and Recovery,* 96. Describing certain aspects of Great War literature, Fussell argues, "The movement was towards myth, towards a revival of the cultic, the mystical, the sacrificial, the prophetic, the sacramental and the universally significant" (*Great War and Modern Memory,* 152). Annette Becker, in a 2000 article in the *Journal of Contemporary History* titled "The Avant-garde, Madness and the Great War," argues that the madness of World War I was the catalyst for surrealism, an art movement fascinated with hallucination, the irrational, and the mysteries of the unconscious. "To psychiatrists, mental confusion and hallucinations were characteristic wartime syndromes, and the numerous case studies discussed seemed to the surrealists to be poems in prose suited just for them" (79). Becker quotes Surrealist poet André Breton: "I insist on the fact that surrealism cannot be understood historically without reference to war — I would say from 1918 to 1938 — both the war it left behind and the one to which it returned" (71–72). Becker goes on to describe the art movement as one created by men haunted by the war: "In the 1920s and 1930s, many surrealist and expressionist artists and poets wrote that they were marked by war, trapped between beauty and violence, between despair and fascination. One case in point is the painter André Masson: 'For me, violence is part of existence, and one must express it. That is why I returned from Switzerland to serve in the army, to be a common soldier, to see violence — not to inflict it, but to see it — but I was in it and had to be in it'" (72).

104 *The day before I hit an IED in Baghdad:* For more on these sorts of compensatory rumors and hallucinations, see the "Myth, Ritual, and Romance" chapter in Fussell's *The Great War and Modern Memory,* specifically pages 148–149.

107 *Modern science tends to look on such episodes:* Personal communication with Steve House.

Perhaps, as Laurence Gonzales wrote: Gonzales, *Surviving Survival.* Gonzales wrote that "dreams can be thought of as conversations between two parts of the brain, the hippocampus . . . and the neo-cortex" (134).

107 *The year after she was raped in a tunnel:* Sebold, *Lucky,* 216. See also ibid., 225–227. Personal communication with Alice Sebold, 2014.

108 *Ambrose Bierce, the most important American writer:* Gilpin Faust, *This Republic of Suffering,* 196, 199.
Freud, a passionately secular man: Caruth, *Trauma,* 115.
Seventy years later, Cathy Caruth, a writer: Ibid., 4–5.
Beliefs about trauma's connection to the spiritual realms: See Percy, *Demon Camp.* Personal communication with Jen Percy, 2014.

109 *Neuroscientists have long known that not all memories:* McGaugh, *Memory and Emotion,* 83. Interview with James McGaugh, 2013.
But the extraordinary flashback memories: See Chris Brewin and Steph J. Hellawell, "A Comparison of Flashbacks and Ordinary Autobiographical Memories of Trauma: Content and Language." *Behaviour Research and Therapy* 42 (2004): 1–12.

110 *"Memories gone wild":* Interview with Clint Van Winkle, 2013.
"In the past six years I've recoiled from remembering": Deraniyagala, *Wave,* 165–166.

112 *By 2007, at the height of the surge:* David H. Petraeus et al., *FM 3-24 Counterinsurgency,* 80, 121.

114 *This situation was not, needless to say, governed by a rational process:* See Gonzales, *Surviving Survival,* 26.
For this reason, cases of chronic PTSD: As Jonathan Shay put it on page 169 of *Achilles in Vietnam:* "PTSD can unfortunately mimic virtually any condition in psychiatry." See also Nicosia, *Home to War,* 182; Sarah Haley, "When the Patient Reports Atrocities: Specific Treatment Considerations of the Vietnam Veteran." *Archives of General Psychiatry* (1974).
So powerful, so transporting, are these intrusive memories: Personal communication with Dewleen Baker, May 2012.

115 *One woman, who had been molested:* Sacks, *Hallucinations,* 238.
Nearly all survivors report that certain: O'Brien, *In the Lake of the Woods,* 79.

116 *Writing about it in an epilogue to his bestselling book:* Simpson, *Touching the Void,* 210.
Needless to say, Simpson, who considers: Personal communication with Joe Simpson, 2013.
One study of 115 combat veterans with PTSD: Holmes and Tinnin, "Problem of Auditory Hallucinations," 1–7.

117 *Douglas Bremner, a researcher at Emory University, makes the point:* Bremner, *Does Stress,* 214.

118 *Post-traumatic hauntings require no such invitation:* Dean, *Shook over Hell,* 104.

119 *Michael Ferrara, a veteran wilderness first responder:* Sides, "The Man Who Saw Too Much," 2011.
As we saw in the previous chapter: Shephard, *War of Nerves,* 85.
An Indiana physician who treated Newell Gleason: Dean, *Shook over Hell,* 151–153.

120 *The dead seem most likely to visit us at night:* Herr, *Dispatches,* 244.

In fact, it was the modern war nightmare: Gay, *Freud,* 400–401; Sacks, *Hallucinations,* 241. Cathy Caruth, on page 24 of *Trauma: Explorations in Memory,* says, *"Beyond the Pleasure Principle* indeed opens with Freud's perplexed observation of a psychic disorder that appears to reflect the unavoidable and overwhelming imposition of violent events on the psyche. Faced with the striking occurrence of what were called war neuroses in the wake of World War I, Freud is startled by the emergence of a pathological condition — the repetitive experience of nightmares and relivings of battlefield events . . . the returning traumatic dream startles Freud because it cannot be understood in terms of any wish or unconscious meaning, but is, purely and inexplicably, the literal return of the event against the will of the one it inhabits."

"Trauma-related anxiety dreams appear": Peretz Lavie, "Sleep Disturbances in the Wake of Traumatic Events." *New England Journal of Medicine* 345 (2001): 1825–1832.

121 *Numerous studies, dating back to the advent of the PTSD:* Herman, *Trauma and Recovery,* 36.

Interestingly, Richard Ross of the University of Pennsylvania: Everly, *Psychotraumatology,* 176–177.

"The bad stuff never stops happening": O'Brien, *Things They Carried,* 32.

For this reason, and the fact that nightmares are difficult: See Friedman, *Handbook of PTSD.*

122 *The most cited studies on traumatic nightmares:* See, for example, Murray A. Raskind et al., "Reduction of Nightmares and Other PTSD Symptoms in Combat Veterans by Prazosin: A Placebo-Controlled Study." *American Journal of Psychiatry* 160 (2003): 371–373.

In a study conducted by therapists: See Lansky, *Posttraumatic Nightmares,* 1995.

123 *This theory helps explain how Caleb Daniels:* See Percy, *Demon Camp,* 2014.

One Iraq veteran I interviewed, who now runs: Interview with Glenn C., 2013.

Audie Murphy, the most decorated American soldier: Graham, *No Name,* 191.

"Something of the working-through process": Solomon, *Combat Stress Reaction,* 76.

124 *"Forty-three years old, and the war occurred":* O'Brien, *Things They Carried,* 38.

Perhaps no one has inhabited this shadowland of dream: See Egremont, *Siegfried Sassoon,* 224, 519–524; Fussell, *Great War and Modern Memory,* 123–127; Ferguson, *Pity of War,* 365.

125 *As a writer, Sassoon turned this backward-looking:* See Fussell, *Great War and Modern Memory,* 112.

These types of obsessions and revisitations all highlight: See Leed, *No Man's Land,* 12–33.

Herein lies the problem: the liminal person: See Karen Samuels, "PTSD as a State of Liminality." *Journal of Military and Strategic Studies* 8, no. 3 (Spring 2006).

126 *Having been unmade and remade by the war:* Leed, *No Man's Land,* 33.

In 1965, one such veteran wrote: Ibid., 14.

"The figure of the veteran is a subcategory": Ibid., 194.

126 *As every military spouse can attest:* Numbers 31:19.

127 *"possessing a great secret which can never be communicated":* Leed, *No Man's Land,* 12.

 "As a man who had lived for years in No-Man's-Land": Ibid., 196.

128 *One war-reporter friend of mine:* Elliott D. Woods, personal communication with the author.

130 *She said, "I want those years back":* Elise Colton, personal communication with the author.

 A better, less venal world: For an examination of the philosophy behind counter-factuals, see Niall Ferguson's provocative *Virtual History: Alternatives and Counterfactuals* (New York: Basic Books, 2000); Michael Chabon's 2007 novel *The Yiddish Policemen's Union;* and my short story "The Counterfactualist" in *War, Literature and the Arts* 25 (2013): 76–97.

5. Modern Trauma

132 *Within the history of psychological trauma:* This section was informed in part by Paul Fussell's August 1989 article in the *Atlantic,* "The Real War 1939–1945," where he argued that "the real war was tragic and ironic beyond the power of any literary or philosophic analysis to suggest, but in unbombed America especially, the meaning of the war seemed inaccessible. Thus, as experience, the suffering was wasted." See also Fussell, *Wartime,* along with my article in the Winter 2007 *Virginia Quarterly Review,* "The Image as History: Clint Eastwood's Unmaking of an American Myth."

 Karl Shapiro, the poet laureate who served in the Pacific: Fussell, *Wartime,* 134.

 Included in this generation of silence: See page 14 of Salinger's story "Last Day of the Last Furlough" as well as Slawenski, *J. D. Salinger,* 139, 185. The Shields and Solerno oral history of Salinger (New York: Simon & Schuster, 2013) is provocative and entertaining, but the authors tend to attribute virtually all of Salinger's eccentricities to his purported PTSD. Salinger's story "For Esmé—With Love and Squalor" is, nevertheless, a fine example of how war trauma was publicly handled by the World War II generation—it was alluded to and generally left off-stage. Interestingly, a number of writers of late have taken on the project of loking for PTSD in history's great actors, including T. E. Lawrence, Ernest Hemingway, Alexander the Great, and Florence Nightingale. For more on this, see Phillip A. Mackowiak et al., "Post-Traumatic Stress Reactions before the Advent of Post-Traumatic Stress Disorder." *Military Medicine* 173 (2009): 1158–1163.

 In America, stories of veterans who came home: See Bradley, *Flags of Our Fathers,* 4, where he says, "He had trained us, as children, to deflect the phone-call requests for media interviews that never diminished over the years ... And this is how we Bradley children grew up: happily enough, deeply connected to our peaceful, tree-shaded town, but always with a sense of an unsolved mystery somewhere at the edges of the picture."

133 *"As long as they could function on a minimum level":* Herman, *Trauma and Recovery,* 26.

Nearly sixty years after the Japanese surrendered: Gladwell, "Getting Over It." Ironically, Gladwell's article came out the day after the second battle of Fallujah began, the deadliest American battle since the Vietnam War.

134 *Why can't we?:* Ibid.

(In 1945, when the U.S. Army learned of John Huston's plan): See Shephard, *War of Nerves,* 271–278. Shephard's examination of Huston's film *Let There Be Light,* which was suppressed by the U.S. government for decades, is both revelatory and instructive.

At the end of the war, General Eisenhower: Shephard, *War of Nerves,* 326.

135 *Subsequent studies into the traumatic experiences:* Hillenbrand, *Unbroken,* 346–351. See also Bernard M. Cohen and Maurice Z. Cooper, *A Follow-up Study of World War II Prisoners of War* (Washington, D.C.: Government Printing Office, 1955); Robert Ursano and James Rundell, "The Prisoner of War," in *War Psychiatry* (Washington, D.C.: Office of the Surgeon General, 1995), 431–456.

As Matthew Friedman, the first executive director: Interview with Gerald Nicosia, November 12, 1988, Dolph Briscoe Center for American History, Austin, Texas (BCAH). I relied heavily on the Nicosia papers, interview tapes, and transcripts stored at the Briscoe in the writing of this section.

A supremely talented soldier: Graham, *No Name,* 70.

136 *"I figured those gentlemen were going to run into trouble":* Ibid., 75.

"War robs you mentally and physically": Ibid., 124.

"In combat, you see, your hearing gets so acute": Ibid., 304.

137 *"They took Army dogs and rehabilitated them for civilian life":* Ibid., 124.

Among the many things that Vietnam changed: Shephard, *War of Nerves,* 355.

This revolution in thinking has even extended into the past: See Winter, *Great War.*

But even beyond the "invention" of PTSD: On page 57 of Rosen's anthology, *Posttraumatic Stress Disorder,* Ben Shephard writes, "Will psychiatrists have the sense to realize that by medicalizing the human response to stressful situations, they have created a culture of trauma and thus undermined the general capacity to resist trauma? They could make a start by dismantling the unitary concept of trauma, an idea that has long outlived its purpose."

138 *Hence,* trauma: In the preface to *The Invisible Bridge: The Fall of Nixon and the Rise of Reagan,* historian Rick Perlstein repeatedly uses the word "trauma" to characterize the period of the 1970s, invoking it to describe Watergate, Nixon's exit from the White House, and the Vietnam War.

"The war itself was a mystery": O'Brien, *In the Lake of the Woods,* 76.

It is this sort of ongoing disagreement: Nash, "Understanding and Treating Post-Deployment Violence." Presentation, Navy Base San Diego, March 2006.

Despite the war's uncertain place in history: As Patrick Bracken put it in a 2001 issue of *Social Science & Medicine,* "The fact that there was a political campaign which looked upon the war in Vietnam as a negative phenomenon meant that there was a political context in which psychiatry could take seriously the negative effects of wartime experiences" (734–735).

139 *One of the great students of this climate:* Nicosia, *Home to War,* 158; Lifton, *Home from the War,* 16. See also Shephard, *War of Nerves,* 356–358.

A practitioner of an unorthodox academic field: Lifton, *Home from the War,* 15.

"I was opposed to the Vietnam War": Robert Lifton interview with Gerald Nicosia, April 20, 1988, BCAH.

The change for Lifton came in November 1969: Lifton, *Home from the War,* 16.

In November 1970, Lifton received a letter from Jan Barry: Nicosia, *Home to War,* 158; Lifton, *Home from the War,* 75.

140 *"there is no anti-war or even anti-establishment group":* Thompson, *Fear and Loathing,* 369.

"the severe psychological problems of many": Lifton, *Home from the War,* 75.

Barry saw the politics of the war and the psychological problems: Nicosia, *Home to War,* 161. See also ibid., 173; Lifton, *Home from the War,* 75.

Some VVAWers, like Joe Urgo, an air force veteran: Nicosia, *Home to War,* 86–87; Scott, *Politics of Readjustment,* 17; Shephard, *War of Nerves,* 356–357.

They didn't belong anywhere: Nicosia, *Home to War,* 164.

141 *"I want to scream at friends and relatives":* See Sarah Haley, "When the Patient Reports Atrocities: Specific Treatment Considerations of the Vietnam Veteran." *Archives of General Psychiatry* 30 (1974): 195. Haley's article is one of the most important documents in the history of PTSD as a formal diagnosis. For a deeper (if skeptical) discussion of Haley's legacy, see Shephard, *War of Nerves,* 369–375.

"Guys are hurting. They're opposed to the war": Robert Lifton interview (BCAH); Nicosia, *Home to War,* 161.

Along with Chaim Shatan, a New York University: Lifton, *Home from the War,* 75–77; Nicosia, *Home to War,* 161.

In Shatan, Lifton had, by sheer accident: Nicosia, *Home to War,* 160–161; Chaim Shatan interview, April 14, 1988 (BCAH).

The first "rap group" met on Saturday, December 12, 1970: Nicosia, *Home to War,* 162. Nicosia's account of this time period is superlative.

142 *"about twelve guys, most of them in fatigue shirts":* Egendorf, *Healing from the War,* 90.

"The explosion of feeling that occurred": Nicosia, *Home to War,* 163; Lifton, *Home from the War,* 76.

Shatan recalled one early meeting: Shephard, *War of Nerves,* 356.

Egendorf, who was an outlier in the group: Nicosia, *Home to War,* 169.

For Egendorf, the rap groups represented: Ibid., 165–169. See also Egendorf, *Healing from the War,* 84–85.

143 *One night, atop his hotel in Saigon:* Egendorf, *Healing from the War,* 67. See also Nicosia, *Home to War,* 166.

Lifton's suggestion that they take place on the veterans': Lifton, *Home from the War,* 76.

"The VVAW crew, like many of their Vietnam veteran": Shephard, *War of Nerves*, 362.

Part of this was due to the fact that in 1966: Shephard, *War of Nerves*, 340; Nicosia, *Home to War*, 170, 175–176. Nicosia: "Lifton went on to denounce the Army's use of 'ostensibly brilliant psychiatric statistics' as a form of 'psychiatric technicism,' the professional equivalent of [a] 'body count'" (177).

At ease in their own territory: Lifton, *Home from the War*, 77.

In fact, what the VVAWers were doing: Egendorf, *Healing from the War*, 130; Egendorf interview, October 3, 1988 (BCAH); see also Schulman, *Seventies*, 159–169. Personal communication with Christine Eubank.

144 *"The idea for rap groups came from"*: Egendorf interview, November 3, 1988 (BCAH). See also Allen, *Free Space*, 5–8.

"we had the women's movement as a constant example": Egendorf, *Healing from the War*, 130.

The women's movement of the 1970s: See Schulman, *Seventies*, 167–168.

In 1971, the first rape crisis center opened: Meredith May, "Oleta Adams — Cofounder of Rape Crisis Center." *San Francisco Chronicle*, January 16, 2005.

145 *Around the same time, Ann Burgess*: Herman, *Trauma and Recovery*, 31; Burgess and Holmstrom, "Rape Trauma Syndrome." *American Journal of Psychiatry* 131 (1974): 981–986.

"One vet would usually begin the conversation by talking": Egendorf interview, October 3, 1988 (BCAH).

One problem that emerged early on: Nicosia, *Home to War*, 162.

146 *This phenomenon is most easily seen*: See Ambrose, *Band of Brothers*, 16–17. The relationship between the Great Depression and the World War II generation's view of trauma is an area that needs to be explored. Ambrose, who was opposed to the Vietnam War, describes the Great Depression in almost positive terms, as if it had the effect of hardening and preparing people for the trials of World War II. Describing the paratroopers of Easy Company, Ambrose said: "They came out of the Depression with many positive features. They were self-reliant, accustomed to hard work and to taking orders" (17). Interestingly, a number of World War II veterans have retroactively embraced the PTSD diagnosis, including some members of Easy Company, 506th PIR, made famous by Stephen Ambrose. One such veteran, Edward "Babe" Heffron, said, "I hear Vietnam vets say they suffer from flashbacks and I think, 'Hey, I've been having them since 1944, I have seniority!'" (Philipps, *Lethal Warriors*, 77). See also Shephard, *War of Nerves*, 356.

One person who was very concerned about where: See Wells, *Battle Within*, 315–317, 489. The Chuck Colson files at the Richard Nixon Presidential Library are filled with memos between Colson and the other members of the White House staff detailing ways to discredit the VVAW, including one undated memo titled "Plan to Counteract Viet Nam Veterans Against the War" (Colson Box 117). Tellingly, Colson and Nixon were both convinced that many of the VVAWers weren't actual U.S. military veterans.

146 *One statement from a VA psychologist in the* Capital Times: Jim Hougan, "Madison's Vietnam Veterans: A Different Breed — Part One: Alienation Follows the Horrors of Asia." *Capital Times,* February 22, 1971.

147 *The man who forwarded the article to Colson:* Memorandum to Colson dated March 9, 1971. Nixon Library, Colson Box 21.

Two months later, soon after the VVAW's highly publicized "Dewey Canyon III": Nicosia: "According to Vietnam veteran and historian Rusty Lindley, Dewey Canyon III had had a profound effect on the Nixon White House and its policies toward Vietnam veterans. Nixon and White House hatchet man Charles Colson became obsessed with the VVAW and its impact on public opinion. The White House launched a concerted effort to discredit not only VVAW, but also the problems the war was creating among returning soldiers. Their position was that 'the Vietnam veteran was too busy in school or on the job to have any readjustment problems' . . . The Nixon administration was adamantly opposed to the provision of any assistance that would indicate that the war was adversely affecting veterans" (200). See also Wells, *Battle Within,* 579–580.

Prior to Dewey Canyon III, members of the Nixon administration had puzzled over the motivations of the antiwar movement besides communist subversion. As Wells put it: "Henry Kissinger felt permissive child-rearing practices were partially responsible for the dissension. Explaining the 'special feeling' he had for antiwar students, Kissinger writes in his memoirs: 'They had been brought up by skeptics, relativists, and psychiatrists; now they were rudderless in a world from which they demanded certainty without sacrifice. My generation had failed them by encouraging self-indulgence and neglecting to provide roots.' [National Security Council staffer Roger] Morris recalled a 'collection of acid Kissinger observations to his staff on the neurotic character of the demonstrators' that fall. '"They don't know who they are," Kissinger said. "They need fathers, not brothers." "They are going through an identity crisis." "This is like dealing with thumb-sucking."' Kissinger's aide Anthony Lake remembered, 'He saw them as spoiled children'" (*Home to War,* 315).

At Colson's request, Herbert Rainwater, head of the VFW: Wells, *Battle Within,* 489.

The effort to undermine the group went well beyond: Nicosia, *Home to War,* 249–254.

Soon after Chaim Shatan began working with the VVAW: Shatan, "Grief of Soldiers," 652–653. See also the Nicosia interview with Shatan, April 14, 1988, found at BCAH.

148 *By Lifton's count, around 115 veterans eventually:* Nicosia, *Home to War,* 163.

On April 30, 1971, Dwight Johnson, a recently discharged army: See Jon Nordheimer, "From Dakto to Detroit: Death of a Troubled Hero." *New York Times,* May 25, 1971. See also Shephard, *War of Nerves,* 357.

149 *In it, Shatan described the work of the rap groups:* Shatan, "Post-Vietnam Syndrome."

According to Shatan, once the op-ed hit newsstands: See Nicosia, *Home to War,* 180. See also Scott, *Politics of Readjustment.*

In April 1973, just as the Watergate scandal: See Nicosia, *Home to War,* 195; see also Shorter, *History of Psychiatry,* 304. See also Scott, *Politics of Readjustment.*

150 *By all accounts, the St. Louis summit was a huge success:* See Nicosia, *Home to War,* 196. Author interview with Floyd "Shad" Meshad, 2013. See also Wilbur J. Scott, "PTSD in DSM-III: A Case in the Politics of Diagnosis and Disease." *Social Problems* 37 (1990): 294–310.

The lone exception to this was the contingent of VA people: Nicosia, *Home to War,* 197.

Speaking of the event years later: See Scott, *Politics of Readjustment,* 46.

151 *As the conference drew to a close:* Ibid., 46.

In Detroit, a Holocaust survivor and psychiatrist: Nicosia, *Home to War,* 180.

It would be years before the members of the VVAW: Tom Wells, speaking of the VVAW and other antiwar groups in *The War Within: America's Battle over Vietnam,* argues, "The American movement against the Vietnam War was perhaps the most successful antiwar movement in history. The movement did not exert its influence in any neat way, but its impact was clearly considerable . . . As Admiral Thomas Moorer, chairman of the JCS [Joint Chiefs of Staff] during the Nixon administration, asserted, 'The reaction of the noisy radical groups was considered all the time. And it served to inhibit and restrain the decision makers.' The movement, Moorer accurately added, 'had a major impact . . . both in the executive and legislative branches of the government'" (579). To this list of accomplishments could clearly be added the eventual creation of the PTSD diagnosis.

Because of its still-speculative nature: See Lifton, *Home from the War,* 420.

152 *It is, perhaps, the fatal flaw of humankind:* In a 2000 article, "The Collective Mind" in the *Journal of Contemporary History,* Catherine Merridale describes the reaction of Russian citizens to the purges and violence of the 1930s: "Time after time, respondents told me that the only way to cope with famine, arrest, hunger and bereavement was 'to get on with our lives'" (46). As Merridale goes on to show, such willful amnesia on the part of these Soviet survivors had the effect of serving the agenda of the Soviet leadership by cultivating an ignorance of its past abuses.

Randy Floyd, a former Marine attack pilot: See Peter Davis's 1974 Academy Award–winning documentary *Hearts and Minds* (available on YouTube) beginning at one hour and forty-six minutes.

153 *What the movement and Shatan, in particular, hadn't counted on:* See Greenberg, *Book of Woe,* 36–43; Shorter, *History of Psychiatry,* 301; Shephard, *War of Nerves,* 362.

"I love controversy! I love it!": Greenberg, *Book of Woe,* 43.

Spitzer had had a number of opportunities to indulge: Ibid., 35–36, 41–42. See also Scott, *Politics of Readjustment,* 39–58.

154 *"If groups of people march and raise hell":* Greenberg, *Book of Woe,* 36. Author interview with Greenberg, April 2013.

In June 1974, Shatan got a phone call: Nicosia, *Home to War,* 202.

Eventually, it came out that Spitzer had no plans: Ibid., 203.

154 *"Trying to understand another human being's emotional life":* Greenberg, *Book of Woe,* 30.

"You don't have any evidence": Nicosia, *Home to War,* 205.

155 *"these guys are all character disorders":* Ibid., 205. See also the transcript of the Nicosia interview with Sarah Haley (April 28, 1988) at BCAH.

"They were reluctant to accept the idea that social": Nicosia, *Home to War,* 205.

156 *Because many of the veterans were hearing voices:* Author interview with Floyd "Shad" Meshad, March 2013. See also Sarah Haley, "When the Patient Reports Atrocities." *Archives of General Psychiatry* (1974); Nicosia, *Home to War,* 182; transcript of the Nicosia interview with Sarah Haley (April 28, 1988) at BCAH. See also Holmes and Tinnin, "Problem of Auditory Hallucinations," 1–7. According to Haley, many Vietnam veterans were misdiagnosed with paranoid schizophrenia in the 1970s. I know of two Iraq veterans who received similar misdiagnoses from the VA as recently as 2013.

Invited to the APA's annual convention in Toronto: Nicosia, *Home to War,* 207–209; Shorter, *History of Psychiatry,* 304; Shephard, *War of Nerves,* 367.

When the committee finally released its findings: Nicosia, *Home to War,* 208.

Shatan would later complain that the diagnosis: Ibid., 208.

Ironically, much of what ended up in the DSM's: Herman, *Trauma and Recovery,* 24.

157 *The post-1980 history of trauma has:* Interview with Greenberg, April 2013. See also Shorter, *History of Psychiatry,* 302.

a "psychological disorder, rather than a biological disorder": Transcript of Nicosia interview with Matthew Friedman (November 12, 1988) at BCAH.

According to Friedman, the first director: Ibid. Ben Shephard, one of PTSD's leading critics, addressed this move toward the biological in increasingly shrill tones throughout the 2000s, at one point declaring in a Rotterdam lecture that "modern psychiatry, for reasons of medical fashion and economic survival, puts its faith in biological research. Its pride and self-respect also; it is relying on biological research to vindicate the whole PTSD project."

Covering more than one thousand male subjects: See Kulka et al., *National Vietnam Veterans.*

158 *In 2006, a Columbia University epidemiologist reworked the data:* B. P. Dohrenwend et al., "The Psychological Risks of Vietnam for U.S. Veterans: A Revisit with New Data and Methods." *Science* 313 (2006): 979–982.

A subsequent reexamination by a Harvard psychologist: See McNally, *What Is Mental Illness?* This debate about the actual traumatic power of Vietnam (and Iraq) was covered in *Scientific American* and by a number of influential neurobloggers, including Jonah Lehrer. In the April 13, 2009, issue of *Scientific American,* David Dobbs argued for a revamped VA PTSD diagnosis system, one that included fewer incentives for a positive PTSD diagnosis, saying, "These changes will be hard to sell in a culture that resists any suggestion that PTSD is not a common, even inevitable, consequence of combat. Mistaking its horror for its prevalence, most people assume PTSD is epidemic, ignoring all evidence to the contrary." He concludes by saying, "PTSD exists. Where it exists we must treat it. But our cultural obsession with PTSD has magnified and finally perhaps become the thing itself a prolonged failure to contextualize and accept our own collective aggression. It may be our own postwar neurosis." See also R. J. McNally, "Progress and Controversy in the Study of Posttraumatic Stress Disorder." *Annual Review of Psychology* 54 (2003): 229–252.

159 *More often than not, it is the powerless:* Transcript of Nicosia interview with Arthur Egendorf (November 3, 1988) at BCAH.

"There are always moral questions, which are inseparable": Quoted in Nicosia, *Home to War,* 173.

An influential 1995 article in the American Journal of Psychiatry: R. Yehuda et al., "Conflict between Current Knowledge," 1705–1713.

160 *And because it is instigated by an external agent:* Author interview with Gaithri Fernando, May 2013.

This has resulted in a clinical culture, especially within psychiatry: See Satel and Lilienfeld, *Brainwashed,* for more on the rise of neuroscience.

"All of us have our own, distinctive mental worlds": Sacks, *Man Who Mistook,* 129.

In 1979, at the dawn of contemporary neuroscience: See Eric R. Kandel, "Psychotherapy and the Single Synapse." *New England Journal of Medicine* 301 (1974): 1028–1037.

161 *In his bestselling book* Listening to Prozac: Kramer, *Listening to Prozac,* x. In 1993, Kramer wrote that "my sense when I began my inquiries — and this is still my sense today — is that the new biological materialism is a cultural phenomenon that goes beyond the scientific evidence. There have always been observations favoring nature over nurture. What changes, in response to the spirit of the times, is the choice of evidence to which we attend" (xiv). Given the rise of the neuroculture in academe as well as in the culture generally, Kramer's words seem prescient.

Between 1987, the year Prozac was introduced: van der Kolk, unpublished manuscript, "The Body Keeps the Score."

This accidental discovery, of a drug associated: Personal communication with Dewleen Baker.

162 *This lack of a scientific basis for using SSRIs to treat PTSD:* See Institute of Medicine, *Treatment of Posttraumatic Stress Disorder,* 2008. See also Shiromani, ed., *Post-Traumatic Stress Disorder,* 338.

As one Oxford University psychiatrist put it recently: See Burns, *Psychiatry,* 2006.

One Manchester, New Hampshire, physician and lawyer argued: Dr. Albert Drukteinis.

In 1995, Cathy Caruth, a trauma scholar at Emory University: Caruth, *Trauma,* 9.

163 *By the 1990s, PTSD as a concept had outgrown:* See Luckhurst, *Trauma Question.*

"After the formulation and extension of PTSD in the 1980s": Ibid., 203–209.

164 *"the timeless time of the post-traumatic condition":* Ibid., 206.

By *September 11, 2001, PTSD as a cultural phenomenon:* See Gonzales, *Surviving Survival,* 7. See also Seeley, *Therapy after Terror,* 2008.

To the dismay of infantrymen who fought in Iraq and Afghanistan: See the late Matt Power's "Confessions of a Drone Warrior" in the October 23, 2013, issue of *GQ.*

165 *"Based on prior experience from other mass disasters":* Watters, *Crazy Like Us,* 69.

Robert Gates, the secretary of defense under Presidents Bush: See Robert Gates, "The Quiet Fury of Robert Gates." *Wall Street Journal,* January 7, 2014.

Once the dream of a handful of Vietnam veterans: See Watters, *Crazy Like Us,* 71.

6. Therapy

166 *The original building, completed in 1972, boasts:* See http://www.sandiego .va.gov/about/ (accessed August 1, 2014).

It serves a regional veteran population of over: Personal communication with VA San Diego staff psychologist; personal communication with Jeanette Steele, staff reporter, *San Diego Union-Tribune;* Iraq and Afghanistan Veterans of America press release, September 23, 2013. "IAVA Leads Events Across San Diego."

169 *"The primary investigator for this study has a résumé":* Personal communication with the author, March 2013.

After guiding me through a thick stack of surveys: See Friedman, *Handbook of PTSD,* 284–285. See also F. W. Weathers et al., "Clinician Administered PTSD Scale (CAPS): A Review of the First Ten Years of Research." *Depression and Anxiety* 13 (2001): 132–156. The VA has a tremendous amount of faith in the CAPS, and it is the cornerstone of its recent evidence-supported therapy campaign. According to the research, the CAPS is very reliable. However, as critics like Gary Greenberg (who's a licensed therapist himself) have pointed out, these sorts of deliberately anonymous, neo-Kraepelinian diagnostic tools are not without their shortcomings. Greenberg argues, in his 2010 book *Manufacturing Depression: The Secret History of a Modern Disease,* that "the trick with the descriptive approach to diagnosis is to keep your eye on the loose-leaf notebook and not on the patient. That's why it didn't really matter whether my doctor knew my name or noticed that I was cracking jokes, engaging him in relatively sophisticated conversation about neurochemistry . . . Details like this would have been inconvenient to say the least . . . The [mental health] industry is working hard to eliminate the human element from psychiatry, but for now the best it can do is to circle the answers in notebooks and train practitioners to ignore what's in front of their eyes" (63–64). Needless to say, the ideal of a diagnosis being arrived at by "a dialogue between patient and doctor," at least with respect to PTSD and the VA, seems to be a thing of the past.

174 *"People with PTSD drink":* Personal communication with the author, March 2013.

175 *"When I started to read the symptoms online":* Author interview with Jessica G., February 2014.

Several years after being raped: Sebold, *Lucky,* 239–240. Author interview with Sebold, July 2013.

176 *"Now, I'm gonna make mistakes and say some stupid things":* All the dialogue between Scott (not his real name) and me was digitally recorded, as were most of the therapy sessions and CAPS interviews at the VA San Diego during my time there. Wherever possible, I have used those recordings to check the accuracy of my reporting. I was admitted into the VA San Diego Healthcare System as a veteran based on my Marine Corps service in the 1990s. I have never sought nor received a disability rating from the VA.

Prolonged Exposure, one of the VA's "gold standard" PTSD therapies: See Follette et al., *Cognitive-Behavioral Therapies,* 66–68, for a succinct overview of the PE therapy; Foa et al., *Treating the Trauma;* Friedman, *Handbook of PTSD,* 475–476; Back et al., *Concurrent Treatment of PTSD;* Finley, *Fields of Combat,* 123. Learning about PE is often difficult for the general researcher because the therapy is referred to by so many different names. Within the scientific literature, one finds references to "prolonged exposure," "exposure therapy," "imaginal therapy," "imaginal exposure," "flooding," and "implosive therapy," and it is often difficult to ascertain exactly what is being discussed. This confusion is exacerbated by the fact that "prolonged exposure" is usually lumped in with the VA's other major therapeutic modality—"cognitive processing therapy"—under the rubric of "cognitive-behavioral therapy," even though the two therapies are very different. PE is largely derived from the work of Ivan Pavlov and Edna Foa, whereas CPT is drawn largely from the work of Aaron Beck and Patricia Resick of the VA's National Center for PTSD.

178 *"In the meantime I experienced eight weeks of mild panic attacks":* Simpson, *Touching the Void,* 213. Simpson's account of his panic attacks is included in the epilogue to the 2004 edition of *Touching the Void.* Simpson's comments in the documentary film *Return to Siula Grande,* included in the DVD extras of the feature film based on his book, are chilling and revelatory.

181 *It was, I would later learn, a "manualized" therapy:* Interview with Gary Greenberg, April 2013; interview with senior VA psychiatrist, April 2013.

183 *Prolonged Exposure, one of the VA's top-tier or "Schedule A":* There are dozens of studies that have shown PE to be effective. Here are a few of the most cited publications: Edna Foa et al., *Prolonged Exposure Therapy for PTSD: Emotional Processing of Traumatic Experiences* (New York: Oxford University Press, 2007); Edna Foa et al., "Randomized Trial of Prolonged Exposure for Posttraumatic Stress Disorder With and Without Cognitive Restructuring: Outcome at Academic and Community Clinics." *Journal of Consulting and Clinical Psychology* 73 (2005): 953–964; Mark B. Powers et al., "A Meta-Analytic Review of Prolonged Exposure for Posttraumatic Stress Disorder." *Clinical Psychology Review* 30 (2010): 635–641. In 2008, the prestigious Institute of Medicine said in its evaluation of the various psychotherapies that "the committee finds that the evidence is sufficient to conclude the efficacy of exposure therapies in the treatment of PTSD." Immediately

after this, in the comment section, it added, "The evidence for efficacy of exposure therapy in veterans — especially in males with chronic PTSD — is less consistent than the general body of evidence" (97).

183 *Derived from the classical conditioning or "learning" theories:* See Friedman, *Handbook of PTSD,* 541.

"Even after a year, I still had an extremely difficult": Foer, *Extremely Loud,* 17.

184 *Created by psychologist Thomas Stampfl in 1967:* Leitenberg, *Handbook of Social,* 300–302; see also Doctor and Shapiro, *Encylopedia of Trauma,* 125.

In 1982, Terry Keane, a psychologist at Boston University: See T. M. Keane et al., "Flooding for Combat-Related Stress Disorders: Assessment of Anxiety Reduction across Traumatic Memories." *Behavior Therapy* 13 (1982): 499–510.

185 *One of the recurring concerns raised by therapists:* See Finley, *Fields of Combat,* 125; personal communication with Caroline F., a psychotherapist in private practice.

One of those most excited by the possibilities of flooding therapy: Finley, *Fields of Combat,* 123; Jeffrey Kluger, "The World's Most Influential People." *Time,* April 29, 2010; Louisa Kamps, "Prolonged Exposure: A Trauma Therapy Has Victims Live Out Life's Blows Again and Again and Again." *Elle,* August 24, 2009; Thomas W. Durso, "A Calming Influence." *Penn Medicine,* Spring 2010, 19–23. Personal communication with VA San Diego research coordinator; personal communication with senior VA psychiatrist.

186 *However, not everyone was convinced about this new therapy:* Everly, *Psychotraumatology,* 363.

"It is not obvious that a rat's display": Stossel, *My Age of Anxiety,* 47.

In 1991, Roger Pitman, a professor of psychiatry: Pitman et al., "Psychiatric Complications During Flooding Therapy for PTSD." *Journal of Clinical Psychiatry* 52 (1991): 17–20; phone interview with Pitman, January 2014.

187 *A lengthier study by Pitman published in 1996:* Pitman et al., "Emotional Processing and Outcome of Imaginal Flooding Therapy in Vietnam Veterans with Chronic Posttraumatic Stress Disorder." *Comprehensive Psychiatry* 37 (1996): 409–418.

Similar research, conducted by Zahava Solomon: Z. Solomon et al., "The 'Koach' Project for Treatment of Combat-Related PTSD: Rationale, Aims, and Methodology." *Journal of Traumatic Stress* 5 (1992): 175–193.

"it is important to emphasize that exposure": See van der Kolk, *Traumatic Stress,* 435.

"You're right. We're seeing the same things": Phone interview with Pitman, January 2014.

In 2008, undeterred by these and other disturbing: See Finley, *Fields of Combat,* 120–127; Kluger, "The World's Most Influential People."

Since the rollout, a number of trauma workers: Finley, *Fields of Combat,* 125.

One research assistant at VA San Diego: Personal communication with the author, January 2014.

An independent survey conducted by the: http://blog.23andme.com/23andme -research/what-works-for-ptsd/ (accessed August 1, 2014).

188 *One rape victim I interviewed, who completed:* Interview with Elise Colton, April 2013.

One senior VA official, who was trained: Interview with senior VA psychiatrist, 2013.

Jonathan Shay, one of the most highly respected: Comments made during presentation given at San Diego State University, "PTSD and Moral Injury: What's the Difference and Does it Matter?" October 4, 2012.

189 *In 2008, the prestigious Institute of Medicine determined:* See Institute of Medicine, *Treatment of Posttraumatic Stress Disorder,* 95–99.

In an August 2002 study in the: Edna Foa et al., "Does Imaginal Exposure Exacerbate PTSD Symptoms?" *Journal of Consulting and Clinical Psychology* 70 (2002): 1022–1028.

"something intended to be effective works better": Greenberg, *Manufacturing Depression,* 306. See also D. Westen et al., "Empirically Supported Complexity: Re-thinking Evidence-Based Practice in Psychotherapy." *Current Directions in Psychological Science* 14 (2005): 266–271.

Greenberg also rails against another statistical procedure: Greenberg, *Manufacturing Depression,* 307. Phone interview with Greenberg, April 2013. Several critics of PE pointed out this experimental design flaw to me. The fact remains that PE has the highest recorded dropout rate of any PTSD therapy, which makes one wonder why the VA chose it as one of its frontline therapies, when there are other, safer, less controversial, and less expensive therapies available.

190 *The controversy surrounding PE also resembles:* See Jonah Lehrer, "The Forgetting Pill Erases Painful Memories Forever." *Wired,* February 17, 2012. While much of Lehrer's work has been retracted due to factual issues, this article was cleared by *Wired*'s editors, according to a review later published at *Slate* magazine. Lehrer's article does a good job of succinctly reviewing the CISD controversy. Another researcher, at UC Irvine, whom I spoke to confirmed Lehrer's assessment of CISD's lack of empirical support.

For his part, Roger Pitman remains skeptical of PE: Phone interview with Pitman, January 2014.

193 *"It is important to emphasize that exposure may":* See van der Kolk, *Traumatic Stress,* 435.

Prior to undergoing PE, I had, in fact, read: See Shephard, *War of Nerves,* 2001. See also Laurent Tatu, "The 'Torpillage' Neurologists of World War I." *Historical Neurology* 75 (2010): 279–283.

194 *There are no documented cases of veterans or other PTSD survivors:* Shay, on page 187 of *Achilles in Vietnam,* says, "During the early days of the current era of PTSD treatment, mental health professionals shared the folk belief that simply 'getting it all out' would result in safety, sobriety, and self-care. The consequences of these well-intentioned 'combat debriefings' were catastrophic, resulting in many suicides, according to veterans in our program who participated." The "combat debriefings" Shay describes are not the same thing as PE therapy, but they seem

to be motivated by the same purgative principle — that the contagion of trauma can be expelled, washed away, "cleaned out" like a festering wound, to use Scott's metaphor. For more on this, see Herman, *Trauma and Recovery,* 172.

194 *"dialectic of trauma":* Herman, *Trauma and Recovery,* 47.

There were the usual introductions: I have changed the names and significant life details of these veterans in order to protect their privacy.

198 *Cognitive Processing Therapy is one of the most popular:* For an overview of CPT, see Victoria M. Follette and Josef Ruzek, eds. *Cognitive-Behavioral Therapies for Trauma,* 100–102. For more on Aaron Beck, see Greenberg, *Manufacturing Depression,* 288–290; Clark and Beck, *Cognitive Therapy of Anxiety Disorders.*

"caught up in the contagion of the times": Quoted in Greenberg, *Manufacturing Depression,* 288.

199 *"therapist and patient work together to identify":* Ibid., 289.

"CBT teaches objectivity": Solomon, *Noonday Demon,* 107.

200 *CPT has been extensively studied:* See P. A. Resick et al., "Cognitive Processing Therapy for Sexual Assault Victims." *Journal of Consulting and Clinical Psychology* 60 (1992): 748–756. See also Candice M. Monson et al., "Cognitive Processing Therapy for Veterans with Military-Related Posttraumatic Stress Disorder." *Journal of Consulting and Clinical Psychology* 74 (2006): 898–907.

A 2002 study by Resick, using a large sample of sexual assault: P. A. Resick et al., "Comparison of Cognitive-Processing Therapy with Prolonged Exposure and a Waiting Condition for the Treatment of Chronic Posttraumatic Stress Disorder in Female Rape Victims." *Journal of Consulting and Clinical Psychology* 70 (2002): 867–879.

201 *Another study, published in* Behavior Therapy *in 2004:* Nicholas Tarrier et al., "Treatment of Chronic PTSD by Cognitive Therapy and Exposure: 5-Year Follow-Up." *Behavior Therapy* 35 (2004): 231–246.

A number of critics, including Gary Greenberg and B. E. Wampold: See Greenberg, *Manufacturing Depression,* 302–314; Wampold, *Great Psychotherapy Debate,* 2001.

One stunningly illuminating study conducted by Hans Strupp: Hans Strupp et al., "Specific vs Nonspecific Factors in Psychotherapy: A Controlled Study of Outcome." *Archives of General Psychiatry* 36 (1979): 1125–1136.

203 *About these sorts of elemental questions:* For more on the idea of moral injury and violation of *themis* (Greek for "justice"), see Shay, *Achilles in Vietnam,* 3–21.

207 *"For most of the 20th century, psychoanalytic theory":* Ghislaine Boulanger, "Witnesses to Reality: Working Psychodynamically with Survivors of Terror." *Psychoanalytic Dialogues* 18 (2008): 640.

The VA, which sets the tone for PTSD treatment worldwide: For the VA's PTSD treatment guidelines, go to: http://www.ptsd.va.gov/professional/treatment/over view/index.asp.; see also Carr, "Combat and Human Existence," 494.

208 *"Biological research is where the money is":* Interview with senior VA psychiatrist, April 2013.

"Sixty years after its introduction": Kandel, *In Search of Memory,* 365.

209 *Russell Carr, a navy psychiatrist at Bethesda–Walter Reed:* Carr, "Combat and Human Existence," 471–496; "The Problem of Therapeutic Alliance When Treating Combat-Related PTSD." Presentation by Commander Russell Carr, MC, USN, Navy and Marine Corps Combat and Operational Stress Control Conference, San Diego, California, May 23, 2012.

Intersubjectivity theory, the school of thought that Carr: See Stolorow, *Trauma and Human Existence.* Carr, in "Combat and Human Existence," said, "As I left for a deployment to Iraq in the summer of 2008, I was wrestling with how to reach soldiers with traumatized experiences that left them with profound shame and difficulties with their relationships with others . . . A few months into the deployment, I developed an even stronger sense of urgency as one of my patients killed himself. I felt the effects of his suicide on his unit, the medical staff who tried to resuscitate him, and the other mental health team on base . . . As I thought of him and continued to meet with my other patients there in Iraq, I felt a strong urgency to find a better way to understand the effects of trauma. I then stumbled upon the writings of Robert Stolorow. I obtained a copy of his recent book, *Trauma and Human Existence.* It fundamentally changed how I work with traumatized military personnel" (473–474).

As Stolorow sees it, everyone wants to be understood: See Carr, "Combat and Human Existence," 475–476.

In his military practice, Carr treats some of the most chronic and complex: Interview with Russell Carr, April 2013.

210 *"Doc, you get this more than anyone I've talked to about it":* Carr, "Combat and Human Existence," 474.

7. Drugs

214 *In the world of memory science, McGaugh:* This chapter is based on my interviews with McGaugh, emails exchanged from 2007 to 2013, the UC Irvine website, and interviews with his colleagues. In his book *Memory and Emotion: The Making of Lasting Memories* (New York: Columbia University Press, 2003), McGaugh describes the thought process behind some of his discoveries and some of the aspects of his academic training. After interviewing McGaugh, I stumbled across a fascinating article published in the *New England Journal of Medicine* by Troy Lisa Holbrook ("Morphine Use after Combat Injury in Iraq and Post-Traumatic Stress Disorder," January 14, 2010), which seemed to confirm much of McGaugh's work and was derived from data collected in Iraq. Holbrook and her colleagues found that giving wounded soldiers and Marines morphine "during early resuscitation and trauma care" cut their risk of getting PTSD by 50 percent. Without realizing it, medics and physicians in Iraq had disrupted traumatic memory overconsolidation in a manner similar to what McGaugh had done in the lab.

If McGaugh's work has a governing principle: McGaugh, *Memory and Emotion,* 83.

214 *"In medieval times, before writing was used to keep"*: McGaugh, *Memory and Emotion*, ix.

Scientists have known for a long time that certain: K. S. Lashley, "The Effects of Strychnine and Caffeine upon the Rate of Learning." *Psychobiology* 1 (1917): 141–170.

McGaugh stumbled across Lashley's research in the fifties: McGaugh, *Memory and Emotion*, 60–61.

215 *Soon after getting his PhD, McGaugh began experimenting*: McGaugh, *Memory and Emotion*, 63–70.

They soon discovered that adrenaline, the chemical released: Ibid., 73, 97–108.

216 *This drug—propranolol, a beta-blocker developed*: Ibid., 100–106. See also L. Cahill and J. L. McGaugh, "Modulation of Memory Storage." *Current Opinion in Neurobiology* 6 (1996): 237–242; Roger K. Pitman, "Pilot Study of Secondary Prevention of Posttraumatic Stress Disorder with Propranolol." *Biological Psychiatry* 51 (2002), 189–192; Friedman, *Handbook of PTSD*, 392.

As I would learn later, the other not-small problem: Phone interview with Roger Pitman, April 2014.

217 *Could trauma—the nightmares, the daemons, the vanished hopes*: McGaugh, *Memory and Emotion*, 122–125.

"will clip an Angel's wings/Conquer all mysteries by rule and line": Quoted in Redfield Jamison, *Touched with Fire*, 259.

218 *While the number of research subjects involved*: Brunet et al., "Effect of Post-Retrieval Propranolol," 503–506.

In January 2014, Pitman told me: Interview with Pitman.

219 *Society, it seems, is not ready for wholesale memory erasure*: See Luckhurst, *Trauma Question*, 204–205.

In October 2003, before the most promising experiments: President's Council on Bioethics, *Beyond Therapy: Biotechnology and the Pursuit of Happiness*. Washington, D.C.: Government Printing Office, 2003.

220 *"Propranolol might be the most philosophically vexing"*: Chuck Klosterman, "Amnesia Is the New Bliss: A Breakthrough Drug Can Erase Your Worst Memories—But Not Everyone Thinks You Have the Right to Take It." *Esquire*, April 10, 2007.

"To be denied a 'normal psychopathology'": Outka, "History, the Posthuman, and the End of Trauma," 76–81.

221 *Trauma, when heard by society, is a form of testimony*: See Herman, *Trauma and Recovery*, 1. See also Caruth, *Trauma*.

Nevertheless, not everyone is convinced that propranolol: Adam Kolber, "Therapeutic Forgetting: The Legal and Ethical Implications of Memory Dampening." *Vanderbilt Law Review* 59 (2006): 1561–1626.

222 *"The original memory is indeed still there, deep inside the brain"*: See Robin Marantz Henig, "The Quest to Forget." *New York Times Magazine*, April 18, 2004.

223 *Prazosin, a drug first used to reduce high blood*: M. A. Raskind et al., "Reduction

of Nightmares and Other PTSD Symptoms in Combat Veterans by Prazosin: A Placebo-Controlled Study." *American Journal of Psychiatry* 160 (2003): 371–373. See also Shiromani, *Post-Traumatic Stress Disorder,* 341–343; Friedman, *Handbook of PTSD,* 392.

224 *Some of the most experienced psychiatrists who treat PTSD:* Comments made by Jonathan Shay during a presentation given at San Diego State University: "PTSD and Moral Injury: What's the Difference and Does it Matter?" October 4, 2012.

The most popular class of drugs prescribed for PTSD: See Friedman, *Handbook of PTSD,* 387. See also Shiromani, *Post-Traumatic Stress Disorder,* 348–352. Friedman asserts, "SSRIs are the treatment of choice for patients with PTSD, as attested by four independent clinical practice guidelines" (387).

"Medication has really changed my life": Interview with Jenny G., March 2013.

225 *Zoloft and other SSRIs have a decent track record with PTSD:* Personal communication with Dewleen Baker, VA San Diego Healthcare System, February 2013. Interview with Jeffrey Matloff, VA San Diego Healthcare System, March 2013.

226 *"Prozac is a very forgiving drug":* Solomon, *Noonday Demon,* 115.

One widely held belief among psychiatrists is: See Redfield Jamison, *Touched with Fire,* 247.

But it wasn't until 2002, some fifteen years after Prozac's: K. Brady et al., "Efficacy and Safety of Sertraline Treatment of Posttraumatic Stress Disorder." *Journal of American Medical Association* 283 (2002): 1837–1844.

Despite these shortcomings, the trials published in 2002: Shiromani, *Post-Traumatic Stress Disorder,* 349.

227 *Seeming to recognize these inconsistencies, in 2008:* See Institute of Medicine, *Treatment of Posttraumatic Stress Disorder,* 67–72. See also Shiromani, *Post-Traumatic Stress Disorder,* 338. The IOM's assessment reads in part, "The committee concluded that the evidence is inadequate to determine the efficacy of SSRIs in the treatment of PTSD based on weaknesses in study designs and inconsistency of results. The committee also observed that SSRIs are widely prescribed, have a good safety profile, and might often find indications for use in veterans with PTSD because of comorbid major depression and anxiety disorders. The committee's conclusion about the SSRI literature was difficult to reach" (71).

As Dewleen Baker, one of the investigators on the original: Personal communication with Dewleen Baker, March 2013.

228 *This frustrating lack of progress with drug research:* See Friedman, *Handbook of PTSD,* 545, where the author argues that "despite great advances in explicating biological alterations associated with PTSD, progress in developing pharmacotherapy has not kept pace ... Our capacity to target key dysregulated pharmacological mechanisms would be greatly enhanced if it was predicated on a more comprehensive and fine-grained understanding of neurobiological abnormalities associated with PTSD." See Rachel Yehuda et al., "Conflict between Current Knowledge about Posttraumatic Stress Disorder and Its Original Conceptual Ba-

sis." *American Journal of Psychiatry* 152 (1995): 1705–1713. Also, interview with Gaithri Fernando, April 2013.

228 *The PTSD diagnosis, from its earliest days:* Nicosia, *Home to War*, 178.

The development of Prozac, for instance, reaches all the way back: See Kramer, *Listening to Prozac*, 60–64.

Matthew Friedman, the first and longest-serving executive: See Friedman, *Handbook of PTSD*, 547.

229 *Is it truly a psychiatric disorder, as we understand them today:* See Shay, *Achilles in Vietnam*; Brett Litz et al., "Moral Injury and Moral Repair in War Veterans: A Preliminary Model and Intervention Strategy." *Clinical Psychology Review* 29 (2009): 695–706.

8. Alternatives

231 *Tall, blonde, and with a gait that makes her look:* This section is based on my interview and personal communications with Elise Colton (not her real name) over the spring of 2013.

237 *"During the early days of the current era of PTSD treatment":* Shay, *Achilles in Vietnam*, 187.

It is almost as if researchers have been talking to Elise: See David Emerson, *Overcoming Trauma through Yoga: Reclaiming Your Body* (Berkeley: North Atlantic Books, 2011).

238 *"after an episode of flow is over":* Csikszentmihalyi, *Flow*, 65.

"To be identified with your mind is to be trapped in time": Tolle, *Power of Now*, 40.

239 *"if many remedies are prescribed for an illness":* Quoted in Solomon, *Noonday Demon*, 135.

"the most striking finding overall is the relative lack of empirical": Strauss et al., "Complementary and Alternative Treatments for PTSD." *PTSD Research Quarterly* 23 (2012): 1–7. See also Friedman, *Handbook of PTSD*, 545.

One crowdsourced website I consulted: http://blog.23andme.com/23andme-research/what-works-for-ptsd/ (accessed August 2, 2014).

240 *"There are numerous new modalities of treatment":* Hoge, *Once a Warrior*, 202–204.

241 *"Each of us has his own rhythm of suffering":* Barthes, *Mourning Diary* (New York: Hill and Wang, 2009), 162.

For example, the idea of training people with PTSD: For more on Todd Vance, see Tony Perry, "Veterans Fight Club." *Los Angeles Times*, September 12, 2012.

244 *"no longer met the diagnostic criteria for PTSD":* Jill E. Bormann et al., "Meditation-Based Mantram Intervention for Veteran with Posttraumatic Stress Disorder: A Randomized Trial." *Psychological Trauma: Theory, Research, Practice, and Policy* 5 (2013): 259–267.

"The seed of EMDR sprouted one sunny afternoon in 1987": Shapiro, *EMDR*, 9.

245 *"84 to 90 percent of the people using EMDR":* Ibid., 5.

Despite these criticisms and complaints about how EMDR: See Foa et al., *Effective Treatments,* 333–334. See also Friedman, *Handbook of PTSD,* which discusses head-to-head comparisons between EMDR and PE, with EMDR coming out slightly ahead in some computer analyses of the data. "Several studies have compared EMDR to various combinations of CBT. Three of these studies report effect size advantages for EMDR in those who complete treatment. Ironson, Freund, Strauss and Williams (2002) compared EMDR to PE in a relatively small mixed sample and found no statistical differences between the two treatments" (344).

"the therapist lets you control your thoughts": See Van Winkle, *Soft Spots,* 206–207.

246 *Indeed, the technique was so well liked:* Shephard, *War of Nerves,* 338. See also Michael M. Phillips's excellent 2013 series of articles in the *Wall Street Journal* on the VA lobotomy program, "The Lobotomy Files." Phillips found that the VA lobotomized at least two thousand veterans over the course of the 1940s.

248 *"My feeling is that therapy is for therapy and that writing":* This quote comes from a 2002 interview with Terry Gross that was included in a reading group guide at the back of the paperback edition of *Lucky.*

"You may well ask why I write. And yet my reasons are quite many": Ford Madox Ford, *The Good Soldier: A Tale of Passion* (Hertfordshire: Wordsworth Editions, 2010), 28.

"EMDR helped a little bit but there was a phase": Interview with Jenny G., Iraq veteran, March 2013.

249 *An ancient tradition within Polynesian cultures, the* haka: See Australian Broadcasting Corporation News, "Giant Haka Honours Fallen NZ Soldiers," August 27, 2012. See also the entry under "HAKA" in *An Encyclopaedia of New Zealand,* edited by A. H. McLintock, originally published in 1966.

250 *In the mid-nineties, a group of clinicians at the VA in West Haven:* David Read Johnson et al., "The Therapeutic Use of Ritual and Ceremony in the Treatment of Post-Traumatic Stress Disorder." *Journal of Traumatic Stress* 8 (1995): 283–298. *One unusually thoughtful therapist I interviewed went so far:* Interview with Gary Greenberg, April 2013.

9. Growth

252 The passages about Steve House are largely derived from my conversations with him, my personal recollections, and his 2009 memoir *Beyond the Mountain.* *"As I fell, I was relaxed at first. A flake had broken":* Steve Casimiro, "Steve House: What It Feels Like to Fall 80 Feet." *Adventure Journal,* June 8, 2010.

253 *"My chest hurt like hell and I knew I didn't have":* Interview with Steve House, February 2014.

His junior year at Evergreen State: House, *Beyond the Mountain,* 27–36.

House's crowning achievement came in September 2005: Interview with Steve House, February 2014. See also House, *Beyond the Mountain,* 229–244.

254 *"The only thing I can compare it to is being on the moon":* Interview with Steve House, February 2014.

256 *A year later, he and Eva founded Alpine Mentors:* See www.alpinementors.org.

257 *"All true wisdom is only to be learned far":* Halifax, *Shamanic Voices,* 6.

"On the occasion of every accident that befalls you": Quoted in Gonzales, *Deep Survival,* 149.

258 *"Some great men and women are fortified and redeemed":* Ha Jin, *Crazed* (New York: Pantheon, 2002), 319.

"It feels to me as if the U.S. civilian population has pathologized": Personal communication with the author.

"There is a misperception of our veterans out there": Jim Michaels, "Mattis: Veterans Are Not Victims." *USA Today,* May 5, 2014.

Perhaps the most radical of these reformulators is Richard Tedeschi: See Calhoun and Tedeschi, *Handbook of Posttraumatic Growth* (New York: Taylor & Francis, 2006).

"I thought, who do I want to know the most about, distressed": Quoted in Jim Rendon, "Post-Traumatic Stress's Surprisingly Positive Flip Side." *New York Times Magazine,* March 22, 2012.

259 *"It is in the realm of existential and, for some persons":* Calhoun and Tedeschi, *Handbook of Posttraumatic Growth,* 6.

"I have no doubt that there are people": Quoted in Rendon, "Post-Traumatic Stress's Surprisingly Positive Flip Side."

260 *"PTSD and post-traumatic growth aren't mutually exclusive":* Interview with Matt Friedman, March 2013.

"Posttraumatic stress disorder is not necessarily indicative": Zahava Solomon et al., "Posttraumatic Stress Disorder and Posttraumatic Growth among Israeli Ex-POWs." *Journal of Traumatic Stress* 20 (2007): 303–312.

261 *"impressed by the number of prisoners of war of the Vietnam":* William H. Sledge et al., "Self-concept Changes Related to War Captivity." *Archives of General Psychiatry* 37 (1980): 430.

One study of Vietnam War ex-POWs even found: Segovia et al., "Optimism Predicts Resilience." *Journal of Traumatic Stress* 25 (2012): 330–336. Interview with Francine Segovia, February 2013.

262 *Holocaust survivor Viktor Frankl, in his classic book:* Frankl, *Man's Search for Meaning,* 137, 155.

264 *"I remembered the basic truth of subjective consciousness":* See Kiland, *Lessons from the Hanoi Hilton,* 2013.

Epilogue: Counterfactuals

269 *"Justice in our minds is strife/We cannot help but see":* Haxton, trans., *Fragments,* 41.

Selected Bibliography

Ackerman, Diane. *An Alchemy of Mind: The Marvel and Mystery of the Brain.* New York: Scribner, 2004.

Allen, Pamela. *Free Space: A Perspective on the Small Group in Women's Liberation.* New York: Times Change Press, 1970.

Ambrose, Stephen E. *Band of Brothers: E Company, 506th Regiment, 101st Airborne from Normandy to Hitler's Eagle's Nest.* New York: Simon & Schuster, 1992.

American Psychiatric Association. *Diagnostic and Statistical Manual of Mental Disorders, III,* 1980.

———. *Diagnostic and Statistical Manual of Mental Disorders, IV-TR,* 2000.

Anderson, Scott. *Lawrence in Arabia: War, Deceit, Imperial Folly and the Making of the Modern Middle East.* New York: Anchor, 2014.

Archer, Dane, et al. "Violent Acts and Violent Times: A Comparative Approach to Postwar Homicide Rates." *American Sociological Review* 41 (1976): 937–963.

Aries, Philippe. *The Hour of Our Death: The Classic History of Western Attitudes toward Death over the Last One Thousand Years.* New York: Vintage, 1982.

Armstrong, Keith. *Courage after Fire: Coping Strategies for Troops Returning from Iraq and Afghanistan and Their Families.* Berkeley: Ulysses Press, 2006.

Back, Sudie E., et al. *Individual Therapy Manual for Concurrent Treatment of PTSD and Substance Use Disorders Using Prolonged Exposure (COPE).* San Diego: VA San Diego Healthcare System, 2013.

Barker, Pat. *Regeneration.* New York: Penguin, 1993.

Ben-Ezra, Menachem. "Traumatic Reactions from Antiquity to the 16th Century: Was There a Common Denominator?" *Stress and Health* 27 (2011).

Bhattacharya, Shaoni. "Molecular Secret of Special Forces Toughness." *New Scientist,* February 18, 2003.

Blom, Jan Dirk. *A Dictionary of Hallucinations.* New York: Springer, 2010.

Blunden, Edmund. *Undertones of War.* Chicago: University of Chicago Press, 2007.

Booth-Kewley, Stephanie, et al. "Factors Associated with Antisocial Behavior in Combat Veterans." *Aggressive Behavior* 36 (2010): 330-337.

Boulanger, Ghislaine. *Wounded by Reality: Understanding and Treating Adult Onset Trauma.* London: Routledge, 2007.

Bowra, C. M. *Classical Greece.* New York: Time-Life, 1965.

Bradley, James. *Flags of Our Fathers.* New York: Bantam, 2000.

Bremner, J. Douglas. *Does Stress Damage the Brain? Understanding Trauma-Related Disorders from a Mind-Body Perspective.* New York: W. W. Norton, 2002.

Brewin, Chris R. *Posttraumatic Stress Disorder: Malady or Myth?* New Haven: Yale University Press, 2003.

Brownmiller, Susan. *Against Our Will: Men, Women and Rape.* New York: Bantam, 1986.

Brunet, A., et al. "Effect of Post-retrieval Propranolol Psychophysiologic Responding during Subsequent Script-driven Traumatic Imagery in Post-traumatic Stress Disorder." *Journal of Psychiatric Research* 42 (2008): 503–506.

Burns, Tom. *Psychiatry: A Very Short Introduction.* New York: Oxford University Press, 2006.

Calhoun, Lawrence G. and Richard G. Tedeschi. *Handbook of Posttraumatic Growth: Research and Practice.* New York: Taylor & Francis, 2006.

Campbell, Joseph. *The Hero with a Thousand Faces.* New York: New World Library, 2008.

Cantwell, John. *Exit Wounds: One Australian's War on Terror.* Melbourne: Melbourne University Publishing, 2012.

Carr, Russell. "Combat and Human Existence: Toward an Intersubjective Approach to Combat-Related PTSD." *Psychoanalytic Psychology* 28 (2011).

Caruth, Cathy. *Unclaimed Experience: Trauma, Narrative and History.* Baltimore: Johns Hopkins University Press, 1996.

———, ed. *Trauma: Explorations in Memory.* Baltimore: Johns Hopkins University Press, 1995.

Chabon, Michael. *The Yiddish Policemen's Union.* New York: Harper Collins, 2007.

Clark, David A., and Aaron T. Beck. *Cognitive Therapy of Anxiety Disorders: Science and Practice.* New York: Guilford, 2010.

Crane, Stephen. *The Red Badge of Courage.* New York: Modern Library, 2000.

Csikszentmihalyi, Mihaly. *Flow: The Psychology of Optimal Experience.* New York: Harper Collins, 1990.

DaCosta, Jacob Mendes. "On Irritable Heart: A Clinical Study of a Form of Functional Cardiac Disorder and Its Consequences." *American Journal of the Medical Sciences* 121, no. 1 (1871).

Damasio, Antonio R. *Descartes' Error: Emotion, Reason, and the Human Brain.* New York: Putnam, 1994.

Dean, Eric T., Jr. *Shook over Hell: Post-Traumatic Stress, Vietnam and the Civil War.* Cambridge: Harvard University Press, 1997.

DeLillo, Don. *Falling Man.* New York: Scribner, 2007.

Deraniyagala, Sonali. *Wave.* New York: Knopf, 2013.

Diamond, Jared. *The World until Yesterday: What Can We Learn from Traditional Societies?* New York: Viking, 2012.

Didion, Joan. *We Tell Ourselves Stories in Order to Live: Collected Nonfiction.* New York: Knopf, 2006.

Dimoulas, E., et al. "Dissociation during Intense Military Stress Is Related to Subsequent Somatic Symptoms in Women." *Psychiatry* 4 (2007): 66–73.

Doctor, Ronald M., and Frank N. Shapiro, eds. *The Encyclopedia of Trauma and Traumatic Stress Disorders.* New York: Facts on File, 2010.

Eagleman, David. *Incognito: The Secret Lives of the Brain.* New York: Pantheon, 2011.

Easwaran, Eknath. *Strength in the Storm: Creating Calm in Difficult Times.* Berkeley: Nilgiri, 2005.

Egendorf, Arthur. *Healing from the War: Trauma and Transformation after Vietnam.* Boston: Shambhala, 1985.

Egremont, Max. *Siegfried Sassoon: A Life.* New York: Farrar, Straus and Giroux, 2005.

Emerson, David. *Overcoming Trauma through Yoga: Reclaiming Your Body.* Berkeley: North Atlantic Books, 2011.

Emerson, Gloria. *Winners and Losers: Battles, Retreats, Gains, Losses and Ruins from the Vietnam War.* New York: W. W. Norton, 1992.

Everly, George S., ed. *Psychotraumatology: Key Papers and Core Concepts in Post-Traumatic Stress.* New York: Plenum, 1995.

Faludi, Susan. *The Terror Dream: Fear and Fantasy in Post-9/11 America.* New York: Metropolitan Books, 2007.

Feitlowitz, Marguerite. *A Lexicon of Terror: Argentina and the Legacies of Torture.* New York: Oxford University Press, 1998.

Fellman, Michael. "Sherman's Demons." *New York Times*, November 9, 2011.

Ferguson, Niall. *The Pity of War.* London: Allen Lane, 1998.

———. *Virtual History: Alternatives and Counterfactuals.* New York: Basic Books, 2000.

Figley, Charles R., ed. *Trauma and Its Wake: The Study and Treatment of Post-traumatic Stress Disorder.* New York: Brunner/Mazel, 1985.

Figley, Charles R., and William P. Nash, eds. *Combat Stress Injury: Theory, Research, and Management.* New York: Routledge, 2007.

Finley, Erin P. *Fields of Combat: Understanding PTSD among Veterans of Iraq and Afghanistan.* Ithaca: ILR Press, 2012.

Fitzgerald, Scott F. *The Great Gatsby: The Authorized Text.* New York: Scribner, 1925.

Foa, Edna B., et al. *Effective Treatments for PTSD: Practice Guidelines from the International Society for Traumatic Stress Studies.* New York: Guilford, 2000.

———. *Treating the Trauma of Rape: Cognitive-Behavioral Therapy for PTSD.* New York: Guilford, 1998.

Foer, Jonathan Safran. *Extremely Loud and Incredibly Close.* New York: Houghton Mifflin Harcourt, 2005.

Follette, Victoria M., and Josef Ruzek, eds. *Cognitive-Behavioral Therapies for Trauma.* 2nd ed. New York: Guilford, 2006.

Frankl, Viktor E. *Man's Search for Meaning.* New York: Simon & Schuster, 1984.

Freud, Sigmund. *Beyond the Pleasure Principle.* New York: W. W. Norton, 1990.

———. *The Collected Papers of Sigmund Freud, Vol. IV.* New York: Basic Books, 1959.

———. *Studies on Hysteria.* London: Hogarth, 1955.

Friedman, Matthew, ed. *Handbook of PTSD: Science and Practice.* New York: Guilford, 2007.

Fussell, Paul. *The Great War and Modern Memory: The Illustrated Edition.* New York: Sterling, 2009.

———. *Sassoon's Long Journey: An Illustrated Selection from Siegfried Sassoon's "The Complete Memoirs of George Sherston."* New York: Faber and Faber, 1983.

———. *Wartime: Understanding and Behavior in the Second World War.* New York: Oxford University Press 1989.

Gates, Robert. *Duty: Memoirs of a Secretary at War.* New York: Knopf, 2014.

Gay, Peter. *Freud: A Life for Our Time.* New York: W. W. Norton, 2006.

Gibson, William. *Pattern Recognition.* New York: Putnam, 2003.

Gilbertson, Ashley. "The Life and Lonely Death of Noah Pierce." *Virginia Quarterly Review* (Fall 2008).

Gilpin Faust, Drew. *This Republic of Suffering: Death and the American Civil War.* New York: Vintage, 2009.

Gladwell, Malcolm. "Getting Over It." *The New Yorker*, November 8, 2004.

Goleman, Daniel. *Emotional Intelligence.* New York: Bantam, 1995.

Gonzales, Laurence. *Deep Survival: Who Lives, Who Dies, and Why.* New York: W. W. Norton, 2004.

———. *Surviving Survival: The Art and Science of Resilience.* New York: W. W. Norton, 2013.

Graham, Don. *No Name on the Bullet: A Biography of Audie Murphy.* New York: Viking, 1989.

Gray, J. Glenn. *The Warriors: Reflections on Men in Battle.* New York: Harper, 1959.

Greenberg, Gary. *The Book of Woe: The DSM and the Unmaking of Psychiatry.* New York: Blue Rider, 2013.

———. *Manufacturing Depression: The Secret History of a Modern Disease.* New York: Simon & Schuster, 2010.

Grinker, Roy R., and John P. Spiegel. *Men under Stress.* Philadelphia: Blakiston, 1945.

Grossman, David. *On Killing: The Psychological Cost of Learning to Kill in War and Society.* New York: Little, Brown, 1996.

Halberstam, David. *The Best and the Brightest.* New York: Ballantine, 1993.

———. *The Fifties.* New York: Ballantine, 1993.

Halifax, Joan. *Shamanic Voices: A Survey of Visionary Narratives.* New York: Penguin, 1991.

Haxton, Brooks, trans. *Fragments: The Collected Wisdom of Heraclitus.* New York: Viking, 2001.

Hearst, Patricia. *Every Secret Thing.* New York: Doubleday, 1981.

Heberle, Mark A. *A Trauma Artist: Tim O'Brien and the Fiction of Vietnam.* Iowa City: University of Iowa Press, 2001.

Hemingway, Ernest. *The Complete Short Stories of Ernest Hemingway: The Finca Vigia Edition.* New York: Scribner, 1998.

Herman, Judith Lewis. *Trauma and Recovery.* New York: Basic Books, 1992.

Herr, Michael. *Dispatches.* New York: Knopf, 1977.

Hillenbrand, Laura. *Unbroken: A World War II Story of Survival, Resilience, and Redemption.* New York: Random House, 2010.

Hipp, Daniel. *The Poetry of Shell Shock: Wartime Trauma and Healing in Wilfred Owen, Ivor Gurney and Siegfried Sassoon.* Jefferson, NC: McFarland & Company, 2005.

Hoge, Charles W. *Once a Warrior, Always a Warrior: Navigating the Transition from Combat to Home.* Guilford, CT: Globe Pequot, 2010.

Hoge, Charles W., et al. "Combat Duty in Iraq and Afghanistan, Mental Health Problems, and Barriers to Care." *New England Journal of Medicine* 351 (2004).

Holmes, Douglas S., and Louis W. Tinnin. "Problem of Auditory Hallucinations." *Traumatology* 1 (1995): 1–7.

House, Steve. *Beyond the Mountain.* Ventura, CA: Patagonia Books, 2009.

———. *Training for the New Alpinism: A Manual for the Climber as Athlete.* Ventura: Patagonia Books, 2014.

Ignatieff, Michael. *Virtual War: Kosovo and Beyond.* New York: Picador, 2001.

Institute of Medicine (IOM). *Treatment of Posttraumatic Stress Disorder: An Assessment of the Evidence.* Washington, DC: National Academies Press, 2008.

Jaffe, Greg. "Marine's Suicide Is Only Start of Family's Struggle." *Washington Post,* January 31, 2012.

Johnson, Denis. *Tree of Smoke.* New York: Farrar, Straus and Giroux, 2007.

Junger, Sebastian. *War.* New York: Twelve, 2010.

Kandel, Eric R. *In Search of Memory: The Emergence of a New Science of Mind.* New York: W. W. Norton, 2007.

Keegan, John. *The Face of Battle.* New York: Penguin, 1978.

Kelly, Diann, ed. *Treating Young Veterans: Promoting Resilience through Practice and Advocacy.* New York: Springer, 2011.

Kiland, Taylor. *Lessons from the Hanoi Hilton.* Annapolis: United States Naval Institute Press, 2013.

Kramer, Peter. *Against Depression.* New York: Viking, 2005.

———. *Listening to Prozac.* New York: Viking, 1993.

Kulka, R. A., et al. *The National Vietnam Veterans Readjustment Study: Tables of Findings and Technical Appendices.* New York: Brunner/Mazel, 1990.

———. *Trauma and the Vietnam War Generation.* New York: Brunner/Mazel, 1990.

Lansky, Melvin. *Posttraumatic Nightmares: Psychodynamic Explorations.* London: Routledge, 1995.

Lasch, Christopher. *The Culture of Narcissism.* New York: W. W. Norton, 1979.

Lawrence, T. E. *Seven Pillars of Wisdom: A Triumph.* New York: Anchor Books, 1991.

le Carré, John. *The Little Drummer Girl.* New York: Scribner, 1983.

LeDoux, Joseph. *The Emotional Brain: The Mysterious Underpinnings of Emotional Life.* New York: Simon & Schuster, 1996.

Leed, Eric. *No Man's Land: Combat and Identity in World War I.* Cambridge: Cambridge University Press, 1979.

Leitenberg, Harold, ed. *Handbook of Social and Evaluation Anxiety.* London: Springer, 1990.

Lethem, Jonathan, ed. *The Vintage Book of Amnesia: An Anthology of Writing on the Subject of Memory Loss.* New York: Vintage, 2000.

Lerner, Paul. *Hysterical Men: War, Psychiatry, and the Politics of Trauma in Germany, 1890–1930.* Ithaca, NY: Cornell University Press, 2003.

Levine, Peter A. *Waking the Tiger: Healing Trauma.* Berkeley: North Atlantic Books, 1997.

Lewis, Lloyd. *Sherman: Fighting Prophet.* Lincoln: Univerity of Nebraska Press, 1993.

Lifton, Robert Jay. *Home from the War: Vietnam Veterans; Neither Victims Nor Executioners.* New York: Other Press, 2005.

Lightman, Alan. *Einstein's Dreams.* New York: Pantheon, 1993.

Lindy, Jacob D. *Vietnam: A Casebook; Psychosocial Stress Series No. 10.* New York: Brunner/Mazel, 1987.

Loyd, Anthony. *My War Gone By, I Miss It So.* New York: Penguin, 1999.

Luckhurst, Roger. *The Trauma Question.* London: Routledge, 2008.

Mack, John E. *Our Prince of Disorder: The Life of T. E. Lawrence.* Cambridge: Harvard University Press, 1998.

Mailer, Norman. *The Time of Our Time.* New York: Random House, 1998.

McCain, John. *Faith of My Fathers: A Family Memoir.* New York: Random House, 2000.

McCarthy, Cormac. *The Crossing.* New York: Vintage, 1995.

McDermott, Terry. *101 Theory Drive: A Neuroscientist's Quest for Memory.* New York: Pantheon, 2010.

McGaugh, James L. *Memory and Emotion: The Making of Lasting Memories.* New York: Columbia University Press, 2003.

McNally, Richard J. *What Is Mental Illness?* Cambridge: Belknap, 2011.

McNamara, Robert S. *Argument without End: In Search of Answers to the Vietnam Tragedy.* New York: PublicAffairs, 2000.

McPherson, James M. *Battle Cry of Freedom: The Civil War Era.* New York: Ballantine, 1988.

Melville, Herman. *Moby-Dick; or, The Whale. The 150th Anniversary Edition.* New York: Penguin, 2001.

Michaels, Jim. *A Chance in Hell: The Men Who Triumphed over Iraq's Deadliest City and Turned the Tide of War.* New York: St. Martin's, 2010.

Morris, David J. *Storm on the Horizon: Khafji — The Battle That Changed the Course of the Gulf War.* New York: Free Press, 2004.

Mukherjee, Siddhartha. *The Emperor of All Maladies: A Biography of Cancer.* New York: Scribner, 2010.

Nash, Bill. "Understanding and Treating Post-Deployment Violence." Presentation, Navy Base San Diego, March 2005.

Nicosia, Gerald. *Home to War: A History of the Vietnam Veterans' Movement.* New York: Three Rivers Press, 2001.

Nietzsche, Friedrich. *The Birth of Tragedy: Out of the Spirit of Music.* New York: Penguin, 1994.

Niffenegger, Audrey. *The Time Traveler's Wife.* New York: Houghton Mifflin Harcourt, 2010.

O'Brien, Tim. *The Things They Carried.* New York: Houghton Mifflin Harcourt, 1990.

———. *In the Lake of the Woods.* New York: Houghton Mifflin Harcourt, 1994.

Outka, Paul. "History, the Posthuman, and the End of Trauma." *Traumatology* 15 (2009): 76–81.

Owen, Wilfred. *The Collected Poems of Wilfred Owen.* New York: New Directions, 1965.

Percy, Jen. *Demon Camp: A Soldier's Exorcism.* New York: Scribner, 2014.

Peretz, Lavie. "Sleep Disturbances in the Wake of Traumatic Events." *New England Journal of Medicine* 345 (2001): 1825–1832.

Perlstein, Rick. *The Invisible Bridge: The Fall of Nixon and the Rise of Reagan.* New York: Simon & Schuster, 2014.

———. *Nixonland: The Rise of a President and the Fracturing of America.* New York: Scribner, 2009.

Petraeus, David H., et al. *FM 3-24 Counterinsurgency.* Chicago: University of Chicago Press, 2007.

Philipps, David. *Lethal Warriors: When the New Band of Brothers Came Home.* New York: Palgrave Macmillan, 2010.

Pinker, Steven. *How the Mind Works.* New York: W. W. Norton, 1997.

Prcic, Ismet. *Shards: A Novel.* New York: Grove Press, 2011.

Putnam, Robert D. *Bowling Alone: The Collapse and Revival of American Community.* New York: Simon & Schuster, 2001.

Ralston, Aron. *Between a Rock and a Hard Place.* New York: Atria, 2004.

Redfield Jamison, Kay. *Night Falls Fast: Understanding Suicide.* New York: Knopf, 1999.

———. *Touched with Fire: Manic-Depressive Illness and the Artistic Temperament.* New York: Free Press, 1993.

———. *An Unquiet Mind: A Memoir of Moods and Madness.* New York: Knopf, 1995.

Remarque, Erich Maria. *All Quiet on the Western Front.* New York: Ballantine, 1987.

Rendon, Jim. "Post-Traumatic Stress's Surprisingly Positive Flip Side." *New York Times Magazine,* March 22, 2012.

Ricks, Thomas E. *Fiasco: The American Military Adventure in Iraq.* New York: Penguin Press, 2006.

Rosen, Gerald M., ed. *Posttraumatic Stress Disorder: Issues and Controversies.* Chichester: John Wiley and Sons, 2004.

Sacks, Oliver. *An Anthropologist on Mars: Seven Paradoxical Tales.* New York: Vintage, 1995.

———. *Hallucinations.* New York: Knopf, 2012.

———. *The Man Who Mistook His Wife for a Hat and Other Clinical Tales.* New York: Harper Collins, 1990.

Salinger, J. D. *Nine Stories.* New York: Little, Brown, 1953.

Samuels, Karen. "Posttraumatic Stress Disorder as a State of Liminality." *Journal of Military and Strategic Studies* 8 (Spring 2006).

Sassoon, Siegfried. *Sherston's Progress.* New York: Doubleday, 1936.

Satel, Sally. "The Battle over Battle Fatigue." *Wall Street Journal,* July 17, 2010.

Satel, Sally, and Scott O. Lilienfeld. *Brainwashed: How We Are Seduced by Mindless Neuroscience.* New York: Basic Books, 2013.

Scarry, Elaine. *The Body in Pain: The Making and Unmaking of the World.* New York: Oxford University Press, 1987.

Schacter, Daniel L. *The Seven Sins of Memory: How the Mind Forgets and Remembers.* New York: Houghton Mifflin Harcourt, 2002.

Schulman, Bruce J. *The Seventies: The Great Shift in American Culture, Society, and Politics.* New York: DaCapo, 2002.

Schwab, Gabriele. *Haunting Legacies: Violent Histories and Transgenerational Trauma.* New York: Columbia University Press, 2010.

Scott, Wilbur J. *The Politics of Readjustment: Vietnam Veterans since the War.* New York: Aldine, 1993.

Sebold, Alice. *Lucky: A Memoir.* New York: Scribner, 2002.

———. "Speaking of the Unspeakable." *Psychiatric Times* (January 1990).

Seeley, Karen M. *Therapy after Terror: 9/11, Psychotherapists, and Mental Health.* Cambridge: Cambridge University Press, 2008.

Shapiro, Francine. *EMDR: The Breakthrough Therapy for Overcoming Anxiety, Stress, and Trauma.* New York: Basic Books, 1997.

Shatan, Chaim. "The Grief of Soldiers: Vietnam Combat Veterans' Self-Help Movement." *American Journal of Orthopsychiatry* 43 (1973).

———. "The Post-Vietnam Syndrome." *New York Times,* May 6, 1972.

Shay, Jonathan. *Achilles in Vietnam: Combat Trauma and the Undoing of Character.* New York: Scribner, 1994.

———. *Odysseus in America: Combat Trauma and the Trials of Homecoming.* New York: Scribner, 2002.

Sheehan, Neil. *A Bright Shining Lie: John Paul Vann and America in Vietnam.* New York: Vintage, 1989.

Shephard, Ben. *A War of Nerves: Soldiers and Psychiatrists in the Twentieth Century.* Cambridge: Harvard University Press, 2001.

Shields, Charles J. *So It Goes: Kurt Vonnegut; A Life.* New York: Henry Holt, 2011.

Shields, David, and Shane Salerno. *Salinger.* New York: Simon & Schuster, 2013.

Shiromani, Priyattam J., ed. *Post-Traumatic Stress Disorder: Basic Science and Clinical Practice.* New York: Humana Press, 2008.

Shorter, Edward. *A History of Psychiatry: From the Era of the Asylum to the Age of Prozac.* New York: John Wiley & Sons, 1997.

Sides, Hampton. "The Man Who Saw Too Much." *Outside,* December 27, 2011.

Simpson, Joe. *Touching the Void.* New York: Harper Perennial, 2004.

Slawenski, Kenneth. *J. D. Salinger: A Life.* New York: Random House, 2010.

Slone, Laurie. *After the War Zone: A Practical Guide for Returning Troops and Their Families.* New York: Perseus, 2008.

Solomon, Andrew. *The Noonday Demon: An Atlas of Depression.* New York: Scribner, 2001.

Solomon, Zahava. *Combat Stress Reaction: The Enduring Toll of War.* New York: Plenum, 1993.

———, et al. "The 'Koach' Project for Treatment of Combat-Related PTSD: Rationale, Aims, and Methodology." *Journal of Traumatic Stress* 5 (1992): 175–193.

Sontag, Susan. *Regarding the Pain of Others.* New York: Picador, 2003.

Spiegelman, Art. *In the Shadow of No Towers.* New York: Pantheon, 2004.

Stanisic, Sasa. *How the Soldier Repairs the Gramophone.* New York: Grove Press, 2008.

Stern, Jessica. *Denial: A Memoir.* New York: Harper Collins, 2010.

Stolorow, Robert. *Trauma and Human Existence: Autobiographical, Psychoanalytic and Philosophical Reflections.* New York: Analytic Press, 2007.

Storr, Anthony. *Solitude: A Return to the Self.* New York: Oxford University Press, 1992.

Stossel, Scott. *My Age of Anxiety: Fear, Hope, Dread and the Search for Peace of Mind.* New York: Knopf, 2014.

Thompson, Hunter S. *Fear and Loathing on the Campaign Trail '72.* New York: Grand Central, 2006.

Tolle, Eckhart. *The Power of Now: A Guide to Spiritual Enlightenment.* Novato, CA: New World Library, 1999.

Turner, Victor. *Betwixt and Between: The Liminal Period in Rites of Passage.* La Salle, IL: Open Court, 1987.

Ursano, Robert J. "Essential Papers on Post Traumatic Stress Disorder." *American Journal of Psychiatry* 157 (2000): 12.

van der Kolk, Bessel. "Posttraumatic Stress Disorder and the Nature of Trauma." *Dialogues in Clinical NeuroSciences* 2 (2000): 7–22.

———. *Traumatic Stress: The Effects of Overwhelming Experience on Mind, Body and Society.* New York: Guilford, 2006.

van Gennep, Arnold. *Rites of Passage.* London: Routledge, 2004.

Van Winkle, Clint. *Soft Spots: A Marine's Memoir of Combat and Post-traumatic Stress Disorder.* New York: St. Martin's, 2010.

Verkamp, Bernard J. *The Moral Treatment of Returning Warriors in Early Medieval and Modern Times.* Scranton: University of Scranton Press, 1993.

Vigarello, Georges. *A History of Rape: Sexual Violence in France from the 16th to the 20th Century.* Cambridge: Polity, 2001.

Vonnegut, Kurt. *Slaughterhouse-Five or The Children's Crusade.* New York: Dell, 1966.

Wampold, B. E. *The Great Psychotherapy Debate: Models, Methods and Findings.* Mahwah, NJ: Erlbaum, 2001.

Watters, Ethan. *Crazy Like Us: The Globalization of the American Psyche.* New York: Free Press, 2008.

Wells, Tom. *The War Within: America's Battle over Vietnam.* Berkeley: University of California Press, 1994.

Wheen, Francis. *Strange Days Indeed: The 1970s; The Golden Days of Paranoia.* New York: PublicAffairs, 2010.

White, Curtis. *The Science Delusion: Asking the Big Questions in a Culture of Easy Answers.* New York: Melville House, 2014.

Wilson, Timothy. *Strangers to Ourselves: Discovering the Adaptive Unconscious.* Cambridge: Harvard University Press, 2002.

Winter, Jay. *The Great War and the Shaping of the Twentieth Century.* New York: Penguin, 1996.

———. "Shell-shock and the Cultural History of the Great War." *Journal of Contemporary History* 35 (2000): 7–11.

Woodward, Bob, and Carl Bernstein. *All the President's Men.* New York: Simon & Schuster, 1974.

Yehuda, Rachel, et al. "Conflict between Current Knowledge about Posttraumatic Stress Disorder and Its Original Conceptual Basis." *American Journal of Psychiatry* 152 (1995): 1705–1713.

Young, Allan. *The Harmony of Illusions: Inventing Post-traumatic Stress Disorder.* Princeton: Princeton University Press, 1995.

Zoroya, Gregg. "Modern Wars Influence Psychiatric Thought." *USA Today,* February 28, 2012.

Index